THEORIES OF DELINQUENCY

THEORIES OF DELINQUENCY

An Examination of Explanations of Delinquent Behavior

FOURTH EDITION

DONALD J. SHOEMAKER

New York   Oxford
OXFORD UNIVERSITY PRESS
2000

Oxford University Press

Oxford   New York
Athens   Auckland   Bangkok   Bogotá   Buenos Aires   Calcutta
Cape Town   Chennai   Dar es Salaam   Delhi   Florence   Hong Kong   Istanbul
Karachi   Kuala Lumpur   Madrid   Melbourne   Mexico City   Mumbai
Nairobi   Paris   São Paulo   Singapore   Taipei   Tokyo   Toronto
Warsaw

and associated companies in
Berlin   Ibadan

Copyright © 1984, 1990, 1996, 2000 by Oxford University Press

Published by Oxford University Press, Inc.,
198 Madison Avenue, New York, New York 10016
http://www.oup-usa.org

Library of Congress Cataloging-in-Publication Data
Shoemaker, Donald J.
Theories of delinquency : an examination of explanations of
delinquent behavior / Donald J. Shoemaker.—4th ed.
p.   cm.
Includes index.
ISBN 0-19-512776-5 (pbk. : alk. paper)
1. Juvenile delinquency.   I Title.
HV9069.S525   2000
364.36—dc21   99-31403

9 8 7 6 5 4 3 2 1

Printed in the United States of America
on acid-free paper

To Robert, my brother and friend

CONTENTS

PREFACE

Since the first edition of this book appeared in 1984, several changes have occurred, not only with respect to patterns of delinquency, but also with conceptualizations and research regarding explanations of delinquent behavior. The second edition of the book built upon the developments in theory and research concerning delinquency from the mid-1980s to the late 1980s. The third edition continued the revision and reconceptualization begun with the second edition, from the late 1980s to the mid-1990s. The fourth edition extends the earlier revisions, updating the literature in most chapters.

In addition to basic updates in most of the chapters, this edition of the book addresses some new developments in the subject of delinquency theory, especially with respect to developmental theories of delinquency. Moreover, there are more extensive updates in some chapters, particularly Chapter 8, Control Theories, Chapter 11, Female Delinquency, and Chapter 12, on integrated theories.

Another feature of this edition is the ever-expanding reference to international examples and research bearing on the theories covered in the volume. International research and theorizing are becoming increasingly important in the area of theoretical development, and this trend is particularly relevant for crime and delinquency.

As is often the case, preparing this revision has involved several people besides the author. In continuing recognition of contributors to earlier editions, I would like to recognize the collegial support and assistance of John Ballweg, Clifton Bryant, Ricardo Zarco of the University of the Philippines, Diliman, the late James K. Skipper, Jr. and the late Edwin Sagarin. I would also like to recognize the efforts of Christina Bao and Laura Montgomery, in the Department of Sociology at Virginia Tech. They have provided invaluable research and secretarial assistance throughout the revision process.

D.J.S.
Blacksburg, Virginia

THEORIES OF DELINQUENCY

1

Explanations
of Delinquency

THE PROBLEM OF DELINQUENCY

Practically no day passes without the appearance of some news item carrying a story of a crime committed by youth. Figures vary from year to year, but generally, rates of delinquency in the United States were higher in the late 1980s and early 1990s than they were a generation ago, particularly for violent offenses (Lundman, 1993:8–15). Although rates of delinquency in the United States, in terms of arrests and referrals to juvenile court, have been declining since the mid-1990s, the rates of delinquency are still higher than they were in the 1980s (Sickmund, 1997; Snyder, 1997). Criminal behavior of juveniles involves all types of activity, and it is committed by youth from all backgrounds. In addition to criminal behavior, juveniles can commit illegal acts that apply only to juveniles. These "crimes" are called status offenses, because they apply only to the status of youth.

Collectively, illegal acts, whether criminal or status, which are committed by youth under the age of 18 are called delinquent behaviors, and the youth committing them are referred to as juvenile delinquents. This terminology officially developed in 1899, when the first code of juvenile delinquency was enacted in Chicago, Illinois.

The problem of juvenile "crime," however, has existed for hundreds of years. Indeed, as Wiley Sanders indicates, juvenile offenders have been noted in many of the written records of human history (1970). Numerous editorials, commission reports, and governmental statistics reveal that juvenile crime, including that of youth gangs, not only existed but was a source of concern to the citizens of Europe and America in the eighteenth and nineteenth centuries. Even early Anglo-Saxon laws contained provisions for the punishment of child offenders (Sanders, 1970).

3

In essence, adults have always been concerned about the miscreant behavior of their youth. Perhaps this worry and attention derive from the perception that a nation's future rests on the development of its youth. Perhaps the concern over youthful deviance stems from the thought (however accurate) that today's delinquent is tomorrow's criminal, if nothing is done to change the antisocial behavior of the youth. Be that as it may, when youngsters are known to have been involved in criminal activity, people become concerned. Why did they do it? What should we do with them? These are the questions adults ask, and the demand for answers seems to become stronger with each new generation of adults.

Proposals for preventing and diminishing delinquency, as well as controlling and punishing the young perpetrators, have assumed so many different forms that any casual reader of the literature can be excused for being totally confused and bewildered. But essentially the question of causation is paramount. In the Middle Ages, and into the nineteenth century, children and adults were lumped together as one group, and whatever explained the misbehavior of older criminals was equally applicable to younger ones. Such was the case with demonology, and it was equally true of the first systematic criminology of the modern era, known as the classical position (Inciardi, 1978; Empey, 1982; Vold and Bernard, 1986).

Demonology assumes that criminal and delinquent behavior is caused by demonic possession. While this view of criminality can be traced to primitive societies, it still maintains some popularity today among laypersons. A recent popular example of demon possession of a child is presented in the novel *The Exorcist.*

The classical school in criminology argues that people, adults and children, act according to free will, rationally exercised, in the pursuit of happiness and the minimization of pain. According to some of the early proponents of this thought, such as Cesare Beccaria, and to some extent his English utilitarian follower, Jeremy Bentham, all persons, including children, are thought to weigh the costs and benefits of their proposed actions before they embark on them, and all persons, it is assumed, possess the ability to do so (see Chapter 2).

Although the American legal system is based on the notions of free will and individual responsibility, it has been recognized for some time that not all individuals have the same ability to reason and weigh the outcome of their behavior; witness, for example, the mentally ill and children (including adolescents). For this reason, juveniles are thought to be less responsible than adults for their behavior, and an entire system of juvenile justice, from separate court proceedings to separate confinement facilities, has been established for them over the past 150 years. Of course, this separate system of handling juvenile offenders does not always result in protective and treatment-oriented practices

(Murphy, 1974; Wooden, 1976; Ayers, 1997). In addition, juvenile court procedures are assuming many of the characteristics of adult courts in response to Supreme Court decisions since the 1960s (Shoemaker, 1988). Whatever changes may have been introduced, the juvenile is still considered by many to be less responsible than the adult, and thus in need of different procedures for adjudication and different policies that emphasize prevention and treatment over punishment.

Along with the assumption that young delinquents need special treatment, the idea has developed that *explanations* of crime among juveniles must be applied specifically to experiences common to youth. Particularly associated with this thought is what came to be known as the Positive School of criminology initiated in the latter half of the nineteenth century (Radzinowicz, 1966). Although some thinkers equate the Positive School with nineteenth-century studies of the criminal personality, the name positive can be applied to any theory that systematically and, in varying degrees, empirically analyzes the causes of crime and delinquency and concludes that personal or social and environmental factors *determine* criminal behavior. As such, many modern theories of delinquency may be called *positivistic.*

Contributions to an understanding of crime and delinquency from a positivist approach have come from a variety of disciplines, most notably biology, psychology, and sociology. While not all positivist theories distinguish juveniles from adults, many do. Some specify several stages of development, from infancy to old age, with accompanying explanations of crime and deviance for each growth period (the psychoanalytic approach, for example). Others focus on pressures, uniquely from an adolescent point of view (such as the middle-class measuring rod theory proposed by Albert Cohen, which is discussed in Chapter 6).

It is the many and varied theories of delinquency, particularly those stemming from the positivist tradition, that create much of the confusion concerning the causes of delinquency. The object of this book is to present the major theories of delinquency to the reader in a manner that is systematic and comparative. Before discussing more fully what will be included in this book, however, a few comments concerning the concepts of causality and theory are in order.

THE ISSUE OF CAUSALITY

The positive school is associated with determinism, that is, the idea that criminal behavior is determined, or caused, by something (Radzinowicz, 1966). It is the identification of that "thing," or set of things, that has elevated the question of causation to a central position in the analysis of crime and delinquency.

A strict interpretation of causality would argue that one phenomenon (the cause) always precedes the result, or the effect, and that the effect never occurs without the previous existence of the cause (MacIver, 1942). For example, broken homes would be considered a cause of delinquency if broken homes always led to delinquency and if all delinquents came from broken homes. In actuality, such an interpretation of causality would eliminate the "causal" explanations of a variety of phenomena, both natural and social. This view of causation is particularly inappropriate for the development of concepts and theories in the social sciences because of the existence of multiple causes, or factors, in human behavior (MacIver, 1942; Hirschi and Selvin, 1978; Gibbons and Krohn, 1986).

In the development of causal explanations of delinquency, the usual procedure is to identify contributory factors, or variables, that are *associated* with delinquency. In identifying these factors, however, some attention must be paid to a minimal set of criteria for the development of causal explanations: (1) there must be an association or connection between the contributory or causal variable and delinquency; (2) the connection must be temporally established such that the causal factor is known to occur before the effect, that is, delinquency; and (3) the original connection between delinquency and the causal variable must not disappear when the influences of other variables, causally located prior to the causal variable, are considered (Hirschi and Selvin, 1978).

Sometimes, correlational data are interpreted in deterministic terms. For example, broken homes are often described as a cause of delinquency because broken homes and delinquency are correlated with one another (that is, delinquents often come from broken homes). The temporal order of this association must be established, however, before causation can be determined. If all we knew was that broken homes and delinquency were correlated, we might just as easily reason that *delinquency* causes broken homes (through parental conflicts over what to do with a troublesome child) or that coming from a broken home causes delinquency (perhaps because trouble and conflict or lack of supervision in the home create problems for a child, which are manifested in the form of illegal behavior).

Even when it has been established that two variables are not only connected, but that one variable precedes another in a time sequence, the preceding variable may not be causal. It could be that a third variable, preceding both of the others, is the real causal agent. When this occurs, it is assumed that the originally identified association between two variables is *spurious*, that is, misleading or false. For example, if a relationship has been established between delinquency and poor grades in school, the relationship may not be a causal one. Perhaps conflicts in the home are contributing to both poor school performance and delinquent behavior. If family conflicts were then introduced into the analysis, the original association between grades and delinquency would disappear, and we would then be able to call that relationship spurious.

In reading the following chapters of this book, the student should be aware of these points. The theories to be discussed are attempts to explain delinquency. While no one theory is able to provide *the* causal answer, some appear to be stronger than others in consideration of the criteria just discussed.

WHAT IS A THEORY?

The word "theory" means many things to different people. To the layperson, a theory often suggests a wild speculation, or set of speculations, an unproved or perhaps false assumption, or even a fact concerning an event or a type of behavior, based on little, if any, actual data. To some scientists, or philosophers of science, a theory consists of a set of descriptions or classification schemes concerning a particular phenomenon (some would call such schemes "taxonomies"; Zetterberg, 1963). To others, a theory is a systematic collection of concepts and statements purporting to explain events or behavior (Timasheff, 1957). Blalock (1969) views theories of this sort as deductive theories, which consist of interrelated propositions. These propositions are described as axioms, or statements of truth, and theorems, which "are derived by reasoning, or *deduced*, from the axioms" (p. 10). Homans takes a similar approach by arguing that theories are essentially deductive explanations of events, and explanations are attempts to test and understand specific parts or sequences of the larger phenomenon, which are organized as propositions (1967:22–27). Other students feel that theories should not only be able to explain phenomena on an abstract level but also should be applicable to practical, everyday situations. In other words, a significant feature of a theory is its ability to explain things for the layperson who may wish to use the theory in an applied setting (Glaser and Strauss, 1967). Some theories concern the activities of individuals, and attempt to explain why individuals commit acts of delinquency. These kinds of theories are often called *microtheories*. Other theories deal with the larger social and cultural context in which humans act, and address the issue of why rates of delinquency are higher in some settings, or among some collections of people, than in others. These theories are called *macrotheories* (Williams and McShane, 1994:8–9; see also, Akers, 1994:4–5; Gibbons, 1994: 8–11). Still other theoretical perspectives focus on the explanations of why laws and norms are established, and in what manner these prescriptions and proscriptions for behavior are enforced (Akers, 1994:3).

Whatever the definition, the social scientist sees a theory, in one way or another, as an attempt to make sense out of observations (Akers, 1994:2; Curran and Renzetti, 1994:2; Gibbons, 1994:6–7). It is in this general sense that the word "theory" will be used in this work. Thus, a view of delinquency will be recognized as a theory if it attempts to explain or understand delinquency, regardless of the level of its causal assumptions and irrespective of the sophistication of its concepts and propositions. It is tempting to adopt a strict interpretation of theory, but to do so would eliminate some useful and interesting approaches to an understanding of delinquency. At one time or another, each of the explanations presented in this book has been referred to as a theory, and it is for this context that the term has been chosen.[1]

VERIFICATION OF THEORIES

The utility of any theory lies in its validity. Can it be verified? Is it true? Will it predict what will be found in groups not yet observed and studied? Theories are analyzed and verified in a variety of ways. Most often, they are verified by gathering data designed to test the validity of their concepts and propositions. This way of testing a theory may be referred to as the empirical method (Akers, 1994:6–12). Validity refers to the extent to which a theory is true (valid). In testing theories, or theoretical propositions, the researcher is often concerned with the validity of the questions and procedures used in the study. That is, do they truly measure what they are purported to measure? For example, do IQ tests actually measure native intelligence, or are they, in part, gauging learned behavior and responsive abilities? A goal of scientific disciplines is to continually test their theories and refine their concepts. To ignore a theoretical explanation of delinquency, or any other type of behavior, because it is unsophisticated or untested would be denying the integrity of the scientific process and foreclosing, perhaps prematurely, what might eventually become a meaningful interpretation of delinquency.

Included in the empirical method of evaluating theories of delinquency is the implementation of a theory's assumptions in prevention or treatment programs. A major concern in this approach to the evaluation of a theory is the gap that can develop among particular questions concerning what the theory proposes, how a practitioner interprets the theory, and how the major elements of the theory are implemented (see, for example, Lilly et al., 1995). While these problems occur in the testing of theories in all disciplines, they are pronounced in the social sciences. The outcomes of practical tests of a theory can be highly affected by the practitioner's understanding of the theory as well as the practitioner's commitment to its success (or failure). What are the chances of a theory being designated successful in reducing delinquency if the practitioner does not believe in the validity of the theory in the first place? Such issues as these make it impractical to evaluate theories of behavior on the basis of their ability to effect changes in behavior in a purposeful manner.[2]

Another method of testing theories is to examine their logical consistency and conceptual clarity. However, some theories are worded so abstractly or with such conceptual unclarity that it is difficult to test them empirically. For instance, theories which argue that behavior is influenced by cultural norms and values are difficult to test with experimental or survey data because the central concepts of the theories are so far removed from day-to-day behavior that it is hard to connect behavior specifically with the concepts. Similarly, psychoanalytical theories which stress unconscious motives for behavior are difficult to test because such motivations are outside the scope of normal observation. These kinds of theories are better evaluated primarily according to their internal logic and consistency rather than their empirical accuracy. These are what McCord describes as "soft theories" (1989:132–133).

THE PLAN OF THIS BOOK

The purpose of this book is to present the student with a systematic discussion of the dominant explanations of delinquency. It is not the intention of the author to develop a new theory of delinquency but, instead, to explain the existing theories in a consistent, organized manner. It is hoped that this procedure will enable the reader not only to obtain an understanding of each theory, but also to be able to compare and contrast these explanations.

It is recognized from the beginning that no single theory will ever be able to explain all types of delinquency. The theories presented are assessed according to their general empirical and logical adequacy. In some cases, such as with theories of lower-class and female delinquency, the evaluation is based on the ability of the theory to explain the specific form of delinquency addressed. The more usual procedure, however, is to discuss each theory in relationship to delinquent behavior in general.

The format of the book is the same in most chapters. First, a brief historical overview of the theory, or set of theories, is presented. Next, the basic assumptions of these theories are examined.[3] These items are followed by discussions of specific theories within the general set, including specific assumptions, key concepts, a general discussion, and an evaluation. Each chapter concludes with a summary and comparative overview. Exceptions to this format occur in the chapters on female delinquency and integrative theory.

This book is not intended to "sell" anyone on the merits of any particular theory, although comparative evaluations will point to the apparent efficacy of one theory over another. Despite the support received from scholarly training or the concentration of experts favoring particular causes of delinquency, students must make up their own minds on explanatory approaches but should reach conclusions based on information and not ignorance, with an open mind and not a rigid one, and free from precommitments and prejudices. If the contents of this book help students in formulating a considered and thoughtful opinion concerning the etiology of delinquency, its purpose will have been fulfilled.

Notes

1. Only in one instance, the discussion of labeling, can it be argued that it is not a theory under consideration (because there is no causal explanation), but a perspective. This problem is considered later.

2. The purpose of this book is to discuss most of the major explanations of delinquency. Of course, this decision forces one to select from the range of potential entries those which are considered representative. In so doing, some theories may be omitted which might be included by other authors. Learning theories of criminality, for example, are not fully covered in this volume. To some extent this interpretation of behavior is addressed in the discussion of differential association theory in Chapter 7. Other versions of learning theories, such as those informed by behavioral psychology, are not included, primarily because the manner in which these theories are used focuses on the treatment, or modification, of delinquent behavior. While the subject of treatment is certainly important, the parameters of this book exclude a detailed examination of treatment or rehabilitation programs. Those interested in such topics may wish to consult other books, such as Lundman (1993) and Morris and Braukmann (1987:especially Chapters 2, 5, 6, 7, 13, 14, 15, and 18).

3. The assumptions listed for each theory cover the causal connections of delinquency. They at times include assumptions of basic human nature (see, for example, Stevenson, 1974) and of the social order, but the focus remains on the theoretical explanation of delinquent conduct.

References

Akers, Ronald L., 1994, Criminological Theories: Introduction and Evaluation. Los Angeles: Roxbury.

Ayers, William, 1997, A Kind and Just Parent. Boston: Beacon.

Blalock, Hubert M., Jr., 1969, Theory Construction: From Verbal to Mathematical Formulations. Englewood Cliffs, N.J.: Prentice-Hall.

Curran, Daniel J. and Claire M. Renzetti, 1994, Theories of Crime. Needham Heights, Mass.: Allyn & Bacon.

Empey, Lamar T., 1982, American Delinquency, second edition. Homewood, Ill.: Dorsey.

Gibbons, Don C., 1994, Talking About Crime and Criminals: Problems and Issues in Theory Development in Criminology. Englewood Cliffs, N.J.: Prentice-Hall.

Gibbons, Don C. and Marvin D. Krohn, 1986, Delinquent Behavior, fourth edition. Englewood Cliffs, N.J.: Prentice-Hall.

Glaser, Barney G. and Anselm L. Strauss, 1967, The Discovery of Grounded Theory. Chicago: Aldine.

Hirschi, Travis and Hanan C. Selvin, 1978, "False Criteria of Causality." Pp. 219–232 in Leonard D. Savitz and Norman Johnston (eds.), Crime in Society. New York: Wiley.

Homans, George C., 1967, The Nature of Social Science. New York: Harcourt, Brace, and World.

Inciardi, James A., 1978, Reflections on Crime. New York: Holt, Rinehart and Winston.

Lilly, J. Robert, Francis T. Cullen, and Richard A. Ball, 1995, Criminological Theory: Context and Consequences, second edition. Thousand Oaks, Calif.: Sage.

Lundman, Richard J., 1993, Prevention and Control of Juvenile Delinquency, second edition. New York: Oxford University Press.

MacIver, R. M., 1942, Social Causation. New York: Ginn and Company.

McCord, Joan, 1989, "Theory, Pseudotheory, and Metatheory." Pp. 127–145 in William S. Laufer and Freda Adler (eds.), Advances in Criminological Theory. New Brunswick, N.J.: Transaction Publishers.

Morris, Edward K. and Curtis J. Braukmann (eds.), 1987, Behavioral Approaches to Crime and Delinquency: A Handbook of Application, Research, and Concepts. New York: Plenum.

Murphy, Patrick T., 1974, Our Kindly Parent—The State. New York: Viking.

Radzinowicz, Leon, 1966, Ideology and Crime. New York: Columbia University Press.

Sanders, Wiley B. (ed.), 1970, Juvenile Offenders for a Thousand Years. Chapel Hill, N.C.: University of North Carolina Press.

Shoemaker, Donald J., 1988, "The Duality of Juvenile Justice in the United States: History, Trends, and Prospects." Sociological Spectrum 8:1–17.

Sickmund, Melissa, 1997, "Offenders in Juvenile Court, 1995." OJJDP Juvenile Justice Bulletin, November:1–12.

Snyder, Howard N., 1997, "Juvenile Arrests, 1996." OJJDP Juvenile Justice Bulletin, November:1–12.

Stevenson, Leslie, 1974, Seven Theories of Human Nature. New York: Oxford University Press.

Timasheff, Nicholas S., 1957, Sociological Theory, revised edition. New York: Random House.

Vold, George B. and Thomas J. Bernard, 1986. Theoretical Criminology, third edition. New York: Oxford University Press.

Williams, Frank P., III and Marilyn D. McShane, 1994, Criminological Theory, second edition. Englewood Cliffs, N.J.: Prentice-Hall.

Wooden, Kenneth, 1976, Weeping in the Playtime of Others. New York: McGraw-Hill.

Zetterberg, Hans L., 1963, On Theory and Verification in Sociology, revised edition. Totowa, N.J.: Bedminster Press.

2

The Classical School:
Issues of Choice
and Reasoning

HISTORICAL OVERVIEW

As mentioned in Chapter 1, the foundation of American jurisprudence is the individual culpability of offenders. Criminal culpability typically rests on the issue of reasoning and criminal intent. That is, legal evidence is based on the degree to which a person is considered to have committed an act, and the degree to which the individual is considered to have committed the act voluntarily, or of free volition.

Many scholars maintain that the legal constructs of free will and reasoning capacity are products of a school of thought named the Classical School (Vold and Bernard, 1986:Chapter 2). The Classical School is characterized by a belief in the influence of free will on the commission of behavior, as well as the use of punishment to deter criminality, but just enough punishment to outweigh the benefits of committing crime. Contemporary systems of criminal justice have been modified to include a variety of "mitigating" circumstances which are thought to reduce the impact of "free will" on behavior.

One of the more common mitigators of criminal responsibility is a person's age, and the corresponding connection between reasoning capability and age. In the United States, historical accounts maintain that beginning in the early nineteenth century, public perceptions of young offenders began to accept the notion of reduced criminal responsibility because of age (Platt, 1977; Krisberg and Austin, 1978). Sanders (1970) demonstrates that age qualifications for punishment were recognized in the laws of the colonies. Specific reform efforts, and institutional structures which focused on the youthful offender, began to appear in the United States during the first third of the nineteenth century. Throughout the twentieth century, a number of legal and social reforms ultimately led to the development of a separate court process for juveniles, first represented in Chicago, Illinois in 1899 (Platt, 1977). However, these reform efforts were not uniformly accepted by all, and even for juveniles, there is the assumption that free will is the basic cause of behavior.

Assumptions

In strictest form, the Classical School argues that all people act according to the exercise of free will and reasoning. Individuals act, furthermore, in order to accomplish some desired goal. Variations of this theme posit that humans behave according to rational considerations of the consequences of their acts, both those results which are beneficial and those which are harmful.

Key Concepts

Free Will Within the concept of classical theory, free will represents individual responsibility for behavior. This does not mean that a person always accepts responsibility for actions. Rather, it means that society holds a person accountable for behavior because this activity is assumed to be the result of conscious, calculating thought.

Rational Choice This concept refers to the method of reaching a decision to commit behavior. It refers to the idea that people act according to a reasoned, logical set of planned calculations (see, for example, Cornish and Clarke, 1986). This choice is based on awareness of potential consequences, positive and negative, of the behavior.

Discussion

The person most often identified with the Classical School is Cesare Beccaria, who outlined his views in a book entitled *On Crimes and Punishments* (1963; originally published in 1764). According to Beccaria, people do what they do because they derive pleasure from their acts, and they voluntarily choose to commit them. In this manner, criminal activity is motivated by the same principles as noncriminal behavior, namely, the gratification of pleasure and the avoidance of pain. The difference between the two is that the law violator chooses to circumvent laws and rules to obtain desired goals, while the law abider stays within the bounds of legal limits to achieve objectives. This position assumes that all people have the same opportunities to exercise choices in their lives. One of the important characteristics of the Classical School is the notion that all people possess the ability to reason and to act on their own volition.

Of course, contemporary social science challenges this conceptualization. While people may exercise reason and choice in pursuing their desires and objectives, these patterns of thought and action are influenced by a host of environmental and individual factors which have been the focus of attention among students of human behavior and society for decades. For example, people from different social status or social class backgrounds may see the availability of legitimate opportunities from very different perspectives (Vold and Bernard, 1986:29). The same may be said of gender differences in society, as well as many other human and social characteristics. Furthermore, this perspective fails to provide meaningful interpretations of why some people choose an illegal path to success, happiness, or whatever else they may be seeking, while others opt for the conformist way, except to contend that this is the way people elect to lead their lives. Moreover, this philosophy does not help to understand why people choose alternating methods of achieving their goals, some legal, some not.

In fairness to Beccaria and his treatise on crimes and punishment, these questions and issues were not foremost in his presentation of arguments. Rather, Beccaria argued that the goal of his essay was to present a plan of jurisprudence which would be fair and effective in controlling crime (Martin et al., 1990:6–15). Thus, we are told that capital punishment is not an effective means for instilling respect for the law in people and preventing crime among the general population, because it is excessive, cruel, and barbaric (Beccaria, 1963:45–52). Throughout this essay, the arguments and comments focus on the proper response to criminality, with an eye toward producing a fair and just system of punishment which would lead to the prevention of future crime among the populace, rather than to disrespect for those charged with enforcing the law, as well as the laws which are being protected. A more complete evaluation of this theory of criminal motivation would encompass the wide range of correctional philosophy which has developed in response to these issues (Martin et al., 1990:16–18). However, the purpose of this book is to present theoretical arguments for the causes of delinquency, not an evaluation of various correctional practices designed to reduce or eliminate crime and delinquent conduct. Consequently, the following evaluation of the Classical School is based on the ideas of this theory which concern the motivations for committing crime, and whether these ideas hold merit when applied to juveniles.

Evaluation

Strict applications of Beccaria's legislative principles, such as the French Penal Code of 1791, have not met with much success (Vold and Bernard, 1986:25). One reason for the inability to hold all people accountable for their actions is the quite human condition of complexity and variability in motivation. Even if the principle of behaving to achieve pleasurable consequences, and to avoid pain, were perfectly valid, there would be the issue of how much and what kinds of pleasure and pain were needed in order to motivate people. Recognition of these difficulties led to revisions of penal codes based on Beccaria's ideas, revisions which incorporated elements of mitigating circumstances and other conditions which might reduce the capacity of people to reason and thus be held fully accountable for their actions. One of the earliest proponents of this view of behavior was Jeremy Bentham, who enunciated his basic philosophy of crime and punishment in a book entitled *An Introduction to the Principles of Morals and Legislation* (1948; originally published in 1789). Bentham is often included as a member of the Classical School, because he believed in the essential freedom of people to chart the course of their actions. In addition, Bentham subscribed to the philosophy that the primary motivation in human behavior is based on pleasure and pain (Bentham, 1948:1). However, Bentham also believed in the **principle of *utility***, by which he meant that the ultimate objective in legislation was to achieve the greatest happiness for the community, or as many members of society as possible (pp. 1–3). This principle is the crux of Bentham's position, for it leads to a consideration of a large number of factors and circumstances concerning crime and its motivation, which a strict classical view cannot entertain. For these reasons, Bentham is more properly classified as a "neoclassical" theorist. The Neoclassical School is characterized by the core belief that people operate according to free will and pleasure-pain, but these principles are modified according to mitigating and extenuating circumstances of a wide range (Vold and Bernard, 1986:26–27; Curran and Renzetti, 1994:15).

Because of these considerations, the contemporary criminal justice system in America and other Western nations is more properly associated with the Neoclassical School. This association extends to the system of juvenile justice as well. Basically, the very existence of a separate system of handling juvenile offenders, apart from adult criminals, is a reflection of a neoclassical view that free will is mitigated by extenuating circumstances, namely, a person's age. However, societal acceptance of the idea of reduced punishment for juveniles based on age is neither automatic nor uniform (Champion, 1992:4–28). Not only was this lack of agreement evident in the earlier stages of the development of juvenile justice concepts (Platt, 1977), but it exists in contemporary times, probably as strongly as ever.

While the juvenile justice system is based on treatment, rehabilitation, prevention, and similar ideas of human correction, efforts continue to be made which would provide punishment to juvenile offenders, even to the extent of providing that juveniles be processed as adults. Most jurisdictions, for example, allow for the transfer of juvenile cases to the adult system, where the juvenile would be then "treated" as an adult (Champion, 1992:210–244). In some states, such as Washington, there have developed strict interpretations of the penalties which should be assessed for the commission of specific offenses, in connection with specific circumstances. The express intent of this legislation, moreover, is based on the assumption that juveniles should be held "accountable" for their acts (Siegel and Senna, 1988:484–485). Thus, while it may be argued that a separate system of juvenile justice recognizes limitations on the influence of free will relative to one's age, court and legislative decisions often work against this philosophy by establishing laws and policies which are based on the assumption that young people should be held accountable for their behavior.

Within the field of social science and theoretical positions on the nature of human action, there also exists considerable argument and debate concerning the impact of free will on behavior. Nearly all the theoretical positions discussed in the remainder of this volume are based on the assumption that, at the very least, people act according to the interaction between free will and a host of factors which operate to constrain the extent to which action is truly "free." These forces are often conceptualized as "determining" factors, and at times it might seem these conditions all but eliminate the option of choice in human behavior.

RATIONAL CHOICE THEORY

In the past few years, an explanation of criminality has emerged which is often referred to as "rational choice theory" (Clarke and Cornish, 1985; Cornish and Clarke, 1986). Basically, this conception of behavior is a modified version of classical theory, in that it suggests that criminal behavior is predicated on the use of calculations, reasoning, and "rational" considerations of choices. In this manner, the theory is similar to the ideas of economists such as Becker (1968), who advocate an economic, calculative approach to the understanding of crime. Rational choices, furthermore, are based on the principle of self-interest (Cornish and Clarke, 1986:1), or what others might refer to as the pleasure-pain principle. Unlike the early classical theorists such as Beccaria, however, the contemporary, "rational choice" view is based largely on, and encourages, empirical investigations into the motives of behavior and the influence of rationality on human actions.

Most of the contemporary literature on rational choice theory addresses the criminal activity of adults. While many attempts to test this perspective report results favorable to its basic assumptions (Cornish and Clarke, 1986), there are exceptions. For example, Piliavin et al. (1986) report data on the connection between self-reported crime, perceived opportunities for committing crime, and the perceived risks of arrest and/or imprisonment for committing crime among samples of previously incarcerated adult offenders, known adult drug users, and adolescent school dropouts. Their analysis failed to support any deterrent effect of perceived punishment on criminal behavior. However, perceived criminal opportunities were related to self-reported crime, especially among adult offenders (pp. 111–117). These findings were particularly relevant for the sample of adult offenders. According to this study, therefore, the assumptions of rational choice theory and classical theory in general, are too simplistic. People may be more affected by perceptions of opportunity for committing crimes than by the prospects of being caught and punished for criminal behavior.

Perceptions of opportunities and risks, furthermore, may be influenced by experiences with committing crime and/or with being punished for crime. Since the results discussed above applied more to adult offenders who had previously been in jail or prison than to adolescents, it may be that perceptions of risks and opportunities relative to crime are more accurate for adult offenders than for adolescents. Also, as Piliavin et al. suggest, people may be sensitive to major shifts in perception, such as a certainty that criminal opportunity exists or that arrest for criminal behavior is imminent, but not to more remote possibilities (1986:115).

These considerations would seem to place even more importance on the impact of age as a conditioning factor for a rational perspective on the understanding of delinquency. If calculations and reasoning are affected by experiences, then it is reasonable to assume these processes are less developed among juveniles than among adults (Paternoster, 1989), which, again, is the basis for according differential corrective responses to delinquent conduct as opposed to adult criminality.

More recent discussions of rational choice theory link the perspective with learning theory, or differential association theory (Akers, 1990; Clarke and Felson, 1993). Paternoster (1989) provides some empirical evidence on the relative effects of deterrence/rational choice variables, compared to social and attitudinal factors, on "common" forms of delinquency. Basically, Paternoster concludes that rational choice and deterrence factors play at best an inconsistent role in the "decision" to commit relatively minor acts of delinquency for the first time, particularly alcohol use and minor theft, as well as for subsequent decision-making, including the notion of repeating delinquent acts, or to stop offending (pp. 22–38).

SUMMARY

It may be difficult to assess the calculative nature of human behavior with any more precision than is currently evident in the literature. These attempts often utilize information gathered from individuals *after* the act has been committed, and sometimes years after the event has occurred. This problem alone should not be sufficient to warrant no further study of a classical, rational choice, or any other similar kind of approach to human behavior. Many attempts to test or examine interpretive explanations of criminal or delinquent behavior incorporate *post hoc* methods which involve recollections or imputations of behavior well after the acts have occurred.

The issue is not as absolute as some positions may imply. Of course, humans act on the basis of reasoning and calculation. Just as certainly, however, people behave in response to habits, suggestions from others in their lives, cultural norms and values, and other environmental stimuli (Harding, 1993). Some refer to this situation as "conditional free will" (Fishbein, 1990:30) or "degree determinism" (Denno, 1988:618, 661–662). These factors and conditions constitute the subject matter of the remainder of this book. People make mistakes in judgment, interpretations of events, assessments of situations, and so on. Some attribute these mistakes to lack of self-control, and contend that criminal behavior occurs early in life and is maintained throughout life (Gottfredson and Hirschi, 1990). Others (Sampson and Laub, 1992, 1993) contend that choices made early in life are often due to the interaction between personal and environmental influences, but that these choices influence other decisions people make throughout their lives, including those which affect social and occupational selections (as well as the reactions of others to these decisions). In Sampson and Laub's view, however, people can also change in their perceptions and views concerning how they should behave, and in their decision making relative to these changes. These fluctuations occur among young people as well as with adults.

It should not be surprising, therefore, to find scholars openly divided about the importance of "free will" versus determinism on the subject of human behavior, for, in fact, humans behave rationally and impulsively, but not robotically.

None of the theories to be discussed in the following chapters should be taken as the ultimate explanation of delinquent behavior. This point of view should become increasingly clear as the reader moves through this book. The presentation concerning "integrated" theories, in the last chapter, attempts to reinforce this position. A reasonable compromise position on this issue is to view human behavior, deviant or conformist, as the result of the exercise of choice within given situations. We may never be able to control the human will; we may never want to reach this level of control. However, we can reasonably expect to reach a clearer understanding of circumstances and situations that are thought to influence delinquent behavior, which is the primary goal of this book.

References

Akers, Ronald L., 1990, "Rational Choice, Deterrence and Social Learning in Criminology: The Path Not Taken." Journal of Criminal Law and Criminology 81: 653–676.

Beccaria, Cesare, 1963, On Crimes and Punishments, translated by Henry Paolucci. New York: Bobbs-Merrill. Originally published in 1764.

Becker, Gary S., 1968, "Crime and Punishment: An Economic Approach." Journal of Political Economy 76:169–217.

Bentham, Jeremy, 1948, An Introduction to the Principles of Morals and Legislation. New York: Hafner. Originally published in 1789.

Champion, Dean J., 1992, The Juvenile Justice System. New York: Macmillan.

Clarke, Ronald V. and Derek B. Cornish, 1985, "Modeling Offenders' Decisions: A Framework for Research and Policy." Pp. 147–185 in Michael Tonry and Norval Morris (eds.), Crime and Justice, Vol. 6. Chicago: University of Chicago Press.

Clarke, Ronald V. and Marcus Felson (eds.), 1993, Routine Activity and Rational Choice. New Brunswick, N.J.: Transaction.

Cornish, Derek B. and Ronald V. Clarke, 1986, The Reasoning Criminal. New York: Springer-Verlag.

Curran, Daniel J. and Claire M. Renzetti, 1994, Theories of Crime. Needham Heights, Mass.: Allyn & Bacon.

Denno, Deborah W. 1988, "Human Biology and Criminal Responsibility: Free Will or Free Ride?" University of Pennsylvania Law Review, 137:615–671.

Fishbein, Diana H., 1990, "Biological Perspectives in Criminology." Criminology 28:27–72.

Gottfredson, Michael R. and Travis Hirschi, 1990, A General Theory of Crime. Stanford, Calif.: Stanford University Press.

Harding, Richard W., 1993, "Gun Use in Crime, Rational Choice, and Social Learning Theory." Pp. 85–102 in Ronald V. Clarke and Marcus Felson (eds.), q.v.

Krisberg, Barry and James Austin (eds.), 1978, The Children of Ishmael: Critical Perspectives on Juvenile Justice. Palo Alto, Calif.: Mayfield.

Martin, Randy, Robert J. Mutchnick, and W. Timothy Austin (eds.), 1990, Criminological Thought. New York: Macmillan.

Paternoster, Raymond, 1989, "Decisions to Participate in and Desist from Four Types of Common Delinquency: Deterrence and the Rational Choice Perspective." Law & Society Review, 23:7–40.

Piliavin, Irving, Rosemary Gartner, Craig Thornton, and Ross L. Matsueda, 1986, "Crime, Deterrence, and Rational Choice." American Sociological Review, 51:101–119.

Platt, Anthony, 1977, The Child Savers, second edition. Chicago: University of Chicago Press.

Sampson, Robert J. and John H. Laub, 1992, "Crime and Deviance in the Life Course." Annual Review of Sociology 18:63–84.

————, 1993, Crime in the Making: Pathways and Turning Points Through Life. Cambridge, Mass.: Harvard University Press.

Sanders, Wiley B. (ed.), 1970, Juvenile Offenders for a Thousand Years. Chapel Hill, N.C.: University of North Carolina Press.

Siegel, Larry J. and Joseph J. Senna, 1988, Juvenile Delinquency, third edition. St. Paul: West.

Vold, George B. and Thomas J. Bernard, 1986, Theoretical Criminology, third edition. New York: Oxford University Press.

3

Biological and
Biosocial Explanations

HISTORICAL OVERVIEW

An essential component of the biological approach to delinquency is that such behavior is caused by some mechanism *internal* to the individual. Biological theories of crime and delinquency (criminality) have been proposed for hundreds of years (Fink, 1938). However, the works of early theorists varied considerably on just exactly what this internal mechanism, or set of mechanisms, might be. Furthermore, many of the early attempts, like those of the eighteenth and nineteenth centuries, made little distinction between biological and psychological characteristics, assuming in general that the criminal's mind is affected by biological composition. Since nearly all of these theorists had been trained as physicians, it is logical that they would focus on the physical properties of the body as the topic of research.

GENERIC ASSUMPTIONS

Besides positing that delinquency is a product of internal, physical properties, modern biological theories usually assume that these properties at least predispose one to criminality. The predispositions, however, are said to interact with environmental factors which can affect the influence of biology on behavior. Prior to the twentieth century, many assumed that biological factors did more than predispose one to crime—they directly caused the behavior. A general diagram of the relationship between biological factors and delinquent behavior should incorporate these two explanatory views (Jeffery, 1979; Denno, 1990; Magnusson et al., 1992; Booth and Osgood, 1993). The assumptions may be depicted as shown in Figure 1.

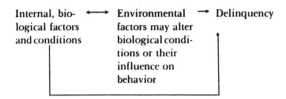

Figure 1

It should be noted that the predisposition connection between biology and delinquency is a reciprocal one. That is, environmental factors (which can be of a wide variety, such as family and peer associations, school performance, and social class membership) may both be shaped by and influence biological factors. It is the result of this reciprocal influence that contributes to delinquency.[1] The direct causation position, however, bypasses environmental situations and suggests that a biological phenomenon, such as a brain tumor or some kind of chemical imbalance, can directly lead to delinquency.

Although numerous biological explanations of crime have been offered in the past (Fink, 1938; von Hentig, 1948), many of these theories made no theoretically substantive distinctions between adult and juvenile offenders. The subjects of this chapter are some of the more dominant biological explanations of *delinquency,* with minimal attention paid to explanations of both crime and delinquency. The specific topics to be discussed are somatotypes and delinquency, the issue of inheritance and delinquency, and emerging trends in biosocial explanations of delinquency.

SOMATOTYPES AND DELINQUENCY

Specific Assumption

A *somatotype is* the overall shape of the body, in consideration of the relative development of the various parts of the body in comparison with each other. An important feature of somatotype explanations of delinquency is that one's character and behavior can be correlated with the shape and structure of the body. One of the foremost supporters of this view, William Sheldon, maintains that the relationship between behavior and one's personality, or character, and physical features, including body shape, can be traced back approximately 2500 years to the works of Hippocrates (1944).

Key Concept

Somatotype or Body Type Numerous body characteristics are included in the analysis of somatotypes, such as arm and leg length, head size, muscle development, and bone structure. Implicit in the concept is that the shape of the body is a reflection of constitutional makeup, that it is strongly influenced by factors present at birth, and that, nutrition notwithstanding, the basic shape, or body type, remains constant.

Discussion

Somatotype theories can be traced to a very influential body of research—the work of the late-nineteenth-century physician and psychiatrist Cesare Lombroso. Even though Lombroso did not analytically separate delinquents from adult criminals, his views are considered "classic" and are thus worthy of some attention at this point. Essentially, Lombroso viewed much criminality as a type of degeneracy. Specifically, he referred to some criminals as "atavists" or throwbacks to an earlier form of human life on the evolutionary scale (Lombroso, 1911). Furthermore, Lombroso maintained that a large portion of criminal behavior was inborn, although he entertained exceptions to this view in the twilight of his career (Lombroso, 1911; Lombroso-Ferrero, 1911).[2]

Although Lombroso did not believe in body type in the manner in which it was developed by Sheldon and others, he did contend that criminals had definite *physical* characteristics that distinguished them from the law-abiding population. The criminal man was supposedly characterized by such features as a large jaw, high cheekbones, handle-shaped ears, and even tattoos (Lombroso, 1911). Obviously, tattoos are not inborn, but were included in the Lombrosoian list because they are physical.

The research conducted by Lombroso and his followers was painstaking but hardly persuasive, because control groups—that is, people selected for comparisons—were rarely used and direct connections between physical features and criminality were never established. While a thorough examination of physical characteristics in relation to criminality questioned several of Lombroso's claims that criminals have distinct physical appearances, it did not diminish and lay to rest the biological orientation to explaining crime (Goring, 1913), and research on this topic continued well into the twentieth century (Fink, 1938; Hooton, 1939; Rafter, 1992).

The first attempt to relate body traits systematically with delinquency came from the work of William Sheldon (1949). Borrowing largely from an earlier attempt to correlate body physiques with general personality and behavior traits (Kretschmer, 1921), Sheldon maintained that elements of three basic body types could be found in all people: (1) *endomorphic*, or soft, round, and fat; (2) *mesomorphic*, or muscular and hard; and (3) *ectomorphic*, or thin, frail, and weak. According to Sheldon, one could not be characterized as totally one or the other of these types, but *relatively* so, on a scale of 1 to 7. Thus, a person might be predominantly mesomorphic, but still possess some endomorphic or ectomorphic traits. His somatotype might thus be 2–6–3. Furthermore, a few people possess no dominant physical shape characteristics and are described as having a mixed or midrange somatotype.

Sheldon viewed body types as inborn. Moreover, the importance of body types in the explanation of behavior lay in the strong association between physique and temperament, or personality. Endomorphy is associated with a viscerotonic temperament, characterized by extroversion and love of comfort. Mesomorphy is related to assertive, aggressive behavior, a somatotonic temperament. Ectomorphs are described as sensitive, shy, and introverted, referred to as a cerebrotonic temperament (Sheldon, 1949; Vold and Bernard, 1986).

Sheldon applied his somatotype theory in a study of 200 young males who had been referred to a specialized rehabilitation home for boys in Boston (Hayden Goodwill Inn). Using subjective assessments of body-typing, that is, the observation of photographs, Sheldon concluded that the mean somatotype for the "delinquent" sample was 3.5–5.6–2.7, "decidedly mesomorphic" (1949:726–729). Furthermore, this mesomorphic nature of delinquents was held in contrast to a more even distribution of body types that was found among 4000 college students.

William Sheldon's study was shortly followed by a massive exploration of delinquency by a husband and wife team at Harvard, Sheldon and Eleanor Glueck (1950). Among dozens of other factors, the Gluecks examined the relationship between body type and delinquency in 500 institutionalized, "persistent" delinquents and a matched control sample of 500 "unquestionable nondelinquents." Measuring body types through examinations of photographs, the Gluecks concluded that over 60 percent of the delinquents were mesomorphic, compared with about 31 percent of the nondelinquents. On the other hand, only 14 percent of the delinquents were ectomorphic, whereas nearly 40 percent of the nondelinquents were so cast.

Further investigation of somatotypes and delinquency, conducted by the Gluecks (1956), revealed that mesomorphy is highly associated with such characteristics as high levels of inadequacy, of "not being taken care of," and of emotional instability. However, whether the mesomorphic body structure determines these characteristics, or whether the personality traits are generated from environmental factors, including being considered "delinquent," or a combination of environmental and constitutional factors, was not determined by the Gluecks. Their conclusion was that delinquency is caused by a combination of environmental, biological, and psychological factors. From their exhaustive research, they concluded that there is no such thing as a "delinquent personality," among mesomorphs or any other body type. Mesomorphs, for example, may be more delinquent than others because their physical and psychological traits "equip them well for a delinquent role under the pressure of unfavorable sociocultural conditions . . ." (Glueck and Glueck, 1956:270).

The social context concerning the relationship between mesomorphy and delinquency has also been interpreted from a developmental perspective. In this view, the physically larger, stronger child, usually a male, can successfully "bully" his way around the playground, and sometimes get into trouble for his efforts. However, this physically aggressive behavioral pattern does not persist into late adolescence, presumably because these youth have learned other ways to obtain their wishes, or perhaps because the availability of weapons for that age group affords the bully an additional tool of persuasion, and the physically weaker youth an opportunity to resist bullying (Killias and Rabasa, 1997).

A third attempt to relate somatotypes to delinquency was proposed as a more definitive approach to the subject by trying to eliminate the problems involved with the research of Sheldon and the Gluecks (Cortès and Gatti, 1972). The method of somatotyping in this study was based on comparative measurements of skin folds, bone structure, muscle development, and body weight and height rather than from observations of photographs. In addition, assessments of temperament were based on self-report inventories, as opposed to subjective opinions of observers. The definition of delinquency in the Cortès and Gatti study, however, was based on the *official* records of institutions or court appearances, which limited the applicability of their findings.

Using these measurements and definitions, Cortès and Gatti found that over half of the 100 delinquents possessed a mesomorphic body type, compared with 19 percent of the 100 nondelinquents. On the other hand, 14 percent of the delinquents were endomorphic, while 37 percent of the nondelinquents were endomorphic.

Cortès and Gatti attempted to provide information on *why* delinquents are predominantly mesomorphic. In this regard, they reported that there is a statistical association between high achievement motivation and mesomorphy, for both delinquent and nondelinquent youth. In addition, delinquents, as a group, have higher achievement motivation than nondelinquents. The association between achievement motivation and mesomorphy, however, is greater for nondelinquents than delinquents, which suggests that other factors, both biological and environmental, are operating in conjunction with achievement orientations to produce delinquency. The explanation of the relationship between body type and delinquency, therefore, remains unsolved. The causal connection has not been established.

Evaluation

What began as an attempt to detail the constitutional, physical, and perhaps hereditary prerequisites to delinquency has developed into a complex bio-psychosocial explanation of delinquent behavior. Over the past 50 to 75 years, during which the somatotype explanations of delinquency have been researched, measurements have become more sophisticated and the biological connection has become less distinct, less powerful, and less imbued with moral and evolutionary characteristics. Nonetheless, the specific physiological connection between body type and behavior is missing. Furthermore, since mesomorphic, aggressive males may be expected to predominate in several competitive fields, such as business and athletics (Cortès and Gatti, 1972), the explanation of the association between physique and delinquent behavior cannot be based solely on internal properties, even if these factors could be identified. To be sure, the importance of both environmental and physical variables in the explanation of delinquency is often readily acknowledged. The specific contribution of biological processes to delinquent behavior, however, can more readily be assessed when *biological* properties are detailed. To say that delinquency is in part caused by biologically "expressive factors" or that the proximate cause of delinquency is some kind of "negative imbalance within the individual" is interesting, but hardly lends itself to empirical testing.

Although officially acknowledged delinquents appear to be disproportionately mesomorphic, a logical, biological interpretation of this relationship has not been established, and thus the theoretical significance of somatotypes as an explanation of delinquency remains questionable.

INHERITANCE AND DELINQUENCY

Specific Assumptions

The assumption of a link between inheritance and delinquency claims that behavior in general is determined by factors that are not only present at birth, but are transmitted, biologically, from parent to child. In some ways this position is a more general statement of the somatotype explanation of delinquency. While it is posited that something inborn is causing delinquency, the specific agent is variously interpreted and only loosely identified. Rarely are such items as male-female contributions isolated and more rarely still are the specific mechanisms explained concerning how inherited factors determine behavior.

The general inheritance explanation also assumes that delinquency is a wrong that must be caused by a bad or negative source, thus ignoring the possibility that a good cultural trait might result in both good and bad consequences. In general, therefore, the inherited factor, or factors, that underlies delinquency is considered abnormal or aberrant.

Key Concept

Concordance Rate Concordance rates refer to the agreement in behavioral outcomes among pairs of individuals—for example, twins or siblings. These rates are significant because they are a major consideration in the analysis of inheritance through studies of twins and other relatives. The behavioral outcome is considered concordant if *both* members of the pair exhibit it—that is, if both members of a set of twins have delinquent records or both are free from such records. When one is delinquent and the other is not, the pair is discordant.

Discussion

The issue of heredity versus environment, nature versus nurture, as the primary cause of behavior has occupied the attention of social and behavioral theorists for hundreds of years. It is not surprising that this debate has also been waged in the literature on crime and delinquency. During the latter part of the nineteenth century and early twentieth century, the nature-nurture debate with respect to criminality was being vigorously waged, mostly in favor of heredity. Besides Lombroso's claims of having discovered the "born criminal," numerous other investigators were trying to establish not only that there was a biological cause of criminality, but that whatever the biological explanation might be, it was inherited (Fink, 1938).

One of the most popular of these studies was Richard Dugdale's late-nineteenth-century analysis of the Jukes in New York (Dugdale, 1888). The lineage of this family included a large number of criminals, prostitutes, and paupers, thus establishing, in Dugdale's mind, that pauperism, illegitimacy, crime, and heredity were all related and fixed in nature.

There were other attempts to establish a hereditary connection with crime using this "family tree" method, most notably the work of H. H. Goddard, who attempted to establish a connection between heredity, *feeblemindedness*, and crime (Goddard, 1912, 1914). These family tree investigations, however, are extremely weak in terms of scientific proof and logic. For example, transmission of criminal, or delinquent, traits may just as easily be explained through processes of social learning and societal reaction rather than biological and genetic processes. Dugdale stated in his study, for instance, that the Juke family had, over several generations, established an infamous reputation in their community. It does not stretch one's imagination much to envision the difficulty a "Juke" boy might have, at the turn of the century, in convincing local residents that he was a bright, "good," promising child with a respectable future. To sort out more accurately the separate effects of heredity and environment on criminality, studies of twins began to emerge early in the twentieth century. The logic behind these studies is that hereditary influences on behavior can be accurately determined by comparing concordance rates of behavior among monozygotic (one-egg, identical, or MZ) twins, dizygotic (two-egg, fraternal, or DZ) twins, and siblings. If heredity influences behavior more than environment, concordance rates should be higher among identical twins than among fraternal twins or siblings.

Numerous studies of criminality among twins have appeared since the 1930s and they have generally, although not invariably, reached the conclusion that higher rates of concordance are found among identical twins than among fraternal twins or siblings (Cortès and Gatti, 1972; Christiansen, 1977b; Reid, 1979; Vold and Bernard, 1986).

When patterns of delinquency are separated from adult criminality, however, other conclusions are often reached. Aaron Rosanoff and colleagues (1934), for example, examined official rates of crime, delinquency, and behavioral problems among 340 pairs of same-sex twins. The twins were classified as "probably monozygotic" or "probably dizygotic." The uncertainty in classification is based on the authors' recognition that look-alike or identical twins are not always MZ, although twins resembling each other very little are likely to be DZ. In fact, they indicate that "physical, intellectual, and temperamental" inequalities among monozygotic twins are the rule rather than the exception (Rosanoff et al., 1934:930).

With these uncertain classifications in mind, the authors generally concluded that adult criminality is mostly inherited but that juvenile delinquency, particularly female delinquency, is largely attributable to environmental factors (the number of female twin pairs included in the study of delinquency, however, was nine, a number too small to yield reliable conclusions).

Such conclusions should be viewed cautiously at this point. With respect to *delinquency*, too few studies have been conducted to reveal a pattern. Data from Japan, for instance, indicate that concordance rates of delinquency are higher for MZ twins than for DZ twins, although the information is not very detailed (Christiansen, 1977b).

Studies of twins and criminality have numerous flaws, which present difficulties in the interpretation of results. The criticisms of this research include: (1) the use of a small number of twin pairs, which prevents adequate statistical comparisons; (2) the difficulty in accurately determining whether twins are one-egg or two-egg (although efforts in this area are improving); (3) the exclusive use of official definitions of crime and delinquency; (4) the inadequate control of environmental factors, particularly since these may affect identical twins and twins reared apart (Sutherland and Cressey, 1978; Reid, 1979). To this list should be added the element of doubt concerning the representativeness of the twins studied. In the Rosanoff study, for example, *all* of the twin pairs had at least one officially identified crime, delinquency, or behavior problem case. This fact suggests that the researchers first checked the official files on crime and delinquency to locate the twins rather than locating the twins first and then checking the files, which is a more valid way of investigating criminality *among* twins.

Some research, particularly in Scandinavia, addresses most of the criticisms of previous studies, thus providing more valid results (Christiansen, 1977a, 1977b). Unfortunately for the purposes of this book, none of these more recent studies deals separately with juvenile delinquency; thus the application of their results to the issue of heredity and delinquency is tentative (Lyons, 1996; Silberg et al., 1996).

A good example of the type of research conducted on twins and criminality is provided by Odd Dalgard and Einar Kringlen (1978). These workers checked the names of all twins born in Norway between 1921 and 1930 with the national criminal record in Norway as of December 31, 1966. The procedure yielded a total of 205 pairs of twins, 134 of which could be included in this study. The results of the comparison indicated that concordance rates for widely sanctioned criminal acts, such as violence, theft, and sexual assault, were higher among 31 pairs of MZ twins than among 54 pairs of DZ twins, although the differences were not statistically significant. The measurement of zygosity in this study was more sophisticated than in most other investigations in that it was based on blood and serum tests, prompting Dalgard and Kringlen to contend that their "zygosity diagnosis" was "almost 100 percent correct" (1978:296).

Dalgard and Kringlen's research also went a step further than previous studies in attempting to control environmental factors. Interviews with the twins elicited information concerning their life histories and experiences, going back to childhood. These interviews allowed the researchers to assess the extent to which the twins felt close to one another or were treated alike during their childhood. The results demonstrated that the MZ twin pairs felt they had been reared as a unit, dressed and treated alike as children, and experienced closeness and common identity as children much more than the DZ twins. When these environmental factors were considered in the analysis, Dalgard and Kringlen observed that the relationship between twin status and recorded criminality was virtually eliminated.

In addition, environmental influence on delinquency may be located among the interactive patterns of the twins themselves. One current line of inquiry in this area focuses on the mutual influence sets of MZ twins may have on each other. Thus, if one of the twin pairs is involved in criminality, the other will be influenced by the first twin's behavior (Carey, 1992).

One investigation of delinquency studied 265 sets of same-sex adolescent twins living in Ohio and concluded that environmental factors had no influence on delinquent behavior (Rowe, 1986). This study addressed the issue of criminality by mailing questionnaires to sets of twins who were in school during the academic years 1978–79 and 1980–81. The twins were identified through the assistance of high schools in Ohio and the Ohio Mothers of Twins Clubs. Those who responded to the study represented middle- and working-class backgrounds. Ten percent of the sample were black. Zygosity was determined on the basis of reported height comparisons, eye color, and general appearance. Uncertain cases (6 percent) were either omitted from the study or subjected to blood analysis for classification.

The measure of delinquency in this study was based on self-reports; that is, respondents were asked to indicate whether they had committed any of a number of delinquent acts within the year prior to the survey. As correlates of delinquency, the investigator utilized several psychological and social-psychological scales, including scale items designed to measure a student's social bonds to society.

Environmental variables were divided into common and within-family categories. Common environmental factors included similar treatment within twin pairs, social class, religion, neighborhood, parental values—in short, "all influences that operate to make siblings alike" (p. 514). Within-family environmental influences included experiences that would be "unique to each individual," such as friends or peer relations (p. 514).

Rowe then compared the simultaneous influence of environmental and hereditary factors on delinquency (antisocial behavior) and the attitudinal correlates of delinquency. His interpretation of the results supported a genetic influence on delinquency and such psychological traits as anger, impulsivity, and deceitfulness, especially among males. However, no such genetic foundations were located for "attitudes toward school," prompting Rowe to conclude that "the genes influencing attitude toward academic work were *not* the same as those influencing delinquent behavior" (p. 528; italics in the original).

In theoretical context, Rowe concludes his results lend support to a genetic cause underlying certain psychological traits, such as impulsivity and deceitfulness, which are connected with conditioning, a topic to be discussed later in this chapter. However, no genetic source was found for the relationship between delinquency and social bonds, a topic which is discussed in more detail in Chapter 8.

While this research provides additional support for a genetic link to delinquency, there are some methodological considerations which lead to precautionary interpretations of the results of this study. First, the sampling procedure yielded a return of under 50 percent (Rowe, 1985). In addition, no inner-city schools were sampled. Second, the determination of zygosity was based primarily on self-report assessments of physical characteristics, not on medical records. Third, the subjects were allowed to respond to questions in an unsupervised setting. Thus, reports of delinquency, attitudes, or experiences may not have been independently expressed. Fourth, environmental influences were not clearly delineated and examined relative to delinquency or other variables in the analysis.

Evaluation

Investigations that attempt to cipher out the unique effects of heredity versus environment on criminality, or behavior in general, are bound to yield conflicting results and conclusions. By now, it is clear that both types of factors influence behavior in a very complex manner. Environmental factors are now thought to exert an influence on behavior before birth, making the determination of hereditary influences even more difficult (Shah and Roth, 1974). Nonetheless, the issue is still important in the view of many scholars, and research continues to be conducted.

In a comparative sense current research on the hereditary influences on criminality is more objective and generally superior to past investigations. As with other areas of biological research, moralistic assumptions tend to be absent from current studies, and conclusions tend to be more tentative. If anything, sweeping statements are beginning to appear *against* the hereditary position, such as the conclusion of the Dalgard and Kringlen study discussed above: *"the significance of hereditary factors in registered crime is non-existent"* (1978:302; italics are in the original).

Although current research on criminality among twins is addressing most of the criticisms of prior studies, several shortcomings still remain. First, the definition of *criminal* or *delinquent* is still primarily based on official records. This situation not only poses the problem of generalizability, but it also raises the question of validity, since concordance of official criminal records may reflect similarities of societal reactions as well as similarities of behavior (see also, Walters and White, 1989).

Second, more careful assessments of environmental influences on criminality are beginning to develop, including studies of criminality among adoptees and among twins reared apart (Christiansen, 1977a, 1977b; Hutchings and Mednick, 1977). For example, a study of criminality among male adoptees in Denmark indicated that the percentage of adoptees with a criminal record increased with an increase in the percentage of biological fathers who also had a criminal record

(Hutchings and Mednick, 1977). This relationship persisted despite the social class of the adoptees' adopted fathers and despite the record of criminality of the adoptive fathers. In no instance, however, did the criminal concordance rate between adoptees and their fathers reach 50 percent.

An extension of the Danish study included all nonrelated adoptions (14,427) which occurred in Denmark between 1924 and 1947 (Mednick et al., 1987a). Using court convictions as the measure of criminality, the researchers concluded that male adoptee and biological father crime rates were higher than the rates for female adoptees, adoptive fathers, and either biological or adoptive mothers. In addition, rates of crime among adopted sons were higher when biological parents had a criminal record, as compared to the criminal background of adoptive parents. However, in this expanded investigation, the highest percentage of adopted sons' criminality was less than 25. Moreover, an examination of genetic and social-class influences on criminality indicated that both factors contributed to criminality among adopted sons. As Mednick et al. conclude, "regardless of genetic background, improved social conditions are likely to lead to a reduction in criminal behavior" (1987a:86).

A review of the literature on genetic influences on crime and delinquency reached a similar conclusion (Cloninger and Gottesman, 1987). These authors, however, take a cautious stance regarding the influence of genetic factors on criminality. They suggest that environmental and hereditary variables interact to produce antisocial behavior, but that such biological influences are limited. The limited influence of genetics is especially evident with delinquency. According to Cloninger and Gottesman, "there is no evidence that genetic factors are important in prepubertal delinquency as a class" (1987:106).

Some call for continued research into the issue of biological, particularly genetic, effects on criminality, and for improved methodological procedures in this research (Denno, 1988; Fishbein, 1990). Others, however, argue that when improved measures of criminality, as well as genetic and environmental factors, are incorporated into research, the estimated influence of genetic variables on crime and delinquency is reduced (Walters and White, 1989).

In a "meta-analysis," that is, a review of existing research, of the "gene-crime relationship," Walters (1992) specifically concludes that there is a measurable and statistically significant hereditary influence on crime. This analysis included 38 published accounts of research on this topic, covering twins, family, and adoption settings. Walters further concludes that the amount of genetic influence on criminal behavior is smaller than previously thought. In addition, this analysis concludes that there may be some type of period effect concerning this relationship. Specifically, Walters concludes that studies conducted prior to 1975 generally used poorer methodological techniques than more recent investigations, and that the higher estimates of genetic influence on criminality typically are found in these earlier publications. However, Walters argues that the decreased significance of genetic factors on criminality is independent of methodological design (p. 607). Ultimately, Walters feels that more fruitful research on this issue will begin to appear when the interaction between genes and environment is considered as the independent variable. No longer should researchers look upon this topic as an either-or relationship, but one which is complex and mutually inclusive of hereditary and environmental influences (p. 609; see also, Denno, 1990).

Nonetheless, detailed and comprehensive assessments of environmental influences on delinquency have not been provided in studies which focus on genetic contributions to criminality. It would seem from the recent literature on the subject, however, that if such detailed observations are included, the relative contribution of genetic influences on delinquency will be lessened.

Most important, there remains the absence of a specific, biological explanation of just *what* is being inherited to produce crime or delinquency. Until such an explanation is developed, the utility of this whole line of research will be little more than that of somatotype research. That is, the delineation of "hereditary" effects on crime and delinquency will only provide a clue to the existence of a biological contribution. The determination of what the biological factor or factors may be or of how it (or they) operates to produce crime or delinquency will have to come from other lines of inquiry.

EMERGING TRENDS IN BIOLOGICAL EXPLANATIONS OF DELINQUENCY

In the last several decades, many developments have occurred that can influence the investigation of biological factors in criminality (Shah and Roth, 1974; Mednick and Christiansen, 1977; Mednick et al., 1987b). Some of these developments, such as research on the XYY chromosomal configuration, do not relate to juvenile delinquency. Two topics that have specifically been related to delinquency are learning disabilities and conditionability factors. Both of these topics will be separately discussed and evaluated. Major assumptions and key concepts are incorporated into the general discussion of each explanation.

Learning Disabilities and Delinquency

The term "learning disability" is a fairly new one, having been coined in the early 1960s (Murray, 1976). Although the concept embodies many diverse elements, and some subjectivity in measurement, it is generally considered to be a disorder or deficiency involving speech, hearing, reading, writing, or arithmetic (Murray, 1976).

While several forms of learning disability are thought to exist, the most common types are *dyslexia*, *aphasia*, and *hyperkinesis*. Dyslexia involves problems in reading, specifically the inability to interpret written symbols. Aphasia includes both visual and auditory deficiencies, which can sometimes lead to speech difficulties. Hyperkinesis is often equated with hyperactivity and comes the closest to overlapping with biochemical deficiencies. It generally refers to "abnormally excessive muscular movement," which can involve both small muscles, such as in the eye, and large muscles, such as leg muscles (Murray, 1976).

The specific cause of learning disabilities is unknown. Conventional wisdom, however, appears to place the greatest confidence in eventually finding an organic or neurological basis for these disorders (Murray, 1976; Cott, 1978; Kelly, 1979). To illustrate this point, many such children are labeled as having "minimal brain dysfunction" or as being "brain injured." Or, these children are considered learning disabled when it looks *as if* there is an organic basis for their learning problems because they are otherwise intelligent and docile. In addition, the presumed biological basis of learning disabilities is illustrated by Charles Murray's contention that hyperkinesis and hyperactivity, though behaviorally similar, are not the same thing because "the hyperkinetic child is thought to have problems which will eventually be traceable to neurological origins" (Murray, 1976:14).

The organic, biological link to learning disabilities is a presumption, albeit a dominant one. Research, however, suggests the possibility of *environmental* factors, particularly family and home conditions, in the etiology (Shah and Roth, 1974). That is, learning disabilities may be connected with deficiencies in early learning settings which leave a child less able to cope with the traditional academic exercises stressed in school.

Whether or not learning disabilities are organically based, there are two theoretical rationales linking such disorders to delinquency. One explanation is that learning disabilities produce poor academic achievement and thus negative attitudes toward the juvenile from relatives, peers, and school officials. The poor grades and negative attitudes, in turn, result in the child's associations with others who are also failing in, and disenchanted with, school, truancy, additional school-related problems, and delinquency (Murray, 1976; Cott, 1978; Holzman, 1979; Fishbein and Thatcher, 1986:258–259; Meltzer et al., 1986: 589–590; Fleener, 1987; Gallico et al., 1988:44–46, 101–18; Fink, 1990).

A second theoretical link stresses that learning disabilities create physical and personal problems, and thus personality characteristics, that can make children susceptible to delinquency. Such children are thought to be impulsive and unable to learn from experience, characteristics which can lead to disruptions in organized settings such as schools, general rule violations, and, of course, delinquency. In short, children with learning disabilities are thought to have a breakdown in the usual sensory-thought processes that enable other children to understand societal punishment-reward systems attached to behavior. Thus, the general effectiveness of sanctions on behavior is lessened (Murray, 1976; Morrison, 1978; Satterfield,1978).

Evaluation

The first theoretical link between learning disability and delinquency basically constitutes a social-psychological explanation. The organic cause of delinquency, the learning disability, is a precondition, and probably only one of many preconditions. The more proximate cause of delinquency is the combination of school failure, social rejection, and association with "bad" companions.

The second theoretical rationale linking learning disabilities with delinquency is more biologically based than the first. The suggestion that learning disabilities affect cognitive development and processes of understanding, which, in turn, render one less appreciative of social rules and sanctions, represents a combination of biological and psychological concepts in the explanation of delinquency. This type of collaborative conceptualization is related to one's ability to learn and appreciate social rules.

The connection between learning disabilities and delinquency, however, must first be clearly established before any plausible theoretical link can be thoroughly developed. This connection has *not* been established to date. Although some researchers maintain that over 90 percent of delinquents have some type of learning disability, these kinds of assertions are based on subjective and uncritical assessments (Murray, 1976).

Very often, the evidence cited to support a link between learning disabilities and delinquency is circumstantial and anecdotal, based on the general opinions and experiences of teachers and clinicians (Murray, 1976; Cott, 1978). Attempts to compare rates of learning disabilities (though still not consistently defined) among delinquent and nondelinquent samples, for the most part, find higher rates of learning disability among the delinquent samples (Slavin, 1978; Holzman, 1979; Fleener, 1987). But further investigation indicates that the disabled juveniles commit the same amount and types of delinquency as other youngsters (Keilitz el al., 1982; Pickar and Tori, 1986). In addition, one assessment of these quantitative studies reveals that the number of delinquents labeled as learning disabled ranges from 22 to over 90 percent (Murray, 1976), while another review concludes that about 35 percent of juvenile offenders are learning disabled (Casey and Keilitz, 1990). Inconsistent methodology and statistical procedures, contradictory results, small sample sizes, narrow definitions of delinquency, and, of course, variable measurements of learning disability associated with these studies all lead to the conclusion that a causal connection between learning disability and delinquency has not been established.

Attempts to reconcile the conflicting evidence regarding the connection between learning disabilities and delinquency suggest that many learning-disabled children are able to overcome their handicap and become good students with satisfying social lives (Perlmutter, 1987; Gallico et al., 1988:47–49). However, some of these youths do not learn to compensate for their handicap in the learning environment, and are at "high risk" of developing emotional and behavioral problems as adolescents. Perlmutter further hypothesizes that there is little "middle ground" for these juveniles. That is, most learn to adapt. The few who do not adjust develop problems later in adolescence. Therefore, the connection between learning disability and delinquency is not automatic, but can be intercepted by a variety of environmental circumstances, including school- and family-based reactive strategies. In short, most of these kids seem to be able to adjust well in the school and peer environments of their lives, given strong encouragement and support in their schools and families.

A longitudinal study of youth in New Zealand supports this developmental perspective on the connection between learning disabilities and delinquency (Moffitt, 1990). This study employed self-reported measures of delinquency, and other antisocial behavior. These estimates of delinquency were supplemented by adult estimates of the juveniles' behavior. In addition, the research included a number of individual characteristics, such as IQ and Attention Deficit Disorder (ADD), and environmental factors, such as family adversity. Subjects were interviewed and tested at various age intervals, starting with age 3, then at ages 5, 7, 9, 11, 13, and 15. This study is rich in detail and the type of information needed to examine various conceptual and theoretical issues in the fields of child development and delinquent behavior.

One important conclusion of this research is that children clinically diagnosed as having ADD, which is related to learning disabilities (see, for example, Barkley, 1990; Campbell, 1990), and delinquent youth are by no means always the same people. In fact, Moffitt suggests that patterns of delinquency may vary significantly, depending upon the presence or absence of ADD. For example, the delinquent youth with ADD began to exhibit antisocial behaviors prior to formal schooling while delinquent youth without ADD began to "behave antisocially" around the time of entry into high school (p. 901). In addition, Moffitt's analysis reports that 46 percent of the ADD youth could be classified as "nondelinquent" (p. 905). Furthermore, the analysis suggests that the presence of positive characteristics, such as "strong verbal skills and/or good family circumstances," can help to offset the potentially negative consequences of ADD (p. 907).

To summarize, the theoretical links between learning disabilities and delinquency are plausible. The basic evidence in support of a statistical connection between delinquency and learning disability is suggestive, but not overwhelming at this point. However, the significant contribution of learning disabilities in the understanding of delinquency seems to lie with its connection to other determinants, such as school failure and social rejection, rather than through its representation of a direct, organic link to delinquency.

Conditionability and Delinquency

One link between learning disabilities and delinquency is the presumed effect that the former may have on attention spans and associations between behavior and sanctions—in other words, the *conditionability* of people. The subject of conditioning and delinquency, of course, can be approached from a variety of social and psychological perspectives. The connection between *organic* or *physiological* factors and conditionability has been the subject of much theoretical and research interest, particularly with respect to crime and delinquency. The general relationship between conditionability and criminality is most often associated with the work of Hans J. Eysenck (1977). To summarize a rather complex theoretical scheme, Eysenck argues that personality influences behavior. Personality, on the other hand, is largely determined by physiological, perhaps even inherited, characteristics. Of central concern in this explanation of criminality is an understanding of two key personality traits, extroversion or extraversion (outgoingness) and introversion (shyness). An extroverted personality is sometimes associated with psychopathy, which, in turn, is associated (not equated) with criminality (Eysenck, 1977; Eysenck and Gudjonsson, 1989:Chapters 3 and 5).

The concept of psychopathy is central to Eysenck's theory, and the term "psychopath" has been widely defined in the literature. Eysenck views the psychopathic personality as including an orientation on the present rather than the future, an inability to develop emotional attachments with others, severe unreliability, and uncontrollable impulsiveness. Essentially, a psychopath is unable to appreciate the feelings of others or to become tractable. These traits, in turn, make one susceptible to criminality (Eysenck, 1977; Eysenck and Gudjonsson, 1989:109–125).

The *biological* component of Eysenck's theory lies in the assumption that defects in the *autonomic nervous system* (ANS), the control center for emotions in the body, are responsible for the extroversion and intractability of criminals and delinquents. Specifically, he maintains that extroverts have low *inhibitory* control and behavior operates without constraint. Furthermore, they need greater amounts of stimulation than others in order to be aroused. The lack of inhibitory controls and the greater need for stimulation reduce conditionability, which in turn increases the chances of criminality (Eysenck, 1977; Eysenck and Eysenck, 1978).[3]

While Eysenck's theory is applied to both adult criminals and juvenile delinquents, others have adopted many of his basic assumptions and applied them specifically to juveniles. Sarnoff Mednick (1977), for example, suggests that fear is a great inhibitor of behavior and thus necessary for the development of conformity among juveniles. The fear response in humans is controlled by the ANS. Normally, the ANS recovers quickly from the experience of punishment, thus facilitating inhibitory control of behavior. The child who possesses an ANS that is slow to recover from punishment is unlikely to develop strong inhibitory controls and is thus a likely candidate for delinquency.

Evaluation

The evidence concerning a connection between the ANS, extroversion, and criminality is suggestive, but not commanding. For instance, Eysenck cites data that indicate that samples of over 1800 prisoners are significantly more extroverted than a sample of over 1800 nonprisoners (Eysenck, 1977). In addition, Eysenck and Eysenck (1978) provide evidence that samples of over 2000 criminals and delinquents are more extroverted than samples of over 2000 controls. Furthermore, this relationship is most pronounced among adolescents and young adults (see also Eysenck, 1989).

In his longitudinal studies of people (that is, the same people followed over a period of time), Mednick (1977) indicates that those who experienced "serious disagreements with the law" have slower "electrodermal recovery" (a measure of ANS) than the controls. In addition, Mednick cites evidence that psychopathic prisoners have slower electrodermal recovery rates than less-psychopathic but "maximum-security prisoners," and that prisoners in general have much slower recovery rates than a sample of college students.

Other studies suggest that officially identified delinquents have slower electroencephalographic (EEG) readings and fewer conditional responses than nondelinquents, even when the response measurements preceded the recorded delinquencies (Loeb and Mednick, 1977; Mednick et al., 1981), and that more repetitive delinquent reformatory inmates have slower skin conductance rates than less repetitive inmates (Siddle et al., 1977).

Not all of the evidence, however, is in support of the basic assumptions behind this theory (Hoghughi and Forrest, 1970; Eysenck, 1977; Eysenck and

Eysenck, 1978). A review of several studies of persistent juvenile property offenders in England and Wales, for example, indicated that most often the delinquents were either no different or more *introverted* than comparison groups of boys (Hoghughi and Forrest, 1970). In addition, the relationships appear to be stronger for some types of criminality than for others. Eysenck maintains, for example, that the relationship between characteristics of the ANS and criminality is particularly strong with the psychopathic offender, juvenile or adult. A considerable body of literature is emerging that documents physiological response differences, associated with the ANS, between psychopaths and others. Moreover, these results appear in studies using different definitions of psychopathy (Hare and Schalling, 1978; Reid, 1978). Thus, Eysenck may be correct, but these reservations should be duly noted in the overall assessment of his theory.

The research that does support an association between the ANS and criminality should be interpreted cautiously at this point. Sample sizes are often small, numbering less than 10 cases in some studies. In addition, the representativeness of the samples, of both offenders and nonoffenders, is unclear. Virtually all of the studies utilize officially identified samples of delinquents or criminals, although not always incarcerated offenders. Not only does this procedure limit the scope of the testing of the theory, but it also raises the question of which came first, the delinquency or the physiological response characteristics. Since the ANS is supposed to govern emotions and reflexes, it is plausible to assume that official identification of one as delinquent or criminal, whether or not incarceration occurs, may alter reflexes and conditioned responses, in contrast to the assumption that slow reflexes and low conditioned response rates lead to the delinquent behavior in the first place. One way to resolve this difficulty would be to conduct longitudinal studies, as is now being done (Mednick, 1977). At this time, however, the temporal order of the relationship between ANS characteristics and criminality remains open to debate.

Even if consistent evidence is produced which indicates that defects in the ANS precede and lead to delinquency, there would still remain the question of environmental influence superseding, or interacting with, physiological influence. Eysenck has considered this prospect, with respect to child-rearing practices in the family, and found it wanting (Eysenck, 1977). In truth, however, Eysenck's consideration of environmental factors is brief and incomplete. Mednick and co-workers (1977) contend that electrodermal recovery rates are "highly related to criminality only in the lower-middle and middle classes" (p. 23), thus suggesting the importance of environmental factors in the etiology of lower-class criminality.

Environmental issues are also indicated in research which utilizes teachers' and parents' assessments and predictions of behavior among youth. Such studies may yield *higher* levels of skin conductance and other measures of response time among middle-class "delinquents" but lower response levels among lower-class antisocial youth. One reason for this type of reversal may be different interpretations of delinquent activity among parents of middle- and lower-social class positions (Venables, 1987). Furthermore, Walsh et al. (1987) suggest that love deprivation in the child-rearing years of psychopathic offenders may later result in slower reactions stemming from the ANS when these individuals encounter uncomfortable circumstances. This situation is particularly addressed to those who are classified as psychopathic and violent delinquents or criminals who have low intellectual abilities.

In another review of research regarding this theory, especially as it pertains to juveniles, some of the criticisms of previous studies are addressed (Eysenck and Gudjonsson, 1989:55–89). For example, research in this review includes studies using larger sample sizes (often numbering in the hundreds and sometimes in the thousands), cross-national research, and self-report assessments of delinquency. Generally, the studies reviewed concluded that delinquency is positively associated with extraversion, although this relationship is not always reported. In addition, the connection between delinquency and extraversion is reported in Western countries (such as France, Germany, Great Britain, Israel, and Spain), Eastern European nations (Czechoslovakia and Hungary), and developing societies (Bangladesh and India).

Eysenck and Gudjonsson also cite studies which conclude that the positive association between criminality and extraversion is not affected by length of incarceration, which they interpret as supportive of a long-lasting connection between personality and criminal behavior (p. 79). Additional "longitudinal" research is cited, but there are few of these and the results are not consistently supportive of the theory.

Another bit of "evidence" mentioned by these reviewers is what they see as a connection between the release of mental patients in the United States and Great Britain during the past three decades, and correlative increases in prison populations (pp. 85–88). This association is offered as supportive of the connection between criminal behavior and personality abnormality. However, in another section of their book, the authors maintain that mental illness and crime are complexly intertwined, and that "it is the exception rather than the rule for criminal behavior to be largely attributable in a simple way to a specific psychiatric diagnosis" (p. 219). Thus the straightforward correlation between psychiatric hospital releases and prison population increases is not as "simple" as it might appear, nor should the association be interpreted in a causal manner. Furthermore, the true complexity of the connection between criminality and psychological traits is another indication of the need to assess the role of environmental factors in the explanation of such behavior.

In summary, the theoretical connection between delinquency and differences in personality and ANS characteristics is plausible. Research evidence relative to the theory is suggestive but not conclusive. This line of inquiry is promising, but firm conclusions cannot yet be reached, particularly regarding the interplay between the ANS and environmental factors in the explanation of delinquency.

SUMMARY

The biological approach to delinquency has undergone several changes in this century. First, modern biological theories seldom display the evolutionary themes so common in the eighteenth and nineteenth centuries. Delinquents are no longer seen as evolutionary throwbacks or degenerates. The modern view characterizes biological factors as predisposing certain individuals toward criminality rather than determining crime and delinquency. Second, modern theories are much more interdisciplinary than in the past. Personality factors and environmental conditions are often considered, if not formally included, in the propositions of the theories and in research designed to test them. Seldom are claims made that solely profess biological explanations of delinquency over all other possible explanations, as was common at the turn of the century. Third, research on the biological contributions to delinquency is more sophisticated than in the past. Control groups are more often used, longitudinal designs are beginning to emerge, and definitions of key variables are being revised and refined.

As these conceptual and methodological changes develop, the overall explanatory power of biological factors appears to diminish. This is not to say that modern theory and research reduce the biological aspects of delinquency to a level of unimportance. Instead, this conclusion is meant to emphasize the relative decline in the overall importance attributed to the biological roots of delinquency, particularly in view of recent theory and research. At the same time, many of the biological explanations that are now emerging are plausible and worthy of continued investigation, particularly those theories which address the biological influences on cognitive development and learning capabilities. It should be anticipated that these aspects of the biological bases of delinquency will continue to be more fully developed in the future and will contribute to a better understanding of delinquent behavior. It should also be anticipated, however, that the importance of biological factors in the explanation of delinquency will increasingly be focused on the connections between these conditions and the more proximate, environmental bases of delinquency rather than on their direct relationship to the antisocial behavior of juveniles.

Notes

1. Some suggest that environmental factors may have different impacts on people depending on their biological characteristics (Rowe and Osgood, 1984). Others suggest that biological and environmental conditions operate independently in their influences on criminality (Gabrielli and Mednick, 1984).
2. For an interesting discussion of a contemporary evolutionary interpretation of crime, and hypotheses based upon an evolutionary perspective, see Ellis and Walsh, 1997.
3. For a similar explanation of crime and delinquency, but without a necessary biological base, see Wilson and Herrnstein (1985:Chapter 2).

References

Barkley, Russell A., 1990, "Attention Deficit Disorders: History, Definition, and Diagnosis." Pp. 65–75 in Michael Lewis and Suzanne Miller (eds.), q.v.

Booth, Alan and D. Wayne Osgood, 1993, "The Influence of Testosterone on Deviance in Adulthood: Assessing and Explaining the Relationship." Criminology 31:93–117.

Brennan, Patricia A. and Sarnoff A. Mednick, 1990, "A Reply to Walters and White: 'Heredity and Crime.'" Criminology 28:657–661.

Campbell, Susan B., 1990, "The Socialization and Social Development of Hyperactive Children." Pp. 77–91 in Michael Lewis and Suzanne Miller (eds.), q.v.

Carey, Gregory, 1992, "Twin Imitation for Antisocial Behavior: Implications for Genetic and Family Environment Research." Journal of Abnormal Psychology 101:18–25.

Casey, Pamela and Ingo Keilitz, 1990, "Estimating the Prevalence of Learning Disabled and Mentally Retarded Juvenile Offenders: A Meta-Analysis." Pp. 82–101 in Peter E. Leone (ed.), q.v.

Christiansen, Karl O., 1977a, "A Review of Studies of Criminality Among Twins." Pp. 45–88 in Sarnoff A. Mednick and Karl O. Christiansen (eds.), q.v.

———, 1977b, "A Preliminary Study of Criminality Among Twins." Pp. 89–108 in Sarnoff A. Mednick and Karl O. Christiansen (eds.), q.v.

Cloninger, C. R. and I. I. Gottesman, 1987, "Genetic and Environmental Factors in Anti-Social Behavior Disorders." Pp. 92–109 in Sarnoff A. Mednick, Terrie E. Moffitt, and Susan A. Stack (eds.), q.v.

Cortès, Juan B., with Florence M. Gatti, 1972, Delinquency and Crime. New York: Seminar Press.

Cott, Allan, 1978, "The Etiology of Learning Disabilities, Drug Abuse and Juvenile Delinquency." Pp. 61–74 in Leonard J. Hippchen (ed.), q.v.

Dalgard, Odd Steffen and Einar Kringlen, 1978, "Criminal Behavior in Twins." Pp. 292–307 in Leonard D. Savitz and Norman Johnston (eds.), Crime in Society. New York: Wiley.

Denno, Deborah W., 1988, "Human Biology and Criminal Responsibility: Free Will or Free Ride?" University of Pennsylvania Law Review 137:615–671.

————, 1990, Biology and Violence: From Birth to Adulthood. Cambridge: Cambridge University Press.

Dugdale, Richard L., 1888. The Jukes: A Study in Crime, Pauperism, Disease and Heredity, fourth edition. New York: Putnam.

Ellis, Lee and Anthony Walsh, 1997, "Gene-Based Evolutionary Theories in Criminology." Criminology 35:229–276.

Eysenck, H. J., 1977, Crime and Personality, third edition. London: Routledge and Kegan Paul.

————, 1989, "Personality and Criminality: A Dispositional Analysis." Pp. 89–110 in William S. Laufer and Freda Adler (eds.), Advances in Criminological Theory. New Brunswick, N.J.: Transaction.

Eysenck, H. J. and S. B. G. Eysenck, 1978, "Psychopathy, Personality, and Genetics." Pp. 197–223 in R. D. Hare and D. Schalling (eds.), q.v.

Eysenck, H. J. and Gisli H. Gudjonsson, 1989, The Causes and Cures of Criminality. New York: Plenum.

Fink, Arthur E., 1938, Causes of Crime. New York: A. S. Barnes.

Fink, Carolyn Molden, 1990, "Special Education Students at Risk: A Comparative Study of Delinquency." Pp. 61–81 in Peter E. Leone (ed.), q.v.

Fishbein, Diana H., 1990, "Biological Perspectives in Criminology." Criminology 28:27–72.

Fishbein, Diana H. and Robert W. Thatcher, 1986, "New Diagnostic Methods in Criminology: Assessing Organic Sources of Behavioral Disorders." Journal of Research in Crime and Delinquency 23:240–267.

Fleener, Fran Trocinsky, 1987, "Learning Disabilities and Other Attributes as Factors in Delinquent Activities Among Adolescents in a Nonurban Area." Psychological Reports 60:327–334.

Gabrielli, William F., Jr. and Sarnoff A. Mednick, 1984, "Urban Environment, Genetics, and Crime." Criminology 22:645–652.

Gallico, Rubin, Thomas J. Burns, and Charles S. Grob, 1988, Emotional and Behavioral Problems in Children with Learning Disabilities. Boston: Little, Brown.

Glueck, Sheldon and Eleanor Glueck, 1950, Unraveling Juvenile Delinquency. New York: Commonwealth Fund.

————, 1956, Physique and Delinquency. New York: Harper and Brothers.

Goddard, Henry H., 1912, The Kallikak Family. New York: Macmillan.

————, 1914, Feeble-Mindedness. New York: Macmillan.

Goring, Charles B., 1913, The English Convict. Reprinted, Montclair, N.J.: Patterson Smith Reprint, 1972.

Hare, R. D. and D. Schalling (eds.), 1978, Psychopathic Behavior. New York: Wiley.

Hippchen, Leonard J. (ed.), 1978, Ecologic-Biochemical Approaches to Treatment of Delinquents and Criminals. New York: Van Nostrand Reinhold.

Hoghughi, M. S. and A. R. Forrest, 1970, "Eysenck's Theory of Criminality: An Examination with Approved School Boys." British Journal of Criminology 10:240–254.

Holzman, Harold R., 1979, "Learning Disabilities and Juvenile Delinquency: Biological and Sociological Theories." Pp. 77–86 in C. R. Jeffery (ed.), q.v.

Hooton, Ernest A., 1939, Crime and the Man. Cambridge, Mass.: Harvard University Press.

Hutchings, Barry and Sarnoff A. Mednick, 1977, "Criminality in Adoptees and Their Adoptive and Biological Parents: A Pilot Study." Pp. 127–141 in Sarnoff A. Mednick and Karl O. Christiansen (eds.), q.v.

Jeffery, C. R. (ed.), 1979, Biology and Crime. Beverly Hills, Calif.: Sage.

Keilitz, Ingo, Barbara A. Zaremba, and Paul K. Broder, 1982, "Learning Disabilities and Juvenile Delinquency." Pp. 95–104 in Leonard D. Savitz and Norman Johnston (eds.), Contemporary Criminology. New York: Wiley.

Kelly, Henry E., 1979, "Biosociology and Crime." Pp. 87–99 in C. R. Jeffery (ed.), q.v.

Killias, Martin and Juan Rabasa, 1997, "Weapons and Athletic Constitution as Factors Linked to Violence Among Male Juveniles." British Journal of Criminology 37:446–457.

Kretschmer, Ernst, 1921, Physique and Character, second edition, translated by W. J. H. Sprott. Reprinted, New York: Cooper Square Publishers, 1936.

Leone, Peter E. (ed.), 1990, Understanding Troubled and Troubling Youth. Newbury Park, Calif.: Sage.

Lewis, Michael and Suzanne Miller (eds.), 1990, Handbook of Developmental Psychopathology. New York: Plenum.

Loeb, Janice and Sarnoff A. Mednick, 1977, "A Prospective Study of Predictors of Criminality: 3 Electrodermal Response Patterns." Pp. 245–254 in Sarnoff A. Mednick and Karl O. Christiansen (eds.), q.v.

Lombroso, Cesare, 1911, Crime, translated by Henry P. Horton. Reprinted, Montclair, N.J.: Patterson Smith Reprint, 1968.

Lombroso-Ferrero, Gina, 1911, Criminal Man. New York: Putnam.

Lyons, Michael J., 1996, "A Twin Study of Self-Reported Criminal Behaviour." Pp. 61–75 in Gregory R. Bock and Jamie A. Goode (eds.), Genetics of Criminal and Antisocial Behaviour. Chichester, Eng.: Wiley.

Magnusson, David, Britt af Klinteberg, and Hakan Stattin, 1992, "Autonomic Activity/Reactivity, Behavior, and Crime in a Longitudinal Perspective." Pp. 287–318 in Joan McCord (ed.), Facts, Frameworks, and Forecasts. New Brunswick, N.J.: Transaction.

Mednick, Sarnoff A., 1977, "A Bio-Social Theory of the Learning of Law-Abiding Behavior." Pp. 1–8 in Sarnoff A. Mednick and Karl O. Christiansen (eds.), q.v.

Mednick, Sarnoff A. and Karl O. Christiansen (eds.), 1977, Biosocial Bases of Criminal Behavior. New York: Gardner Press.

Mednick, Sarnoff A., William F. Gabrielli, Jr., and Barry Hutchings, 1987a, "Genetic Factors in the Etiology of Criminal Behavior." Pp. 74–91 in Sarnoff A. Mednick, Terrie E. Moffitt, and Susan A. Stack (eds.), q.v.

Mednick, Sarnoff A., Lis Kirkegaard-Sorensen, Barry Hutchings, Joachim Knop, Raben Rosenberg, and Fini Schulsinger, 1977, "An Example of Bio-social Interaction Research: The Interplay of Socioenvironmental and Individual Factors in the Etiology of Criminal Behavior." Pp. 9–23 in Sarnoff A. Mednick and Karl O. Christiansen (eds.), q.v.

Mednick, Sarnoff A., Terrie E. Moffitt, and Susan A. Stack (eds.), 1987b, The Causes of Crime: New Biological Approaches. Cambridge: Cambridge University Press.

Mednick, Sarnoff A., Jan Voluka, William F. Gabrielli, Jr., and Turan M. Itil, 1981, "EEG as a Predictor of Antisocial Behavior." Criminology 19:219–229.

Meltzer, Lynn J., Bethany N. Roditi, and Terence Fenton, 1986, "Cognitive and Learning Profiles of Delinquent and Learning-Disabled Adolescents." Adolescence XXI:581–591.

Moffitt, Terrie E., 1990, "Juvenile Delinquency and Attention Deficit Disorder: Boys' Developmental Trajectories from Age 3 to Age 15." Child Development 61:893–910.

Morrison, Helen L., 1978, "The Asocial Child: A Destiny of Sociopath?" Pp. 22–65 in William H. Reid (ed.), q.v.

Murray, Charles A., 1976, The Link Between Learning Disabilities and Juvenile Delinquency. Washington, D.C.: U.S. Department of Justice.

Patterson, Gerald R. and Karen Yoerger, 1993, "Developmental Models for Delinquent Behavior." Pp. 140–172 in Sheilagh Hodgins (ed.), Mental Disorder and Crime. Newbury Park, Calif.: Sage.

Perlmutter, Barry F., 1987, "Delinquency and Learning Disabilities: Evidence for Compensatory Behaviors and Adaptation." Journal of Youth and Adolescence 16:89–95.

Pickar, Daniel B. and Christopher D. Tori, 1986, "The Learning Disabled Adolescent: Eriksonian Psychosocial Development, Self-Concept, and Delinquent Behavior." Journal of Youth and Adolescence 15:429–440.

Rafter, Nicole Hahn, 1992, "Criminal Anthropology in the United States." Criminology 30:525–545.

Reid, Sue Titus, 1979, Crime and Criminology, second edition. New York: Holt, Rinehart and Winston.

Reid, William H. (ed.), 1978, The Psychopath. New York: Brunner/Mazel.

Rosanoff, Aaron J., Leva M. Handy, and Isabel Avis Rosanoff, 1934, "Criminality and Delinquency in Twins." Journal of Criminal Law and Criminology 24:923–934.

Rowe, David C., 1985, "Sibling Interaction and Self-Reported Delinquency Behavior: A Study of 265 Twin Pairs." Criminology 23:223–240.

———, 1986, "Genetic and Environmental Components of Antisocial Behavior: A Study of 265 Twin Pairs." Criminology 24:513–532.

Rowe, David C. and D. Wayne Osgood, 1984, "Heredity and Sociological Theories of Delinquency." American Sociological Review 49:526–540.

Satterfield, James H., 1978, "The Hyperactive Child Syndrome: A Precursor of Adult Psychopathy?" Pp. 329–346 in R. D. Hare and D. Schalling (eds.), q.v.

Shah, Saleem A. and Loren H. Roth, 1974, "Biological and Psychophysiological Factors in Criminality." Pp. 101–173 in Daniel Glaser (ed.), Handbook of Criminology. Chicago: Rand McNally.

Sheldon, William H., 1944, "Constitutional Factors in Personality." Pp. 526–549 in J. McV. Hunt (ed.), Personality and the Behavior Disorders, Vol. 1. New York: Ronald Press.

————, 1949, Varieties of Delinquent Youth. New York: Harper and Brothers.

Siddle, David A. T., Sarnoff A. Mednick, A. R. Nicol, and Roger H. Foggitt, 1977, "Skin Conductance Recovery in Anti-Social Adolescents." Pp. 213–216 in Sarnoff A. Mednick and Karl O. Christiansen (eds.), q.v.

Silberg, Judy, Joanne Meyer, Andrew Pickles, Emily Simonoff, Lindon Eaves, John Hewitt, Hermine Maes, and Michael Rutter, 1996, "Heterogeneity Among Juvenile Antisocial Behaviours: Findings from the Virginia Twin Study of Adolescent Behavioural Development." Pp. 76–86 in Gregory R. Bock and Jamie A. Goode (eds.), Genetics of Criminal and Antisocial Behaviour. Chichester, Eng.: Wiley.

Slavin, Sidney, H., 1978, "Information Processing Defects in Delinquents." Pp. 75–104 in Leonard J. Hippchen (ed.), q.v.

Sutherland, Edwin H. and Donald R. Cressey, 1978, Criminology, tenth edition. New York: Lippincott.

Venables, Peter H., 1987, "Autonomic Nervous System Factors in Criminal Behavior." Pp. 110–136 in Sarnoff A. Mednick, Terrie E. Moffitt, and Susan A. Stack (ed.), q.v.

Vold, George and Thomas J. Bernard, 1986, Theoretical Criminology, third edition. New York: Oxford University Press.

von Hentig, Hans, 1948, The Criminal and His Victim. New Haven: Yale University Press.

Walsh, Anthony, J. Arthur Beyer, and Thomas A. Petee, 1987, "Violent Delinquency: An Examination of Psychopathic Typologies." Journal of Genetic Psychology 148:385–392.

Walters, Glenn D., 1990, "Heredity, Crime, and the Killing-of-the-Bearer-of-Bad-News Syndrome: A Reply to Brennan and Mednick." Criminology 28:663–667.

————, 1992, "A Meta-Analysis of the Gene-Crime Relationship." Criminology 30:595–613.

Walters, Glenn D. and Thomas W. White, 1989, "Heredity and Crime: Bad Genes or Bad Research?" Criminology 27:455–485.

Wilson, James D. and Richard J. Herrnstein, 1985, Crime and Human Nature. New York: Simon and Schuster.

4

Psychological Theories

HISTORICAL OVERVIEW

Many scholars, policymakers, and laypersons have argued that there are individual differences in intelligence, personality, or other factors that not only separate delinquents from all other youths but that are, directly or indirectly, the causes of their delinquency. These can be summarized as psychological theories, and while it is possible that some of these factors are hereditary or inborn, and hence can be thought of as biological, this is not necessarily the case.

Perhaps the earliest attempt to isolate the psychological or mental aspects of criminal behavior was the development of the concept of insanity, particularly moral insanity (Fink, 1938). It was typically suggested that criminals and delinquents were deficient in basic moral sentiments and that, furthermore, this condition was inherited. The assumption that the lack of basic moral sentiments was an inherited trait contributed to the fusion of biological and psychological properties in the explanation of criminality.

With the introduction of intelligence tests around the turn of the twentieth century, students of crime and delinquency began to concentrate on the specific mental aspects of aberrant behavior, although, again, earlier analyses of the intellectual capacities of criminals and delinquents assumed that intelligence was inherited and thus, essentially, a biological component of behavior.

Toward the end of the nineteenth century, Sigmund Freud and others began to write of the internal workings of the mind and personality configurations, and how these components of the human condition affected behavior, including criminality. Collectively, this position is often referred to as the psychiatric-psychoanalytic approach, although it is generally recognized that psychoanalysis is a form of psychiatry, which is focused on the treatment of human behavioral problems. With the establishment of the juvenile court concept in 1899, the influence of the psychiatric position relative to delinquency became prominent. Delinquents were viewed as behaving under the influence of a disease, a condition which would become worse if it were not treated. In accordance with this philosophy, psychiatrically influenced child-guidance clinics were established during the first third of the twentieth century, often as extensions of the juvenile court (Krisberg and Austin, 1978).

GENERIC ASSUMPTIONS

Throughout the twentieth century, the psychological approach to delinquency developed and, at times, flourished. Some of the more prominent variations of this overall approach included concepts of mental deficiency, psychiatric disturbances, and general personality configurations. Generically they shared some common, basic assumptions: (1) The basic cause of delinquency lies *within* the individual's patterns and developments. Delinquent behavior, in other words, is a manifestation of internal, underlying disturbances. (2) Whatever the specific psychological disturbance which might exist in any particular delinquent behavior pattern, it most probably began to develop not later than early childhood and has become a fairly characteristic feature of the individual. (3) While allowance is given for the potential modifying effects of external, environmental factors, it is the individual who has the problem and it is thus on the individual that one must focus if the problem is to be resolved and the consequent delinquent behavior is to be changed.

The causation chain that links psychological theories to delinquency may be depicted as shown in Figure 2. Thus, the proximate cause of delinquency, and the appropriate focus of concern, is the psychological abnormality, not the factors which produced it. The psychological abnormalities may be considered as responses to biological or environmental conditions. Delinquency, in turn, may be seen as a response to psychological problems. It is recognized that both the psychological conditions and the delinquent behavior may affect the antecedent biological and environmental factors, thus generating new psychologi-

Diverse Factors	Psychological Abnormalities	
a. Biological	a. Mental ability	
b. Environmental $\rightarrow$	b. Subconscious conflicts	$\rightarrow$ Delinquency
	c. General personality traits	

Figure 2

cal and behavioral adjustments. From this perspective, however, the focus remains on the psychological conditions and their effect on delinquency.

INTELLIGENCE AND DELINQUENCY

Specific Assumptions

At the turn of the century, a number of investigators concluded that a general lack of intelligence was an important contributing factor to crime, delinquency, and a host of assorted social ills. A basic assumption of these earlier investigations was that lack of intelligence directly led to criminal behavior by rendering one less capable of appreciating the immorality of behavior or the complexity of a particular situation. Second, it was assumed that those of low intelligence were less able to control their emotions and desires, and were thus more likely to engage in criminality, not because they particularly wanted to, but because they could rarely keep their behavior in check. Later investigations have assumed that intelligence affects delinquency *indirectly*, because it affects other factors which have a more direct connection with delinquency.

Key Concept

Intelligence In the literature connecting intelligence with delinquency, the key concept is *intelligence*. Besides the issue of whether intelligence is innately or environmentally determined, which goes beyond the scope of this book, there remains the crucial question of how to measure the concept.

Many of the earlier investigations of criminality utilized definitions of intelligence that were based on logic; that is, low intelligence was often associated with placement in institutions for those of low intelligence (the feebleminded) or with some similar "official" judgment. Typically, these judgments were based on commonsense observations, association and memory tests, or just plain guesswork (Fink, 1938).

At the turn of the century, Alfred Binet, and later Theodore S. Terman, devised intelligence tests (IQ tests), which have come to be used, in modified versions, in most intelligence tests today. IQ tests have themselves become the center of much controversy and debate in terms of their reliability and validity (Jensen, 1969; Richardson and Spears, 1972; Senna, 1973; Whimbey and Whimbey, 1975; Block and Dworkin, 1976; Jensen, 1980; Eysenck and Kamin, 1981; Grace and Sweeney, 1986; Haynes et al., 1986; Haynes and Howard, 1986), but, again, these issues lie on the periphery of the present discussion. The main point to be made for now is that the dominant measurement of intelligence today is that which an IQ test measures and that the validity of these tests is still being examined.

Discussion

With the introduction of IQ tests as the basic measure of intelligence, the investigation between intelligence and criminality began to flourish. This interest in the intellectual characteristics of criminals and delinquents was spearheaded by H. H. Goddard, an administrator of the New Jersey School for the Feeble-Minded. In 1912, Goddard published an examination of the Kallikak family, a member of whom had been sent to the school. This family had two lines of progeny, one emanating from a "feebleminded" barmaid and the other from a "respectable girl of good family." The former line "produced" an assorted array of illegitimate children, prostitutes, alcoholics, criminals, and other deviants. The latter lineage consisted of a variety of governors, senators, doctors, and "good" people.

Two years later, Goddard (1914) published a study on the intellectual capacities of inmates in 16 reformatories. He found the percentage of "defectives," of feebleminded inmates, to range from 28 to 89, with an estimated average of 50 percent. The results of these studies led Goddard to conclude that criminal behavior was largely attributable to weak intelligence.

Although Goddard's study of the Kallikak family employed a subjective definition of feeblemindedness, the later investigation identified feeblemindedness on the basis of the IQ distributions among those in institutions for the feebleminded. These distributions yielded an IQ of 75 or less, or a mental age of 12 or below, as the cutoff points for classifying one as feebleminded.

The initial wave of research which followed Goddard's earlier studies reported that feebleminded prisoners constituted from about 25 to 90 percent of prison populations (Fink, 1938). The validity of this research, however, came into question when the U.S. Army began to administer IQ tests to Army draftees during World War I. These tests indicated that roughly one-third of the draftee population was feebleminded, according to the definition of feeblemindedness then in use (Zeleny, 1933). Clearly, this was an unsettling proposition for most people to accept. Accordingly, the definition of feeblemindedness was revised downward to an IQ of 50, or a mental age of 8 or below, to conform to more trustworthy proportions. This readjustment cast doubt on the earlier work of Goddard and others which had so often linked low intelligence and feeblemindedness with delinquency.

Subsequent investigations, armed with the revised guidelines for feeblemindedness, and using direct comparisons between criminals and delinquents and other population subgroups, have generally failed to establish any clear, consistent connection between IQ and criminality (Zeleny, 1933; Tulchin, 1939; Sutherland and Cressey, 1978; Vold and Bernard, 1986). Some studies, for example, have found criminals to be of higher intelligence than Army draftees (Murchison, 1926).

Besides numerous methodological problems, such as sampling design and definitions of criminality, the inconsistent findings of these latter studies tended to focus attention on causative factors other than intelligence. For several decades, therefore, scant attention was paid to the intelligence of delinquents and criminals. Recently, however, several investigators have begun to include intellectual functioning in their theories of criminality, and nearly all of these formulations have been addressed to delinquency. Roy Austin (1975), for example, suggests that intelligence is a major factor in the development of interpersonal maturity levels.

In a discussion of delinquency rate measurement, Robert Gordon (1976) examines delinquency *prevalence* rates, in contrast to delinquency incidence rates. Prevalence rate is a measurement of the proportion of a given age cohort, or specific age category of people, that have committed delinquent acts by a certain age in life. Gordon proceeds to analyze existing delinquency prevalence figures, based on official accounts, and concludes that nonwhite juvenile males have uniformly higher arrest rates and court appearance rates than white males or females, regardless of any specific geographical location, rural or urban.

Gordon proposes that differences in IQ may provide the greatest explanation of the persistent differences that he sometimes documents and sometimes assumes. Differences in IQ distributions in specific populations are offered as the basic explanation for differences in delinquency rates between these same populations for the following reasons: (1) the IQ distribution in a population is constant across time and geographical location; (2) IQ is directly associated with delinquency among whites (which, Gordon suggests, also explains the consistently higher official delinquency rates among lower-class, as opposed to middle-class, whites); (3) low IQ could be responsible for the higher crime and delinquency concordance rates among monozygotic twins compared to dizygotic twins; (4) low IQ might explain the results of one study wherein a higher rate of criminality was found among adoptees of unknown parentage; (5) IQ differences in general between racial groups are in the same direction and of similar magnitude as the differences between these racial groups in terms of delinquency (when differences in IQ between blacks and whites are controlled, differences in delinquency prevalence rates disappear); (6) there is a relatively high rate of delinquency in middle-class African-American neighborhoods (which some would challenge; Gordon, 1976:256–265).

Although Gordon raises the issue of innate ability as a basic component of IQ, he eventually appears to be implicating IQ in the causation of delinquency because *low IQ* is presumed to inhibit the socialization process of children. Not only are low-IQ children less likely to comprehend the world in which they are forced to live (particularly those whose IQ score falls between 50 and 90), but they will more likely be raised by parents whose IQ is also low. Thus, the ability of these parents to socialize their children appropriately is diminished. It should be noted that many of Gordon's assertions, especially the idea that low-IQ parents are poor socializers, are conjectural (Sampson and Laub, 1993:529). As Edward Sagarin states:

> We have no empirical proof—or disproof—that low-IQ parents are ineffective socializing agents. We do not have evidence that low-IQ delinquents have low-IQ parents or that high-IQ delinquents (yes, there are such) have high-IQ parents. . . . We do not know whether high-IQ children or children of high-IQ parents have greater opportunities to escape official recognition as delinquents. The entire argument suffers from a lack of parsimony: Occam's razor has never been so dull as in the hands of Gordon. (Sagarin, 1980:17)

In another article, Travis Hirschi and Michael Hindelang (1977) analyze earlier studies of the relationship between intelligence and delinquency and conclude that the available evidence does support a connection between the two variables.

As far as official rates of delinquency are concerned, Hirschi and Hindelang conclude from their secondary analysis that IQ predicts delinquency as well as do race and social class and better than other variables, such as family status, which has traditionally been linked with delinquency.

With respect to self-report or unofficial delinquency, the relationship with intelligence is evident, but not as strong as the relationship between intelligence and official records. Hirschi and Hindelang offer two suggestions for this discrepancy: (1) those with low IQs may be the least able or the least willing to respond meaningfully to a self-report questionnaire but still be the most delinquent youth in a sample and (2) IQ is a better predictor of multiple-offense delinquents (as officially recorded) rather than delinquency in general. Since self-report surveys typically reveal less serious and less repetitive instances of delinquency (see Elliott and Ageton, 1980), this measure of delinquency may be less sensitive to the effects of IQ than official indices. It is also possible to postulate that adolescents with high IQs have the cunning to conceal their delinquent acts on a self-report questionnaire. This possibility would also reduce the connection between IQ and delinquency.

Hirschi and Hindelang conclude that after the initial popularity of IQ as a cause of criminality, subsequent research failed to support the existence of a consistent relationship between the two variables. At the same time, sociological theories began to dominate the literature on delinquency, and these theories, *ostensibly*, have ignored IQ as a causal factor. In actuality, Hirschi and Hindelang argue that recent research has established a consistent eight-point IQ difference between delinquents (presumably official delinquents) and non-delinquents, a difference they argue is too large to be ignored. Furthermore, they argue that many sociological theories *implicitly* recognize the importance of IQ on delinquency, but for different reasons, especially those theories which focus on class-based strains and conflicts.

Hirschi and Hindelang do not attribute any direct effects of IQ on delinquency. Instead, like Gordon, they suggest an indirect effect, especially via the school system and the juvenile's ability to function well in that arena of competition.[1] Juveniles with low IQs do poorly in school, become discouraged and develop a negative attitude toward schoolwork, and search elsewhere for acceptance and activity. More and more, "acceptable" alternatives such as work become unavailable to these youth, leaving unacceptable choices, such as delinquency, as more likely (see also, Wilson and Herrnstein, 1985:166–172). This is a far cry from Gordon's race and heredity theories, and it allows for a host of intervening factors connecting the influence of the low IQ to delinquency.

Furthermore, a consideration of the mutual effects of IQ, academic performance and ability, peer associations, perceived labeling by teachers, parents, and peers, school alienation, and perceived academic and employment opportunities on a self-report measure of delinquency led Menard and Morse (1984) to conclude that IQ does indirectly influence delinquency, through academic abilities, but only mildly. Basically, they find that peer associations and school practices with respect to academic abilities are more directly associated with delinquent behavior and that the IQ-delinquency connection has "weak support" (p. 1375).

Other research maintains that the IQ–school performance–delinquency connection should add more variables (Ward and Tittle, 1994). Specifically, Ward and Tittle suggest that school performance contributes to attitudes toward school, which, in turn, have a more direct effect on delinquency. Overall, however, their conclusion is similar to that of other researchers on this topic, namely, that IQ has a relatively weak impact on delinquency, even indirectly through school-related variables (pp. 206–208).

An investigation of the contributing factors to delinquency, as measured by police contacts, among a sample of 800 African-American youth in Philadelphia also revealed an indirect connection between IQ and delinquency, but only for males (Denno, 1985). Among females no connection between IQ and delinquency was found. The indirect connection between IQ and male delinquency involved academic achievement as the mediating variable. Among both sexes, the primary precursor to delinquency was disciplinary problems in school, but this factor was not connected to IQ among girls.

The indirect relationship between IQ and delinquency, through school achievement, seems plausible, and has some theoretical support. However, empirical attempts to test this relationship have failed to identify strong and consistent support for the hypothesis. Thus, while the hypothesized indirect connection between IQ and delinquency more than likely does exist, the force of the relationship is relatively weak and more operative for some juveniles than for others.

Evaluation

The history of research on the relationship between IQ and delinquency shows an uneven pattern. The original studies claimed to demonstrate a consistently strong inverse relationship between the two variables, such that those with low IQs had higher rates of delinquency. With the introduction of more reliable measures of IQ, the strength of the association between IQ and delinquency was reduced to insignificance. This conclusion was reinforced by the introduction of self-report studies of delinquency, which have consistently yielded lower levels of association with IQ than official measures of delinquency. More recently, analyses have begun to resurrect the importance of IQ in the explanation of delinquency, although the bulk and persuasiveness of these arguments rest with official measures of delinquency.

In a field with as few absolutes as the subject of juvenile delinquency, sweeping conclusions either for or against the validity of a theoretical position, such as the inverse relationship between IQ and delinquency, should be greeted with caution. It is probably true that many students of delinquency have "thrown the baby out with the bathwater," so to speak, with respect to the influence of IQ on delinquency. The issue has frequently assumed racial, even moral, overtones and has thus been shrouded with emotional judgments. This situation has tended to obscure the factual elements of the studies that have been conducted.

The relatively moderate conclusions reached by more recent analyses must be carefully weighed for two reasons: (1) they are largely based on official measures of delinquency, which might reflect the tendency of those with low intellect to be caught more often than others; and (2) they are based on a number of assumptions concerning IQ that are still unresolved. Two of these assumptions are that IQ scores are constant over time and experience, and that IQ scores are culturally unbiased measures of native intellect. Although Gordon tends to deny that these factors influence the results, which indicate a low IQ-high delinquency correlation, and Hirschi and Hindelang acknowledge the existence of doubt, they all nevertheless brush the issues aside and determine that the case is settled. ~~Suffice it to say that the validity and reliability of IQ scores are still in question, and any attempt to deal with the connection between IQ and delinquency must account for these questions.~~

THE PSYCHIATRIC-PSYCHOANALYTIC APPROACH

Specific Assumptions

The field of psychiatry is quite broad, encompassing several different orientations and approaches to an understanding of human personalities. One of these psychiatric perspectives is referred to as the psychoanalytic perspective. Although derived from a single source, the seminal teachings of Sigmund Freud, it has developed different orientations, which can lead to different causal explanations of delinquency (Feldman, 1969).[2]

The psychoanalytic approach received wide support in the delinquency literature and in treatment programs for several decades; although in the 1970s it appeared to be losing adherents, it survived, particularly in modified neo-Freudian form. The basic assumptions of the psychoanalytic approach to delinquency include the following points: (1) each person (presumably, other than the severely retarded) grows and develops in stages, particularly in stages which focus on sexual development; (2) in some cases, and for a variety of specific reasons, abnormalities occur that create conflict within a person's developing personality, usually at an early age (preadolescence); (3) these conflicts arise generally from the interplay between instinctual drives and societal restraints; (4) the conflicts, and the specific reasons for their development, become painful to the individual's awareness and are pushed into the realm of the unconscious; and (5) attempts to handle the painful conflicts are developed within the personality in the form of defense mechanisms, and these mechanisms can lead to abnormal personality patterns, of which delinquency is one behavioral manifestation.

Key Concepts

Unconscious The concept of the unconscious is essential to psychoanalysis. By the unconscious, Freud referred to that which was repressed but ultimately capable of becoming conscious, although not always in ordinary ways (S. Freud, 1927).

Id, Ego, Superego According to Freud, all people have three personality components, called the id, the ego, and the superego. Essentially, the id refers to the basic instinctual drives and motivations of humans, the "passionate" aspect of the human psyche. An element of the id is the libido, the constellation of sexual drives and energies. The ego assumes the role of regulating the id's potentially damaging impulses. The ego represents "reason and sanity" within the personality. The superego is the individual's inner restraints, derived from societal norms and the fear of sanctions. It is equated with the human *conscience,* the sense of guilt for perceived or contemplated transgressions (S. Freud, 1920, 1927, 1930; A. Freud, 1935).

Oedipus Complex   Among several conflicts that develop during the process of sexual growth, one of the most significant, according to Freud, is the Oedipus complex. The term refers to the one-sided rivalry a son feels with his father for the attention of his mother, which develops in the second or third year of life. For Freud, the resolution of the oedipal conflict determined the development of the socially restraining superego (S. Freud, 1927); failure to resolve this conflict could, however, lead to serious personality and behavioral disorders. While many of these ideas were known and utilized in psychiatry before Freud, the terminology and the influence of the psychoanalytic approach in the delinquency literature are attributable largely to the work of Freud and twentieth-century psychoanalytic studies.

Discussion

Two conclusions can be drawn from the foregoing discussion: (1) that delinquency is *symptomatic* of underlying conflicts (often unconscious) and emotional stress, and (2) that these conflicts and stresses can be compared to a *disease*, which, if untreated, will become progressively worse. These two conclusions regarding delinquency are predominant in the psychoanalytic literature.

Franz Alexander and William Healy (1935) offer an example of the symbolic nature of delinquency when they conclude in a particular case that the real motivation behind a juvenile's repeated thefts was a repressed sexual desire for his mother. To these psychiatrists, the conflicts over a forbidden sexual object were so painful that stealing, as a "lesser crime," took the place of the forbidden sexual desires. In another instance, August Aichhorn (1925) relates the account of a 17-year-old who repeatedly stole denatured alcohol from his father's carpenter shop and urinated into the empty bottles, presumably to cover up the thefts. Aichhorn concluded from his analysis of the case that the urination was probably a symbolic way of striking back at a father whom the boy perceived as a rival for the affections of a young stepmother. Another psychoanalyst, Kate Friedlander (1947), relates the history of a 7-year-old antisocial boy who was constantly involved in fights with other children, cruelty to animals, exhibitionism in front of adults, property destruction, and truancy. After an extensive analysis of the boy's life and his family relationships, Friedlander concluded that the antisocial behavior was a reaction to an unconscious oedipal conflict with the boy's father and to an imperfect superego.

The conception of delinquency as the outward manifestation of a disease is advocated by many proponents of psychoanalysis. William Healy and Augusta Bronner (1936), for example, compare delinquency and tuberculosis. Just as fever may be a symptom of TB, delinquency is a symptom of psychological conflicts and illnesses. Similarly, Aichhorn (1925) argues that *delinquency* is the disease and the "dissocial" behavior of a delinquent is the outward sign of the disease. To complete this analogy, Aichhorn argues that there are two kinds of delinquency, latent and manifest. Latent delinquency refers to potential delinquency, the situation Aichhorn refers to as a disease. Manifest delinquency refers to "overt bad behavior" (1925:41).

Explicit in the distinction between latent and manifest delinquency is a recognition of the connection between predisposing, underlying conditions and environmental stimuli needed to transform the potential behavior problems into actual ones (see also, Alexander and Healy, 1935; Friedlander, 1947).

An example of the interplay between internal and environmental factors in the psychoanalytic approach to delinquency is provided by Richard Jenkins' analysis of three behavioral-personality types identified by Lester Hewitt and Jenkins (1947). In a study of 500 juveniles referred to the Michigan Child Guidance Institute, they identified the following problem behaviors: (1) over-inhibited, shy, seclusive; (2) unsocialized aggressive and assaultive; and (3) socialized delinquent gang. The last two are clearly delinquent behavior patterns, according to the authors, while the first is more of a neurotic behavior pattern. Although some psychoanalytic proponents make a clear distinction between delinquent and neurotic behavior (Friedlander, 1947), the two terms have often been used interchangeably in the literature.

Jenkins describes these three behavior patterns in terms of their psychoanalytically derived personalities. The overinhibited behavior pattern is referred to as a Type I personality and is characterized as having an excessive shell of inhibition (superego). The Type II personality corresponds to the unsocialized aggressive behavior pattern and is characterized by the relative lack of inhibitions, or an underdeveloped superego. The Type III personality is associated with the socialized gang delinquent or "pseudo-social" person and is characterized by a dual superego configuration. In this individual there is a normal superego with respect to fellow gang members but an inadequate superego in regard to others. Out-group members may thus be victimized by this person who feels no sense of guilt or restraint toward the victim (Hewitt and Jenkins, 1947). Thus, the personality configuration of the gang delinquent depends on the setting in which behavior occurs.

Although many psychoanalytic explanations of delinquency recognize environmental factors in the etiology of delinquency, the focus of attention is on the internal psychological conflicts that the factors influence.

Evaluation

One of the most critical drawbacks of psychoanalytic theory is the difficulty encountered in attempts to measure key concepts and to test basic assumptions and specific hypotheses. Concepts such as "superego," "id," "unconscious conflicts," among others, are, by their very nature, incapable of being directly observed. Their existence and influence must be inferred rather than observed through overt means. The inference of "hidden" motives is often made from subjective techniques, such as dream analysis, hypnosis, and Rorschach tests. Since these techniques are largely subjective, they are susceptible to great variations in interpretation (Hakeem, 1957–58; Waldo and Dinitz, 1967). The field of psychotherapy thus becomes based more on art than on science.

In lieu of using objective measurements of concepts, psychoanalysts often use analogies to illustrate a point, such as a connection between various parts of the personality. Freud, for example, compared the connection between the id and the ego to that of the relationship between a horse and its rider. The horse (id) is stronger, but the rider (ego) is more intelligent and able to control and guide the potentially dangerous impulses of the horse. Sometimes, however, the horse is able to assume command over the rider, just as the id is sometimes able to overcome the ego (S. Freud, 1927). In another example, Aichhorn likened the relationship between the superego and the ego to a radio. The superego is the societal broadcast (radio), while the ego is the receiver and interpreter of social messages (Aichhorn, 1925).

All of these concepts are to be interpreted as metaphors. While metaphors can be very enlightening, they can also be misleading, particularly when they are interpreted literally rather than as figures of speech, and when not supported with empirical evidence. Most of the literature documenting a connection between psychoanalytic concepts and delinquency is based on detailed examinations of a few case histories. A disturbing element in these analyses is that they start from a presumed consequence—delinquency—and proceed to develop an elaborate explanation of why the event occurred, or what the behavior really meant, by using essentially anecdotal evidence. In short, the connection between unconscious conflicts and repressed experiences and delinquency is tautological or circular; that is, the effect (delinquency) is taken *as evidence* of the presumed cause (unconscious personality conflicts).

Besides the use of anecdotal and analogous evidence and tautological explanations of delinquency, the psychoanalytic approach has been criticized for its strong emphasis on early childhood experiences rather than current situations in the explanation of behavior (Parsons, 1954; Cohen, 1966; Clinard and Meier, 1979). A basic tenet of the sociological position is that people act in accordance with their perceived role expectations (Goffman, 1961; Inkeles, 1964). Roles are attached to the positions and situations people occupy, and these positions can vary widely. Of course, some sociologists, for example Talcott Parsons (1954), find psychoanalytic concepts to be somewhat useful in the explanation of human behavior, such as aggression. Also, Albert Cohen (1955) incorporates psychoanalytic terms into a largely sociological explanation of delinquency (see Chapter 6).

Even though psychoanalysis emphasizes early childhood influences, it does not fail to recognize the effects of environmental factors on personality and behavior. The major focus of attention in psychoanalysis, however, is on the internal mechanisms of the mind as these are influenced and developed early in life. As such, this theory is most aptly applied to small numbers of delinquents who truly do have personality problems. To the extent that these factors are stressed, the utility of the psychoanalytic position for an understanding of delinquency in general can be questioned.

GENERAL PERSONALITY CHARACTERISTICS

Specific Assumptions

In many ways, the assumptions of the general personality approach to delinquency are similar to those of psychoanalysis. Typically proponents of the personality trait approach assume that delinquency is a manifestation of underlying conflicts within the individual's psychological framework. Unconscious drives and motives and analogous imageries, however, are not part of the general personality perspective, in contrast to the psychoanalytic approach.

Second, and also similar to psychoanalysis, it is assumed that the genesis of one's personality is in childhood, although some of the proponents of this approach recognize the influence of ongoing life experiences in the development of personality characteristics.

A third assumption of the general personality perspective is that a specific trait, or a coherent set of traits, characterizes a person's general outlook on life and consequently his or her overall behavior.

Finally, it is assumed that a "negative" consequence, such as delinquency, must be preceded by a "negative" cause. Those personality traits that are characteristic of delinquents, therefore, are considered aberrant. This assumption is also similar to that of psychoanalysis, although the specific nature of the "disease" is not always explained. Instead, it is assumed that negative or abnormal personality traits act in a general way to produce delinquency.

Key Concept

Core Personality   The general personality trait approach to delinquency is rather straightforward. There are few entangled pathways that must all converge to produce delinquency. One is delinquent because of who he is—a delinquent "kind of person" (Cohen, 1966). This perspective is focused on the general concept of the *core personality*; that is, the delinquent, like others, is seen as possessing a dominant, overriding set of values and attitudes that guide his behavior. As will be demonstrated below, dependence on the existence of a core personality among delinquents has often caused problems of interpretation and understanding. Nevertheless, the concept remains a vital component of this approach and should be so recognized.

Discussion

The predominant view within the general personality perspective is that delinquents are disturbed, but very seldom psychotic. Sheldon and Eleanor Glueck, for example, concluded from their comparison of 500 delinquents and a matched sample of nondelinquents that less than 1 percent of the delinquents could be characterized as psychotic, although 1.6 percent of the nondelinquents were thus classified (Glueck and Glueck, 1950). In another controlled study, William Healy and Augusta Bronner (1936) compared the psychological characteristics of 105 delinquents (who had been referred to child guidance clinics) and 105 sibling nondelinquents. Their conclusion was that less than 7 percent of the delinquents were mildly psychotic, as compared with none of the controls.

The Healy and Bronner study is also known for the conclusion that 91 percent of the delinquents were unhappy and discontented with their lives or emotionally disturbed. In contrast, only 13 percent of the control siblings were so characterized (1936). In terms of personality characteristics, the delinquents were variously described as jealous, feeling personally inadequate, and guilt ridden. While this study has been used to demonstrate a strong link between personality characteristics and delinquency, there are some methodological problems that tend to cast doubt on its validity: (1) the personality differences between the delinquents and the nondelinquents were noted by a clinical staff of psychiatrists and psychologists; (2) the staff had much greater opportunity to observe and analyze the delinquents because they were clients (or patients) at the clinic; (3) the staff of the clinics knew the identity of the delinquents and the nondelinquents (Sutherland and Cressey, 1978). In short, the striking personality differences between the delinquents and nondelinquents could have been as much a result of the expectations (even though unintended) of the psychiatrically trained observers as a result of basic personality differences between the two groups.

A more recent analysis compared personal and social characteristics of a small (N = 31) collection of incarcerated delinquents with a like number of "nondelinquents" (Lewis et al., 1987). The two samples were matched relative to age, sex, social class, and race/ethnicity, a procedure which would tend to emphasize the influence of personal variables on delinquency. An examination of differences between the two samples located few neurological differences, but the delinquents were more often classified as having auditory hallucinations and paranoid thoughts. Overall, however, the factor which most clearly differentiated the two sets of juveniles was the presence of violence and abuse in the homes of the delinquents. Thus, while some psychiatric differences between the two samples were observed, the abusive atmosphere of the home and family emerged as the strongest indicant of delinquency.

Beyond the establishment of quantitative differences in personality characteristics between delinquents and nondelinquents, research in this area has attempted to specify those personality traits that particularly distinguish delinquents. There have been several reviews of these efforts and they generally demonstrate inconsistencies and difficulties in identifying a coherent "personality type" among delinquents. Walter Bromberg (1953), for example, listed 14 identifiable personality traits of delinquents including aggressiveness, emotional instability, immaturity, egocentricity, lack of ethics or inhibitions, suggestibility, and passivity. Not only is this list rather long, but it includes some patently contradictory traits, such as aggressiveness and passiveness. Although it may be true that contradictory personality traits are present in different delinquents, a general theory of delinquency based on that fact would have little predictive power.

Another review of the personality trait literature covered 113 comparisons of delinquents (and criminals) and nondelinquents using 30 personality tests (Schuessler and Cressey, 1950). In only 42 percent of the comparisons were any significant differences found. Furthermore, there was no evidence that any particular personality inventory or trait best identified delinquents or criminals.

The Schuessler and Cressey review was updated by Gordon Waldo and Simon Dinitz (1967). In addition, the Waldo-Dinitz review assessed the research according to its methodological characteristics, such as sample size, the use of control groups, and the consideration of other variables which might also influence criminality. In contrast to the earlier review, Waldo and Dinitz concluded that 81 percent of the post-1950 studies differentiated delinquents (criminals) from nondelinquents. They further noted that the differences between their conclusion and that of Schuessler and Cressey lay mainly in the greater sophistication of personality tests developed between 1950 and 1967. In particular, Waldo and Dinitz singled out "objective tests" as better discriminators between offenders and nonoffenders than performance tests or projective tests.

The objective personality test that Waldo and Dinitz selected as the most reliable was the Minnesota Multiphasic Personality Inventory (MMPI). The results of the use of the MMPI in distinguishing delinquents and other offenders from nonoffenders are rather impressive, particularly for the psychopathic deviation (Pd) subscale. Of the 29 reviewed instances in which the Pd scale of the MMPI was used, it significantly discriminated offenders from nonoffenders in 28 cases (Waldo and Dinitz, 1967). The developers of the inventory, Starke Hathaway and Elio Monachesi, and others have applied it to thousands of juvenile delinquents and nondelinquents with consistent discriminatory results, again mostly with the Pd subscale (Hathaway and Monachesi, 1963).

Another personality explanation of delinquency is commonly known as "interpersonal maturity" (Sullivan et al., 1957). According to the proponents of this explanation, it is possible for people to attain a maturity in social or interpersonal skills in the form of seven progressive stages or levels of development, each one being associated with a "core personality."

Although no specific names were originally given to these personality levels, later modifications and discussions of the theory began to isolate specific descriptive components, in the form of subtypes, of those personality levels within which most officially defined delinquents were located, Levels 2 to 4. In these classifications, those in maturity Level 2 are seen as asocial, aggressive, and power oriented, those in Level 3 are most often identified as conformist to the rules of delinquent groups, and those in Level 4 are typically called neurotic (Warren, 1970; Palmer, 1974). Since these three maturity levels represent close to 90 percent of officially identified delinquents (Warren, 1970; Palmer 1974), it may be surmised that the personality of the delinquent is not only "immature," but simultaneously aggressive, passive, and neurotic.

A Note on Psychopathy

Perhaps no other criminological term exerts more interest and fascination from the public than "psychopath." The term developed in the latter part of the nineteenth century to refer to aggressive criminals who acted impulsively with no apparent reason or goal (Fink, 1938). Since that time, it has been used widely in the mass media, often referring to murders such as those depicted in Alfred Hitchcock's *Psycho*. Clinically, however, the term has referred to a veritable host of attitudinal and behavioral characteristics. Over 200 terms have been used to describe people and to link them as a result of these descriptions with psychopathy, and of these it can be said that 55 are generally agreed on as describing the psychopathic personality (Sutherland and Cressey, 1978). Furthermore, several synonyms have appeared in the literature and in clinical manuals, particularly "sociopath" and "antisocial personality," which add to the confusion.

While it seems that such a wide range of attributes cannot produce a meaningful entity, there are some particularly recurring themes that provide a limited degree of intuitive understanding of the concept. Themes such as impulsiveness, inability to relate to others, inability to learn or profit from experiences, lack of guilt or remorse for harmful behavior, insensitivity for pain of others (and even relative insensitivity to pain experienced by oneself), and repeated transgressions are often used in scholarly treatises on the subject (McCord and McCord, 1956; Robins, 1966; Cleckley, 1976; Eysenck, 1977). The American Psychiatric Association's Diagnostic and Statistical Manual of Mental Disorders (1994) utilizes these characteristics, and a few others, such as irresponsibility, in its clinical definition of the antisocial personality, or sociopath among adults.

Some investigators wish to arrange psychopathy on a scale (Robins, 1966; Cleckley, 1976). Robins, for example, selected 19 life circumstances as the symptomatic criteria for identifying sociopathy, including the use of aliases, a "wild" adolescence, suicide attempts, and financial dependency. Arbitrarily, Robins decided that anyone whose behavior fit any 5 of the 19 symptoms would be under *consideration* as a sociopath. Other criteria, unspecified, were thus apparently utilized in arriving at a final conclusion that one had the "disease" of sociopathy.

Whether students of psychopathy regard the concept as an illness, almost all *associate* it with criminality. There is disagreement, however, over whether psychopathy or sociopathy pertains to juveniles as well as adults. On the one hand, Lewis Yablonsky (1970) argues that core members of violent gangs are so psychopathic and emotionally disturbed that they cannot even form primary groups. He thus refers to these types of gangs as "near groups." In addition, Hans and Sybil Eysenck (1978) are somewhat emphatic on the point that psychopathy is inversely related to age (that is, psychopathy is reduced as one gets older), although they cite some literature that is unable to find psychopathic personality differences among adolescents.

On the other hand, Robins (1966) is equally convinced that sociopathy is an adult disease and that juveniles can only be considered potentially sociopathic. The behavior that might be regarded as sociopathic in an adult is only symptomatic of sociopathy among juveniles. Moreover, the clinical definition of sociopathy or the antisocial personality seems to associate the condition with adulthood. Those children who are impulsive, self-centered, and apparently guiltless are often referred to as having a "tension-discharge disorder" or an "impulse-ridden personality" (Hare, 1970:5), or as having "conduct problems"

(White et al., 1990; Maughan, 1993; Robins, 1993), as opposed to a sociopathic personality. Consistent with this view is the Diagnostic and Statistical Manual of Mental Disorders, which reserves the term "antisocial personality disorder" for adults, as discussed earlier. For those under age 18, however, the term used to describe these personality characteristics is "conduct disorder." (1994:645–646).

Evaluation

The nature of the personality explanations of delinquency allows for more direct testing of assumptions than is true of psychoanalytic theories. Indeed, the literature on this topic is much more quantified and empirical than the psychoanalytic literature. Thus, the validity of the assumptions and concepts can be more confidently assessed. This evaluation focuses on two major concerns relative to the validity of personality theories: (1) the problem of *personality* classification and (2) the documented relationship of personality patterns to delinquency.

The idea that people have a dominating, "core" personality can sometimes lead to forced judgments and, ultimately, to misclassification. For example, several attempts have been made to test the validity of the I-level explanation of delinquency, and a recurring problem has been interjudge agreement on just what a person's personality is (Butler and Adams, 1966; Jesness, 1971; Beker and Heyman, 1972). Inventories or paper and pencil tests are quite unlikely to capture the core identity of people. It is difficult, even with in-depth interviews, to measure the variability of thought, mood, and behavior which people experience and express as they go through their daily lives.

The problem in adequately measuring and classifying one's personality is indicated in the numerous personality types and subscales that have been related to delinquency, some of which are contradictory (see, for example, Block et al., 1988). With so many dimensions and attributes assigned to the *criminal* and *delinquent* personality, much less to human personality in general, it is hard to imagine that any one characteristic or coherent set of attributes can accurately summarize a person's feelings and relationships with others. Perhaps misclassifications, or incomplete classifications, are the reasons for changes in the personality types of delinquents (Butler and Adams, 1966; Beker and Heyman, 1972). Of course, changes in personality can occur because of treatment interventions. Indeed, such change is at the heart of most treatment programs. But noted changes in personality classifications do occur in the absence of specific treatment. Robins' longitudinal examination of sociopathy (1966) noted that 39 percent of those diagnosed as sociopathic improved or "remitted" (changed, presumably) with age and with no apparent organized treatment, other than perhaps the help and guidance of ministers, friends, and relatives.

Large rates of change, with no programmatic treatment, were also noted for those diagnosed as psychotic and alcoholic. Clearly, such changes in personality cannot be supportive of a permanent core personality concept. Nor does such evidence provide trust in the accuracy of original diagnoses.

Even if core personalities existed and could be accurately identified, the relationship between personality differences and delinquency is far from conclusive. The demonstration of personality or emotional differences between delinquents and nondelinquents by Healy and Bronner has already been critiqued and found methodologically questionable. The two literature reviews mentioned earlier reached somewhat different conclusions regarding the relationship between personality and delinquency. The review that was more favorable to the significance of personality differences among delinquents (Waldo and Dinitz, 1967), however, was supportive only of personality differences measured by objective tests. Furthermore, Waldo and Dinitz note that the control study of the Gluecks (mentioned earlier) concluded that delinquents were more assertive, hostile, defiant, suspicious, and less cooperative than nondelinquents, using the Rorschach test as a measure. But they did *not* note that the Gluecks also found that nondelinquents were more neurotic than delinquents and that, overall, nearly half of the delinquents had "no conspicuous pathology," as compared with nearly 56 percent of the nondelinquents (Glueck and Glueck, 1950).

The two specific examples of personality explanations discussed earlier, MMPI and interpersonal maturity or I-level, have also been questioned regarding their connection with delinquency. Differences between delinquents and nondelinquents on the Pd subscale of the MMPI, for example, are often *statistically* significant, but numerically small. The scoring procedure of the inventory is such that a difference in responses to 4 items out of 50 between delinquents and nondelinquents would give statistically significant results. Considering the wording of the items ("I like school"; "My sex life is satisfactory"), such small differences in responses are hardly indicative of basic personality differences (Waldo and Dinitz, 1967; Vold and Bernard, 1986). Furthermore, since the Pd subscale was originally developed from "asocial" young patients, many of whom were delinquent, and since one of the items on the subscale is "I have never been in trouble with the law" (Hathaway and Monachesi, 1963; Waldo and Dinitz, 1967), it is not surprising that investigators, using this subscale, have often found significant differences between delinquents and nondelinquents. Some have noted, moreover, that much of the relationship that exists between delinquency and MMPI scores can be attributed to exaggerated responses, if such manipulations are not controlled (Rathus and Siegel, 1980). Finally, the MMPI comparisons often yield greater differences among various delinquent populations than between delinquents and nondelinquents (Waldo and Dinitz, 1967; see also, Tennenbaum, 1977:227–228).

The interpersonal maturity explanation of delinquency has attracted a great deal of attention in treatment programs (Jesness, 1971; Palmer, 1974). Its relationship to delinquency, however, has not been established, nor has it even been tested systematically (Gibbons, 1970; Beker and Heyman, 1972). Damaging to this theory is the difficulty in connecting I-level classifications with either traditional psychiatric concepts or with similar personality conceptualizations (Butler and Adams, 1966). In fact, an attempt to assess the construct validity of "interpersonal maturity" characteristics among institutionalized male delinquents in California failed to confirm "maturity" as an important characteristic of the I-level classification of delinquents. While there was a slight positive association between maturity level and I-level classification (as predicted), its importance was minuscule and ranked far below other variables, such as verbal aptitude, reasoning ability, and concern over right and wrong (Austin, 1975).

Along with all these shortcomings is the problem of cause and effect. The vast majority of delinquency research informed by personality theories and concepts has been conducted with *officially* defined delinquents, mostly those who have been referred to court or institutionalized. Consequently, it is possible that whatever personality differences have been detected in these studies between delinquents and nondelinquents may stem from the effects of identifying juveniles as delinquents.

The overall assessment of personality theories is that their validity is not very strong. Although personality differences between delinquents and nondelinquents have been noted, these differences are often numerically small, inconsistent in meaning, and possibly influenced by the effects of labeling juveniles as delinquents.

More recent studies address some of these issues by incorporating alternative measures of personality and by using self-report indices of delinquency. Some utilize multidimensional scales and refer to the "temperament" of individuals. Windle (1992), for example, used a 54-item temperament scale which identified 10 attributes, including such characteristics as sleep and eating habits, overall energy and activity levels, distractibility, and persistence. Responses to these items were correlated with self-report delinquency items, and measures of depression, among a sample of 975 high school students (who were mostly white, *middle-class* youth). Those who reported irregular sleeping and eating habits, high energy levels, high levels of distraction, low levels of task orientation, and so on, were considered as having a "difficult temperament." Using this scheme, Windle found significant correlations between difficult temperament and high levels of delinquency and depression. In addition, however, Windle found significant associations between difficult temperament and low levels of peer and familial emotional support. Furthermore, both temperament and family support exhibited significant and independent effects on delinquency and depression. Peer support yielded an interesting pattern with delinquency in that high peer support was associated with high levels of delinquency (pp. 9–13).

These results suggest that the connection between personality factors and delinquency is neither simple nor direct. Rather, these relationships involve a complex pattern of general psychopathology which can operate independently of, or in conjunction with, environmental factors such as peer and familial support (see also, Jones and Heaven, 1998; Loeber et al., 1998).

The interest in personality features and delinquency is more and more being couched in terms of general individual characteristics, but not necessarily a "core" personality, which contribute to delinquency early in life, throughout adolescence and into adulthood. An emerging theme is the existence of such personality traits as impulsivity, lack of control, hyperactivity, and so on, which distinguish delinquent behavior from nondelinquency (Tremblay, 1992; Caspi et al., 1994). In fact, the life course perspective is now applied to an understanding of personality characteristics in general, whether or not these lead to delinquency (Caspi, 1998). Even some traditional sociological explanations of delinquency, such as strain theory (see Chapter 5), are being reconceptualized to incorporate psychological dimensions of frustration and "strain" (Agnew, 1992).

For the past several years, a debate has been developing over whether crime and deviance, or "antisocial behavior" (Farrington, 1992), are the result of some underlying personal characteristic which emerges early in life and persists well into adulthood (Gottfredson and Hirschi, 1990), or whether deviance and its causative forces can be modified over the life course (Sampson and Laub, 1993).

Some are pursuing the view that there are multiple pathways to offending, in particular an early path and a later stage of involvement in delinquency (Moffitt, 1993; Simons et al., 1994). A biopsychological view of these pathways focuses on individual characteristics of early offenders, as opposed to more situational manifestations of delinquency. Using data from the New Zealand longitudinal study discussed in Chapter 3, Terrie Moffitt and associates, for example, argue that youth who show "persistent" signs of antisocial behavior (before adolescence) are significantly different on neuropsychological measures, such as verbal and memory abilities, compared to later offenders (Moffitt et al., 1994).

Another longitudinal study examined patterns of hyperactivity, autonomic nervous system functioning (as measured by levels of adrenaline excretion), and delinquency among all male youth living in a middle-sized city (population approximately 100,000) in Sweden (Magnusson et al., 1992), and reached a conclusion similar to Moffitt et al. Data were obtained from teacher evaluations of juveniles at ages 10 and 13. Estimates of criminality were generated from police and social service records of the youth up to age 15. The results of this study indicate a significant association between delinquency, hyperactivity, and lower levels of adrenaline excretion (pp 290–297). The longitudinal patterns, however, indicated that there were two sets of associations. In a limited number of cases, delinquency and other antisocial behaviors appeared early in life and persisted into adulthood. Among these boys there were high levels of hyperactivity and low levels of adrenaline excretion, or "autonomic reactivity." However, among a slightly larger number of males, a second pattern emerged. In this case, delinquency occurred only during adolescence and ceased by adulthood. In this situation, the adrenaline excretions were *higher* than among nonoffenders. The delinquency of these offenders was thus attributed to environmental factors, or essentially to variables other than low adrenaline excretion and hyperactivity (pp. 298–305).

Magnusson et al. offer the interpretation that low autonomic reactivity, as measured by adrenaline excretion, is an inborn trait which leads to hyperactivity, which leads to "persistent" criminality in some cases. This view is similar to the biological component of Eysenck's theory, discussed in Chapter 3. However, these authors offer other explanations for their findings, which involve environmental assessments of delinquency causation. For example, they suggest that one possible causal pattern is that low autonomic reactivity may be *learned* as a result of inconsistent patterns of discipline and socialization. According to this view, normal autonomic reactivity depends, at least to a degree, on consistent patterns of socialization in early childhood, even in infancy (pp. 309–310). Or, delinquency may be a result of both biological traits and inconsistent patterns of socialization. While these latter two interpretations are offered as explanations for both situational and persistent offenders, it would seem more likely that they would explain situational patterns of delinquency. Furthermore, these authors assume that negative biological factors may be offset by positive environmental factors, thus reducing the risk of delinquency. This conclusion is similar to the conclusions of Moffitt, as discussed in Chapter 3.

Evidence is becoming increasingly clear that "chronic" or repeat offenders, especially aggressive or violent youth, begin displaying delinquent behaviors or conduct problems at an early point in life, often preadolescence, and continue into late adolescence or young adulthood. Moreover, these early beginners usually have a combination of physical, psychological, and environmental risk factors which separate them from late starters and/or one-time offenders (Loeber and Hay, 1994; Thompson et al., 1996; Bender and Losel, 1997; Raine et al., 1997; Stattin et al., 1997; Vitelli, 1997; Coie and Dodge, 1998; Loeber et al., 1998).

Added to this picture of multiple pathways to delinquency is the presence of toxic chemicals and/or metals in the environment. In particular, exposure to lead has been connected with hyperactivity, impulsivity, and eventually delinquency, especially among youth in early to middle adolescence (Needleman et al., 1996).

SUMMARY

The traditional view that delinquents, and criminals in general, are produced from degenerate stock is no longer evident in modern psychological theories. IQ theories have been modified to include indirect influences through socialization and school experiences. While the emphasis on individual differences between delinquents and nondelinquents remains strong in these theories, there is an increasing recognition that personality and behavior are complex phenomena.

Nonetheless, the search for a unique set of personal, psychological antecedents of delinquency continues and remains unfulfilled. The psychoanalytic approach, once so popular in the literature and so influential in juvenile courts and institutional settings, has tended to give way to newer personality images of the delinquent. The contributions of Freud, his students, and subsequent generations of psychoanalysts will not be lost in the search for the psychological roots of delinquency. We will probably always be mindful of the possibility of underlying, "hidden" motives of behavior. Newer conceptions of the delinquent personality, however, have focused more on the objective, cognizant meanings of behavior. But these conceptions have lacked convincing evidence, particularly when it is argued that a core personality exists which is formed early and dominates one's behavior through most of life.

At the same time, few would suggest that juveniles, and adults for that matter, do not have personalities, as well as values and outlooks that can influence social relationships. These constructs are probably variable and malleable, and contingent on social roles and experiences. They are to be located on a continuum, not dichotomized (Gough, 1960). Indeed, many of the theories to be discussed in subsequent chapters assume, at least implicitly, that attitudes, personalities, and the like play some role in the translation of external events into individual behavior. The emphasis in these other theories, however, is on the external, social antecedents to delinquency.

Newer lines of inquiry are using longitudinal data, multiple indicators of delinquency or antisocial behavior (such as self-reports, teacher evaluations, and parental assessments), and are done in consideration of social and environmental factors. Consequently, the findings and conclusions of this research are not as vulnerable to the criticisms of earlier psychological and biopsychological studies, such as those discussed earlier in this chapter and in Chapter 3. An encouraging aspect of this research, furthermore, is the willingness to include environmental conditions on the personality and/or biological characteristics which are thought to be major contributors to delinquency (Caspi et al., 1994). That traditional sociological explanations of delinquency are being reconceptualized to include individualistic constructs is further indication of the potential for true interdisciplinary conceptualization and investigation of the contributions to delinquency.

Not all the investigations into life course patterns of delinquency contain biopsychological focuses. Sampson and Laub (1993), for example, have developed a view of life patterns of crime and delinquency which essentially focuses on situational and environmental influences that can have an impact on one's life and opportunities for conventional and nonconformist paths of behavior (see also, Kaplan et al., 1983:39–44; Huizinga et al., 1991).

Furthermore, as with the research of Magnusson et al., some contend that early and late paths of delinquency can be explained by patterns of child-rearing and other parental and familial influences, rather than by biopsychological factors alone (see also, Patterson et al., 1991; Simons et al., 1994). Patterns of familial relationships and socialization practices will be discussed in more detail in Chapter 8. For the moment, however, it is important to stress that modern psychological and biopsychological investigations of delinquent and antisocial behavior are addressing many of the criticisms of earlier studies, and this research is becoming more interdisciplinary in conceptualization.

Notes

1. A detailed examination of this proposition was provided by John Conger and Wilbur Miller's longitudinal analysis of IQ, personality, and official delinquency in Denver (1966). Their analysis, however, indicated that the relationship that exists among IQ, school performance, and delinquency characteristics is neither linear nor simple. IQ, for example, was found to clearly differentiate future delinquents from nondelinquents (basically through social adaptation, school performance, and so forth) in kindergarten through third grade. In grades 1 to 6, however, the importance of IQ as a direct or indirect predictor of future delinquency diminished in favor of social class status. In grades 7 to 9 both IQ and social class status combined to explain observed delinquent behavior.

2. It would be impossible to discuss all of the published psychoanalytic studies of delinquency. Some of the more notable analyses which are not cited elsewhere in this chapter include Lindner (1944), Redl and Wineman (1951), Abrahamsen (1952), and Halleck (1967, especially Chapters 9 and 10).

References

Abrahamsen, David, 1952, Who Are the Guilty? New York: Rinehard.

Agnew, Robert, 1992, "Foundation for a General Strain Theory of Crime and Delinquency." Criminology 30:47–87.

Aichhorn, August, 1925, Wayward Youth. Reprinted, New York: Viking, 1965.

Alexander, Franz and William Healy, 1935, Roots of Crime. Reprinted, Montclair, N.J.: Patterson Smith Reprint, 1969.

Austin, Roy L., 1975, "Construct Validity of I-Level Classification." Criminal Justice and Behavior 2:113–129.

Beker, Jerome and Doris S. Heyman, 1972, "A Critical Appraisal of the California Differential Treatment Typology of Adolescent Offenders." Criminology 10:3–59.

Bender, Doris and Friedrich Losel, 1997, "Protective and Risk Effects of Peer Relations and Social Support on Antisocial Behaviour in Adolescents from Multi-Problem Milieus." Journal of Adolescence 20:661–678.

Block, Jack, Jeanne H. Block, and Susan Keyes, 1988, "Longitudinally Foretelling Drug Usage in Adolescence: Early Childhood Personality and Environmental Precursors." Child Development 58:336–355.

Block, N. J. and Gerald Dworkin (eds.), 1976, The IQ Controversy. New York: Pantheon.

Bromberg, Walter, 1953, "American Achievements in Criminology." Journal of Criminal Law, Criminology and Police Science 47:166–176.

Butler, Edgar W. and Stuart N. Adams, 1966, "Typologies of Delinquent Girls: Some Alternative Approaches." Social Forces 44:401–407.

Caspi, Avshalom, 1998, "Personality Development Across the Life Course." Chapter 6 in William Damon and Nancy Eisenberg (eds.), q.v.

Caspi, Avshalom, Terrie E. Moffitt, Phil A. Silva, Magda Stouthamer-Loeber, Robert F. Krueger, and Pamela S. Schmutte, 1994, "Are Some People Crime-Prone? Replications of the Personality-Crime Relationship Across Countries, Genders, Races, and Methods." Criminology 32:163–195.

Cleckley, Hervey, 1976, The Mask of Sanity, fifth edition. St. Louis: Mosby.

Clinard, Marshall B. and Robert F. Meier, 1979, The Sociology of Deviant Behavior, fifth edition. New York: Holt, Rinehart and Winston.

Cohen, Albert K., 1955, Delinquent Boys: The Culture of the Gang. New York: Free Press.

———, 1966, Deviance and Control. Englewood Cliffs, N.J.: Prentice-Hall.

Coie, John D. and Kenneth A. Dodge, 1998, "Aggression and Antisocial Behavior." Chapter 12 in William Damon and Nancy Eisenberg (eds.), q.v.

Conger, John Janeway and Wilbur C. Miller, 1966, Personality, Social Class and Delinquency. New York: Wiley.

Damon, William and Nancy Eisenberg (eds.), 1998, Handbook of Child Psychology, fifth edition, Vol. 3. New York: Wiley.

Denno, Deborah W., 1985, "Sociological and Human Developmental Explanations of Crime: Conflict or Consensus." Criminology 23:711–741.

Diagnostic and Statistical Manual of Mental Disorders, DSM-IV-R, 1994, fourth edition. Washington, D.C.: American Psychiatric Association.

Elliott, Delbert S. and Suzanne S. Ageton, 1980, "Reconciling Race and Class Differences in Self-Reported and Official Estimates of Delinquency." American Sociological Review 45:95–110.

Eysenck, H. J., 1977, Crime and Personality, second edition. London: Routledge and Kegan Paul.

Eysenck, H. J. and S. B. G. Eysenck, 1978, "Psychopathy, Personality, and Genetics." Pp. 197–223 in R. D. Hare and R. Schalling (eds.), Psychopathic Behavior. New York: Wiley.

Eysenck, H. J. and Leon Kamin, 1981, The Intelligence Controversy. New York: Wiley.

Farrington, David P., 1992, "Explaining the Beginning, Progress, and Ending of Anti-social Behavior from Birth to Adulthood." Pp. 253–286 in Joan McCord (ed.), q.v.

Feldman, David, 1969, "Psychoanalysis and Crime." Pp. 433–442 in Donald R. Cressey and David A. Ward (eds.), Delinquency, Crime and Social Process. New York: Harper & Row.

Fink, Arthur E., 1938, Causes of Crime. New York: A. S. Barnes.

Freud, Anna, 1935, Psycho-Analysis for Teachers and Parents. New York: Emerson Books.

Freud, Sigmund, 1920, A General Introduction to Psycho-Analysis, translated by Joan Riviere. New York: Liveright, 1935.

———, 1927, The Ego and the Id, translated by Joan Riviere. London: Hogarth, 1949.

———, 1930, Civilization and Its Discontents, edited and translated by James Strachey. New York: Norton, 1961.

Friedlander, Kate, 1947, The Psycho-Analytical Approach to Juvenile Delinquency. London: Routledge and Kegan Paul.

Gibbons, Don C., 1970, "Differential Treatment of Delinquents and Interpersonal Maturity Levels Theory: A Critique." Social Science Review 44:22–33.

Glueck, Sheldon and Eleanor Glueck, 1950, Unraveling Juvenile Delinquency. Cambridge, Mass.: Harvard University Press.

Goddard, H. H., 1912, The Kallikak Family. New York: Macmillan.

———, 1914, Feeble-Mindedness. New York: Macmillan.

Goffman, Erving, 1961, Asylums. Garden City, N.Y.: Doubleday/Anchor.

Gordon, Robert A., 1976, "Prevalence: The Rare Datum in Delinquency Measurement and Its Implications for the Theory of Delinquency." Pp. 201–284 in Malcolm Klein (ed.), The Juvenile Justice System. Beverly Hills, Calif.: Sage.

Gottfredson, Michael and Travis Hirschi, 1990, A General Theory of Crime. Stanford, Calif.: Stanford University Press.

Gough, Harrison G., 1960, "Theory and Measurement of Socialization." Journal of Consulting Psychology 24:23–30.

Grace, William C. and Mary E. Sweeney, 1986, "Comparisons of the P>V Sign on the WISC-R and WAIS-R in Delinquent Males." Journal of Clinical Psychology 42:173–176.

Hakeem, Michael, 1957–58, "A Critique of the Psychiatric Approach to the Prevention of Juvenile Delinquency." Social Problems 5:194–205.

Halleck, Seymour L., 1967, Psychiatry and the Dilemmas of Crime. New York: Harper & Row.

Hare, Robert D., 1970, Psychopathy. New York: Wiley.

Hathaway, Starke R. and Elio D. Monachesi, 1963, Adolescent Personality and Behavior. Minneapolis: University of Minnesota Press.

Haynes, Jack P. and Rodney C. Howard, 1986, "Stability of WISC-R Scores in a Juvenile Forensic Sample." Journal of Clinical Psychology 42:534–537.

Haynes, Jack P., Rodney C. Howard, and Suzanne M. Haynes, 1986, "Internal Reliability of the WISC-R with Male Juvenile Delinquents." Journal of Clinical Psychology 43:496–499.

Healy, William and Augusta F. Bronner, 1936, New Light on Delinquency and Its Treatment. New Haven: Yale University Press.

Hewitt, Lester E. and Richard L. Jenkins, 1947, Fundamental Patterns of Maladjustment. Springfield, Ill.: State of Illinois.

Hirschi, Travis and Michael J. Hindelang, 1977, "Intelligence and Delinquency: A Revisionist Review." American Sociological Review 42:571–587.

Hodgins, Sheilagh (ed.), 1993, Mental Disorder and Crime. Newbury Park, Calif.: Sage.

Huizinga, David, Finn-Aage Esbensen, and Anne Wylie Weiher, 1991, "Are There Multiple Paths to Delinquency?" Journal of Criminal Law and Criminology 82:83–118.

Inkeles, Alex, 1964, What Is Sociology? Englewood Cliffs, N.J.: Prentice-Hall.

Jensen, A. R., 1969, "How Much Can We Boost IQ and Scholastic Achievement?" Harvard Educational Review 39:1–123.

———, 1980, Bias in Mental Testing. New York: Free Press.

Jesness, Carl F., 1971, "The Preston Typology Study: An Experiment with Differential Treatment in an Institution." Journal of Research in Crime and Delinquency 8:38–52.

Jones, Suzanne P. and Patrick C. L. Heaven, 1998, "Psychological Correlates of Adolescent Drug-Taking Behavior." Journal of Adolescence 21:127–134.

Kaplan, Howard B., Cynthia Robbins, and Steven S. Martin, 1983, "Toward the Testing of a General Theory of Deviant Behavior in Longitudinal Perspective: Patterns of Psychopathology." Research in Community and Mental Health 3:27–65.

Krisberg, Barry and James Austin (eds.), 1978, The Children of Ishmael: Critical Perspectives on Juvenile Justice. Palo Alto, Calif.: Mayfield.

Lewis, Dorothy Otnow, Jonathan H. Pincus, Richard Lovely, Elinor Spitzer, and Ernest Moy, 1987, "Biopsychosocial Characteristics of Matched Samples of Delinquents and Nondelinquents." Journal of the American Academy of Child and Adolescent Psychiatry 26:744–752.

Lindner, Robert, 1944, Rebel Without a Cause. New York: Grove Press.

Loeber, Rolf, David P. Farrington, Magda Stouthamer-Loeber, Terrie E. Moffitt, and Avshalom Caspi, 1998, "The Development of Male Offending: Key Findings from the Pittsburgh Youth Study." Studies in Crime and Crime Prevention 7:141–171.

Loeber, Rolf and Dale F. Hay, 1994, "Developmental Approaches to Aggression and Conduct Problems." Pp. 488–516 in Michael Rutter and Dale F. Hay (eds.), Development Through Life: Handbook for Clinicians. Oxford: Blackwell Scientific Publications.

Magnusson, David, Britt af Klinteberg, and Hakan Stattin, 1992, "Autonomic Activity/Reactivity, Behavior, and Crime in a Longitudinal Perspective." Pp. 287–318 in Joan McCord (ed.), q.v.

Maughan, Barbara, 1993, "Childhood Precursors of Aggressive Offending in Personality-Disordered Adults." Pp. 119–139 in Sheilagh Hodgins (ed.), q.v.

McCord, Joan (ed.), 1992, Facts, Frameworks, and Forecasts. New Brunswick, N.J.: Transaction.

McCord, William and Joan McCord, 1956, Psychopathy and Delinquency. New York: Grune and Stratton.

Menard, Scott and Barbara J. Morse, 1984, "A Structuralist Critique of the IQ-Delinquency Hypothesis: Theory and Evidence." American Journal of Sociology 89:1347–1378.

Moffitt, Terrie E., 1993, "'Life-Course-Persistent' and 'Adolescent-Limited' Antisocial Behavior: A Developmental Taxonomy." Psychological Review 100:674–701.

Moffitt, Terrie E., Donald R. Lynam, and Phil A. Silva, 1994, "Neuropsychological Tests Predicting Persistent Male Delinquency." Criminology 32:277–300.

Murchison, Carl, 1926, Criminal Intelligence. Worcester, Mass.: Clark University Press.

Needleman, Herbert L., Julie A. Reiss, Michael J. Tobin, Gretchen E. Blesecker, and Joel B. Greenhouse, 1996, "Bone Lead Levels and Delinquent Behavior." Journal of the American Medical Association (JAMA) 275:363–369.

Palmer, Ted, 1974, "The Youth Authority's Community Treatment Project." Federal Probation 38:3–14.

Parsons, Talcott, 1954, "Certain Primary Sources and Patterns of Aggression in the Social Structure of the Western World." Pp. 298–322 in Talcott Parsons (ed.), Essays in Sociological Theory, revised edition. New York: Free Press. Originally published in 1947.

Patterson, Gerald R., Deborah Capaldi, and Lou Bank, 1991, "An Early Starter Model for Predicting Delinquency." Pp. 139–168 in Debra J. Pepler and Kenneth H. Rubins (eds.), The Development and Treatment of Childhood Aggression. Hillsdale, N.J.: Erlbaum.

Raine, Adrian, Patricia A. Brennan, David P. Farrington, and Sarnoff A. Mednick (eds.), 1997, Biosocial Bases of Violence. New York: Plenum.

Rathus, Spencer A. and Larry J. Siegel, 1980, "Crime and Personality Revisited: Effects of MMPI Response Sets in Self-Report Studies." Criminology 18:245–251.

Redl, Fritz and David Wineman, 1951, Children Who Hate. Glencoe, Ill.: Free Press.

Richardson, Ken and David Spears (eds.), 1972, Race and Intelligence. Baltimore: Penguin.

Robins, Lee N., 1966, Deviant Children Grown Up. Baltimore: Williams and Wilkins.

———, 1993, "Childhood Conduct Problems, Adult Psychopathology, and Crime." Pp. 173–193 in Sheilagh Hodgins (ed.), q.v.

Sagarin, Edward, 1980, "Taboo Subjects and Taboo Viewpoints in Criminology." Pp. 7–21 in Edward Sagarin (ed.), Taboos in Criminology. Beverly Hills, Calif.: Sage.

Sampson, Robert J. and John H. Laub, 1993, Crime in the Making: Pathways and Turning Points Through Life. Cambridge, Mass.: Harvard University Press.

Schuessler, Karl and Donald R. Cressey, 1950, "Personality Characteristics of Criminals." American Journal of Sociology 55:476–484.

Senna, Carl (ed.), 1973, The Fallacy of IQ. New York: Third Press.

Simons, Ronald L., Chyi-In Wu, Rand D. Conger, and Frederick O. Lorenz, 1994, "Two

Routes to Delinquency: Differences Between Early and Late Starters in the Impact of Parenting and Deviant Peers." Criminology 32: 247–276.

Stattin, Hakan, Anders Romelsjo, and Marlene Stenbacka, 1997, "Personal Resources as Modifiers of the Risk for Future Criminality: An Analysis of Protective Factors in Relation to 18-Year-Old Boys." British Journal of Criminology 37:198–223.

Sullivan, Clyde, Marguerite Q. Grant, and J. Douglas Grant, 1957, "The Development of Interpersonal Maturity: Applications to Delinquency." Psychiatry 20:373–385.

Sutherland, Edwin H. and Donald R. Cressey, 1978, Criminology, tenth edition. New York: Lippincott.

Tennenbaum, David J., 1977, "Personality and Criminality: A Summary and Implications of the Literature." Journal of Criminal Justice 5:225–235.

Thompson, Laetitia L., Paula D. Riggs, Susan F. Mikulich, and Thomas J. Crowley, 1996, "Contribution of ADHD Symptoms to Substance Problems and Delinquency in Conduct-Disordered Adolescents." Journal of Abnormal Child Psychology 24:325–347.

Tremblay, Richard E., 1992, "The Prediction of Delinquent Behavior from Childhood Behavior: Personality Theory Revisited." Pp. 193–230 in Joan McCord (ed.), q.v.

Tulchin, Simon H., 1939, Intelligence and Crime. Chicago: University of Chicago Press.

Vitelli, Romeo, 1997, "Comparison of Early and Late Start Models of Delinquency in Adult Offenders," International Journal of Offender Therapy and Comparative Criminology 41:351–357.

Vold, George B. and Thomas J. Bernard, 1986, Theoretical Criminology, third edition. New York: Oxford University Press.

Waldo, Gordon and Simon Dinitz, 1967, "Personality Attributes of the Criminal: An Analysis of Research Studies, 1950–65." Journal of Research in Crime and Delinquency 4:185–202.

Ward, David A. and Charles R. Tittle, 1994, "IQ and Delinquency: A Test of Two Competing Explanations." Journal of Quantitative Criminology 40:189–212.

Warren, Marguerite Q., 1970, "The Case for Differential Treatment of Delinquents." Pp. 419–428 in Harwin L. Voss (ed.), Society, Delinquency, and Delinquent Behavior. Boston: Little, Brown.

Whimbey, Arthur, with Linda Shaw Whimbey, 1975, Intelligence Can Be Taught. New York: Dutton.

White, Jennifer L., Terrie E. Moffitt, Felton Earls, Lee Robins, and Phil A. Silva, 1990, "How Early Can We Tell?: Predictors of Childhood Conduct Disorder and Adolescent Delinquency." Criminology 28:507–533.

Wilson, James and Richard J. Herrnstein, 1985, Crime and Human Nature. New York: Simon and Schuster.

Windle, Michael, 1992, "Temperament and Social Support in Adolescence: Interrelations with Depressive Symptoms and Delinquent Behaviors." Journal of Youth and Adolescence 21:1–21.

Yablonsky, Lewis, 1970, The Violent Gang, revised edition. Baltimore: Penguin.

Zeleny, L. D., 1933, "Feeble-Mindedness and Criminal Conduct." American Journal of Sociology 38:564–576.

5

Social Disorganization and Anomie

HISTORICAL OVERVIEW

The suggestion that delinquency is caused by environmental factors has a long history. Urban studies in the nineteenth century, particularly in Europe, regularly demonstrated correlations between delinquency (and crime) and such factors as population density, age and sex composition, poverty, and education. Morris (1958) maintains that the three dominant nineteenth-century hypotheses concerning crime causation were poverty, ignorance, and population density. Largely because of the academic and public popularity of individualistic explanations of delinquency, this earlier interest in environmental research became eclipsed for several years (Voss and Petersen, 1971b).

A distinguishing feature of the earlier, European environmental analyses of criminality, particularly by A. M. Guerry and Adolphe Quetelet, was the extensive use of maps and charts to demonstrate the quantitative distribution of crime and delinquency. The use of such research methods has prompted some to name this approach the "Cartographic School" (Sutherland and Cressey, 1978).

While the results of research conducted within the Cartographic School supported environmental explanations of criminality, there was no underlying theory that guided the interpretation of these results. Often the findings were used to indicate the lack of morality in certain parts of a city or region of a country, or among members of certain population categories. The late-nineteenth-century theoretical development of the concept of "anomie" by the Frenchman Emile Durkheim and the Marxist theory of class-based behavior patterns, plus the later work in America of Clifford Shaw and Henry McKay, contributed to the merger of fact with theory in this area of delinquency research.

Thus, the theoretical constructs that underlie social disorganization and anomie as explanations of delinquency extended from prior methodological, but essentially atheoretical, environmental-ecological studies of criminality. At the same time, these explanations represent the earliest modern sociological and social psychological explanations of crime and delinquency. The concepts, hypotheses, and research generated from these theories have influenced the analysis of delinquency and crime for most of this century.

GENERIC ASSUMPTIONS

As explanations of delinquency, social disorganization and anomie share a common set of assumptions. First, delinquency is assumed to be *primarily* caused by social factors. Both explanations consider personal or situational influences in delinquency, but the dominant factor is social. Second, the structure and institutions of society are assumed to be in disarray or disorganization. Just specifically what component of society is thought to be in a state of disorganization is one of the factors that distinguishes the two explanations. Third, the uncertainty and confusion that accompany social disorganization and anomie are said, in this approach, to leave one vulnerable or susceptible to delinquent behavior. In essence, it is assumed that social factors control delinquency and, when these factors become unstable, juveniles are rendered less able to resist deviant temptations. Fourth, it is implied that the erosion of stability in social structure is most pronounced among the lower classes, an assumption made because these theories were developed to explain a disproportionate rate of delinquency (and crime) among the working and lower classes. This excess of criminality among the lower classes of society was partly the result of using police and court records as the measure of delinquency. Nonetheless, both explanations assume that criminality is inversely related to social class, although, *in the abstract,* this assumption is not necessary for either theory.

These assumptions are diagrammed in Figure 3.

It is apparent from the preceding discussion that social disorganization and anomie are partly *social control* theories of delinquency. That is, it is assumed

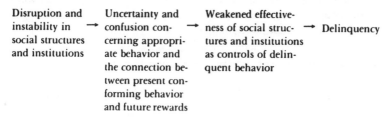

| Disruption and instability in social structures and institutions | → | Uncertainty and confusion concerning appropriate behavior and the connection between present conforming behavior and future rewards | → | Weakened effectiveness of social structures and institutions as controls of delinquent behavior | → | Delinquency |

Figure 3

that delinquency results, in part, from a lack of significant attachment to social institutions, such as the family and school. The thrust of these explanations, however, is on the social factors that produce weakened controls on delinquency. The specific processes and dimensions of weakened controls in relationship to delinquency will be discussed in Chapter 8.

SOCIAL DISORGANIZATION

Specific Assumptions

The foremost assumption of social disorganization as an explanation of delinquency is that delinquency is primarily the result of a breakdown of institutional, community-based controls. The individuals who live in such situations are not necessarily themselves personally disoriented; instead, they are viewed as responding "naturally" to disorganized environmental conditions. A second assumption of this approach to delinquency is that the disorganization of community-based institutions is often caused by rapid industrialization, urbanization, and immigration processes, which occur primarily in *urban* areas. Third, it is assumed that the effectiveness of social institutions and the desirability of residential and business locations correspond closely to natural, ecological principles, which are influenced by the concepts of competition and dominance. Largely because of this assumption, the social disorganization explanation of delinquency is associated with the term "ecological approach." A fourth assumption is that socially disorganized areas lead to the development of criminal values and traditions, which replace conventional ones, and that this process is self-perpetuating.

The causal chain depicting the assumptions of social disorganization in relationship to delinquency is presented in Figure 4.

Key Concepts

Social Disorganization   This term is variously defined throughout the literature, but in relationship to delinquency, it typically refers to either: (1) a breakdown in conventional institutional controls, as well as informal social control forces, within a community or neighborhood (cf. Thomas and Znaniecki, 1927) or (2) the inability of organizations, groups, or individuals in a community or neighborhood to solve common problems collectively.

Growth Zones   As formulated by Burgess (1967), this concept refers to concentric zones that represent distinctive characteristics and that are thought to appear in successive stages as the result of growth and expansion in a city.

Rapid changes in industrialization or urbanization or increased immigration → Decline in the effectiveness of institutional and informal social control forces in communities or neighborhoods—that is, social disorganization →

Development of delinquency areas, as exemplified by high rates of delinquency, and the existence of delinquent traditions and values in specific geographical areas or neighborhoods

Figure 4

Ecological Approach This term refers to the systematic analysis of delinquency *rates* as these are distributed geographically within a city or locality. The distribution of rates is often mapped, or spotted, and correlated with other community characteristics, and the results are used to describe patterns of delinquency in a statistical fashion.

Delinquency Area A geographical unit (often approximately a square mile) that has a higher than average rate of delinquency is referred to as a delinquency area. It is also presumed that delinquency areas are characterized by traditions and values that support or even encourage criminality.

Discussion: The Work of Shaw and McKay

While the mapping of crime, delinquency, and other "social ills" has been in existence for over a hundred years, the connection between social disorganization and delinquency is associated with the work of Clifford Shaw and Henry McKay, two sociologists connected with the University of Chicago and the Illinois Institute for Social Research during the early to mid-twentieth century.

Starting with *Delinquency Areas* (Shaw et al., 1929), Shaw, and later McKay, produced a number of books and reports that described the distribution of delinquency rates in Chicago and that also discussed the processes which delinquent values and traditions developed and continued. The bulk of this work culminated in a detailed investigation of delinquency rates in Chicago covering a period of over 30 years, as well as descriptions of the distribution of rates in 20 other American cities (Shaw and McKay, 1942). This work has also been revised and updated to include data through the mid-1960s (Shaw and McKay, 1969).

The work of Shaw and McKay was decidedly influenced by the principles of human ecology enunciated by Robert Park and his associates at the University of Chicago during the early part of the twentieth century (Park, 1936, 1967).

For example, they utilized the depiction of urban growth outlined by Burgess (1967). This analysis of urban growth identified five concentric zones characterizing growth in American cities in the 1920s, particularly in Chicago. Zone I was called the central business district or the "Loop" and was located at the center of the city. Zone II was termed the zone of transition, the oldest section of the city, and the one being "invaded" by business and industrial expansion. The residential attractiveness of this zone had declined and it had become inhabited by recent migrants and the poor. Zone III was referred to as the zone of working-class homes, usually those in skilled and semi-skilled occupations. Zone IV was the location of single-family homes and more elegant apartments. Zone V was called the commuter's zone, consisting of suburbs and satellite cities surrounding the central city.

Of course, this depiction of urban growth is not complete. Even where the pattern does appear to be accurate, the specific dimensions of the zones can be influenced by numerous conditions, such as historical landmarks and natural barriers. The point is, however, that this analysis of urban growth was used by Shaw and McKay not only to describe the distribution of delinquency, but also to explain why delinquency was distributed in urban areas as it was. For their purposes, each zone in Chicago was assumed to be 2 miles in width.

The culminating work of Shaw and McKay presented detailed discussions of delinquency rates in Chicago over three time periods: 1900–1906, 1917–1923, and 1927–1933. "Delinquency" in these analyses was first measured by the number of young males, under a specified age, depending on time period and location, who were petitioned to juvenile court, whether or not their case was actually heard by a judge. Delinquency rate was the percentage of 10- to 16-year-old boys in an area or zone who had been petitioned to court in the mid-year of the time series under investigation (Shaw and McKay, 1969). Thus, delinquency was measured in terms of official criteria and in terms of where delinquents *lived* rather than where the offense was committed.

The results of Shaw and McKay's investigations revealed that rates of delinquency decreased as one moved from the zones located at or near the central business district outward to the commuter's zone, as Figure 5 demonstrates. This pattern was replicated for all three time series under investigation. Although changes in areas or neighborhoods occurred during the three time periods, 75 percent of the neighborhoods with the highest delinquency rate in 1900–1906 were among the highest delinquency areas in 1927–1933, with a total correlation of .61 between the two time periods.

In addition to the distributions charted for court petitions, Shaw and McKay measured the distribution of rates of males committed to correctional institutions and the rate of males who appeared in police records for the various time periods between 1900 and 1935. The results were essentially the same as for the earlier analyses of juvenile court petition rates. That is, the highest rates were found in the center of the city, near the central business district, and the rates decreased regularly by zone as one moved farther out from the center of the city. Furthermore, the correlations between the three separate measures of delinquency and the various time periods ranged from .81 to .97.

Despite skepticism as to the applicability of the concentric zone theory to other cities, research conducted in American cities, such as Philadelphia, Boston, Cleveland, and Richmond, Virginia, also concluded that official rates of delinquency decreased from the center of the city outward to the suburbs (Shaw and McKay, 1969). Follow-up studies in Chicago during the 1950s and 1960s, for both male *and* female delinquents, also confirmed the conclusions of the earlier studies in Chicago, although these later analyses did not compare delinquency rates by concentric zones.

Thus, the ecological research by Shaw, McKay, and others conducted in a number of American cities over a period of 60 years has consistently demonstrated one basic fact concerning delinquency—that official rates of delinquency *decline* with movement away from the inner city. By itself, this finding, apart from its remarkable consistency, is interesting, but hardly theoretically significant.[1] A number of related findings reported by Shaw and McKay, however, point to the theory of social disorganization as a basic explanation of delinquency.

First, when delinquency rates were observed according to square-mile areas, the highest rate areas were usually located near or adjacent to industrial or commercial sites, such as the Chicago stock yards and steel mills. On the other hand, those areas with low rates of delinquency were primarily residential neighborhoods (Shaw and McKay, 1969).

Second, the persistence of high delinquency rates in Chicago neighborhoods or areas from 1900 to 1933 occurred despite the predominance of several *different* ethnic and racial categories of people. At the turn of the century, the predominant populations in high-delinquency areas were of northern European background, such as German, Irish, and English-Scotch. By 1920, the ethnic composition had changed to eastern and southern European nationalities, such as Polish and Italian. By the 1930s, the increased presence of African-Americans was beginning to appear (Shaw and McKay, 1969). Since certain areas were characterized by high delinquency rates regardless of ethnic or racial predominance, Shaw and McKay concluded that delinquency was more a product of economic conditions and locality-based traditions and values than ethnic culture. This view was reinforced by the observation that delinquency rates among African-Americans and the members of various nationality groups varied considerably throughout the city and in accordance with the general geographic distribution of overall delinquency rates.

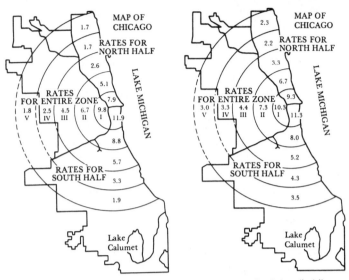

A. Zone rates of male juvenile delinquents, 1927-33 series

B. Zone rates of male juvenile delinquents, 1917-23 series

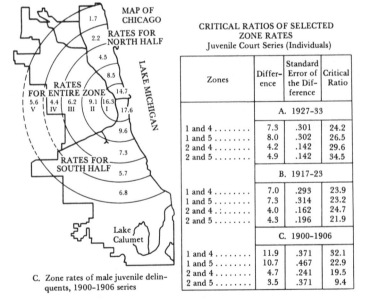

C. Zone rates of male juvenile delinquents, 1900-1906 series

CRITICAL RATIOS OF SELECTED ZONE RATES
Juvenile Court Series (Individuals)

Zones	Difference	Standard Error of the Difference	Critical Ratio
A. 1927-33			
1 and 4	7.3	.301	24.2
1 and 5	8.0	.302	26.5
2 and 4	4.2	.142	29.6
2 and 5	4.9	.142	34.5
B. 1917-23			
1 and 4	7.0	.293	23.9
1 and 5	7.3	.314	23.2
2 and 4 .:......	4.0	.162	24.7
2 and 5	4.3	.196	21.9
C. 1900-1906			
1 and 4	11.9	.371	32.1
1 and 5	10.7	.467	22.9
2 and 4	4.7	.241	19.5
2 and 5	3.5	.371	9.4

Figure 5. Zone maps for three juvenile court series.

(Source: Clifford R. Shaw and Henry D. McKay, *Juvenile Delinquency and Urban Areas.* Revised edition. Chicago: University of Chicago Press, 1969. Copyright, 1942, 1969, University of Chicago Press.)

Third, delinquency rates by areas were highly correlated with the rates and severity of other "community problems." Included in this list of additional problems were rates of school truancy (which they apparently had separated from delinquency), young adult (17 to 20 years of age) criminality, infant mortality, tuberculosis, and mental disorders (Shaw and McKay, 1969; see also, Farris and Dunham, 1939).

Fourth, delinquency rates were also correlated with a number of economic characteristics, thought by Shaw and McKay to be indicators of stability or growth, or their opposites. For example, delinquency rates were generally associated with population decline, although the relationship was not consistent. In addition, delinquency was positively associated with the percentage of families on relief and rates of financial dependency. Finally, delinquency rates were inversely related to median monthly rental values and percentage of home ownership, although in the case of the latter the relationship was not consistent.

All of these relationships concerning rates of delinquency did not *prove* delinquency causation to Shaw and McKay. What the relationship did was to point to an underlying or overriding condition that led directly to delinquency. Just what to call this factor, and how best to describe it, presented Shaw and McKay with some difficulty. Their earlier analyses, their supporters (see Burgess, 1942), and later their reviewers (Voss and Petersen, 1971b; Finestone, 1976), all seem to have agreed on one term to describe the set of conditions evident in Shaw and McKay's data—namely, *social disorganization*.

Nonetheless, it should be noted that the later work of Shaw and McKay did not stress social *disorganization*. Instead, they referred to concepts such as differential social organization (a term also used by Edwin Sutherland; see Chapter 7) and value differences to explain their position. The term social disorganization has persisted in the literature, however, and, for the sake of discussion, it will be the frame of reference for the rest of this section of the chapter.

According to Shaw and McKay the economic instability and social pathology which characterize delinquency rates lead to conflicting moral and value systems for young children. These conflicting standards are reflected in the influence that individuals and informal groups exert in the areas, in addition to, or opposed to, the traditional institutionalized social control forces emanating from churches, schools, and families. In delinquency areas, a young child is as likely to see economic success and personal reputation earned by criminal behavior as by school success and hard work in legal occupations (Shaw and McKay, 1969).

The extent to which children in a delinquency area may choose to identify with a conventional or criminal life-style depends on the particular strength of the legitimate social control forces in their lives, particularly those within their *family* settings. In addition, the choice of one life-style over another depends on the amount of support for a particular pattern of behavior the children receive from their associates and peers. Since, by definition, delinquency areas are characterized by a concentration of delinquents and criminals in a small geographical area, the chances would be slim of a child growing up in such a setting and not coming into contact with values and behavior that supported criminality.

The persistence of high delinquency rates in certain areas decade after decade prompted Shaw and McKay to suggest that a tradition of criminality eventually develops in these neighborhoods, which becomes transmitted from one generation to another. The medium of this transmission is largely the structure of juvenile and adult gangs in the areas. This conclusion was derived from in-depth case studies of juvenile delinquents (see also, Shaw, 1930; Shaw et al., 1938). In addition, Shaw and McKay noted that not only were most delinquent offenses committed in group settings but that, in most such settings, specific older and younger boys regularly appeared together in court records "backward in time in an unbroken continuity" (1969:175).

Evaluation

The empirical and theoretical work of Shaw and McKay has generated a substantial amount of literature in the field of delinquency (Wilks, 1967; Voss and Petersen, 1971a; Finestone, 1976). Their work has also generated what some would regard as a successful delinquency intervention program, the Chicago Area Projects, which have been operative for over 60 years (Kobrin, 1959; Finestone, 1976; V. I. P. Examiner, 1992:6–17; Lundman, 1993:Chapter 3). The data and conceptualization surrounding the work of Shaw and McKay, however, have not been without critical comment. The adequacy of this approach to an understanding of juvenile delinquency can be evaluated according to three factors: (1) the influence of cultural factors in the effects of social disorganization on delinquency; (2) the presence of nondelinquency in "delinquency areas"; and (3) the question of whether socially disorganized areas produce delinquency traditions or attract delinquent individuals.

One of the strongest criticisms of social disorganization as an explanation of delinquency is that it tends to downplay the significance of ethnic and cultural factors. The replication of Shaw and McKay's work in different countries has generally supported their contention that delinquent rates are highest in areas marked by economic and population decline or instability (Morris, 1958; DeFleur, 1967). Such research, however, has not duplicated the American findings of decreasing rates from the center of the city outward. In Argentina, for example, the highest rates of delinquency have been found in interstitial and peripheral sections of the city, partly because the wealthy are often found near the center of the city, while the poorer sections of the city are found near its outskirts (DeFleur, 1967).

Obi Ebbe's research (1989) in Lagos, Nigeria, yields additional information on the cultural aspects of the ecological patterns of delinquency. Using juvenile court statistics, Ebbe found that the residences of delinquents tended to be concentrated in "high- and medium-grade residential districts" (p. 760), which were scattered throughout the metropolitan area of Lagos. More importantly, however, he noted that the delinquents in these higher-income areas were typically the servants of the owners of the homes, servants who lacked transportation and mobility to move or travel to other parts of the city. Furthermore, Ebbe observed that in "low-grade residential areas" (p. 763) neighborhoods are more homogeneous and socially integrated. Informal social controls are stronger and rates of delinquency are lower. In effect, he maintains that these lower-income areas are well organized, a conclusion opposite to that reached by Shaw and McKay.

Also, Johnstone (1978), using self-report measures of delinquency, noted that it was not the lower-class neighborhoods in Chicago which had the highest rates of delinquency. Rather, the most delinquent youth were those who were classified as lower-class but who lived in "middle- or high-status communities rather than in the heart of a slum area" (p. 65), although not as servants, as in Nigeria. The situation Johnstone identifies is a form of anomie, a concept which will be discussed in the next section of this chapter.

Besides differences in the physical location of delinquency, the influence of cultural factors can alter the basic effects area of residence may have on delinquent tendencies. In a strong critique of Shaw and McKay's work, Jonassen (1949) argues that Shaw and McKay's own data reveal marked ethnic differences in delinquency rates *within* areas. In addition, Shaw and McKay concede the importance of ethnic differences when they note the unusually low rates of delinquency among Oriental juveniles found in Hayner's studies of Pacific Northwest communities (Hayner, 1942; Shaw and McKay, 1969). The overall significance of ethnicity as a determining or mitigating factor in the explanation of delinquency, however, was not developed by Shaw and McKay.

The influence of race and ethnicity on rates of delinquency has been studied extensively and has indicated a variety of ways in which such cultural factors can influence delinquent behavior. The low rates of delinquency among Orientals have been noted by others (Smith, 1937; Chambliss, 1974) and have usually been interpreted as reflecting strong familial controls as well as a strong network of informal groups and organizations. However, studies have indicated an increase in the presence of Asian gangs in America during the past 20 years (Miller, 1975; Sheu, 1986; Chin, 1990).

The influence of cultural factors has also been examined relative to the delinquency-producing effects of *cultural conflicts* (Sellin, 1938). Such conflicts are thought to have either direct effects, especially on second-generation juveniles, or assimilative effects, in which the extent of delinquency in a minority group becomes similar to that of a dominant group as cultural assimilation occurs (Smith, 1937; Young, 1967; Sheu, 1986:Chapter 5; Wong, 1997).

Cultural factors are also apparent in the type of delinquency in which members of various ethnic groups engage. This influence can derive both from the process of assimilation with other cultural groups (Sellin, 1938; Sutherland and Cressey, 1978) and from the distinctive experiences and value systems of particular racial and ethnic groups. In a study of the emergence of African-Americans and Hispanics in organized crime, for example, Ianni (1974) argues that the process of transmitting criminal values from adults to juveniles and from older to younger juveniles does not always occur in the streets of local neighborhoods but often through prison experiences. In fact, he argues that, while some similarities exist between Italian and African-American-Hispanic structures of organized crime, there are also numerous differences, some of which have a direct bearing on the type of criminal activity committed.

More recently, Curry and Spergel (1988) contend that social disorganization, as measured by the "concentration of Hispanics" (p. 387) in a locality, is strongly associated with gang-related homicides in Chicago, but not with overall patterns of delinquency. For non-Hispanic neighborhoods, poverty is strongly associated with delinquency and gang homicides. Overall, they conclude that population shifts in certain parts of cities, as they may be differentially distributed by race and/or ethnicity, may explain youth participation in gang violence.

In addition, some cultural contexts might encourage criminal activity, whether committed by adults or juveniles. In this case, the illegal acts would not be considered criminal, or morally wrong, within the social or cultural context that such behavior is committed. An example of this situation may be found among Gypsies, who, according to Anne Sutherland, value making money from non-Gypsies, regardless of the "legality of a scheme or occupation" (1975:73). This cultural value, however, does not extend to violent acts, especially murder. Thus, while it would be erroneous to attribute a strong deterministic influence to cultural factors, it would be equally wrong to discount or ignore the effect of such variables on delinquency, as Shaw and McKay tended to do.

Another question about the conclusions of Shaw and McKay concerns the extent of nondelinquency in "delinquency areas" (Stark, 1987:904–906). Certainly, it is unrealistic to expect a theory to explain all cases of a phenomenon. Much of sociological theory and research is based on correlations and relationships, not total explanation and prediction. Inasmuch as Shaw and McKay's own data reveal that no more than 30 percent of the 10- to 16-year-old males appeared in juvenile court records, even in high delinquency rate areas, their contention that something about the culture of a geographical area contributes to its rate of delinquency is subject to challenge. Admittedly, the use of official court records lowers the percentage of recognized delinquency in a study, as compared to unofficial measures (Robison, 1936). The point remains, though, that the large percentage of "nondelinquents" in delinquent areas should be addressed if this theory is to be considered a major explanation of delinquency. In part, the difference between geographical, or ecological, rates of behavior and individual actions of those living in those localities is a reflection of what Robinson (1950) demonstrated. That is, the collective behavior of the residents may differ, even sharply, from the activity of any one resident, or a small group of people. This situation is now clearly understood among sociologists. However, specific instances of criminality must also be explained, especially if this behavior runs counter to the patterns of activity existing in a neighborhood or community.

The development of a cultural tradition of delinquency transmitted through gangs was a primary effort of Shaw and McKay to explain *why* delinquency areas developed and continued. This explanation was largely based on case analyses, such as *The Jack-Roller* (Shaw, 1930). Although these analyses can be very useful in theory building, the method here often failed to define terms or to quantify concepts in replicable fashion. These types of shortcomings have prompted some, such as Kobrin (1971), to argue that the delinquency tradition argument is the weakest link in Shaw and McKay's theory.

Part of the reason for the unsystematic accounting of the development of delinquent traditions was Shaw and McKay's failure to develop more specifically some of the institutional and social-psychological factors which they merely seemed to suggest in their work. Institutional factors, such as family, school, and religious disorganization, were often linked with delinquent traditions. By implication, the presence of greater controls through these institutions over juveniles residing in delinquency areas would lessen their chances of committing delinquency. Similarly, peer relationships and personalities, including self-concept, may also explain why many nondelinquents exist in delinquency areas. Later theoretical developments, such as Sutherland's theory of differential association, Reckless' self-concept theory of delinquency, and a whole battery of theory and research on the effects of institutional attachments and commitments (social control through social bonds) on delinquency, have contributed considerably to our understanding and most certainly can be used to distinguish those who have conflict with the law from those who do not in delinquency areas. These theories are discussed in detail in subsequent chapters.

The consideration of institutional and other specific variables, however, might not always yield clear distinctions. An ecological study of delinquency rates in Philadelphia, for example, compared officially defined delinquents with nondelinquents in a "high delinquent area" of African-Americans according to the following variables: presence of parents, presence of adult males in home, gender of household head and of main decision maker, household size, ordinal position, occupation and education of main wage earner, home ownership, and room density (Rosen, 1978). The basic conclusion of this study was that no variable distinguished delinquents from nondelinquents in the area studied, prompting the author to conclude that perhaps the "area" itself should be the proper focus of attention. Nonetheless, this interpretation would not resolve the question at hand, and presumably factors other than those measured should be studied.

An analysis of official and self-report delinquency among over 500 male youth aged 11½ to 17½ in New York City attempted to clarify the effects of various neighborhood and individual conditions (Simcha-Fagan and Schwartz, 1986). The results indicated that different factors affected general self-report delinquency versus official (arrest) or serious self-report youth crime, at the *neighborhood* level. In the case of the former, rates of organizational participation in the neighborhood and level of residential stability were important correlates. With respect to the other two measures of delinquency, however, only one neighborhood condition exerted any significant effect, and that was the presence of disorder or a criminal subculture. At the neighborhood level, these results tend to support the social disorganization theory of delinquency, but specify the theory according to the measure of delinquency utilized.

Individually, that is, for individual assessments of delinquency, age had the most significant effect on all three measures of delinquency, with older youth being more delinquent, but the relationship was strongest for the two self-report measures. Moreover, the effect of age was independent of all neighborhood conditions. This result is difficult to interpret using social disorganization theory, unless one is willing to conclude that perhaps the cumulative personal effects of community disorganization begin to take their toll at later ages of adolescence. Further analysis implicated negative school experiences and delinquent peer associations as being influenced by neighborhood conditions of stability and conformity, while school experiences and delinquent peers, in turn, had more direct effects on delinquency, especially self-report delinquent behavior (Simcha-Fagan and Schwartz, 1986:689–693).

Thus, some of the neighborhood conditions which may affect individual patterns of delinquency are being isolated, and this deficiency of social disorganization theory is being corrected. At the moment, evidence is pointing to the deleterious effects that community-based characteristics may have on the school and peer relations of young people. Again, these factors will be analyzed at further points in this book.

Sampson and Groves (1989) report additional evidence which supports social disorganization theory, although, by their own admission, their measures of community structure were only approximations of the concepts suggested by Shaw and McKay. Using survey responses of nationwide samples of people aged 16 and over in England and Wales, Sampson and Groves determined crime rates of specific communities and neighborhoods. An interesting feature of this study is that it measured crime by the self-reports of the sample, as well as by their indications of the extent to which they had been victimized by criminal behavior.

Overall, Sampson and Groves found that crime rates were lower in areas characterized by higher friendship ties in a locality, higher levels of participation in organizations, and greater control of teenage groups. These factors were considered indications of social organization; thus, their relative absence suggested social disorganization. Again, however, these concepts are only approximations of community structure. In fact, in some cases, they were measured by responses to just one statement.

Additional information on this issue is supplied by Gottfredson et al. (1991). Their research is based on self-report estimates of delinquency among purposive, predominantly minority samples of youth in Baltimore, Kalamazoo (Michigan), Christiansted, St. Croix, and the Charleston, South Carolina metropolitan area. Basically, this study finds that social disorganization contributes little in the way of direct influence on delinquency, explaining perhaps 1 to 2 percent of the variation in individual rates of delinquency (p. 221). Rather, the greater impact of social disorganization is found in the effects of neighborhood organization on more proximate contributions to delinquency, in particular social bonds (to parents, the school, and the community) and peer influences. Furthermore, among males in the sample, living in more affluent areas is correlated with *higher* rates of delinquency, particularly property offenses, a finding similar to that of Ebbe. Unlike Ebbe's conclusion, however, Gottfredson et al. suggest that delinquency is more common in affluent neighborhoods because that is "where the money is," so to speak (p. 218). This conclusion is consistent with the rational choice theory discussed in Chapter 2.

A closely related issue is whether the rates of delinquency for an area should be based on where the delinquent act occurs or where the identified delinquent lives. This would not be an issue if the two rates of delinquency were the same, or if delinquents lived near the locus of their deviant acts. The available evidence on this question is not clear. For example, some argue that very often the area of a delinquent's home is the same as the area where he commits offenses (Morris, 1958; Sutherland and Cressey, 1978; Fabrikant, 1979). These statements are qualified, however, to include mostly serious felonies (such as murder, rape, and robbery), acts in large cities, or inadequate transportation facilities and opportunities. In addition, not all research has found that delinquent acts are committed in proximity to the residences of delinquents (Morris, 1958; DeFleur, 1967). In these cases, it is argued that delinquency areas are more likely to attract than produce delinquents.

In a similar sense, it could even be argued that areas tend to attract social misfits and the disadvantaged as a place to reside. As Sutherland and Cressey (1978) contend, however, the observation that delinquent areas remained such for nearly 30 years, despite numerous turnovers in dominant ethnic composition, provides strong support for the contention that they contain delinquent traditions. Moreover, the case study material mentioned earlier frequently reflects pride and determination in the people who live in these areas rather than fatalism and apathy. In fact, the whole premise of the Chicago Area Projects is based on the use of local lay leaders and other residents as the basic source of neighborhood reorganization.

Research continues to build upon the connection between neighborhood organizational conditions and patterns of delinquency. Much of this analysis focuses on the negative impact of neighborhood disorganization on the amount of informal social control and social integration that exist in a neighborhood, which supports Shaw and McKay's original speculations. Such areas may lose the interest of their residents in keeping up with the activities and general welfare of their neighbors, including what is happening to the youth in the neighborhood (Elliott et al., 1996). Taylor (1997) presents an interesting argument in support of the impact of socioeconomic conditions at the *block* level of residence, and the small-group patterns of behavior control generated at this level of community organization.

Added to this situation is the fact that crime and socially disorganized areas can interact to produce varying patterns of residential mobility. Crime, such as homicide, may generate personal levels of fear, less neighborhood commitment, and more desire to move away from the high crime area(s), although this movement may be easier to accomplish among whites than among African-Americans (Morenoff and Sampson, 1997). This movement, in turn, may result in even less commitment to residential stability and conformity among those left in the neighborhood.

Of course, these conceptualizations of the negative effects of neighborhood organization can be turned around to generate ideas regarding the *positive* impacts of residential wills on reducing crime and delinquency in a neighborhood (Donnelly and Kimble, 1997). Indeed, this outcome is what the Chicago Area Projects (see above) have intended to accomplish. However, attempts to build successful neighborhood, or block, responses to crime and delinquency may depend on physical structures and social characteristics such as local leadership and residential interest in reducing criminality (Donnelly and Kimble, 1997; Taylor, 1997:121–131), characteristics which disorganization seems to affect negatively.

Furthermore, some neighborhoods may develop into what Suttles calls a "defended neighborhood" (1972:21). In such cases, residents may actually encourage delinquency, especially violent activity, in an effort to help protect their neighborhood from the perceived advances of undesirable racial or ethnic intruders. This possibility has been supported in ecological studies of delinquency in Chicago (Heitgerd and Bursik, 1987) and Dayton, Ohio (Baker and Donnelly, 1986). In essence, as Heitgerd and Bursik (1987) observe, the traditional notion that social disorganization of a neighborhood contributes to higher rates of delinquency should be amended to address the possibility that stable, "defended" neighborhoods may also have high rates of delinquency in response to perceived external threats from nearby neighborhoods or communities.

While the separation of offense from residence is important for a fuller understanding of delinquency, the definition of delinquency based on residential location is better when the explanation is focused on the development *and* transmission of traditions within geographical areas. If one were solely interested in charting the distribution of delinquent offenses, then a definition of delinquency based on location of delinquent acts would be more appropriate. On this issue, then, it would seem that Shaw and McKay's methods and observations are justified.

In summary, the theory of social disorganization, as principally developed by Shaw and McKay, has merit in that it has pointed to social causes of delinquency that seem to be located in specific geographical areas. In this sense, the theory makes a contribution to an understanding of delinquency. On the other hand, the lack of specification of just why delinquent rates are concentrated in certain areas of a city reduces the merits of the theory. In effect, the theory would appear to be generally accurate, but incomplete (see also, Bursik, 1988). Social disorganization as an explanation of delinquency thus offers a good starting point, but leaves to other analyses—whether they are individualistic, cultural, institutional, or social-psychological—the task of more clearly specifying differences between delinquents and nondelinquents, whether or not they live in delinquent areas.

ANOMIE AND DELINQUENCY: DISCONTINUITIES IN SOCIETY

Specific Assumptions

A sociological construct closely related to, but conceptually distinct from, social disorganization is *anomie*. Social disorganization often applies to localized institutional conditions, while anomie usually refers to larger, societal conditions. A major assumption of anomie as an explanation of delinquency and crime is that large numbers of people who find themselves at a disadvantage relative to legitimate economic activities are seen as being motivated to engage in illegitimate, delinquent activities. These individuals may be willing to work or otherwise be productive members of society but, because of the unavailability of employment or an opportunity to develop job skills, they turn to criminality, perhaps out of frustration with their situation or perhaps because of economic necessity.

Although anomie theory is oriented toward conditions in society generally, some researchers have attempted to combine the theory of anomie with the ecological method, that is, the study of neighborhood rates of delinquency. These studies are discussed in this section. With anomie theory, however, there is no basic assumption that delinquency becomes embodied in localized traditions, which reflect divergent economic classes and value systems. According to anomie theory, while such traditions may develop, they might more accurately be described as consequences of broader social conditions that affect a society's economy and the distribution of work and economic rewards within that society.

The relationship between anomie and delinquency may be presented as shown in Figure 6. As Figure 6 shows, the relationship between anomie and delinquency is straightforward. On the surface, it makes no specifications concerning states of mind or intervening conditions. Many of those who have utilized this explanation of delinquency have attempted to "flesh it out," so to speak, but such modifications are not an actual component of anomie theory per se.

Key Concepts

Anomie This construct refers to inconsistencies between societal conditions and individual opportunities for growth, fulfillment, and productivity within a society. The term *anomia* has been used to refer to those who experience personal frustration and alienation as a result of anomie within a society.

Opportunity Structure This concept is defined as the availability of legitimate work and other activity to attain the goals that are inculcated into the people of a society.

Discussion

The introduction of the concept of anomie to sociology is generally attributed to the French sociologist Emile Durkheim. In a classic volume entitled *The*

Societal (mostly economic) conditions that affect one's access to legitimate activities (anomie)	→	Pressures to engage in illegitimate (mostly economic) activity or delinquency

Figure 6

Division of Labor in Society (1933), Durkheim detailed a thesis which argued that societies normally develop or change from a relatively simple, uncomplicated state of existence to a complex state. The first condition Durkheim referred to as a state of *mechanical solidarity*, in which societies are held together, so to speak, by forces of similarities and likenesses. In this state of affairs, the biological endowments of people are roughly equal to the roles in life they are expected to perform (Durkheim, 1933).

As societies become larger and population more dense, and as economic and technological advances develop, the structure of social relationships changes to what Durkheim called *organic solidarity*. In this situation, society is held together through a system of functional interdependence. Roles and positions become divided and specialized, and people come to depend on one another for their survival.

Durkheim viewed this change as natural for a variety of reasons. For one thing, he equated the development of division of labor with the insatiable human desire to be happy. Thus, the more work is divided and specialized, the more people can produce and consume for their enjoyment. The natural development of division of labor, however, does not always occur smoothly. Under certain conditions, the division of labor develops "abnormally" and the society is said to be in a "pathological state."

Durkheim outlined three situations that could lead to an abnormal division of labor. The first comes from financial crises and failures, as well as industrial conflicts and disputes. The second comes from unnatural class and caste divisions, in which those in the lower classes rebel against the arbitrary boundaries placed on their aspirations and abilities. The third abnormal form of a division of labor occurs when duplication and lack of coordination within and among businesses result in a breakdown of social cohesion. In a sense, workers become alienated from their jobs.

In part, all three conditions of an abnormal division of labor have been associated with anomie by subsequent analysts (Taylor et al., 1973). Durkheim's own terminology, however, suggests that the term anomie is to be reserved for times of financial and industrial crises. In a lengthy discussion of the social causes of suicide, Durkheim specifically refers to *anomic* suicide as the result of a lack of societal regulation over people's desires and aspirations. Furthermore, this societal deregulation arises from economic crises, either depressions or rapid periods of prosperity (Durkheim, 1951).

While Durkheim failed explicitly to relate conditions of anomie to crime or deviance, with the exception of suicide, later writers did utilize the term to explain the presence of crime and deviance. The most significant of these contributions was provided by Robert Merton, whose article on social structure and anomie, first published in 1938, has become a classic.

The basic argument of Merton's theory is that there often exists within a society a discrepancy, or disjunction, between its goals and its system of legitimate means for achieving those goals. In the United States, Merton reasons, the dominant goal is the achievement of economic success. At the same time, the system of legitimate opportunities for achieving success, such as the availability of educational and occupational pursuits, is not evenly distributed within the society (Merton, 1957). Although most people can obtain some type of job, the ability to secure a high-paying position, or one with advancement potential, is dependent on a variety of conditions that a large part of the population does not possess.

The goal of economic success is placed within the realm of culture, while the system of legitimate opportunities is classified as part of the society's social structure. Anomie is defined, according to this theory, as the disjunction between cultural goals and structured means for achieving these goals, as it affects a large number of people. For this reason, Merton's theory is also known as the means-end theory of deviance.

The reactions or adaptations to a state of anomie can vary within a society, according to Merton, and these reactions help describe the types of crime and deviance that exist in society. These responses are described in terms of accepting or rejecting cultural goals or structural means.

The first reaction is not considered deviant at all, but is termed *conformity*. It is characterized by accepting, not necessarily achieving, both goals and means, and by attempting to abide by one's lot in life, so to speak. Merton argues that this reaction is the most common form of behavior in anomic, yet stable, societies. Thus, the theory would appear to be aimed at a minority of a population that is faced with a condition of anomie. In many ways, this is the same condition with which Shaw and McKay were faced in their explanation of delinquency as the result of social disorganization. It must be remembered, however, that the theories of both Merton and Shaw and McKay were based on observations of *official* rates of criminality and deviance. While conformity may appear on the surface to be a dominant reaction among people in "crime-prone" situations, in actuality it may be a minority reaction. In any case, the point to be noted here is that conformity to rules and regulations, even when they appear to place one in disadvantageous and undesirable positions, is a form of behavior that many people adopt.

The other four reactions to anomie, as identified by Merton, are considered deviant, in one way or another. The first of these is called *innovation*, in which there is an acceptance of cultural goals but a rejection of legitimate means. The second is termed *ritualism*, in which the goals are sometimes rejected while the means are rigidly obeyed. Another reaction is *retreatism*, in which both the goals and the means are rejected. The final response is labeled *rebellion*, which involves not only a rejection of goals and means, but also a desire to substitute new goals and means in place of the established ones.

Of the four "deviant" responses to anomie just described, all but one point to some evident example of a criminal or delinquent act. The "innovator," for example, would be expected to engage in theft. Retreatism would involve illegal drug use. Rebellion would include property destruction and crimes of public disorder. The ritualist, however, displays no clear-cut example of criminal or delinquent behavior. It is plausible to connect ritualism with neuroticism and claim a deviant connection in that sense. Since Merton's purpose was to outline a general theory of deviance, the inclusion of ritualism as a basic "deviant" reaction would thus seem appropriate.

A test of this theory using a national self-report data set (Menard, 1995) concludes that anomie theory is as good an explanation of delinquency, particularly minor forms of offenses, as are other explanations, such as social bond theory (see Chapter 8). In addition, Menard's analysis indicates that anomie theory is stronger as an explanation of delinquency among younger juveniles, compared to older youth (p. 166).

The concept of anomie has also been used in connection with ecological studies of delinquency. One such ecological investigation was Bernard Lander's (1954) analysis of juvenile court statistics among the census tracts of Baltimore. Some results were similar to the studies of Shaw and McKay. For example, he found large inverse correlations between the delinquency rates of a census tract and median education, median rental values, and the percentage of home ownership; positive correlations were found between delinquency and overcrowding and substandard housing in census tracts.

In other respects, however, Lander's study did not support Shaw and McKay's findings. Delinquency rates only generally conformed to concentric zone patterns, and they were not uniformly highest in or near industrial or commercial zones. In general, Lander's results questioned the validity of social disorganization and transitional zones as major explanations of the distribution of delinquency rates.

As an alternative explanation, Lander offered the concept of anomie, which he conceptualized in terms of social and community stability. Community, or neighborhood, stability is in part exemplified by home ownership, a factor which had the highest overall correlation with delinquency. Thus, a stable, or less anomic, community would tend to have lower rates of delinquency *in spite* of socioeconomic characteristics potentially capable of producing delinquency, such as substandard housing, poverty, and overcrowding (pp. 55–58).

The ecological construct of anomie is in some respects so similar to the social disorganization perspective that a detailed evaluation of its logical properties would be redundant. There have been several replications of Lander's Baltimore study and they have essentially supported the ecological correlations reported earlier (Bordua, 1958–59; Chilton, 1964). These analyses, and other discussions of Lander's study (Gordon, 1967), however, question the legitimacy of using home ownership and percent nonwhite as indicators of anomie. In addition, statistical manipulations often produce diverse findings and can lead to the conclusion that socioeconomic variables, such as rental value and median education, are as strongly related to delinquency as Lander's anomie constructs.

Overall, it would appear that the ecological definition of anomie, and its relationship to delinquency, has run its course. This approach to delinquency seems to have no real "home," as it were, in theoretical classification schemes. Using anomie as an *ecological* concept is inconsistent with a social disorganization perspective. At the same time, to compare anomie with ecological characteristics is incongruous with the dominant usage of the term. Even Merton, for example, criticizes Lander's conceptualization on the ground that it represents, at best, only an indirect measure of social relationships, which represent only one component (actually, result) of anomie (Merton, 1957). The urgings of Chilton (1964) and Rosen and Turner (1967) for an end to ecological-anomic studies of delinquency appear to have been heeded. While the investigation of delinquency still sometimes utilizes ecological measurements, and is more often informed by anomie theory, the specific search for statistical indices of anomie in neighborhood or census tract settings has become virtually nonexistent.

Evaluation

The Durkheim-Merton formulations of anomie have received a substantial amount of attention in the field of crime and deviance (Cole and Zuckerman, 1964). Much of this literature has indicated a general acceptance of anomie as an explanation of criminality. At the same time, several problems exist that limit the explanatory power of anomie theory.

One of the foremost concerns is how social conditions become translated into forces that can influence individual behavior. For Durkheim, the issue was not an idle one, but one which presented many problems to those who would wish to reduce suicide in their society. For the most part, Durkheim viewed the corporate entity, as opposed to other institutions such as government, education, the family, and religion, as the most practical source of efforts to control suicide (Durkheim, 1951). Whether such entities actually are society's best defense against suicide, the point to be stressed here is the recognition by Durkheim that individual adjustments to societal conditions should be considered as part of a full development of socially constructed theories of behavior.

While Durkheim argued that institutional collectivities are major connectors between social structure and individual behavior, Merton's views on the subject are more general. In the initial explication of his theory, Merton has conceded that little attention was paid to the individual interpretations of anomic conditions and the effect such interpretations might have on behavior (Merton, 1964). For him, however, the principal consideration of anomie theory is that it is based on conditions that characterize society, or the "social surround" (Merton, 1964). Some maintain that Merton's version of anomie theory is actually a dual theory, with motivational (individual) and structural (social organization) components (Messner, 1988). Messner also argues that these two dimensions of the theory are independent and that different research strategies are needed to test each facet of this explanation of criminality.

Still, the question remains, what is the relationship between anomie and individual behavior? A tentative answer for Merton lies in the interaction patterns generated by individuals living in "collectivities" of varying degrees of anomie (Merton, 1964). Thus, the influence of societal conditions on individual behavior is evident in *interaction* patterns, however these may be specifically generated.[2]

In a lengthy analysis of reference groups, Merton discusses a concept that could influence patterns of interaction, although he does not pursue the connection with respect to his anomic theory of deviance. This concept is called *relative deprivation*, which refers to comparisons an individual makes personally, or of the social situation relative to associates, or others, who are in some respects similar to the person (Merton, 1957). This concept can be used to explain why some people in "anomic" situations do not resort to criminality to resolve their dilemma. They do not perceive the dilemma as others might or as a structural, "objective" assessment of the situation might suggest. According to the logic of relative deprivation, the poor, or those in the lower class, do not compare their condition with middle- and upper-class life-styles, even when they are aware of such values and behaviors. Instead, the poor compare themselves with each other or those just above poverty. In other words, the poor, and other social classes as well, will compare themselves more to those with whom they interact and associate than to those whom they only know through mass media accounts. It may be argued, for example, that labor union workers compare their economic situation more with the members of other unions than with management. A young lower-class offender may not be comparing himself with a specific victim who is also poor and resides nearby, but in relation to the general conditions of peers and associates, as opposed to those in the middle- or upper-middle class.

Actually, Durkheim's concern with institutional factors and Merton's use of relative deprivation could be combined to produce another anomic view of delinquency. If one does not focus on economic issues, it is possible to conceptualize anomie in terms of specific organizational goals and means. With respect to delinquency, therefore, the means-end theory may be more appropriately applied to school problems, peer relationships, and other youth-oriented concerns, rather than to economic issues.

Robert Agnew (1985) takes another position relative to Merton's theory by conceptualizing a connection between delinquency and blocked opportunities to *leave* aversive situations. In essence, Agnew argues that a youth's inability to escape unpleasant home or school experiences leads to anger and frustration, which then lead to delinquency. As such, Agnew's refinement addresses the individual adaptation to anomie or strain rather than the societal sources of anomie. In an investigation of this hypothesis, using self-reported measures of delinquency among a sample of 10th-grade boys, Agnew reports significant positive associations between unhappy home and school environments and feelings of anger. In addition, anger was significantly, and positively, related to delinquency. Furthermore, these relationships persisted even when other possible explanatory factors were considered, such as grades in school, aspirations, and attachments to parents. However, the overall coefficients were modest or low, suggesting that other factors, not included in the study, were contributing to delinquency within the sample. Furthermore, the study was limited to males, and the pain-avoidance measures were not very direct.

Agnew modified this position by conceptualizing three kinds of strain, and naming the idea a "general strain theory," or GST (Agnew, 1992). The first type is the discrepancy between societal means and goals, which is the traditional view developed by Merton. A second source of strain is the loss of something positive in one's life, such as the breakup of a relationship with a girlfriend or boyfriend. The third kind of strain results from the presence of negative events, such as criminal victimization, or intimidation from parents or peers.

This conceptualization of strain theory was tested on a longitudinal sample of 12- and 15-year-old males and females in New Jersey (Agnew and White, 1992). The results of this investigation support Agnew's position that an expanded conceptualization of strain to include the loss of positive factors in one's life, and the presence of negative stimuli, can contribute to delinquency, as measured by self-reports. In addition, these results were still present when controlling for other possible contributing factors, such as relationships with deviant peers and the relative absence of positive associations with conventional aspects of society (differential association theory and social control or social bond theory, respectively; see Chapters 7 and 8 in this volume).

Using a national, longitudinal data set, the National Youth Survey, Paternoster and Mazerolle (1994) reach a similar conclusion. Their study confirms positive associations between general strain and several forms of self-reported delinquency, controlling for the effects of competing factors, such as deviant peer associations and weakened social bonds. In fact, their analysis suggests that general strain leads to weakened bonds and to greater delinquent peer associations, which in turn contribute to delinquency (p. 251; see also, Brezina 1996).

This research demonstrates continued interest in reconceptualizing Merton's theory as it applies to the experiences of youth, and the institutional components of society which are meaningful at an adolescent stage in life.[3]

SUMMARY

As social explanations of delinquency, social disorganization and anomie offer significant contrasts to individualistic explanations. In both instances, the logic of the theory appears to be fairly sound, if not complete. Furthermore, in the case of social disorganization, there has appeared a rather impressive collection of supporting evidence (the empirical assessment of the anomic theory of delinquency is discussed in Chapter 6).

A persistent problem of both explanations of delinquency, however, is the lack of explanation as to how social or societal conditions exert an influence over one's behavior. In this sense, both theories are incomplete. While they provide a solid base from which to launch other theoretical explanations of delinquency, they should not be interpreted as providing the ultimate sociological understanding of delinquency.

In particular, the theory of social disorganization has provided the basis for many significant contributions to delinquency theory and research in the latter half of the twentieth century. The explanatory value of social disorganization lies in its implication of institutional factors in the etiology of delinquency. Although these factors were largely invoked in an attempt to explain the ultimate acceptance of delinquent behavior in delinquency areas, subsequent research has pointed to institutional factors as significant influences in their own right. In addition, the cultural transmission aspect of social disorganization utilizes interpersonal concepts in describing the process of learning and conveying criminal values. These concepts have also proved useful in explaining delinquency.

The theory of anomie, particularly Merton's means-end interpretation, is also not without promise as an explanation of delinquency. Anomie theory might best be applied to delinquency in the form of means and goals that are relevant to the status of youth, such as pressures and expectations associated with school or home, rather than solely in terms of economic issues.

Within the context of general strain theory, delinquency, or youth deviance in general, is viewed as an escape mechanism from the negative aspects in one's life, or as a kind of compensation for the loss of a loved one, or a prized goal.

As such, this conceptualization of anomie stresses the individual adaptations to personal strain, rather than to the societal factors which produce the stress in the first place. Nonetheless, a large part of the literature relating anomie to delinquency has focused on the distribution of economic opportunities in society, particularly among lower-class youth. The applications of anomie theory, and other theories, to delinquent behavior among lower-class youth is presented in the following chapter.

Notes

1. Bursik (1984, 1986, 1988) points out that changes in economic, racial/ethnic, and other socioeconomic conditions within urban areas may alter the geographic distribution of delinquency rates. Furthermore, such changes may not always result from "natural" competition for limited space, but might also reflect the intentional efforts of those who have some control over land-use patterns. Walker (1994) reaches a similar conclusion in a study of delinquency in Little Rock, Arkansas. The analysis supported many of Shaw and McKay's earlier findings. However, the distribution of delinquency rates within the metropolitan area of Little Rock did not correspond to a concentric pattern. Walker suggests this finding is the result of newer patterns of dispersed social life-styles and economic opportunities in modern urban areas (pp. 68–69).

2. Lemert (1964) argues that individual choices are also controlled by calculated risk assessments and awareness of the opportunity to commit illegal or deviant acts. In this analysis, cultural or societal conditions are relatively noninfluential in the explanation of individual behavior, especially in a complex, technologically advanced society, such as the United States.

3. An interesting collection of essays on anomie theory has been published (Adler and Laufer, 1995). Among other papers, this book contains a fascinating account by Merton of the development of opportunity structure (anomie) theory, from the 1930s through the 1950s. In addition, there are papers that address the social-psychological and peer aspects of anomie or strain theory, including Agnew's revised strain theoretical perspective (Agnew, 1995; Hoffman and Ireland, 1995).

References

Adler, Freda and William S. Laufer (eds.), 1995, The Legacy of Anomie Theory. New Brunswick, N.J.: Transaction.

Agnew, Robert, 1985, "A Revised Strain Theory of Delinquency." Social Forces 64:151–167.

———, 1992, "Foundation for a General Strain Theory of Crime and Delinquency." Criminology 30:47–87.

———, 1995, "The Contribution of Social-Psychological Strain Theory to the Explanation of Crime and Delinquency." Pp. 113–137 in Freda Adler and William S. Laufer (eds.), q.v.

Agnew, Robert and Helen Raskin White, 1992, "An Empirical Test of General Strain Theory." Criminology 30:475–499.

Baker, Daniel and Patrick G. Donnelly, 1986, "Neighborhood Criminals and Outsiders in Two Communities: Indications that Criminal Localism Varies." Sociology and Social Research 71:59–65.

Bordua, David J., 1958–59, "Juvenile Delinquency and 'Anomie': An Attempt at Replication." Social Problems 6:230–238.

Brezina, Timothy, 1996, "Adapting to Strain: An Examination of Delinquent Coping Responses." Criminology 34:39–60.

Burgess, Ernest W., 1942, "Introduction." Pp. ix–xiii in Clifford R. Shaw and Henry D. McKay, q.v.

———, 1967, "The Growth of the City: An Introduction to a Research Project." Pp. 47–62 in Robert E. Park, Ernest W. Burgess, and Roderick D. McKenzie (eds.), q.v.

Bursik, Robert J., Jr., 1984, "Urban Dynamics and Ecological Studies of Delinquency." Social Forces 63:393–413.

———, 1986, "Ecological Stability and the Dynamics of Delinquency." Pp. 35–66 in Albert J. Reiss, Jr. and Michael Tonry (eds.), Communities and Crime, Vol. 8. Chicago: University of Chicago Press.

———, 1988, "Social Disorganization and Theories of Crime and Delinquency: Problems and Prospects." Criminology 26:519–551.

Chambliss, William J., 1974, "Functional and Conflict Theories of Crime." MSS Modular Publications, Module 17:1–23.

Chilton, Roland J., 1964, "Continuity in Delinquency Area Research: A Comparison of Studies of Baltimore, Detroit, and Indianapolis." American Sociological Review 29:71–83.

Chin, Ko-Lin, 1990, Chinese Subculture and Criminality: Non-Traditional Crime Groups in America. New York: Greenwood.

Clinard, Marshall B. (ed.), 1964, Anomie and Deviant Behavior. New York: Free Press.

Cole, Stephen and Harriet Zuckerman, 1964, "Inventory of Empirical and Theoretical Studies of Anomie." Pp. 243–283 in Marshall B. Clinard (ed.), q.v.

Curry, G. David and Irving A. Spergel, 1988, "Gang Homicide, Delinquency, and Community." Criminology 26:381–405.

DeFleur, Lois B., 1967, "Ecological Variables in the Cross-Cultural Study of Delinquency." Social Forces 45:556–570.

Donnelly, Patrick G. and Charles E. Kimble, 1997, "Community Organizing, Environmental Change, and Neighborhood Crime." Crime and Delinquency 43:493–511.

Durkheim, Emile, 1933, The Division of Labor in Society, translated by George Simpson. London: The Free Press of Glencoe. Originally published in 1893.

———, 1951, Suicide, translated by John A. Spaulding and George Simpson. New York: Free Press. Originally published in 1897.

Ebbe, Obi N. I., 1989, "Crime and Delinquency in Metropolitan Lagos: A Study of 'Crime and Delinquency' Theory." Social Forces 67:751–765.

Elliott, Delbert S., William Julius Wilson, David Huizinga, Robert J. Sampson, Amanda

Elliott, and Bruce Rankin, 1996, "The Effects of Neighborhood Disadvantage on Adolescent Development." Journal of Research in Crime and Delinquency 33:389–426.

Fabrikant, Richard, 1979, "The Distribution of Criminal Offenses in an Urban Environment: A Spatial Analysis of Criminal Spillovers and of Juvenile Offenders." American Journal of Economics and Sociology 33:32–48.

Farris, R. E. L. and H. W. Dunham, 1939, Mental Disorders in Urban Areas. Chicago: University of Chicago Press.

Finestone, Harold, 1976, Victims of Change. Westport, Conn.: Greenwood.

Gordon, Robert A., 1967, "Issues in the Ecological Study of Delinquency." American Sociological Review 32:927–944.

Gottfredson, Denise C., Richard J. McNeil, III, and Gary D. Gottfredson, 1991, "Social Area Influences on Delinquency: A Multilevel Analysis." Journal of Research in Crime and Delinquency 28:197–226.

Hayner, Norman S., 1942, "Five Cities of the Pacific Northwest." Pp. 353–387 in Clifford R. Shaw and Henry D. McKay, q.v.

Heitgerd, Janet L. and Robert J. Bursik, Jr., 1987, "Extra-Community Dynamics and the Ecology of Delinquency." American Journal of Sociology 92:775–787.

Hoffman, John P. and Timothy Ireland, 1995, "Cloward and Ohlin's Strain Theory Reexamined: An Elaborated Theoretical Model." Pp. 247–270 in Freda Adler and William S. Laufer (eds.), q.v.

Ianni, Francis A. J., 1974, Black Mafia. New York: Simon and Schuster.

Johnstone, John W. C., 1978, "Social Class, Social Areas and Delinquency." Sociology and Social Research 63:49–72.

Jonassen, Christen T., 1949, "A Re-Evaluation and Critique of the Logic and Some Methods of Shaw and McKay." American Sociological Review 14:608–617.

Kobrin, Solomon, 1959, "The Chicago Area Project—A 25 Year Assessment." The Annals of the American Academy of Political and Social Science 322:20–29.

———, 1971, "The Formal Logical Properties of the Shaw-McKay Delinquency Theory." Pp. 101–131 in Harwin L. Voss and David M. Petersen (eds.), q.v.

Lander, Bernard, 1954, Towards an Understanding of Juvenile Delinquency. New York: Columbia University Press. Reprinted by AMS Press, 1970.

Lemert, Edwin M., 1964, "Social Structure, Social Control, and Deviation." Pp. 57–97 in Marshall B. Clinard (ed.), q.v.

Lundman, Richard J., 1993, Prevention and Control of Delinquency, second edition. New York: Oxford University Press.

Menard, Scott, 1995, "A Developmental Test of Mertonian Theory." Journal of Research in Crime and Delinquency 32:136–174.

Merton, Robert K., 1957, Social Theory and Social Structure, revised and enlarged edition. London: Free Press of Glencoe.

———, 1964, "Anomie, Anomia, and Social Interaction: Contexts of Deviant Behavior." Pp. 213–242 in Marshall B. Clinard (ed.), q.v.

Messner, Steven F., 1988, "Merton's 'Social Structure and Anomie': The Road Not Taken." Deviant Behavior 9:33–53.

Miller, Walter B., 1975, Violence by Youth Gangs and Youth Groups as a Crime Problem in Major American Cities. Washington, D.C.: U.S. Government Printing Office.

Morenoff, Jeffrey D. and Robert J. Sampson, 1997, "Violent Crime and the Spatial Dynamics of Neighborhood Transition: Chicago, 1970–1990." Social Forces 76:31–64.

Morris, Terence, 1958, The Criminal Area. London: Routledge and Kegan Paul.

Park, Robert E., 1936, "Human Ecology." American Journal of Sociology 42:1–15.

———, 1967, "The City: Suggestions for the Investigation of Human Behavior in the Urban Environment." Pp. 1–46 in Robert E. Park, Ernest W. Burgess, and Roderick D. McKenzie (eds.), q.v.

Park, Robert E., Ernest W. Burgess, and Roderick D. McKenzie (eds.), 1967, The City. Chicago: University of Chicago Press. Originally published in 1925.

Paternoster, Raymond and Paul Mazerolle, 1994, "General Strain Theory and Delinquency: A Replication and Extension." Journal of Research on Crime and Delinquency 31:235–263.

Robinson, W. S., 1950, "Ecological Correlations and the Behavior of Individuals." American Sociological Review 15:351–357.

Robison, Sophia M., 1936, Can Delinquency Be Measured? New York: Columbia University Press.

Rosen, Lawrence, 1978, The Delinquent and Non-Delinquent in a High Delinquent Area. San Francisco: R&E Research Associates.

Rosen, Lawrence and Stanley H. Turner, 1967, "An Evaluation of the Lander Approach to Ecology of Delinquency." Social Problems 15:189–200.

Sampson, Robert J. and W. Byron Groves, 1989, "Community Structure and Crime: Testing Social Disorganization Theory." American Journal of Sociology 94:774–802.

Sellin, Thorsten, 1938, Culture Conflict and Crime. New York: Social Science Research Council.

Shaw, Clifford R., 1930, The Jack-Roller. Chicago: University of Chicago Press.

Shaw, Clifford R. and Henry D. McKay, 1942, Juvenile Delinquency and Urban Areas. Chicago: University of Chicago Press.

———, 1969, Juvenile Delinquency and Urban Areas, revised edition. Chicago: University of Chicago Press.

Shaw, Clifford R., Henry D. McKay, and James F. McDonald, 1938, Brothers in Crime. Chicago: University of Chicago Press.

Shaw, Clifford R., Frederick M. Zorbaugh, Henry D. McKay, and Leonard S. Cottrell, 1929, Delinquency Areas. Chicago: University of Chicago Press.

Sheu, Chuen-Jim, 1986, Delinquency and Identity: Juvenile Delinquency in an American Chinatown. New York: Harrow and Heston.

Simcha-Fagan, Ora and Joseph E. Schwartz, 1986, "Neighborhood and Delinquency: An Assessment of Contextual Effects." Criminology 24:667–703.

Smith, William Carlson, 1937, Americans in Process. Ann Arbor, Mich.: Edwards Brothers.

Stark, Rodney, 1987, "Deviant Places: A Theory of the Etiology of Crime." Criminology 25:893–909.

Sutherland, Anne, 1975, Gypsies: The Hidden Americans. London: Tavistock.

Sutherland, Edwin H. and Donald R. Cressey, 1978, Criminology, tenth edition. New York: Lippincott.

Suttles, Gerald D., 1972, The Social Construction of Communities. Chicago: University of Chicago Press.

Taylor, Ian, Paul Walton, and Jock Young, 1973, The New Criminology. New York: Harper & Row.

Taylor, Ralph B., 1997, "Social Order and Disorder of Street Blocks and Neighborhoods: Ecology, Microecology, and the Systemic Model of Social Disorganization." Journal of Research in Crime and Delinquency 34:113–155.

Thomas, William I. and Florian Znaniecki, 1927, The Polish Peasant in Europe and America, Vol. 2. New York: Knopf.

V. I. P. Examiner, 1992, "Chicago Area Project: A Delinquency Prevention Project." Summer:6–17.

Voss, Harwin L. and David M. Petersen (eds.), 1971a, Ecology, Crime, and Delinquency. New York: Appleton-Century-Crofts.

———, 1971b, "Introduction." Pp. 1–44 in Harwin L. Voss and David M. Petersen (eds.), q.v.

Walker, Jeffery T., 1994, "Human Ecology and Social Disorganization Revisit Delinquency in Little Rock." Pp. 46–78 in Gregg Barak (ed.), Varieties of Criminology: Readings from a Dynamic Discipline. Westport, Conn.: Praeger.

Wilks, Judith A., 1967, "Ecological Correlates of Crime and Delinquency." Pp. 138–156 in The President's Commission on Law Enforcement and Administration of Justice, Task Force Report: Crime and Its Impact—An Assessment. Washington, D.C.: U.S. Government Printing Office.

Wong, Siu Kwong, 1997, "Delinquency of Chinese-Canadian Youth: A Test of Opportunity, Control, and Intergeneration Conflict Theories." Youth and Society 29:112–133.

Young, Pauline V., 1967, The Pilgrims of Russian-Town. New York: Russell and Russell. Originally published in 1932.

6

Lower-Class-Based Theories of Delinquency

HISTORICAL OVERVIEW AND GENERIC ASSUMPTIONS

Beginning in the 1950s, several causal theories of juvenile delinquency were developed in an attempt to explain delinquent, and typically delinquent gang, behavior of lower-class males. Such explanations concentrated on the social nature of delinquency, much like the social disorganization and anomie theories offered 20 or 30 years earlier. Indeed, they may be viewed as modifications and extensions of sociological perspectives that developed in the 1920s. In this context, a "juvenile gang" is often described as a "delinquent subculture," or at least as being the gang part of such a subculture. For this reason, these are referred to as "subcultural theories" of delinquency. This terminology suggests one major assumption—namely, that most delinquent behavior occurs within a group or gang setting. Delinquents, it is said, typically act together, or when they act alone, their behavior is strongly influenced by groups, gangs, peers, and the general ambience of their lives and associations.

While the majority of the discussion to follow in this chapter pertains to delinquency within group, or gang, contexts, this discussion is not intended to provide an extensive analysis of gangs. For more detailed information on gang structures and gang developments, including the impact of gang membership on delinquency, see, for example, Klein, 1995; Yablonsky, 1997; and Battin et al., 1998).

Another basic assumption of these theories is that delinquency is overwhelmingly a *lower-class*, *male* phenomenon. As Albert Cohen, the developer of one such theory, put it: "It is our conclusion, by no means novel or startling, that juvenile delinquency and the delinquent subculture in particular are overwhelmingly concentrated in the male, working-class sector of the juvenile population" (1955:371). Here, as elsewhere, Cohen uses the term "working class" more or less interchangeably with "lower class," although many sociologists make a rather strong distinction. Whatever the terminology, *all* theories of lower-class juvenile misconduct are based on the assumption that delinquency, particularly gang delinquency, is concentrated in the lower class, as measured by a variety of economic and social factors.

Of course, some investigators are skeptical of the validity of this assumption (Vaz, 1967). Surely, they argue, delinquency occurs among all social classes, and the official estimates of delinquency, which so regularly indict the lower classes, are more reflections of the biases of the police, courts, and others than the actual behavior of lower-class juveniles. Theorists who contend that the delinquency of lower-class youth is relatively high are not unmindful of such charges. Upon examination of the evidence, their conclusion remains, however, unchanged: serious and repetitive juvenile delinquency is predominantly a lower-class phenomenon.

Similar arguments and charges are sometimes raised with respect to the distribution of delinquency by gender, although the evidence here is not as much in doubt as with the question of social class. Much of the controversy regarding the increased involvement of females in crime and delinquency is built around the suspected influence of the changing gender roles of women on the opportunity and motivation for deviance (delinquency in this case) among the distaff side of the population (Adler, 1975; Simon, 1975; Steffensmeier and Steffensmeier, 1980). Data on the increase of female delinquency indicate that female rates of delinquency are still lower than male rates. Furthermore, the increase in female delinquency has been primarily in property- and drug-related crimes. Females have not been involved in violent offenses to the same extent as males, and female delinquency has not been considered as threatening as male delinquency (Chesney-Lind and Shelden, 1998:7–72).

Certainly, there is enough delinquency among the lower-class male segment of the population, whether it has been officially recorded or not, to warrant concern and investigation. To the extent that delinquency occurs among lower-class youth, it may well be that experiences of the lower class, including values and life-styles, contribute significantly to this behavior.

A sound explanation of delinquency within a particular segment of the population, therefore, may be useful in the search for delinquency causation. Such an explanation would not only be useful in its own right, but it might also provide insightful clues for the explanation of delinquency among other groups of people.

There are three major concepts and ideas in the subcultural explanations of lower-class delinquency: the middle-class measuring rod theory of Cohen, the opportunity theory of Richard Cloward and Lloyd Ohlin (partly based on Merton's anomie theory of deviance), and the lower-class value system explanation of Walter Miller.

COHEN AND THE MIDDLE-CLASS MEASURING ROD

Specific Assumptions

The middle-class measuring rod theory has four basic assumptions: (1) that a relatively high number of lower-class youth (males in particular) do poorly in school; (2) that poor school performance is related to delinquency; (3) that poor school performance is mostly attributable to a conflict between the dominant middle-class values of the school system and the values of lower-class youth; and (4) that lower-class male delinquency is largely committed in a gang context, partly as a means of developing more positive self-concepts and nurturing antisocial values.

Key Concepts

Reaction Formation   This is a Freudian term that describes the process in which a person openly rejects that which he wants, or aspires to, but cannot obtain or achieve.

Middle-Class Measuring Rod   The evaluations of school performance or behavior according to norms and values thought to be associated with the middle class, such as punctuality, neatness, cleanliness, nonviolent behavior, and so on, constitute a middle-class measuring rod.

Discussion

The gist of Cohen's (1955) argument is that social class membership is associated with social values and life-styles. With respect to child-rearing in the middle class, the working-class (and presumably lower-class) child is likely to be taught that behavior should be spontaneous and aggressive. Values are focused on the present with little emphasis placed on long-range planning. Socialization, or training, in the lower class is "easy going." The child learns to obey commands because of the immediate, practical value of obedience, not because of the intrinsic worth or "good" associated with conformity in and of itself, or because obedience will generate warm, affectionate reactions from a parent who is loving and on whom the child has become dependent.

By contrast, Cohen maintains that middle-class socialization or child-rearing stresses values and life-styles that are often quite opposite to those found within the lower class. Specifically, he suggests that middle-class values can be summed up in nine concepts: (1) drive and ambition, (2) individual responsibility, (3) achievement and success, whether at work, in the classroom, on the field, or in any other arena of competition, (4) the willingness to postpone immediate satisfaction of wants and desires for future profit or gain (the deferred gratification pattern), (5) rationality in the form of long-range planning and budgeting, (6) exercise of courtesy and self-control in association with others, particularly strangers, (7) control of violence and aggression, verbal or physical, in all social settings, (8) "wholesome" recreation, that is, constructive use of leisure time, such as in a hobby, and (9) respect for the property of others, perhaps the most basic value of all. Here, Cohen is suggesting that the middle-class members of society admire and try to promote more than simple, basic honesty. The value of property rights extends to the right of the owner of an article or thing to do as he or she wishes with it, with little interference from others.

While these two separate class-related value systems exist, middle-class values predominate within the school context. Consequently, the lower-class youth finds himself "measured" and evaluated by middle-class standards. This situation would present no problems to the lower-class young were it not for two conditions. First, middle-class values are the generally accepted ones in society, even among those of the lower class. Thus, standards of acceptance, achievement, and reward, as established by middle-class values and norms, are adopted and *aspired* to by members of the lower class. Second, personal failure alone, at the immediate level of the school setting, can lead to other problems, not excluding delinquency.

So strongly does the lower-class boy initially aspire to the middle-class standards of success that his repeated failures in the school system, both academically and otherwise, lead him to reject the school and the system of values it represents (a reaction formation). In this case, Cohen argues, the lower-class boy repudiates middle-class values and becomes malicious and hostile toward a now hated set of standards and all things which symbolize those standards. Cohen stresses three descriptive words to denote the extent to which the lower-class delinquent boy rejects middle-class status symbols: *malicious, negativistic,* and *nonutilitarian.* In other words, delinquent boys are "just plain mean." Middle-class standards are not only to be rejected, they are to be *flouted.* Thus, "good" children are to be terrorized, playgrounds and gyms are to be taken over for aimless use, golf courses are to be torn up, library books are to be stolen and destroyed, and so on. But perhaps the most graphic display of contempt and malice shown by lower-class gang boys toward the school system is defecating on a teacher's desk.

The final element of Cohen's theory is the introduction of a peer group or, more accurately, a gang context through which the rejected and resentful lower-class boy can nurture his growing feelings of hostility and bolster a damaged self-concept. At this point, Cohen is careful to specify that not all working- or lower-class boys caught in this predicament begin to associate with delinquent peers. Because of family, neighborhood, personality, and other conditions, some working-class males adopt a "college-boy" response, which is based on success at school and in the conventional, middle-class world altogether. Others, perhaps most, adopt a "corner-boy" response, which represents an acceptance of the lower-class male's situation and an attempt to make the best of a bad situation. The residue, a numerical minority, turn to delinquency.

The theoretical scenario of Cohen's explanation of delinquency is depicted graphically in Figure 7.

Evaluation

Recall that Cohen's theory is based on several assumptions. Evidence on the first assumption is fairly clear; lower-class youth generally *do* perform poorly in school relative to other students. From the early studies of sociologists at the University of Chicago, from which there came such works as *The Gang* by Frederick Thrasher (1927) and *Elmtown's Youth* by August Hollingshead (1949), to more recent research of a wide methodological variety (Polk and Schafer, 1972; Harvey and Slatin, 1975; Liazos, 1978), there emerges the conclusion that lower-class youth (and often ethnic minority youth) perform poorly, academically and socially, in school. Indeed, much of this evidence suggests that lower-class juveniles are expected by teachers and school administrators to perform at academic levels below those of middle-class students, and the effect of such lower expectations on eventual performance cannot be ignored.

One example of the influence of school administration expectations on student performance is the tracking system, in which students are placed into a multi-year program of instruction which is typically divided into college-oriented and trade or technical training-oriented curricula. While a number of academic factors have been related to the assignment of juveniles to particular

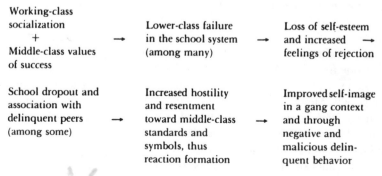

Working-class
socialization
+   →   Lower-class failure
Middle-class values   in the school system   →   Loss of self-esteem
of success   (among many)   and increased   →
                                                          feelings of rejection

School dropout and   Increased hostility   Improved self-image
association with   and resentment   in a gang context
delinquent peers   toward middle-class   →   and through
(among some)   →   standards and   negative and
                             symbols, thus   malicious delin-
                             reaction formation   quent behavior

Figure 7

tracks, social factors have also been found to play a part in this selection, including social class (Schafer et al., 1972; Kelly, 1978).

The second basic point of Cohen's thesis, that school performance is related to delinquency, has also been supported by research. In fact, this has been one of the most consistently documented relationships in recent literature (Hirschi, 1969; Offord et al., 1978; Wiatrowski et al., 1982; Rogers and Mays, 1987; Tygart, 1988).[1]

An acceptance of Cohen's thesis leads to the conclusion that school failure leads to dropping out, which leads to delinquency. In one of the most careful analyses of this relationship, Delbert Elliott and Harwin Voss (1974) provide some very interesting information. They investigated the correlation between school dropout and delinquency by closely monitoring the annual school performance and delinquency records of 2000 students in California, from the ninth grade to one year after the expected date of graduation from high school (twelfth grade).

As with several other studies, these researchers found that those students who had dropped out of school during this monitored time had higher rates of delinquency than those who had graduated. The expected causal ordering of this relationship, however, was not supported. Instead, the study revealed that rates of delinquency (as measured by police contacts and self-reports) *peaked* in the time just *before* dropping out and *declined* in each subsequent check period. According to this study, then, dropping out may be a *delinquency-reducing solution* to school problems rather than the starting point for a delinquent career, as Cohen's theory suggests. This conclusion is further justified by the finding that delinquency rates of dropouts are lower for those who married and, to some extent at least, found employment. That is, dropouts who not only eliminate school problems by dropping out but who also bolster their efforts to assume adult status by marrying or gaining employment have the lowest rates of delinquency.

The causes of school problems which led to dropping out were analyzed according to a variety of possibilities, including self-esteem, academic abilities, feelings of isolation and alienation (at home, in the community, or at school), and peer associations. In general, Elliott and Voss conclude that low academic achievement is strongly related to dropping out, as are isolation and alienation from the school. Social class is not examined relative to dropping out per se, but Elliott and Voss did find that social class is related to exposure to dropouts. Moreover, in another investigation of school dropout and delinquency, Elliott (1966) found that the relationship between dropping out and delinquency was stronger for lower-class boys than for middle-class youth, a finding which supports Cohen's thesis.

A replication of the Elliott and Voss study, however, failed to duplicate their findings. Using arrest records of 567 male youth in Philadelphia, Thornberry et al. (1985) assessed the short- and long-term effects of dropping out of high school among those who left school at ages 16, 17, and 18. In general, the results indicated that arrest rates increased soon after dropping out of school and remained relatively high until the youth reached their early 20s. Furthermore, the data indicated a general increase in arrest rates among all youth, whether or not they dropped out of school, from about age 13 to 16, with a leveling off and gradual decline until age 25, when the follow-up period ended. This age pattern of criminality is consistent with other longitudinal studies (see, for example, Gottfredson and Hirschi, 1986; Tracy and Kempf-Leonard, 1996:46–48). The pattern, however, was affected by dropping out of school, after which arrests increased. Furthermore, the impact of school dropout was present regardless of the social class background of the dropouts.

In addition, arrest rates were compared simultaneously with school dropout, marriage, and unemployment among those in their early 20s. The results showed that arrest rates were significantly higher among dropouts than high school graduates, even when the dropouts became employed. Marital status did not affect arrest rates much at all, among dropouts or graduates.

Thornberry et al. conclude that the results offer no support for Cohen's theory, but that the data do lend support to other interpretations of delinquency, such as control theory (discussed in Chapter 8). However, Cohen predicted that rates of delinquency would increase after dropping out of school, particularly if the dropout became involved in a delinquent gang or subculture. While Thornberry et al. do not offer any data on this subject, their general finding of increased rates of delinquency among high school dropouts can be interpreted as providing support for Cohen's arguments.

Moreover, a longitudinal analysis of male English students who had left school showed significantly lower rates of offending (according to official records) among youth who were employed (Farrington et al., 1986). The lower rates of offending among the employed were particularly pronounced for 15- to 16-year-olds, those who were regarded as "delinquent-prone," and for property offenses. The relationship between unemployment and criminality, however, was not affected by in-school or dropout status. Again, though, the English data do not address the issue of joining gangs upon leaving school, nor do they assess the school experiences of the youth before they left school. Since the unemployed 15- to 16-year-old school dropouts had high rates of delinquency, however, Farrington et al. suggest this subsample of youth may be more "susceptible" to influence by delinquent peers (1986:351), a proposition which would support Cohen's thesis.

Continued research on this topic clearly indicates that the relationship between dropping out of school and delinquency is complex, and is moving beyond the conceptualization that school dropout is merely a cog in a larger explanation of delinquency. As noted previously, there are several reasons for dropping out of school. Some research indicates that non-school reasons may have more significance for delinquency than do school-based factors (Fagan and Pabon, 1990), while other studies reach the same conclusion as Elliott and Voss, namely, that school-based reasons for leaving school have the strongest connection with delinquency (Jarjoura, 1993). In addition, several investigations point to a variety of personal, environmental, and economic conditions which can have important consequences for dropping out of school and for the rate of delinquency among school dropouts (Hartnagel and Krahn, 1989; Figueira-McDonough, 1993; Jarjoura, 1993; Kaplan and Liu, 1994). Also, Jarjoura (1996) presents longitudinal data which suggest that dropping out of school is associated with higher rates of offending among nonpoverty (based upon family income) juveniles, compared to youth living in poverty. Consequently, that school dropouts have higher rates of delinquency than do graduates, or that dropping out of school is followed by decreases or increases in delinquency, is not necessarily explained by the frustrating experiences of lower-class youth in school, or by the lack of bonding with the school setting, or by any particular theoretical explanation of delinquency.

We should also be mindful that there could be longer-term consequences of delinquency and dropping out of school, which might be masked by present feelings of peer acceptance and reduced strain from continued negative experiences at school. It may be the case that those youth who derive little satisfaction from school, and who see dim prospects of a successful life based upon school achievement, will seek others with similar attitudes and values, and associate more with these youth, in out-of-school activities. They may be encouraged to seek employment, at lower-paying jobs, but with more prospects for peer acceptance and short-term achievement than school could provide (Ellenbogen and Chamberland, 1997). In the long run, however, these short-term choices could result in adult patterns of unemployment, feelings of despair, and low levels of life satisfaction (Hagan, 1997; Lawrence, 1998:94–98).

Nonetheless, the documentation of *class-related* school problems, the third assumption, is generally problematic. Several darts have been thrown at the ineffectiveness of public education to reach and develop the potential of *all* youth (Polk and Schafer, 1972; Liazos, 1978; Polk, 1984). Some of those criticisms, such as irrelevant instruction, improper motivation, and intolerance of nonconformity to rigid rules, would certainly suggest that *differential class values between pupils and school officials* might be a major influence on the higher failure rates of lower-class youth. But this class connection, which is clearly at the heart of Cohen's argument, has not been carefully researched or well documented.

The fourth major component of Cohen's theory, that delinquency is a gang phenomenon and that gang members derive psychological gratification from gang membership, has received mixed support from other studies. On the one hand, there is considerable research evidence that delinquency is *social* in nature, occurring in the presence of at least two adolescents. However, the extent to which delinquency, even lower-class male delinquency, is part of structured, antisocial gangs is debatable (Jensen and Rojek, 1992).

Aside from the question of how much of lower-class male delinquency is gang related, there is mixed opinion concerning the psychological states of gang members. Somewhat consistent with Cohen's thesis, Lewis Yablonsky (1970) contends that juvenile gangs, particularly lower-class violent gangs, are best described as "near groups" because their core members are psychopathic and unable to establish primary, stable relationships, even with each other, and hence do not have the close interweaving of members with one another that would characterize true groups. This view of gang personalities, however, is contrary to most other studies of gangs (Thrasher, 1927; Bordua, 1961; Short and Strodtbeck, 1965; Klein, 1971). Actually, few delinquents, lower-class males or otherwise, are considered psychopathic or even seriously disturbed, as Yablonsky maintains. In addition, there is inconsistent evidence to support the contention that delinquency helps to bolster one's self-esteem (see Chapter 8). But whereas Cohen's thesis suggests inner conflict and psychological problems in the delinquent, it does not require that we find psychopathology to maintain its basic tenets. It does seem to require the search for an explanation related to neurosis to solve a class-based problem, and personality studies do not appear to validate that aspect of his theory.

On balance, the totality of Cohen's theory has not been empirically verified. There is little doubt that America is socially stratified and that class differences are observed with respect to school performance. However, that such differences are the cause of both school problems and, subsequently, of delinquency, particularly among lower-class males, has not been consistently substantiated. Nor has it been demonstrated that male youth who have failed in school seek peer associations through which aggressive and hostile acts of delinquency are committed against an overtly hated, but unconsciously admired, middle-class value system. It is also problematic to try to explain just how failure in school becomes interpreted in terms of a delinquent response, as opposed to what Cohen feels is a more common response among lower-class males, the adaptive, corner-boy response. As Hyman Rodman (1963), Elliot Liebow (1967), and others suggest, the disadvantaged often display an ability to incorporate a basic conformity to a dominant, middle-class value system with the exigencies of their everyday lives.

Cohen's thesis has merit, however, in that it has pointed to a critical source of adolescent problems and juvenile delinquency—lack of status and failure within the school system. And to the extent that he highlights the qualitative distinction between youthful and adult lawbreaking, in both motivation and pattern of conduct, Cohen made an important contribution to the understanding of delinquency. If this observation is accepted, then no theory of delinquency is adequate that does not account for Cohen's measuring rod.

CLOWARD AND OHLIN'S THEORY OF DIFFERENTIAL OPPORTUNITY STRUCTURE

Specific Assumptions

The differential opportunity theory has two basic assumptions: (1) that blocked economic aspirations cause poor self-concepts and general feelings of frustrations, and (2) that these frustrations lead to delinquency in specialized gang contexts, the nature of which varies according to the structure of criminal and conventional values in the juvenile's neighborhood.

Key Concepts

Differential Opportunity Structure   The uneven distribution of legal *and* illegal means of achieving economic success in a society, particularly as these opportunities or means are unequally divided by social class positions, represents a differential opportunity structure.

Criminal Gang   A juvenile gang primarily involved in theft activity is a criminal gang.

Conflict Gang   A conflict gang engages largely in violent behavior.

Retreatist Gang   A retreatist gang is primarily involved in drug-related behavior.

Discussion

In contrast to Cohen's explanation of lower-class delinquency, the explanation of Cloward and Ohlin (1960) suggests that lower-class male delinquents are goal-oriented beings, who are able rationally to assess their *economic* situation and to plan for their future accordingly.

This theory stems from a combination of two theoretical positions, which are discussed elsewhere in this book. One position is that of Robert K. Merton (1957), who argues that lower-class crime and delinquency result from a systematic exclusion of the lower class from competitive access to legitimate channels that lead to economic success in this society (see Chapter 5). The other position, brought forth by Edwin Sutherland (1939), maintains that criminal and delinquent behavior, like all other behavior, is learned, primarily in close, primary group relationships and associations (see Chapter 7). The specific content, degree, and duration of delinquent behavior depends on these associations.

Cloward and Ohlin combine the essential elements of Merton's theory of anomie and Sutherland's theory of differential association to propose that lower-class male gang delinquency is *generated* from blocked legitimate economic opportunities through America's conventional institutions, and that the specific *nature* of this delinquency is dependent on the *characteristics of the neighborhoods* in which the delinquent adolescents live (and to a slighter extent, on other significant associations, particularly with peers, that the adolescents make). These characteristics affect the opportunities for committing *illegal* acts. A major contribution of this theory is the contention that the opportunity to commit illegal acts is distributed unevenly throughout society, just as are opportunities to engage in conformist behavior.

Essentially, Cloward and Ohlin argue that lower-class gang delinquency occurs in three dimensions: *criminal, conflict,* and *drug-oriented* or *retreatist.* They also contend that the *predominance* of one or other delinquent behavior patterns is largely dependent on the *integration of conventional and organized illegitimate values and behavior systems and the integration of offenders of different ages in a neighborhood.* Previous studies of gangs and general delinquent behavior in lower-class neighborhoods have emphasized the close connection that often exists between gang behavior and conventional, legitimate business and governmental concerns (Kobrin, 1951; Whyte,1955). Furthermore, years earlier Thrasher, Shaw, and others of the influential school of sociology located at the University of Chicago had consistently documented associations between delinquent gangs of different age levels and between older gangs and adult offenders (Thrasher, 1927; Shaw, 1930, 1931; Shaw and McKay, 1942). Cloward and Ohlin took this work a step further by systematically connecting neighborhood integration patterns with specific types of gang behaviors and by tying all of this in with Merton's theory of means-end societal discrepancies as the generating force of delinquent gangs.

According to the theory, a *criminal* pattern of gang behavior emerges when there is the presence of organized, adult criminal activity in a lower-class neighborhood. In this situation, adult criminals become the success role models of the juvenile gangs. These adult role models serve as the tutors for the juveniles and as the developers of criminal skills within that group. The relationship between the adult criminals and conventional adults in these neighborhoods is described as "stable." A pattern of accommodation and mutual interdependence emerges between these two adult groups, which filters down to the juvenile gangs that flourish in the area. This accommodation is exemplified by the "fence," who makes a little extra income by disposing of stolen goods through a conventional business. Of course, local political and criminal justice officials are also accommodative of the criminal behavior in their neighborhoods, often offering protection and other preferred treatment to the criminals in exchange for personal gain and community stability. The integration and accommodation between criminal and conventional forces in a neighborhood combine to produce an emphasis on neighborhood stability and order. Thus, gang behavior will become theft oriented, not violence oriented. Behavior is supposed to be businesslike and disciplined, not irrational or tempestuous. As Cloward and Ohlin put it, "there is no place in organized crime for the impulsive, unpredictable individual" (1960:167). And while gang behavior is not organized crime in the sense in which that term is widely used, to connote powerful families in virtual control of large-scale criminal activity, Cloward and Ohlin find that the organization and discipline necessary in fruitful gang conduct preclude the impulsive and irrational people.

In some lower-class neighborhoods a stable, organized pattern of adult criminality fails to develop, although the discrepancy between societal success goals and accessibility to legitimate means of achieving success still exists for the local residents. Furthermore, in these areas living conditions in general are unstable and transient. Adult role models for juveniles, either criminal or conventional, do not develop. The result is the emergence of what Cloward and Ohlin call a *conflict* form of gang behavior. In this type of gang, violence becomes predominant. The violent behavior in these gangs, however, is *not* characterized as stemming primarily from psychopathic personalities or from reaction formation, although the youths in these gangs are described as "acutely frustrated." The major reason for the emergence of conflict gangs in these lower-class neighborhoods is the absence of a stable system of social control, which can be exerted by either criminal adult or conventional adult models. Adolescents use violence as a means of obtaining some kind of status and success because nonviolent, theft-oriented avenues of success are not available to them.

To illustrate their point, Cloward and Ohlin assert that violence within gangs declines when a detached street worker is assigned to work with them. This reduction in violence might reflect not only the abilities of the street worker, but also recognition by the gang members that the street worker represents the end of rejection and the beginning of access to legitimate success opportunities in their lives.

In some neighborhoods, *whether or not they are characterized by stable adult success opportunities (criminal or conventional)*, gangs develop that are dominated by drug use. These are the *retreatist* gangs, according to Cloward and Ohlin. Their members are described as "double failures" because they cannot succeed in either the conventional or the criminal world. The authors caution that not all double failures become members of retreatist gangs. Some scale down their aspirations and become "corner boys," as Cohen has suggested. The extent to which adolescents adopt a corner-boy or a retreatist response varies not only according to the personality of the youth, but particularly according to his associations and circumstances.

An indication that retreatism is largely a response to one's associations and circumstances is provided in the assertion of Cloward and Ohlin that retreatist gangs often emerge *after* involvement with criminal or conflict gangs. In fact, they suggest that inappropriate behavior by some in the gang, abusive drug behavior or otherwise, can lead to a rejection by the gang members and the subsequent development of a retreatist life-style. It is also for this reason that Cloward and Ohlin hedge on the description of these doubly rejected youths as members of a retreatist gang or subculture. Although most gangs use drugs, it is doubtful whether there are many drug-oriented gangs, as such. It would be more accurate, therefore, to use the word "response" or "adaptation" when referring to retreatism through drug use.

In summary, the basic components of Cloward and Ohlin's theory of lower-class gang delinquency may be diagrammed as shown in Figure 8.

Evaluation

The assumption that blocked economic aspirations affect attitudes and cause frustration has been tested in a variety of ways and has basically been found

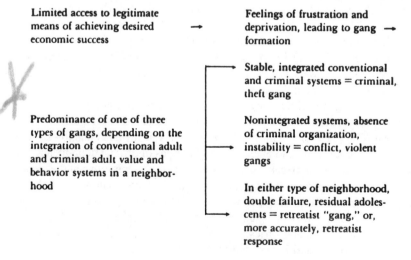

Figure 8

lacking. Interviews with lower-class youth, delinquent youth, or gang members simply fail to support the basic assumption that lower-class youth hinge their feelings and behavior on the door of perceived economic opportunity in their lives. One reason for this conclusion is the interaction among aspirations, *expectations*, and behavior. In a comparative study of high school seniors from working- and middle-class neighborhoods in Atlanta, for example, Wan Sang Han (1969) found that working-class and middle-class students aspired to essentially the same goals several years after graduation. When asked what they *expected* to have after graduation, however, there were marked differences among the students. Working-class seniors expected to have less than they desired. Middle-class students, on the other hand, still continued to expect what they desired 10 years upon graduation, almost as if they considered these goals a right or a natural phase of life.

An attempt to assess the interrelationship among a juvenile's aspirations and expectations and subsequent delinquency was reported in the previously discussed study by Elliott and Voss (1974). These researchers assessed the actual and anticipated amount of success or failure among their sample with respect to educational and occupational status. Simply put, the results of this test failed to demonstrate a relationship between failure and self-reported delinquency in support of the thesis of Cloward and Ohlin. If anything, what little relationship did emerge tended to support an opposite conceptualization—that lowered perceptions of occupational success *follow* delinquency rather than precede delinquency. A similar conclusion was reached by another investigation of self-reported delinquency, with the qualification that delinquency was more strongly related to perceived lower educational opportunities than to occupational aspirations (Quicker, 1974)

Elliott and Voss did find that educational and occupational perceptions of success were lower for lower-class youth than for middle-class adolescents. The relationships were not very strong, however, and should not be used in support of class-linked theories of delinquency.

A study of gang delinquency in Chicago provides conflicting evidence concerning the relationship between delinquency and perceived opportunities for success (Short, 1964). On the one hand, the analysis revealed that lower-class gang boys, both white and black, had higher rates of official delinquency and higher average discrepancies between occupational aspirations and expectations than nongang boys, although the discrepancies were small. When the boys' aspiration levels were compared with their fathers' occupational levels, however, it was found that white gang members had the smallest discrepancy of all groups studied, including African-American gang juveniles, lower- and middle-class black youth, and lower- and middle-class white boys. With respect to perceived educational opportunities, the highest rates of delinquency were recorded for those juveniles who perceived educational opportunities as closed to them, in agreement with the theory. However, among those who perceived educational opportunities as closed, those who had the lowest aspirations also had the highest rates of delinquency, contrary to the thesis.

Other studies, either of delinquency in general (Hirschi, 1969) or of gang delinquency (Short et al., 1965), provide further evidence refuting Cloward and Ohlin's argument. In these studies, the most delinquent juveniles are those with both low aspirations and expectations rather than those with high aspirations and low expectations, as the thesis would predict.

Perhaps the difficulty in this area lies with the imprecision of paper and pencil measures of values. It may well be that lower-class and middle-class adolescents, as well as adults, *do* have different goal perceptions and that the perception of blocked opportunities may lead to feelings of hostility and frustration. On the other hand, the perceptions and values of those in the lower class, including lower-class delinquents, are adapted from basic support of middle-class or conventional standards. Those in the lower class must come to grips with the reality of the situation and "stretch" or alter their values to accommodate their present behavior (Rodman, 1963). Excellent literary and ethnographic descriptions of this process are found in Joyce Carol Oates' *Them* (1969) and Elliot Liebow's *Tally's Corner* (1967). Paper and pencil tests, it may be argued, simply cannot measure or describe the complexities of these relationships.

Another view is that the *wrong* dimensions of opportunity have been used in studying the attitudes of juveniles. Farnworth and Leiber (1989), for example, argue that contrasts between economic goals and educational expectations yield the best indicators of delinquency. Using self-reported measures of delinquent behavior among a sample of 15- to 18-year-olds in Seattle, Farnworth and Leiber report that rates of delinquency were particularly high among those youth who had high economic aspirations but low educational expectations. Thus, they argue, blocked opportunities may indeed be predictive of delinquency, but previous measures of these blockages were conceptually flawed. To these authors, therefore, the difficulties in finding support for this type of theory have stemmed from the questions asked and the relative significance of these items to the juveniles' lives.

One trend in this line of investigation is to increase the scope of concern to include other structural conditions, particularly race and ethnicity. La Free et al. (1992), for example, conducted a longitudinal study of the impact of increased educational and economic opportunities from 1957 to 1988 on rates of crime and delinquency. To summarize a complex analysis scheme, the results of this investigation support the contention that increased opportunities correlate with lower rates of crime and delinquency among whites. Among

African-Americans, however, the results were different. For this group, crime rates *increased* with increased educational and economic opportunities. More to the point of this discussion, among African-American youth, rates of delinquency *decreased* in association with "female-headed families" (p. 177). This conclusion is contrary to strain theory and most particularly to Moynihan's analysis (see next section). The authors suggest that strain theory might be an adequate explanation of criminality among whites, but not among African-Americans. They further suggest that among African-Americans the *perception* of blocked opportunities might be a better predictor of crime and delinquency than the actual existence of these barriers (p. 178). This view has some support in the literature (Simons and Gray, 1989).

Furthermore, Emilie Allan and Darrell Steffensmeier (1989) provide evidence which suggests that youth in America are motivated by economic considerations. In essence, they conclude that arrest rates (for economic crimes) of juveniles (13–17) are lower when full-time employment is high, even when controlling for minority status, household activities, residential mobility, region, prison commitments, and relative size of police force. For young adults, however, "marginal employment" (for example, low wages and hours) is more strongly related to arrest rates than is the condition of employment per se.

The results for youth are consistent with anomie theory. Employed youth, for instance, may be less "susceptible to peer subcultures and to the attractions of illegitimate alternatives to the labor market" (p. 119). In addition, these youth would likely have less-stigmatizing backgrounds and more reasons for continued legitimate employment than would unemployed juveniles. While none of these factors demonstrates that today's young people are only, or even primarily, motivated by economic considerations, the results of this study certainly give credence to the view that employment is important to American youth today. The important point, of course, is the continued investigation of delinquency to monitor such factors and to adapt or adjust relevant theories accordingly.

Cross-cultural research might shed additional information on the impact of strain or blocked opportunities on delinquency, especially in societies with different cultural and/or economic characteristics than might be found in Western countries. The importance of economic success to youth in the Philippines, for example, must be couched within a larger sociocultural framework which emphasizes social and familial cooperation and support. Thus, the importance of strain theories to explain delinquency in this society is lessened (Shoemaker, 1992). Of course, international studies of all explanations of crime and delinquency are needed for a fuller appreciation of the strengths and weaknesses of these theories.

The second assumption of Cloward and Ohlin's argument, that lower-class gangs become specialized according to the type of neighborhood in which they exist, has received more support in the literature than the first assumption. Irving Spergel (1964) examined the nature of juvenile gangs in three predominantly lower-class neighborhoods and concluded that gang specialization did appear. The specific content of these gangs, however, did not duplicate Cloward and Ohlin's criminal, conflict, and drug typology. For example, Spergel could not detect a specific drug subculture, or juvenile gang, in any of the three neighborhoods, although drug use was practiced in a limited way in each area.[2] In addition, Spergel's analysis differentiated the criminal subculture of Cloward and Ohlin into a *racket* subculture and a general *theft* subculture.

Spergel's study also demonstrated a connection between gang delinquency and neighborhood integration, both conventional-criminal integration and age-level integration. The racket (career theft, organized crime) subculture was found in a neighborhood having residential stability and organized crime. In this neighborhood, Spergel noted a connection between both conventional and criminal adult activities and between the criminal activities and the dominant forms of conduct in the juvenile gangs, such as loan sharking, policy or numbers games, off-track betting, drug selling, and prostitution. The gang members from "Racketville" exhibited a stronger criminal orientation (although no more delinquent behavior) than the gang members in the other two neighborhoods. A dominant role model for the delinquents in Racketville was the adult racketeer, and the major means of getting ahead for them were "connections," as opposed to luck, ability, or education.

A fighting or conflict subculture was found in an area with high rates of public assistance, psychiatric treatment, infant mortality, congestion, physical deterioration, and low income. The delinquents in these neighborhoods also had the least amount of stability of all three areas. Consistent with Cloward and Ohlin's predictions, the integration of "Slumtown" was very low. Petty criminals occupied the streets. Respected adults in the area, conventional or criminal, were hard to locate. Deference to older delinquents by younger ones was also not in evidence.

The third neighborhood studied by Spergel, "Haulburg," was lower-class by some economic criteria, but in many ways more middle-class than the other two areas, standing midway between Racketville and Slumtown in terms of neighborhood integration and adult criminal organization. Gang behavior in Haulburg was composed of some violence but more theft, such as car theft, apartment burglary, and store holdups. This type of gang was not predicted by Cloward and Ohlin, but the relationship between this gang's behavior and its neighborhood characteristics does not contradict the thesis.

A study by James Short and Fred Strodtbeck in Chicago also generally supports the idea of gang specialization, although the specific nature of the specialization is, again, not in perfect agreement with Cloward and Ohlin (Short and Strodtbeck, 1965). In this study no criminal subculture, as such, was discovered. Instead, several cliques within conflict gangs would break off and engage in "semi-professional theft," such as burglary, auto stripping, and shoplifting. To some extent, Short and Strodtbeck feel that there may be a "parent delinquent subculture" which characterizes all gangs in general and from which more specialized gang activity may develop.

On many other accounts, however, this research lends little support to Cloward and Ohlin's thesis. There was no evidence that these gang boys were driven by frustrations derived from perceived blocked economic aspirations.

Because dominant themes among these gangs were fighting and sexual activity, Short and Strodtbeck point out that a major concern among lower-class gang members is the development and maintenance of a "rep" for both physical and sexual prowess. This concern is highlighted by the general description of adolescent gang behavior as "risk-taking," with little long-term profit making involved.

Research using mathematical models has also shown that delinquent behavior is somewhat specialized (Wolfgang et al., 1972; Bursik, 1980; Rojek and Erickson, 1982; Tracy et al., 1990). Other analyses have also noted specialization among juvenile offenders, but have concluded that a more predominant "career" pattern is offense versatility which tends to stabilize in more specialized categories with increasing age (Farrington et al., 1988; Rankin and Wells, 1985). Others suggest that there are different age peaks for particular crimes. Steffensmeier et al. (1989), for example, report that arrest rates for public order offenses have a higher age apex than do such "youth-oriented" crimes as automobile theft, burglary, and vandalism (p. 817). They also speculate that "lucrative" crimes, such as embezzlement, have relatively high age peaks, but this conclusion is not firm (p. 827). This research does not focus on lower-class gang behavior, however, nor does it specify any connection between delinquency specialization and neighborhood integration patterns.

Overall, it would seem that Cloward and Ohlin's theory has not stood up to the test, a view fortified by an effort in New York City to utilize it as the basis for a massive program, known as Mobilization for Youth, which did not seem to have a significant effect on reducing serious delinquency (Empey, 1982). The paper and pencil tests of the aspiration-expectation component of the thesis may not be adequate to measure complex psychological processes. It is most difficult to capture all the nuances in human behavior and its motivation by asking people to respond yes, no, or maybe to short questions or statements. Gang members may indeed share the feelings and attitudes predicted by the theory; it is difficult to know for sure when using attitude scales.

There is support, however, for the contention that lower-class gang behavior is specialized and that the specialization is somewhat connected with neighborhood characteristics. In fact, connection between gang delinquency and neighborhood organization is the strongest feature of Cloward and Ohlin's theory. In other words, the theory offers a reasonably good explanation of the *content* of gang delinquency, with the possible exception of drug use in gangs; it falls short in providing an adequate explanation of *why* the delinquency originally develops.

MILLER'S THEORY OF LOWER-CLASS CULTURE AND DELINQUENCY

Specific Assumptions

The lower-class culture explanation of delinquency rests on two very basic assumptions: (1) that clear-cut lower-class focal concerns or values exist, independent of other values, and (2) that female-dominated households constitute an integral feature of lower-class life-styles and, as such, represent a primary reason for the emergence of street-corner male adolescent groups in lower-class neighborhoods.

Key Concepts

Focal Concerns   Predominant values and norms that guide the day-to-day behavior of people are referred to as focal concerns; in this context, such concerns are thought to be characteristic of various social classes, with attention devoted to the lower class.

One-Sex Peer Unit   This is a social unit that serves as an alternative source of companionship and male role model development outside the home.

Discussion

Both Cohen, on the one hand, and Cloward and Ohlin, on the other, have brought forward what have been termed "strain" theories. For different reasons, both propose that a basic cause of lower-class gang delinquency is a structurally imposed barrier or obstacle to success in the society. That such a structural strain is not a requisite for an explanation of lower-class gang delinquency is the contention of Walter Miller.

In 1958, Miller summarized the tenets of what was to become a highly politicized explanation of lower-class gang delinquency. Essentially, his thesis was that lower-class gangs are male-oriented and street-oriented groups, and that these characteristics do not develop by chance. The characteristics of lower-class gangs, including their behavior, reflect the characteristics *not* of the gangs' neighborhoods but, instead, of a generic lower-class cultural system.

According to Miller, the key components of the lower-class culture are best described as "focal concerns," of which there are six: (1) trouble, (2) toughness, (3) smartness, (4) excitement, (5) fate, and (6) autonomy.

Trouble involves run-ins with authority, police, bureaucratic personnel, or others. It also includes, for men, problems associated with fighting or sexual activity accompanied by drinking and, for women, complications associated with sexual activity.

Toughness is characterized as a concern for physical prowess and strength, so-called masculine traits (as exhibited by bravery and sexual skills, often symbolized through tattooing and shown by lack of emotion).

Smartness represents an ability to outwit someone through mental gymnastics. It involves being able to "play the game," to hustle the John, so to speak, particularly in the setting of the street.

Excitement represents a heightened interest in the "thrill"—particularly experienced through alcohol, sex, gambling, "making the rounds," and "going out on the town." It is considered a periodic adventure, often followed by, or preceded by, a period of inaction, referred to as "hanging out."

Fate includes the feeling that one's future is out of his hands, beyond his control, not necessarily because of religious powers, but more because of the strong forces of destiny or magic.

The last focal concern, autonomy, contains paradoxical elements. On the surface, Miller argues that autonomy represents a strong desire on the part of lower-class people to be independent of external controls (the "boss" or a spouse, for example). Underneath all this manifested independence, however, is a consistent pattern of seeking out nurturing situations, such as a steady job or a comforting wife, or perhaps a period of confinement, particularly after a round of trouble or excitement.

The focal concerns of a lower-class culture relate to delinquency in two ways. First, the values of lower-class life often result in the absence of the father, or any other significant male role model, in the home. Thus, many adolescent boys leave the home in search of male identities in street gangs, called by Miller "one-sex peer units" (1958:14). Second, within the gang, needs and behaviors develop that are *consistent with* the focal concerns of the lower class. According to Miller, lower-class gang members are not psychologically disturbed. Instead, gang members typically represent the most "able" male youngsters in a neighborhood, in terms of both physical abilities and "personal competence."

The motivation for delinquency, in this theoretical context, is the need among most adolescents, but heightened for lower-class males because of female-oriented households, to "belong" and to be positively recognized—that is, to have "status" among their peers. Fulfillment of these needs is sought in street-corner gang membership. Because the behavior in these gangs is guided by lower-class focal concerns, it will "automatically" go against certain laws, such as laws regulating aggressive behavior. Rather than being nonconformist and "driven," gang members are behaving in stable, conforming, and "normal" fashion, according to the norms and values of their "most significant cultural milieu" (Miller, 1958:18).

Diagrammatically, Miller's thesis can be presented as shown in Figure 9.

Evaluation

With respect to the first assumption of the theory, the reader might be of the opinion that the focal concerns described above are, to some extent, as much a part of the middle class as the lower class. This situation indicates a blending of class-related cultural values and life-styles. The blending can occur as a result of the incorporation of middle-class values among the lower class, or vice versa.

There are many social commentators who basically agree with the notion that there is a lower-class culture, a set of life-styles and values unique to the lower class. A popularized version of this concept is the "culture of poverty," most often associated with Oscar Lewis' ethnographic studies of poverty in Latin American cultures (Lewis, 1961, 1966). Later, Edward Banfield (1968) took up this theme in describing the ills of the modern urban center. In this treatise, Banfield suggests that poverty represents a cycle in which lackadaisical attitudes and present-time orientations produce low educational aspirations and achievements, which result in low occupational attainment, which is equated with low social class attainment and, often, with poverty.

In addition, Marvin Wolfgang and Franco Ferracuti (1967) contend that violence, manifested criminally in such acts as homicide and assault, is part of a subculture of values and norms that legitimate the use of violence in various social situations. Moreover, this theory explicitly locates the subculture of violence among young males in the lower social classes of Western societies, as

Lower-class focal concerns + Female-dominated households	→	Desire of lower-class male adolescents to seek male identity and status in "one-sex peer unit" street-corner gangs	→
Behavior in accordance with lower-class focal concerns	→	Behavior that is often delinquent and criminal	

Figure 9

well as in the populations of many developing nations. Furthermore, according to some research (Heimer, 1997), the mechanism for transmitting attitudes and values favorable to violence involves peer associations, which is consistent with a learning theory, or differential association, approach to delinquency (see Chapter 7). While there has been inconsistent support for this theory (Shoemaker and Williams, 1987), the fact remains that it represents another attempt to locate specific values and behavioral norms in the lower social classes of developed countries.

Whether the life-style of the poor represents a cultural set of values consciously passed along from one generation to the next, or whether this life-style is a rational, logical adaptation to a continuous set of problems and obstacles to achievement, is subject to debate (Liebow, 1967). In either case, research evidence accumulated since the end of World War II has supplied *some* support for a basic tenet of Miller's thesis—that a definite set of values and life-styles exists among the poor of Western societies.

The rich, detailed ethnographic accounts of the lower class do not, of course, duplicate the specific focal concerns outlined in Miller's thesis. More importantly, these accounts rarely discuss crime and delinquency as separate aspects of lower-class behavior, sometimes barely at all. Poverty engenders a variety of problems, it would seem, while crime and delinquency, in this view, are manifestations of the larger problem of poverty.

It is with regard to the second assumption of Miller's thesis that any direct attention has been applied. This assumption, again, is that a common facet of lower-class culture and life-styles is the matriarchal home, and the presence of female-led households contributes directly to lower-class male delinquency. Attempts to test this proposition, however, have largely focused on the issue of race rather than social class. This attention to the relationship between family structure and delinquency, *by race*, is largely attributable to a controversial report issued by Daniel Patrick Moynihan in 1965. In essence, Moynihan argued that the contemporary urban African-American population was becoming divided into two definite sections, a stable middle class and a deteriorating lower class. This deteriorating lower-class segment of blacks was directly related to the presence of *female-dominated households*, which, in turn, was traceable in American history to the breakup of the African-American family structure during the period of slavery (Moynihan, 1965). The presence of female-dominated households leads Moynihan to conclude that the lower-class African-American family is inordinately involved in a "tangle of pathology" (1965:29), which includes, among a host of social problems, a high rate of delinquency. A major attack on Moynihan was not a repudiation of his factual information as much as a shifting of responsibility for the plight of African-American from the contemporary white-dominated society to an unalterable historical legacy.

Now, instead of describing the roots of *lower-class* male delinquency, a central component of Miller's thesis had been transformed into a *racial* issue, at the apex of racial problems in America, no less.[3] Besides this transformation, Moynihan failed to make any reference to Miller's thesis in his report, a point which further allowed the ensuing controversy to take on racial tones rather than class issues.

The issue of family structure and delinquency has a lengthy research tradition of its own.[4] For the moment, it is sufficient to discuss attempts to test the assumption that female-dominated households lead to, or correlate with, delinquency among blacks, or within the lower class. Actually, the presence of female-dominated households within the lower class or among African-Americans has been less than half, on an absolute scale (Rosen, 1969), although it has been higher than among whites.

In 1990, 64 percent of African-American children were living with both natural parents, and this figure was 81 percent for Hispanic children (Statistical Abstracts, 1994:63, 66). In 1997, 35 percent of African-American children and 64 percent of Hispanic children were living with both parents (U.S. Bureau of the Census, March Current Population Survey, 1998: Figure POP5).

While poverty is not the only measure of lower class, government statistics usually report household characteristics relative to official definitions of poverty. In 1996, 10 percent of children in "married-couple families" were classified as living in poverty. Among female-headed families, the percentage of children living in poverty was 49 percent, while this figure was 58 percent for African-American families and 67 percent for Hispanic families (U.S. Bureau of the Census, March Current Population Survey, 1998: Table ECON1.A).

Clearly, there are economic difficulties for families headed by females, no matter what race or ethnicity is involved. Governmental poverty figures, however, do not indicate rates of delinquency within family structures, and the direct correlations among poverty or social class, race and ethnicity, family structure, and delinquency have to be established by other sources of data.

It has been pointed out that the *relative* proportion of female-dominated homes among African-Americans or the lower class is much greater than among middle-class whites (Moynihan, 1965; Rosen, 1969), and thus the relatively higher rates of delinquency among these groups may be related to matriarchal homes. When this assumption has been tested, it has received contradictory support. Some research has noted no evidence that young males from lower-class or nonwhite homes are delinquent because of female dominance in the households, whether delinquency is measured in official terms or through self-reports (Rosen, 1969; Berger and Simon, 1974; Austin, 1992). Other studies indicate that lower-class juvenile males have stronger images of masculinity and are more aggressive than middle-class youth (Fannin and Clinard, 1967), and that incarcerated delinquents from female-based homes are more concerned with masculine images and are more hostile than delinquents from other home situations (Silverman and Dinitz, 1974).

On the whole, Miller's thesis remains speculative and interesting, often substantiated more by common sense and haphazard, perhaps stereotypical, observations than by systematic research. Although there is some evidence that a lower-class culture of poverty does exist, it is difficult to determine how influential this set of values and norms may be on behavior, including delinquent behavior, when counterposed with other norms and values, such as middle-class and racial/ethnic standards and moral codes.

As mentioned earlier, there is a large amount of research on the topic of family structure and delinquency. This topic is addressed in more detail in Chapter 8, Control Theories. For the present discussion, it is *incorrect* to assume that (a) single-parent homes are always found in lower-class settings and (b) that single parents are incapable of controlling their children and thus reducing the risks of these youth becoming involved in delinquency.

SUMMARY

It would be easy to criticize all of the theoretical positions on lower-class delinquency on the grounds that *none* of them provides an adequate explanation of delinquency among all adolescents, particularly middle-class juveniles. This type of criticism, however, is irrelevant in that the theories were not intended to explain middle-class delinquency. A theory should be evaluated in terms of what it purports to explain, not in terms of anything else.

Scholars have debated the degree to which social class is a determinant of delinquency (Tittle et al., 1978; Hindelang et al., 1979; Elliott and Ageton, 1980; Krohn et al., 1980; Akers et al., 1981; Braithwaite, 1981; Thornberry and Farnworth, 1982). Two reviews of this literature by Tittle and Meier (1990, 1991) fail to identify social class as a meaningful determinant of delinquency. Others, however, conclude that social class does affect delinquency, particularly when class is conceptualized in terms of poverty and unemployment, rather than as a position on a status scale, and when serious and repetitive measures of delinquency are considered in the relationship (Farnworth et al., 1994; see also, Hagan, 1992).

However, few would contend that delinquency in middle-class settings is a rarity, or should not be addressed. Theoretical explanations of middle-class delinquency have been offered since the 1960s, when self-report surveys and simple observations led people to conclude that this kind of behavior was, in fact, a reality. Moreover, middle-class delinquency is not a thing of the past, but is clearly evident in contemporary self-report surveys, not only in Western societies, but in developing countries as well (Shoemaker, 1992). One explanation of such behavior is the influence of what some term a "youth culture" (Flacks, 1971). Basically, this view of delinquency focuses on the impact of industrialization and social changes in the twentieth century, particularly on the class structure in society and on the socialization of youth. Youth are being categorized and treated as a separate entity, which allows them to establish their own set of norms and values, and many of these young people are living in middle-class homes. This situation then leads to a separate youth culture, which can lead to the development of norms which permit, or even encourage, deviance among middle-class youth.

Of course, the youth culture theory is not the only explanation of why youth from middle-class backgrounds commit delinquent or criminal acts. However, theoretical efforts to identify factors specifically within a middle-class setting may be misguided. Some may argue that individual traits, such as biological or psychological characteristics, offer a better explanation of middle-class delinquency. A more persuasive explanatory path, however, is to be found in the factors which are addressed in the next two chapters, Chapter 7, differential association theory, and Chapter 8, control theory (particularly social bond theory). Neither of these explanations is based on specific class backgrounds, and the strength of these theories should not be evaluated on their application to any one social-class setting. Rather, one of the attractions of these two theoretical explanations lies in their identification of motivating factors which would seem to be independent of class parameters (Albanese, 1993:59).

Considering only the basic assumptions and explanatory goals of the subcultural theories of lower-class delinquency, several difficulties emerge in attempts to establish the veracity of their propositions. In addition to the previously discussed shortcomings of each theory, any attempt to explain a complex behavioral phenomenon on a grand and largely static condition is unlikely to be persuasively supported by research evidence. Why, for example, do most delinquent youth, in gangs or otherwise, "reform," so to speak, and abstain from criminality when reaching young adulthood, as the theorists themselves suggest is the case? Surely one would not argue that *social class* conditions change so dramatically for these youth in a span of four or five years. The paradox here is that the larger, social class conditions remain relatively stable while the behavior these conditions are proposed to influence changes.

Of the three theories discussed in this chapter, the one that is best able to handle this paradox is Cohen's middle-class measuring rod theory. In this case, delinquent youth would be expected to move away from delinquency when pressures to achieve through the school system were lessened, such as upon reaching adulthood. In fact, some research has shown that delinquency is immediately reduced when the youth are removed from the stress-producing conditions of school. The value of Cohen's thesis, however, resides in its connection with an institutional factor, the school setting, as a basic element in the causation of delinquency.

The utility of Cohen's theory underscores another significant shortcoming of subcultural theories of delinquency. That is, whatever the content of class values may be, their *interpretation is* almost always derived from interpersonal and institutional experiences. It is one thing to suggest that social class values and norms exist; it is quite another matter to maintain that such values serve as the prime motivators of thought and behavior, separately from other social or personal conditions. Such powers of persuasion would be difficult enough to establish in a culture literally dominated by social class distinctions. Frankly, to attribute to social class factors an overriding influence on behavior in any complex, modern Western society is unrealistic. Some maintain that strain theories do not address individual responses and that attempts to test these theories with individual-level data are misguided (Bernard, 1987). As Agnew (1987) points out, however, attention to individual responses to blocked opportunities is necessary in testing strain theories, otherwise the "causal chain would break down" (p. 282).

All of these comments should not be construed as suggesting that social class values do not exist, or that such values may not be mutually incompatible. Of course, there are different values in different social classes. The accommodations people make relative to class values, or conflicts among values, however, reduce the explanatory power of social class-generated theories of behavior.

The strength of these theories lies in their *sensitizing* qualities. That is, each suggests that a broad-based societal condition is responsible for a significant proportion of delinquent behavior. To rest an explanation of delinquency *solely* on such factors is inadequate. To ignore societal conditions in the explanation of delinquency, however, would be myopic and, most probably, unproductive. In other words, attention to institutional conditions, such as school problems or family relationships, in the explanation of delinquency may be generated from an analysis of the structure of social class values. However, the desire to focus attention on social class values and life-styles is quite strong, particularly among sociologists. The use of social class as a basis for explaining delinquency is addressed again in Chapter 10, when the radical approach to youthful misconduct is examined, although the issues raised from Marxist, or neo-Marxist, and other radical perspectives are not the same as those discussed here.

Notes

1. The subject of school-related factors and delinquency is also discussed in Chapter 8, which looks at control theories. The relationship between poor school performance and delinquency is mentioned at this point only to document the validity of this aspect of Cohen's thesis.

2. The inability to find an exclusive drug or "retreatist" subculture is not too surprising to some (Lindesmith and Gagnon, 1964). Drug use and addiction have long preceded the blocked economic opportunity conditions spelled out in Cloward and Ohlin's thesis. In addition, relatively high rates of addiction have been found among upper-middle-class occupational groups, such as physicians, whose legitimate opportunities for economic success would be much greater than for lower-class juveniles (Lindesmith and Gagnon, 1964). Furthermore, the effects of drugs, including addictive drugs, vary according to the social situations in which drug use occurs and can range over a variety of reactive moods. Thus, to conceptualize drug use as a retreatist reaction to failure is inaccurate.

3. Another example of transforming the problem of delinquency into a racial issue is the previously discussed analysis of IQ, race, and delinquency presented by Gordon (1976); see also Sagarin (1980).

4. Parsons (1954), for example, presents an interesting theoretical connection among family structure, gender roles, and aggression. Parsons' discussion, however, covers Western society in general and is not confined to criminal behavior among lower-class males.

References

Adler, Freda, 1975, Sisters in Crime. New York: McGraw-Hill.

Agnew, Robert, 1987, "On 'Testing Structural Strain Theories.'" Journal of Research in Crime and Delinquency 24:281–286.

Akers, Ronald L., Marvin D. Krohn, Marcia Radosevich, and Lonn Lanza-Kaduce, 1981, "Social Characteristics and Self-Reported Delinquency: Differences in Extreme Types." Pp. 48–62 in Gary F. Jensen (ed.), Sociology of Delinquency. Beverly Hills, Calif.: Sage.

Albanese, Jay, 1993. Dealing with Delinquency: The Future of Juvenile Justice, second edition. Chicago: Nelson-Hall.

Allan, Emilie Anderson and Darrell J. Steffensmeier, 1989, "Youth, Underemployment, and Property Crime: Differential Effects of Job Availability and Job Quality on Juvenile and Young Adult Arrest Rates." American Sociological Review 54:107–123.

Austin, Roy L., 1992, "Race, Female Headship, and Delinquency: A Longitudinal Analysis." Justice Quarterly 9:585–607.

Banfield, Edward C., 1968, The Unheavenly City. Boston: Little, Brown.

Battin, Sara R., Karl G. Hill, Robert D. Abbott, Richard F. Catalano, and J. David Hawkins, 1998, "The Contribution of Gang Membership to Delinquency Beyond Delinquent Friends." Criminology 36:93–115.

Berger, Alan S. and William Simon, 1974, "Black Families and the Moynihan Report: A Research Evaluation." Social Problems 22:145–161.

Bernard, Thomas J., 1987, "Testing Structural Strain Theories." Journal of Research in Crime and Delinquency 24:262–280.

Bordua, David J., 1961, "Delinquent Subcultures: Sociological Interpretations of Gang

Delinquency." Annals of the American Academy of Political and Social Science 33:119–136.

Braithwaite, John, 1981, "The Myth of Social Class and Criminality Reconsidered." American Sociological Review 46:36–57.

Bursik, Robert J., Jr., 1980, "The Dynamics of Specialization in Juvenile Offenses." Social Forces 58:851–864.

Chesney-Lind, Meda, and Randall G. Shelden, 1998, Girls, Delinquency, and Juvenile Justice, second edition. Belmont, Calif.: West/Wadsworth.

Clinard, Marshall B. (ed.), 1964, Anomie and Deviant Behavior. New York: Free Press.

Cloward, Richard A. and Lloyd E. Ohlin, 1960, Delinquency and Opportunity. New York: Free Press.

Cohen, Albert K., 1955, Delinquent Boys: The Culture of the Gang. New York: Free Press.

Ellenbogen, Stephen and Claire Chamberland, 1997, "The Peer Relations of Dropouts: A Comparative Study of At-Risk and Not At-Risk Youths." Journal of Adolescence 20:355–367.

Elliott, Delbert S., 1966, "Delinquency, School Attendance, and Dropout." Social Problems 13:307–314.

Elliott, Delbert S. and Suzanne S. Ageton, 1980, "Reconciling Race and Class Differences in Self-Reported and Official Estimates of Delinquency." American Sociological Review 45:95–110.

Elliott, Delbert S. and Harwin L. Voss, 1974, Delinquency and Dropout. Lexington, Mass.: D. C. Heath.

Empey, Lamar T., 1982, American Delinquency, second edition. Homewood, Ill.: Dorsey.

Fagan, Jeffrey and Edward Pabon, 1990, "Contributions of Delinquency and Substance Abuse to School Dropout Among Inner-City Youth." Youth & Society 21:306–354.

Fannin, Leon F. and Marshall H. Clinard, 1967, "Differences in the Conception of Self as a Male Among Lower and Middle Class Delinquents." Pp. 101–112 in Edmund W. Vaz (ed.), q.v.

Farnworth, Margaret and Michael J. Leiber, 1989, "Strain Theory Revisited: Economic Goals, Educational Means, and Delinquency." American Sociological Review 54:263–274.

Farnworth, Margaret, Terence P. Thornberry, Marvin D. Krohn, and Alan J. Lizotte, 1994, "Measurement in the Study of Class and Delinquency: Integrating Theory and Research." Journal of Research in Crime and Delinquency 31:32–61.

Farrington, David P., Bernard Gallagher, Lynda Morley, Raymond J. St. Ledger, and Donald J. West, 1986, "Unemployment, School Leaving, and Crime." British Journal of Criminology 26:335–356.

Farrington, David P., Howard N. Snyder, and Terrence A. Finnegan, 1988, "Specialization in Juvenile Court Careers." Criminology 26:461–485.

Figueira-McDonough, Josefina, 1993, "Residence, Dropping Out, and Delinquency Rates." Deviant Behavior 14:109–132.

Flacks, Richard, 1971, Youth and Social Change. Chicago: Markham.

Gordon, Robert A., 1976, "Prevalence: The Rare Datum in Delinquency Measurement and Its Implications for the Theory of Delinquency." Pp. 210–284 in Malcolm W. Klein (ed.), The Juvenile Justice System. Beverly Hills, Calif.: Sage.

Gottfredson, Michael and Travis Hirschi, 1986, "The True Value of Lambda Would Appear to Be Zero: An Essay on Career Criminals, Criminal Careers, Selective Incapacitation, Cohort Studies, and Related Topics." Criminology 24:213–234.

Hagan, John, 1992, "The Poverty of a Classless Criminology—The American Society of Criminology 1991 Presidential Address." Criminology 30:1–19.

———, 1997, "Defiance and Despair: Subcultural and Structural Linkages Between Delinquency and Despair Throughout the Life Course." Social Forces 76:119–134.

Han, Wan Sang, 1969, "Two Conflicting Themes: Common Values Versus Class Differential Values." American Sociological Review 34:679–690.

Hartnagel, Timothy F. and Harvey Krahn, 1989, "High School Dropouts, Labor Market Success, and Criminal Behavior." Youth & Society 20:416–444.

Harvey, Dale G. and Gerald T. Slatin, 1975, "The Relationship Between Child's SES and Teacher Evaluations." Social Forces 54:140–159.

Heimer, Karen, 1997, "Socioeconomic Status, Subcultural Definitions, and Violent Delinquency." Social Forces 75:799–833.

Hindelang, Michael J., Travis Hirschi, and Joseph G. Weis, 1979, "Correlates of Delinquency." American Sociological Review 44:995–1014.

Hirschi, Travis, 1969, Causes of Delinquency. Berkeley: University of California Press.

Hollingshead, August E., 1949, Elmtown's Youth. New York: Wiley.

Jarjoura, G. Roger, 1993, "Does Dropping Out of School Enhance Delinquent Involvement? Results from a Large-Scale National Probability Sample." Criminology 31:149–172.

———, 1996, "The Conditional Effect of Social Class on the Dropout Delinquency Relationship." Journal of Research in Crime and Delinquency 33:232–255.

Jensen, Gary F. and Dean G. Rojek, 1992, Delinquency and Youth Crime, second edition. Prospect Heights, Ill.: Waveland.

Kaplan, Howard B. and Xiaoro Liu, 1994, "A Longitudinal Analysis of Mediating Variables in the Drug Use–Dropping Out Relationship." Criminology 32:415–439.

Kelly, Delos H., 1978, "Status Origins, Track Position and Delinquency." Pp. 446–452 in Leonard D. Savitz and Norman Johnston (eds.), Crime in Society. New York: Wiley.

Klein, Malcolm W., 1971, Street Gangs and Street Workers. Englewood Cliffs, N.J.: Prentice-Hall.

———, 1995, The American Street Gang. New York: Oxford University Press.

Kobrin, Solomon, 1951, "The Conflict of Values in Delinquency Areas." American Sociological Review 16:653–661.

Krohn, Marvin D., Ronald L. Akers, Marcia J. Radosevich, and Lonn Lanza-Kaduce, 1980, "Social Status and Deviance: Class Context of School, Social Status, and Delinquent Behavior." Criminology 18:303–318.

La Free, Gary, Kriss A. Drass, and Patrick O'Day, 1992, "Race and Crime in Postwar

America: Determinants of African-American and White Rates, 1957–1988."
Criminology 30:157–185.

Lawrence, Richard, 1998, School Crime and Juvenile Justice. New York: Oxford
University Press.

Lewis, Oscar, 1961, The Children of Sanchez. New York: Random House.

———, 1966, La Vida. New York: Random House.

Liazos, Alexander, 1978, "School, Alienation, and Delinquency." Crime and Delinquency 24:355–370.

Liebow, Elliot, 1967, Tally's Corner. Boston: Little, Brown.

Lindesmith, Alfred R. and John Gagnon, 1964, "Anomie and Drug Addiction."
Pp. 158–188 in Marshall B. Clinard (ed.), q.v.

Merton, Robert K., 1957, Social Theory and Social Structure, revised and enlarged
edition. New York: Free Press.

Miller, Walter B., 1958, "Lower-Class Culture as a Generating Milieu of Gang Delinquency." Journal of Social Issues 14:5–19.

Moynihan, Daniel Patrick, 1965, The Negro Family. Washington, D.C.: U.S. Department of Labor.

Oates, Joyce Carol, 1969, Them. New York: Vanguard.

Offord, D. R., Mary F. Poushinsky, and Kathryn Sullivan, 1978, "School Performance,
I.Q., and Delinquency." British Journal of Criminology 18:110–127.

Parsons, Talcott, 1954, "Certain Primary Sources and Patterns of Aggression in the
Social Structure of the Western World." Pp. 298–322 in Talcott Parsons (ed.),
Essays in Sociological Theory, revised edition. New York: Free Press. First
published in 1947.

Polk, Kenneth, 1984, "The New Marginal Youth." Crime and Delinquency 30:462–480.

Polk, Kenneth and Walter Schafer (eds.), 1972, Schools and Delinquency. Englewood
Cliffs, N.J.: Prentice-Hall.

Quicker, John C., 1974, "The Effect of Goal Discrepancy on Delinquency." Social
Problems 22:76–86.

Rankin, Joseph H. and L. Edward Wells, 1985, "From Status to Delinquent Offenses:
Escalation?" Journal of Criminal Justice 13:171–180.

Rodman, Hyman, 1963, "The Lower Class Value Stretch." Social Forces 42:205–215.

Rogers, Joseph W. and G. Larry Mays, 1987, Juvenile Delinquency and Juvenile Justice.
New York: Wiley.

Rojek, Dean G. and Maynard L. Erickson, 1982, "Delinquent Careers: A Test of the
Escalation Model." Criminology 20:5–28.

Rosen, Lawrence, 1969, "Matriarchy and Lower-Class Negro Male Delinquency."
Social Problems 17:175–189.

Sagarin, Edward, 1980, "Taboo Subjects and Taboo Viewpoints in Criminology."
Pp. 7–21 in Edward Sagarin (ed.), Taboos in Criminology. Beverly Hills, Calif.:
Sage.

Schafer, Walter, Carol Olexa, and Kenneth Polk, 1972, "Programmed for Social Class:
Tracking in High School." Pp. 33–54 in Kenneth Polk and Walter Schafer
(eds.), q.v.

Shaw, Clifford R., 1930, The Jack-Roller. Chicago: University of Chicago Press.

————, 1931, The Natural History of a Delinquent Career. Chicago: University of Chicago Press.

Shaw, Clifford and Henry D. McKay, 1942, Juvenile Delinquency and Urban Areas. Chicago: University of Chicago Press.

Shoemaker, Donald J., 1992, "Delinquency in the Philippines: A Description." Philippine Sociological Review 40:83–103.

Shoemaker, Donald J. and J. Sherwood Williams, 1987, "The Subculture of Violence and Ethnicity." Journal of Criminal Justice 15:461–472.

Short, James F., Jr., 1964, "Gang Delinquency and Anomie." Pp. 98–127 in Marshall B. Clinard (ed.), q.v.

Short, James F., Jr., Ramon Rivera, and Ray A. Tennyson, 1965, "Perceived Opportunities, Gang Membership, and Delinquency." American Sociological Review 30:56–67.

Short, James F., Jr. and Fred L. Strodtbeck, 1965, Group Process and Gang Delinquency. Chicago: University of Chicago Press.

Silverman, Ira and Simon Dinitz, 1974, "Compulsive Masculinity and Delinquency: An Empirical Investigation." Criminology 11:498–515.

Simon, Rita, 1975, Women and Crime. Lexington, Mass.: Lexington Books.

Simons, Ronald L. and Phyllis A. Gray, 1989, "Perceived Blocked Opportunity as an Explanation of Delinquency Among Lower-Class Black Males: A Research Note." Journal of Research in Crime and Delinquency 26:90–101.

Spergel, Irving, 1964, Racketville, Slumtown, and Haulburg. Chicago: University of Chicago Press.

Statistical Abstracts of the United States, 1994, 114th edition. Washington, D.C.: U.S. Government Printing Office.

Steffensmeier, Darrell J., Emilie Anderson Allan, Miles D. Haver, and Cathy Streifel, 1989, "Age and the Distribution of Crime." American Journal of Sociology 94:803–831.

Steffensmeier, Darrell J. and Renee Hoffman Steffensmeier, 1980, "Trends in Female Delinquency: An Examination of Arrest, Juvenile Court, Self-Report, and Field Data." Criminology 18:62–85.

Sutherland, Edwin H., 1939, Principles of Criminology, third edition. Philadelphia: Lippincott.

Thornberry, Terence P. and Margaret Farnworth, 1982, "Social Correlates of Criminal Involvement: Further Evidence on the Relationship Between Social Status and Criminal Behavior." American Sociological Review 47:505–518.

Thornberry, Terence P., Melanie Moore, and R. L. Christenson, 1985, "The Effect of Dropping Out of High School on Subsequent Criminal Behavior." Criminology 23:3–18.

Thrasher, Frederick M., 1927, The Gang. Chicago: University of Chicago Press.

Tittle, Charles R. and Robert F. Meier, 1990, "Specifying the SES/Delinquency Relationship." Criminology 28:271–299.

————, 1991, "Specifying the SES/Delinquency Relationship by Social Characteristics of Contexts." Journal of Research in Crime and Delinquency 28:430–455.

Tittle, Charles R., Wayne J. Villemez, and Douglas A. Smith, 1978, "The Myth of Social Class and Criminality: An Empirical Assessment of the Empirical Evidence." American Sociological Review 43:643–656.

Tracy, Paul E. and Kimberly Kempf-Leonard, 1996. Continuity and Discontinuity in Criminal Careers. New York: Plenum.

Tracy, Paul E., Marvin E. Wolfgang, and Robert M. Figlio, 1990, Delinquency Careers in Two Birth Cohorts. New York: Plenum.

Tygart, Clarence E., 1988, "Strain Theory and Public School Vandalism: Academic Tracking, School Social Status, and Students' Academic Achievement." Youth and Society 20:106–118.

U.S. Bureau of the Census, March Current Population Survey, 1998. www.bls.census.gov/cps/cpsmain.htm.

Vaz, Edmund W. (ed.), 1967, Middle-Class Juvenile Delinquency. New York: Harper & Row.

Wiatrowski, Michael D., Stephen Hansell, Charles R. Massey, and David L. Wilson, 1982, "Curriculum Tracking and Delinquency." American Sociological Review 47:151–160.

Whyte, William F., 1955, Street Corner Society. Chicago: University of Chicago Press.

Wolfgang, Marvin E. and Franco Ferracuti, 1967, The Subculture of Violence. London: Tavistock.

Wolfgang, Marvin E., Robert Figlio, and Thorsten Sellin, 1972, Delinquency in a Birth Cohort. Chicago: University of Chicago Press.

Yablonsky, Lewis, 1970, The Violent Gang, revised edition. Baltimore: Penguin.

———, 1997, Gangsters. New York: New York University Press.

7

Interpersonal and Situational Explanations

HISTORICAL OVERVIEW

Interpersonal and situational theories of delinquency are historically placed in time between the development of individualistic theories and the more recent labeling and radical perspectives. The interpersonal theory of Edwin Sutherland, *differential association*, was developed during the 1920s, from Sutherland's earlier education at the University of Chicago and from his continued contact with those associated with ecological studies of criminality in Chicago, such as Henry McKay (Schuessler, 1973a, 1973b; Sutherland, 1973).

In Chapter 5, which examined social disorganization and anomie, it was stressed that community- and social-based explanations of delinquency were unable to explain the behavior of individuals. In other words, these relatively macro-level explanations did not provide a theoretical mechanism for the translation of environmental factors into individual motivations.

Sutherland was well aware of the deficiencies of the ecological studies of crime in Chicago. He was also well informed of the ethnographic studies of Shaw and McKay, which represented an effort to supply some of the missing links in a total explanation of delinquency. Sutherland's theory of differential association, therefore, was an attempt to "bridge the gap," so to speak, between the atomistic, individualized explanations of the turn of this century and the emerging environmental theories of delinquency of the 1920s and 1930s.

In a similar vein, the situational explanation of delinquency, most often associated with David Matza's use of the term *drift* (Matza, 1964), represents an effort to focus on the connection between internally based and societally based theories of delinquency. A major difference between Matza's situational explanation and other explanations of delinquency developed in the twentieth century, including Sutherland's, is the importance of human will and choice in behavior. According to Matza, all explanations of delinquency are too deterministic. While it is true that some external, or perhaps uncontrollable, factors influence human behavior, it is also true that people have the capacity to modify these influences and to choose what will affect their decisions and behavior. Since human behavior is extremely complex, the specific determination of any particular delinquent act must be based on the influences that are in effect in a particular situation.

Matza's explanation of delinquency was proposed during the mid-1960s, at a time when sociologists were becoming more and more dissatisfied with sociological and psychological causal explanations. The theory itself stands as a transitional statement between the earlier, deterministic depictions of delinquency and later perspectives on delinquency, which have tended to focus more on factors that influence the description of behavior as delinquent rather than on the causes of the behavior in the first place.

GENERIC ASSUMPTIONS

A major assumption of interpersonal and situational theories of delinquency is the belief that human behavior, including delinquent behavior, is flexible and not fixed. Behavioral inclinations change according to circumstances or situations. A second assumption of these theories is that neither the delinquent nor the society in which he lives is deviant or "bad." Delinquency arises from the same general social conditions as does nondelinquent behavior, and the same person may be committing both kinds of acts at different times. A third assumption of these theories is that most delinquent behavior is committed in a group or gang context. While the particular situation in which delinquent behavior appears may fluctuate, the general setting will most typically include group norms and behavioral patterns.

Figure 10 depicts the causal flow of delinquency according to these assumptions.

Two points should be stressed relative to Figure 10. First, both peer associations and situational factors may independently lead to delinquent acts, even though they are thought to be related to each other. Second, the proper termi-

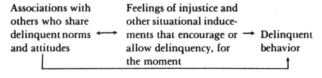

Figure 10

nology to use in connection with these theories is delinquent *behavior,* because such activity is presumed to be situational, not indicative of long-term behavioral patterns or personal character (Sagarin, 1975); that is, the behavior is delinquent, but the individual ought not to be characterized *as a delinquent,* in the sense of a continuing identity.

DIFFERENTIAL ASSOCIATION

Specific Assumptions

The best known interpersonal theory of delinquency (and adult crime as well) is the theory of differential association, developed by Edwin H. Sutherland. Unlike the developers of many other theories of delinquency, Sutherland outlined the major components of his theory in the form of propositional statements. These propositions also represent the basic assumptions of the theory, and they are discussed in detail here. Some of the major overriding assumptions of the theory, however, include the following: (1) all behavior is learned (that is, not genetically programmed) and, hence, delinquent acts are learned behavior; (2) the learning of delinquent behavior primarily occurs in small, informal group settings; and (3) the learning of delinquent behavior develops from collective experiences as well as from specific situational, current events.

Key Concepts

Differential Association   According to the concept of differential association, a youth commits an act of delinquency in response to an *excess* of attitudes favoring law or norm violation, *at that time,* and that principally he has attained this excess in association with others. Since this idea also appears in the list of propositions which collectively define the theory, it will be elaborated on later.

Differential Social Organization   This concept represents an alternative to social disorganization. Rather than arguing that certain environmental settings are disorganized, Sutherland reasoned that such areas are organized differently from other areas. In other words, there is some organization in any social setting, whether or not that setting is conducive to criminality. This concept reflects the societal dimension of the theory of differential association. At the individual level, young people commit delinquent acts in accordance with delinquent associations. At the community or societal level, norms, values, and behavior patterns are differentially organized to make it more or less likely that a juvenile will come into contact with, and be influenced by, delinquent values.

This concept is an important one. However, differential social organization has been neglected in most studies of differential association theory, and is difficult to analyze. Part of the difficulty is how best to measure differential organization. One effort addressed the concept by examining the social class composition of neighborhoods. This study failed to support any differential impact of social class composition on a sample of "serious juvenile offenders" (Reinarman and Fagan, 1988). However, as the authors acknowledge, it is difficult to capture the complexity of a construct such as differential social organization with a single measure. In fact, social class may at best be an approximation of differential social organization. Other variables, such as the existence of crime prevention groups, levels of tolerance of crime in a neighborhood, and so on, may be better indices of this variable. As indicated in Chapter 5, many of the contemporary studies of community and neighborhood influences on delinquency focus on the concept of social *dis*organization. Future research in this area may continue along this line of thought, but it does seem that a productive approach would be to refocus attention on Sutherland's idea, namely, that areas are not disorganized so such as they are organized differently, some better for the prevention of crime, others for the encouragement of criminality.

Discussion

Sutherland formally proposed the theory of differential association in 1939, in a new edition of his already successful textbook, *Principles of Criminology*. This first enunciation of the theory contained seven propositions. In subsequent editions of that book, as well as in other publications, the theory was revised to include nine propositions. These nine statements represent the theory as it is currently conceptualized (Sutherland and Cressey, 1978:80–83; italics specify words from the original).

Proposition 1. *Criminal behavior is learned*, not inherited. Put in another way, people do not commit crime because of in-born predispositions. Instead, they utilize previously acquired experiences in the commission of crime and delinquency.

Proposition 2. *Criminal behavior is learned in interaction with other persons in a process of communication.* This communication can be either verbal (or direct) or indirect.

Proposition 3. *The principal part of the learning of criminal behavior occurs within intimate personal groups.* This statement allows for the influence of impersonal, mass media influences on behavior, but it clearly stresses the overwhelming importance of personal relationships on norms and action.

Proposition 4. *When criminal behavior is learned, the learning includes* (a) *techniques of committing the crime, which are sometimes very complicated, sometimes very simple,* and (b) *the specific direction of motives, drives, rationalizations, and attitudes.* Thus, the learning of criminal behavior involves not only how the behavior is to be committed, but also why it is to be done.

Proposition 5. *The specific direction of motives and drives is learned from definitions of the legal codes as favorable or unfavorable.* "Definitions," in this statement, refer to attitudes toward the law. This statement also recognizes that definitions or attitudes are not consistently or entirely favorable or unfavorable, but are most often, at least in American society, mixed and conflicting for an individual.

Proposition 6. *A person becomes delinquent because of an excess of definitions favorable to violation of law over definitions unfavorable to violation of law.* This statement represents the main point of the theory. It stresses the transient nature of delinquency and it casts the delinquent in a situational mold. This statement further illustrates a point made in connection with Proposition 5—that exposure to delinquent norms and behavior is likely to be inconsistent and mixed with simultaneous exposure to nondelinquent norms and behavior.

Proposition 7. *Differential associations may vary in frequency, duration, priority, and intensity.* These terms exhibit an effort to qualify the effect of definitions concerning the law on behavior. Frequency and duration have the same meanings they do in common usage. Priority indicates that associations (whether delinquent or nondelinquent) formed in early childhood may take precedence in influence over later associations. Intensity refers to the prestige of an association or, actually, to the power of influence one person or group may have over another.

Proposition 8. *The process of learning criminal behavior by association with criminal and anticriminal patterns involves all of the mechanisms that are involved in any other learning.* Learning among humans, in other words, is complex and includes much more than mere imitation or copying. At the same time, delinquent and criminal acts are learned in the same manner as all other human acts. The behavior may be different, but the learning process through which the behavior develops is the same.

Proposition 9. *While criminal behavior is an expression of general needs and values, it is not explained by those general needs and values, since noncriminal behavior is an expression of the same needs and values.* Theft and honest labor both have the same goal—making money to obtain some measure of happiness and satisfaction in life. Thus, the goals of delinquents and nondelinquents are often the same; the means, however, are different. Of course, this view of criminality is not unique to Sutherland but has been offered by other sociologists, most notably by Robert Merton in the means-end theory of deviance discussed in Chapter 5. Sutherland offers this proposition, however, in an effort to persuade criminologists not to separate delinquent and nondelinquent acts on the basis of different drives and goals. If we all behave according to the same general goals, then other factors must be identified to explain delinquent and nondelinquent choices for reaching the same goal.

Some criminologists have suggested modifications of the concept of differential association for the purpose of greater precision or in order to expand the scope of the theory. Melvin DeFleur and Richard Quinney (1966), for example, reformulated the nine propositions. Using the logic and symbols of set theory, DeFleur and Quinney argue that the theory of differential association could be formally tightened if it were based on the concepts of symbolic interaction and attitude formation. Their basic statement of crime causation, based on the principle of differential association, is that criminal behavior stems from the learning of "criminal motivations, attitudes and techniques" through the processes of symbolic interaction in close-knit, informal primary groups (DeFleur and Quinney, 1966:14).

Daniel Glaser (1956) offers the concept of "differential identification" as a more inclusive conceptualization of differential association. The theory of differential identification is stated as follows: *"a person pursues criminal behavior to the extent that he identifies himself with real or imaginary persons from whose perspective his criminal behavior seems acceptable"* (Glaser, 1956:440; italics in the original). The concept of differential identification stresses the importance of group memberships and social roles in shaping one's behavioral choices. In addition, the concept allows for the influence of *reference groups*— groups to which a youth looks for general evaluation and approval, whether or not he is in direct contact with the group (see also, Haskell, 1960).

However, the largest number of suggested reformulations of differential association has been based on the principles of behavioral conditioning or "learning theory." In heeding the earlier advice of C. R. Jeffery (1965) to couch the concepts and principles of differential association in terms of operant behavior theory, Robert Burgess and Ronald Akers (1966) proposed a step-by-step *restatement* of differential association according to such ideas as reinforcement and punishment. The use of these concepts does not offer a new theory, but they were substituted in an effort to place the key elements of the theory into testable constructs. Thus, instead of saying that criminal behavior is learned mostly in primary groups, Burgess and Akers contend that criminal behavior is primarily learned "in those groups which comprise the individual's major source of reinforcements" (1966:146). This theme has also been applied by Reed Adams (1973) in a call for the use of learning principles in general criminological research.

While all of these suggested revisions have added some insight into Sutherland's formulations of differential association, they have not significantly altered the basic principles of the theory. The identification of reference group and nonsocial influences on attitudes and behavior is quite important, but not entirely unrecognized by Sutherland. Essentially, the reformulations of differential association according to the concepts of set theory or learning theory have formally stated what was already implicit, if not explicit, in Sutherland. In addition, not all are in agreement that the formalistic features of learning theory offer the most insightful interpretation of human learning (Halbasch, 1979). The argument here is that Sutherland's theory of differential association allowed for the influence of human emotion and interpersonal feedback in the explanation of behavior, whereas behaviorist concepts imply an animalistic, noninterpretive response to stimuli, characteristics which do not apply to humans. For these reasons, the following evaluation of differential association is based on the theory as proposed by Sutherland.

Evaluation

The theory of differential association has not been totally accepted by criminologists. Some of the sharpest attacks have focused on the contention that criminal behavior is learned. It is argued by some that this view is either too simplistic, in consideration of the complexity of crime patterns and motivations, or that the gist of the statement adds nothing new to an understanding of criminality, and that it downplays the influence of individualistic factors. According to these criticisms, the theory may serve as a better explanation of why juveniles do *not* commit acts of delinquency than of why they do commit offenses (Glueck, 1962; Radzinowicz, 1966).

Sutherland and his collaborator, Donald R. Cressey, have catalogued challenges to differential association on at least a dozen points of wording, logic, and scope (Sutherland and Cressey, 1978). According to Sutherland and Cressey, some of these criticisms arise from errors of interpretation. For example, a common misinterpretation of the theory is that it deals only with actual contacts or associations with criminal or delinquent behavior. Were this the case, the theory would not be able to account for the conforming behavior of most police officers and court personnel, as well as the differential involvement in delinquency of children from the same family. Differential association, however, refers to association with attitudes and values (definitions) that are connected with patterns of behavior, through secondary as well as primary contacts, and criminality results from an excess of procriminal definitions over neutral or anticriminal definitions.

Another erroneous criticism, according to Sutherland and Cressey, is the failure of differential association to account for why people have the associations they have. Two rebuttals are offered for this charge. One, the concept of differential social organization, defined earlier, does somewhat account for variations in associations. Unfortunately, the significance of this concept has been lost in comparison to the attention given to differential association. Consequently, research concerning differential association has virtually ignored this principle. Second, the individualized aspect of the theory is self-contained and does not have to account for why or how associations develop. Technically, this assertion is correct. It would seem, however, that if a theory as broad in scope as differential association is to be accepted, it needs to stress why associations arise as well as what the consequences of the associations might be.

Another argument is that differential association does not account for the influence of personality variables in the development of definitions relative to law violation. This criticism is a rather strict one inasmuch as the theory does allow for individual interpretations and applications of definitions of legal codes. At one time, Sutherland felt it necessary to incorporate personality traits into his theory, but later reflections caused him to question the wisdom of such modifications (Sutherland, 1973). Part of the difficulty with incorporating personality variables into the theory lies in determining which traits to include and under what conditions to include them—that is, how they are to be measured. To move beyond such particular traits and to charge that the theory generally ignores individual interpretations is, again, erroneous. The question then becomes not whether individual responses to situational conditions affect behavior, but what kinds of responses affect behavior and in what ways.

Other complaints against the theory concern the measurement of key concepts. For example, if, as the theory suggests, certain characteristics of associations are to have more influence on behavior than other characteristics, such as intensity and priority, how are such qualities to be measured and compared? Similarly, how is an *excess* of definitions to be objectively measured *and applied* to a particular act (Sutherland and Cressey, 1978)?

Of all the criticisms levied at the theory of differential association, the problem of measurement is the most serious. Several investigators have commented on the difficulty of measuring a person's definitions of the law, their sources, and their qualifications (Cressey, 1952; Short, 1960; Stanfield, 1966). A major problem of measurement with this theory is its historical and situational focus. Since most criminal offenders are discovered after the fact, so to speak, reconstruction of thoughts and moods at the time the act was committed is exceedingly difficult to develop. When one adds to this difficulty the problem of reconstructing prior events and influences on one's attitudes and behavior, the task becomes almost impossible.

Despite these methodological difficulties and shortcomings, there have been empirical attempts to test the validity of the theory, with juveniles as well as adults. One empirical assessment of differential association relative to delinquency is the well-documented fact that most delinquency is committed in a group context (Weis, 1980; Jensen and Rojek, 1992). The overall significance of this finding for the theory of differential association, however, is questionable. For one thing, the relationship does not speak to the issue of shared attitudes and values, nor to the matter of excess of definitions favorable to law violation, either within the group or individually. In addition, the group nature of delinquency does not specify temporal conditions of causality—that is, whether the associations occurred before or after delinquency was first or most often committed.

Specifically, with reference to delinquency, those issues concerning the relationship between peer group associations and delinquency have been empirically studied. These investigations have *generally supported* the basic propositions of the theory (Short, 1957, 1960; Reiss and Rhodes, 1964; Voss, 1964; Jensen, 1972; Hepburn, 1977). For the most part, however, the research has indicated that differential association is only one of two or three causal explanations that is supported. In a study of nearly 1600 white male junior and senior high school students in California, for example, Gary Jensen (1972) found support for the *independent* effects of differential association variables and family supervision variables on self-reported delinquency. That is, each set of factors had a separate, unique influence on delinquent behavior. Differential association variables were measured according to number of close delinquent friends, perceptions of "trouble" in the neighborhood, official delinquency rates of the schools attended, and measures of the acceptance of attitudes or definitions favorable to the violation of laws.

Research continues to document the importance of peer attachments, and definitions favorable to law violation, in the explanation of delinquency. In a study of police records in Sweden, for example, Sarnecki (1986) concludes that group activity is more important to the offender than is the act of committing a delinquent offense.

Some comparative examinations of differential association and other theories, especially social control theory (see Chapter 8), conclude that differential association is a better explanation of self-report delinquency than are such social control factors as attachment to parents and broken homes (Matsueda, 1982; Matsueda and Heimer, 1987; Paternoster and Triplett, 1988; Cashwell and Vacc, 1996). Furthermore, Matsueda and Heimer (1987) maintain that the important impact of differential association lies in the concept of definitions favorable to law violation.

A similar conclusion is reached by Thompson et al. (1984), who conclude that differential association theory is a better explanation of delinquency than is social control theory. In this study, self-report delinquency questionnaires were given to 724 male and female high school students. The primary measure of differential association was delinquent companions, and this factor was substantially more associated with delinquency than were such other variables as conventional attitudes and attachment to parents, school, and peers.

In addition, Johnson et al. (1987) conclude that associations with peers who use drugs are strongly connected with usage of a variety of drugs. The sample in this study was a collection of 768 students in a private western high school. Differential association was measured by peer associations and definitions favorable to drug use. The researchers also incorporated other variables into their study, such as parental, religious, and educational attachments and conventional beliefs. They concluded that differential association variables, especially peer associations, were more strongly related to delinquency than were attachments or beliefs. Nonetheless, Johnson et al. argue that their analysis supports attempts to combine differential association with social control theory to produce a "superior" explanation of delinquency (see also, Marcos et al., 1986; Aseltine, 1995).

In a related study, Dembo et al. (1986) investigated the relationship between attachment to drug-using parents and drug use among a sample of junior high school youth (average age of 13) in South Bronx, New York. In this investigation, differential association was conceptualized as a learning theory, and it was hypothesized that children of drug-using parents would exhibit greater levels of drug use than would the offspring of non-drug-using adults (all such behaviors were based on the responses of the youths). The results indicated that adolescent drug use was highly related to parental attachment, among those juveniles who indicated their parents were low or moderate drug users. Among these youth, drug use was quite low. The children of high-drug-using parents, however, were themselves high drug users, but drug use among these youth was not significantly related to attachment to their parents. These results suggest, again, some interactive effect between differential association and social bond theory, relative to adolescent drug use. Among the children of low-drug-using parents, a combination of conformist behavior and strong parental attachments tended to inhibit drug use. Those living in families where parents are high drug users, however, may have learned to use drugs, perhaps by observation, despite the level of attachment to their parents.

The theory of differential association appears to offer a reasonable explanation of individual delinquency within environmental contexts, although the numerous critical comments concerning its scope and logic cannot be ignored. Empirically, the theory is difficult to test, yet several attempts to assess its validity have generally been supportive. (See Orcutt, 1987, for a defense of the testability of differential association theory.) That differential association is not the only valid explanation of delinquency is indicated by the importance of other variables simultaneously compared with differential association items.

Some have challenged the often-noted group nature of delinquency by asserting that delinquency is *inversely* related (delinquents have low group involvement) to peer group associations (Hirschi, 1969). In part, these inconsistent predictions have been resolved by research which concludes that delinquency is more common among those youth who report having friendships with other delinquent, or unconventional, youth. On the other hand, associations with more conformist, or conventional, peers is correlated with lower rates of delinquency (Hirschi, 1969; Hindelang, 1973; Gardner, 1984; Thompson et al., 1984; Elliott et al., 1985; Matsueda and Heimer, 1987).

A conceptually sophisticated analysis of friendship patterns and self-report delinquency revealed differences by delinquency status, such as more delinquent youth reporting more "conflicts" with friends (Giordano et al., 1986). Nonetheless, there were many similarities in friendship patterns between delinquent and nondelinquent youth. For example, both youth expressed similar estimates regarding time spent with friends, length of friendship, or caring and trustworthiness of friends. Thus, while the normative content of peer interaction may differ between delinquents and others, the patterns and dynamics of friendship groupings may be similar. The conceptualization of friendship patterns in terms of a dynamic process promises to enrich the understanding of the connection between peer relationships and delinquency (see also, Meier et al., 1984; Dishion et al., 1995).

The investigation of the dynamics of peer relationships continues to be an important topic of research on differential association theory. For example, two analyses of a longitudinal, national survey of over 1700 youth (the National Youth Survey) support the influence of peer associations on delinquency, but specify this influence. Agnew (1991) concludes that high levels of interaction, as opposed to moderate or low levels of interaction, with peers who are involved in serious forms of delinquency (burglary, selling "hard" drugs, theft of items worth $50 or more, p. 57) contribute significantly to committing serious acts of delinquency on the individual level. However, such peer interactions do not have an impact on minor acts of delinquent behavior.

In another analysis of the National Youth Survey data, Warr contends that peer relationships dominate adolescent lives during the mid- to late teen years. Also, the impact of peers is more important in the explanation of delinquency than is age (Warr, 1993). Furthermore, Warr's analysis finds that despite a trend for delinquency and the impact of peers on behavior to decline after adolescence, friendships, particularly recent ones, even among delinquent peers, tend to last beyond adolescence. Warr acknowledges that these findings may be tapping into what some refer to as a "party culture" among modern North American youth (Hagan, 1991), a subculture which emphasizes the importance of peer friendships in finding ways, including illegal activity, to spend leisure time.

While Warr contends that the conclusions of this analysis support some of the principles of differential association, it is recognized that the study does not irrefutably prove the theory. Nor does the study overcome the many criticisms which have been aimed at this explanation, such as those mentioned earlier in this chapter, and raised by others (Matsueda, 1988). In particular, the finding that delinquent peers tend to remain friends, what Warr refers to as the "sticky friends" (p. 35) concept, seems to contradict the conclusion that delinquency declines with age. It is likely that both delinquent friends and delinquency decline after adolescence, but that for some, sticky friends remain, and delinquency continues into adult patterns of crime.

The continued analysis of peer relationships, particularly the dynamics of these associations, may or may not always be in accordance with the principles of differential association theory. At times, it seems the interest in peer relations has become a separate conceptual issue. For example, studies conducted at the Oregon Social Learning Center indicate that even discussing deviance among male friendship groups in early adolescence is associated with self-reported delinquency in mid-adolescence (Dishion et al., 1996).

In some ways, this shift of focus may not be altogether a bad idea, particularly since the total context of differential association theory is difficult to operationalize. As Matsueda (1988:294) indicates, the current state of research on this topic is becoming more integrated (see Chapter 12). Thus, peer relations are studied in combination with important concepts connected with other theories, such as social bond theory (see Chapter 8), with the aim of obtaining a more complete explanation of delinquency. In this context, for example, the *loss* of delinquent friends is associated with other changes in a juvenile's life, such as changes in attitude, job prospects, relationships with family members, particularly with parents, and so on (Mulvey and LaRosa, 1986). Conceptualizing peer relationships in this manner provides an explanation for why delinquency begins and continues, as well as for why it tends to decline in late adolescence.

Increasingly, the impact of peers, and differential association in general, is understood to be a factor of social and cultural context. The meaning, and importance, of friendships may vary by sociocultural settings. In the Philippines, for example, the peer group is known as a *barkada*. While the barkada is considered an important social grouping in this country, especially among males, its existence has also been implicated in studies of delinquency in the Philippines (Albada-Lim, 1969; Shoemaker, 1992, 1994). The barkada may not cause one to commit crime, because almost all males, and many females, belong to such a group from childhood through life. However, committing delinquent acts as a member of the barkada would likely be supported by group members and intensify delinquent behavior, especially during adolescence. Again, however, there needs to be a better understanding of how such intense social pressure and support can be turned from criminal to conventional activities, as people leave adolescence and enter adulthood.

In the inner cities of the United States, youth groups may serve a totally different function than what is assumed in differential association theory, or in studies of peer relationships in general. Among Hispanic youth, for example, it is contended that an almost constant threat of violence and criminal victimization pushes one into group memberships for protection, rather than for social and emotional support. In this context, criminal behavior may be as much an attempt to survive and protect oneself as an effort for personal gain at the expense of others (Pabon et al., 1992).

These findings and considerations do not signal the demise of differential association theory, nor of the importance of peer relations in the explanation of delinquency. The trend in delinquency research is to provide clarification of elements of existing theoretical explanations, as well as to develop models which attempt to combine or integrate several theories. In this regard, it would seem differential association theory is very much alive.

DRIFT AND DELINQUENCY

Specific Assumptions

Matza's concept of drift shares many of the assumptions found in the theory of differential association. A central difference between the two theories, however, is that the notion of drift assumes delinquency to be based largely on the exercise of a juvenile's choices, depending on the situation or circumstances at a particular moment. The importance of individual judgment on behavior in this explanation differs from virtually all other theories of delinquency, which stress the influence of deterministic forces, individualistic or environmental, on the behavior of juveniles.

Another assumption of drift theory, which tends to separate it from differential association, is that delinquents are angered over a sense of injustice they feel from discriminatory law enforcement practices and community reactions to their misbehaviors. In other words, delinquents are somewhat psychologically alienated from society.

Key Concepts

Drift The concept of drift asserts that delinquent behavior and law-abiding behavior are both characteristics of delinquents. Thus, juveniles drift in and out of delinquency, depending on the situation and their mood or feelings. They do not have a commitment to delinquency, even when deeply immersed in the behavior.

Neutralization   A central factor in the decision to commit a delinquent act is the juvenile's ability to neutralize, or explain away, the moral reprehension felt to be associated with the act. There are several types of neutralization. Their existence may be encouraged by feelings of injustice, but the factor of neutralization is a key link between emotional states and delinquent behavior.

Discussion

According to Matza, delinquency is best viewed as occasional and associated with particular situations and circumstances. In other words, juveniles do not commit acts of delinquency because a group set of norms dictates that they do, but because the nature of a particular time, place, and setting encourages the commission of delinquent acts at that time. Group membership may promote a delinquent response in certain situations, but it does not mandate such behavior.

Because of their status in Western societies, juveniles are lodged in a transitional state between total dependence on adults and freedom of thought and action. Opposition to adult rules is likely to develop among juveniles and will sometimes be expressed in the form of delinquency. The emergence of delinquent subcultures, however, with totally oppositional values to conventional, adult values is not likely to happen. Delinquent (oppositional) subcultures do not emerge because adolescents are too closely supervised by, or otherwise connected with, adults for that to happen.

This view of delinquency is also characterized as drift, in which delinquency is seen as the result of vacillation within a juvenile between the conforming expectations of adults and the peer-dominated, situational demands and opportunities that encourage delinquency. In this view, delinquency is committed not because a juvenile is driven by wicked internal or external forces, but because it seems more profitable and correct to do so at the moment.

Juveniles are able to drift into and out of delinquency through a number of rationalizations or neutralizations (Sykes and Matza, 1957; Matza, 1964). These rationalizations and neutralizations, respectively, provide excuses for having committed delinquency and justifications for committing delinquency before the fact. Gresham Sykes and Matza (1957) concentrate on the justifications for delinquency and propose five types of "techniques of neutralization": (1) *denial of responsibility*, in which the juvenile fails to accept personal blame for his actions, attributing them instead to forces beyond his control, such as having bad parents or living in poverty; (2) *denial of injury*, in which the juvenile does not deny the act but maintains that no one was really physically hurt or economically harmed; (3) *denial of a victim*, in which the harm of injury caused by the act is felt to be deserved because the "victim" deserved it, such as stealing from a "crooked" store owner; (4) *condemnation of condemners*, which involves a view of disapproving others as hypocrites and hidden deviants, a view which sometimes becomes cynical of authority figures, such as the police and school officials; (5) *appeal to higher loyalties*, which argues that the immediate demands of the group take precedence over familial, community, or societal values and rules, and that these group demands sometimes call for the commission of delinquent acts. Hamlin (1988) argues that the value of "neutralization theory" lies in conceptualizing these techniques as rationalizations which are utilized *after* delinquent acts have been committed.

While Sykes and Matza did not dwell on the factors that contribute to the techniques of neutralization, subsequent comments have tended to focus on the existence of a "subterranean" adult value system which tacitly encourages the pursuit of thrills and irresponsibility among juveniles (Matza and Sykes, 1961). This underground system of values, as it were, also contributes to adolescent justifications for delinquency by allowing one to charge that "Everyone is doing it, so why can't I?"

The later work of Matza (1964) implicates the lack of family supervision in the development of neutralization techniques, but more emphatically suggests the role of peer-dominated social settings and the operations of the juvenile justice system in the emergence of such justifications.

Peer-group situations are characterized by the concept of "situation of company," in which the delinquent is depicted as constantly exposed to tests or "soundings" designed to challenge his masculinity and group loyalty. Ironically, however, Matza contends that each member of the group personally adopts conventional adult values but that public expressions to the contrary lead to group shared misunderstandings of just what others in the group actually feel.

To summarize, Matza's theory of drift suggests that most delinquents are not alienated from adult, conventional values but, instead, that they are susceptible to both the conforming influences of adults and the delinquent influences of peer pressure. Opportunities for delinquency emerge out of situational contexts. These opportunities can assume more importance for a juvenile when he has established a set of justifications, or moral neutralizations, which temporarily sanction delinquent behavior. The neutralization of conventional values, in turn, is facilitated by several factors, including perceived discriminatory enforcement of the law and perceived implicit adult acceptance of many "delinquent" acts, which represent what conventional adults often do or encourage rather than what they publicly proclaim to be their values and attitudes.

Evaluation

The theory of drift assumes that juveniles live in a state of flux and uncertainty, and this notion is convincing (Goodman, 1962). Furthermore, some research has documented the general acceptance of middle-class, conventional values among juvenile gang members and their leaders (Short and Strodtbeck, 1965; Krisberg, 1974). In addition, Cohen's (1955) argument that a common trait in juvenile gangs is short-run hedonism is consistent with Matza's conceptualization of drift (although on other particulars Cohen and Matza are at odds). Even though these characteristics apply to gang delinquency, it is possible that they apply to other examples of delinquency as well.

An implicit assumption of Matza's drift theory is that delinquency will decline as adolescents approach adulthood. This is a very involved issue and it is definitely influenced by the effects of official intervention and treatment efforts on the part of society in an effort to "reform" delinquents. Certainly gang members tend to disassociate from the gang as adulthood approaches, and delinquency, gang or otherwise, does decline with advanced age status, through marriage, employment, or perhaps general maturation (McCord et al., 1959; Briar and Piliavin, 1965; Laub and Sampson, 1993). Edwin Schur (1973) advocates an approach of "radical nonintervention" toward delinquents, an approach which is in part based on Matza's theory, including the implicit notion of natural reformation.

Those who have attempted to study specifically the concepts of drift and neutralization, however, have not consistently supported Matza's assertions. In an investigation of rural and urban youth and institutionalized delinquents, Michael Hindelang (1974) failed to find any support for Matza's contention that delinquents are basically disapproving of delinquency but go along with it because they think their friends would approve. Those who admitted involvement in delinquency were more likely to approve personally of such behavior than those not involved in delinquency, and this finding remained constant for a variety of offense behaviors, for males and females, rural and urban youngsters, and institutionalized youth as well as juveniles in public schools (see also, Hindelang, 1970). Richard Ball (1983) found that neutralization was less related to "basic norm violation" among young adolescents than was their self-concept.

Peggy Giordano (1976) surveyed the attitudes of public school students and juveniles who had been processed through various stages of the juvenile justice system (police contact, court contact, institutionalization, and so on). She found no significant attitudinal differences between the students and the official delinquents. These delinquents did not perceive their handling as unfair or unjust. If anything, they developed more positive feelings toward the juvenile justice system as they experienced more contact with it. Such results question the foundation on which Matza's theory of drift and neutralization is based.

Landsheer et al. (1994), however, differentiated techniques of neutralization according to the victim's status and the nature of the offense. They applied these separations in a self-report study of delinquency involving nearly 2700 youth and young adults, aged 12–25, in the Netherlands. Their results indicate that the respondents could be classified into three categories: nondelinquency, low delinquency, and high delinquency. The nondelinquents were uniform in their lack of permissiveness for any act of criminality. Delinquents tended to view crimes as permissible, or acceptable, in support of neutralization theory. However, for crimes causing personal injury and in which the victim was "familiar" or known to the offender, all respondents, including delinquents, indicated nonpermissiveness toward the offense. Thus, while this study provides general support for neutralization theory, it fails to distinguish attitudes of delinquents and nondelinquents relative to criminal acts causing personal injury to an associate of the offender.

Agnew (1994) sheds some light on this situation by demonstrating that most adolescents disapprove of violence. Consequently, committing acts of violence is enhanced through neutralization. Neutralization, in turn, is encouraged by associations with delinquent peers, a connection which would also lend support to differential association theory. Agnew's data source is a longitudinal survey (the National Youth Survey), and the analysis indicates that neutralization precedes violent acts. However, his analysis does not indicate whether association with peers precedes using techniques of neutralization. Logically, one would expect to find this causal pattern, but the published results do not clearly point in this direction.

A difficulty with Matza's theory lies in its focus on psychological motivations and intentions regarding behavior, both before *and* after the act. In this respect, Matza's theory of drift shares the same difficulty as Sutherland's theory of differential association—namely, the assessment of one's *prior* state of mind from a vantage point far removed from the commission of an act.

Matza's conceptualization of the delinquent adolescent portrays a rather free-floating individual who is being buffeted about by diverse influences. While this view may be somewhat appealing, it seems to allow for too much individual freedom of choice without suggesting a rationale for explaining the choices which are made.

The issue of choice is an important theoretical concept, but, as was argued in Chapter 2, choice must be considered relative within social contexts. Choice among contained populations, such as native North Americans, may not be as free and relevant as among other people, and this fact of life may have significant effects on the impact of drift on delinquency among native North American youth (Ratner, 1995).

Some have suggested that drift theory is actually a type of social control theory of delinquency (see Chapter 8), in which the delinquent is seen as relatively uncommitted or unattached to conventional social institutions and peer groups (Briar and Piliavin, 1965; Schur, 1973). In fact, this type of theoretical framework does seem to be beneficial to a better understanding of delinquency if the two perspectives are merged. For example, drift theory proposes that juveniles may be delinquent at any given time. It does not provide a systematic account, however, of why delinquency is defined as acceptable by a group or an individual. Social control theory argues that delinquency occurs after disaffiliations develop between juveniles and representatives of social institutions, such as parents and school authorities. Youngsters who are thus unattached are more likely to be attracted to delinquency than others. Those who "drift" into delinquency are those who are relatively more disenchanted with traditional institutions in society.

SUMMARY

Differential association and drift as explanations of delinquency differ from previously discussed explanations in that they are essentially *social psychological*. That is, the primary cause of delinquency lies *with* the individual, but not within him. While these theories maintain that individuals commit delinquent acts, they also acknowledge the importance of social factors in the decision to commit delinquency. Furthermore, the influential individuals or groups typically are significant others (meaningful people in one's life, such as peer group members and authority figures).

In Sutherland's theory of differential association, the influence of significant others on a juvenile is in the direct encouragement of delinquency. For Matza and his theory of drift, the influence of significant others can be either an actual encouragement of delinquency or an indirect contribution to delinquency through the development of resentment of authority figures.

Both theories attempt to provide a link between the broad, ill-defined effects of social class and social structure and the atomistic, overly deterministic conceptualizations of biological and psychological theories of delinquency, such as psychoanalytic interpretations. In this respect, they make a contribution to the explanation of delinquency.

A difficulty with both theories, however, lies with the measurement and testing of basic concepts and propositions. Of the two theories, differential association is presented in a more rigorous fashion, and it has been researched more thoroughly than has Matza's drift theory. Nonetheless, it seems as if both explanations are trying to explain too much by attempting to account for the vagaries of human behavior from an open and situational point of view.

Both differential association and drift appear to be well grounded in their attempts to understand the more proximate causes of delinquency. It would appear, however, that these theories would be enhanced by being attached to a more measurable and fixed social entity, as opposed to broadly conceived societal factors. This type of foundation may perhaps best be supplied by control theories, particularly *social* control theories, of delinquency. These explanations are considered in the next chapter.

References

Adams, Reed, 1973, "Differential Association and Learning Principles Revisited." Social Problems 20:458–470.

Agnew, Robert, 1991, "The Interactive Effects of Peer Variables on Delinquency." Criminology 29:47–72.

———, 1994, "The Techniques of Neutralization and Violence." Criminology 32: 555–580.

Albada-Lim, Estefania, 1969, Toward Understanding the Filipino Delinquent. Quezon City, Philippines: Bustamante.

Aseltine, Robert H., Jr., 1995, "A Reconsideration of Parental and Peer Influences on Adolescent Behavior." Journal of Health and Social Behavior 36:103–121.

Ball, Richard A., 1983, "Development of Basic Norm Violation: Neutralization and Self-Concept Within a Male Cohort." Criminology 21:75–94.

Briar, Scott and Irving Piliavin, 1965, "Delinquency, Situational Inducements, and Commitment to Conformity." Social Problems 13:35–45.

Burgess, Robert L. and Ronald L. Akers, 1966, "A Differential Association-Reinforcement Theory of Criminal Behavior." Social Problems 14:128–147.

Cashwell, Craig S. and Nicholas A. Vacc, 1996, "Family Functioning and Risk Behaviors: Influences on Adolescent Delinquency." The School Counselor 44: 128–147.

Cohen, Albert, 1955, Delinquent Boys: The Culture of the Gang. New York: Free Press.

Cressey, Donald R., 1952, "Application and Verification of the Differential Association Theory." Journal of Criminal Law, Criminology and Police Science 43:43–52.

DeFleur, Melvin and Richard Quinney, 1966, "A Reformulation of Sutherland's Differential Association Theory and a Strategy for Empirical Verification." Journal of Research in Crime and Delinquency 2:1–22.

Dembo, Richard, Gary Grandon, Lawrence La Voie, James Schmeidler, and William Burgos, 1986, "Parents and Drugs Revisited: Some Further Evidence in Support of Social Learning Theory." Criminology 24:85–104.

Dishion, Thomas J., David W. Andrews, and Lynn Crosby, 1995, "Antisocial Boys and Their Friends in Early Adolescence: Relationship Characteristics, Quality, and Interactional Process." Child Development 66:139–151.

Dishion, Thomas J., Kathleen M. Spracklen, David W. Andrews, and Gerald R. Patterson, 1996, "Deviancy Training in Male Adolescent Friendships." Behavior Therapy 27:373–390.

Elliott, Delbert S., David Huizinga, and Suzanne A. Ageton, 1985, Explaining Delinquency and Drug Use. Beverly Hills, Calif.: Sage.

Gardner, Robert Le Grande, III, 1984, Social Bonding and Delinquency: A Multivariate Analysis. Unpublished Ph.D. Dissertation. Blacksburg, Va: Virginia Polytechnic Institute and State University.

Giordano, Peggy C., 1976, "The Sense of Injustice? An Analysis of Juveniles' Reactions to the Justice System." Criminology 14:93–112.

Giordano, Peggy C., Stephen A. Cernkovich, and M. D. Pugh, 1986, "Friendships and Delinquency." American Journal of Sociology 91:1170–1202.

Glaser, Daniel, 1956, "Criminality Theories and Behavioral Images." American Journal of Sociology 61:433–444.

Glueck, Sheldon, 1962, "Theory and Fact in Criminology: A Criticism of Differential Association." Pp. 91–95 in Marvin E. Wolfgang, Leonard Savitz, and Norman Johnston (eds.), The Sociology of Crime and Delinquency. New York: Wiley.

Goodman, Paul, 1962, Growing Up Absurd. New York: Random House (Vintage).

Hagan, John, 1991, "Destiny and Drift: Subcultural Preferences, Status Attainments, and the Risks and Rewards of Youth." American Sociological Review 56:567–582.

Halbasch, Keith, 1979, "Differential Reinforcement Theory Examined." Criminology 17:217–229.

Hamlin, John E., 1988, "The Misplaced Role of Rational Choice in Neutralization Theory." Criminology 26:425–438.

Haskell, Martin R., 1960, "Toward a Reference Group Theory of Juvenile Delinquency." Social Problems 8:220–230.

Hepburn, John R., 1977, "Testing Alternative Models of Delinquency Causation." Journal of Criminal Law and Criminology 67:450–460.

Hindelang, Michael J., 1970, "The Commitment of Delinquents to Their Misdeeds: Do Delinquents Drift?" Social Problems 17:502–509.

———, 1973, "Causes of Delinquency: A Partial Replication and Extension." Social Problems 20:471–487.

———, 1974, "Moral Evaluations of Illegal Behaviors." Social Problems 21:370–385.

Hirschi, Travis, 1969, Causes of Delinquency. Berkeley: University of California Press.

Jeffery, C. R., 1965, "Criminal Behavior and Learning Theory." Journal of Criminal Law, Criminology and Police Science 56:294–300.

Jensen, Gary F., 1972, "Parents, Peers, and Delinquent Action: A Test of the Differential Association Perspective." American Journal of Sociology 78:562–575.

Jensen, Gary F. and Dean G. Rojek, 1992, Delinquency and Youth Crime, second edition, Prospect Heights, Ill.: Waveland.

Johnson, Richard E., Anastasios C. Marcos, and Stephen J. Bahr, 1987, "The Role of Peers in the Complex Etiology of Adolescent Drug Use." Criminology 25:323–340.

Krisberg, Barry, 1974, "Gang Youth and Hustling: The Psychology of Survival." Issues in Criminology 9:115–129.

Landsheer, J. A., H't Hart, and W. Kox, 1994, "Delinquent Values and Victim Damage: Exploring the Limits of Neutralization Theory." British Journal of Criminology 34:44–53.

Laub, John H. and Robert J. Sampson, 1993, "Turning Points in the Life Course: Why Change Matters to the Study of Crime." Criminology 31:301–325.

Marcos, Anastasios C., Stephen J. Bahr, and Richard E. Johnson, 1986, "Test of a Bonding/Association Theory of Adolescent Drug Use." Social Forces 65:135–161.

Matsueda, Ross L., 1982, "Testing Control Theory and Differential Association: A Causal Modeling Approach." American Sociological Review 47:489–504.

———, 1988, "The Current State of Differential Association Theory." Crime and Delinquency 34:277–306.

Matsueda, Ross L. and Karen Heimer, 1987, "Race, Family Structure, and Delinquency." American Sociological Review 52:826–840.

Matza, David, 1964, Delinquency and Drift. New York: Wiley.

Matza, David and Gresham M. Sykes, 1961, "Juvenile Delinquency and Subterranean Values." American Sociological Review 26:712–719.

McCord, William, Joan McCord, and Irving K. Zola, 1959, Origins of Crime. New York: Columbia University Press.

Meier, Robert F., Steven R. Burkett, and Carol A. Hickman, 1984, "Sanctions, Peers, and Deviance: Preliminary Models of a Social Control Process." The Sociological Quarterly 25:67–82.

Mulvey, Edward P. and John F. LaRosa, Jr., 1986, "Delinquency Cessation and Adolescent Development: Preliminary Data." American Journal of Orthopsychiatry 56:212–224.

Orcutt, James D., 1987, "Differential Association and Marijuana Use: A Closer Look at Sutherland (with a Little Help from Becker)." Criminology 25:341–358.

Pabon, Edward, Orlando Rodriquez, and Gerald Gurin, 1992, "Clarifying Peer Relations and Delinquency." Youth & Society 24:149–165.

Paternoster, Raymond and Ruth Triplett, 1988, "Disaggregating Self-Reported Delinquency and Its Implications for Theory." Criminology 26:591–620.

Radzinowicz, Leon, 1966, Ideology and Crime. New York: Columbia University Press.

Ratner, R. S., 1995, "Drift, Delinquency, and Destiny." Pp. 332–341 in James H. Creechan and Robert A. Silverman (eds.), Canadian Delinquency. Scarborough, Ontario: Prentice-Hall Canada.

Reinarman, Craig and Jeffrey Fagan, 1988, "Social Organization and Differential Association: A Research Note from a Longitudinal Study of Violent Juvenile Offenders." Crime and Delinquency 34:307–327.

Reiss, Albert J., Jr. and A. Lewis Rhodes, 1964, "An Empirical Test of Differential Association Theory." Journal of Research in Crime and Delinquency 1:5–18.

Sagarin, Edward, 1975, Deviants and Deviance. New York: Praeger.

Sarnecki, Jerzy, 1986, Delinquent Networks. Stockholm, Sweden: The National Council for Crime Prevention, Sweden.

Schuessler, Karl (ed.), 1973a, Edwin H. Sutherland on Analyzing Crime. Chicago: University of Chicago Press.

————, 1973b, "Introduction." Pp. ix–xxxvi in Karl Schuessler (ed.), q.v.

Schur, Edwin M., 1973, Radical Non-Intervention. Englewood Cliffs, N.J.: Prentice-Hall (Spectrum).

Shoemaker, Donald J., 1992, "Delinquency in the Philippines: A Description." Philippine Sociological Review 40:83–103.

————, 1994, "Male-Female Delinquency in the Philippines: A Comparative Analysis." Youth & Society 25:299–329.

Short, James F., Jr., 1957, "Differential Association and Delinquency." Social Problems 4:233–239.

————, 1960, "Differential Association as a Hypothesis: Problems of Empirical Testing." Social Problems 8:14–25.

Short, James F., Jr. and Fred L. Strodtbeck, 1965, Group Process and Gang Delinquency. Chicago: University of Chicago Press.

Stanfield, Robert E., 1966, "The Interaction of Family Variables and Gang Variables in the Aetiology of Delinquency." Social Problems 13:411–417.

Sutherland, Edwin H., 1939, Principles of Criminology, third edition. Philadelphia: Lippincott.

————, 1973, "Development of the Theory." Pp. 13–29 in Karl Schuessler (ed.), q.v.

Sutherland, Edwin H. and Donald R. Cressey, 1978, Criminology, tenth edition. New York: Lippincott.

Sykes, Gresham M. and David Matza, 1957, "Techniques of Neutralization: A Theory of Delinquency." American Journal of Sociology 22:664–670.

Thompson, William E., Jim Mitchell, and Richard A. Dodder, 1984, "An Empirical Test of Hirschi's Control Theory of Delinquency." Deviant Behavior 5:11–22.

Voss, Harwin L., 1964, "Differential Association and Reported Delinquent Behavior: A Replication." Social Problems 12:78–85.

Warr, Mark, 1993, "Age, Peers, and Delinquency." Criminology 31:17–40.

Weis, Joseph G., 1980, Jurisdiction and the Elusive Status Offender. Washington, D.C.: U.S. Government Printing Office.

8

Control Theories

HISTORICAL OVERVIEW

Control theories of delinquency cover a wide range of topics. Lamar Empey (1982) characterizes nineteenth-century and early-twentieth-century individualistic theories of delinquency as "control" theories, especially psychoanalytic explanations. Travis Hirschi (1969) traces the ideas of control theory as far back as Durkheim in the nineteenth century. The core ideas of control theories, therefore, have a rather long history. Most often, however, control theories of delinquency are equated with self-concept research and social control mechanisms, such as family and school experiences. In this context, control theories may be historically placed in the 1950s and early 1960s, with the development of Walter Reckless' self-concept or containment explanation of delinquency. In the late 1960s Travis Hirschi extended Reckless' ideas to broader social contexts, thus leading to the social or psychosocial perspective, which became synonymous with control theory (see also, Toby, 1957).

The idea that juveniles commit delinquency because some controlling force is absent or defective has been generally supported for some time. The *focus* of attention on social or social-psychological control factors, however, is relatively new. Although family factors were prominent in late-nineteenth and early-twentieth-century explanations of delinquency (Sanders, 1970; Krisberg and Austin, 1978), they were either not carefully researched or were of secondary importance to the psychoanalytic interpretation of delinquency as an *individual* problem.

Among sociological perspectives, interest in family factors gave way to broader social and economic conditions in the 1940s and 1950s and all but disappeared from the literature (Wilkinson, 1974). Current interest in family variables, as well as other institutional factors, such as religious and school influences, is often couched in terms of the control perspective.

For the most part, therefore, control theories of delinquency represent a relatively modern development. This statement is most particularly appropriate for social control factors, the subject of considerable research and discussion since the early 1970s.

GENERIC ASSUMPTIONS

Control theories all assume one basic point. Human beings, young or old, must be held in check, or somehow controlled, if criminal or delinquent tendencies are to be repressed.

A related assumption of control theories is that delinquency is to be expected, considering all of the pressures and inducements toward delinquency to which most juveniles are exposed. To control theories, the explanation of delinquency is based not on the question of "*Why* did he do it?" but, instead, "Why did he *not* do it?" In other words, control theories assume that the tendency to commit delinquent acts is well-nigh universal. Since delinquent behavior is to be expected, the crucial explanation of it is to be found in searching for *missing* factors in delinquents that separate them from nondelinquents.

The first two assumptions logically point to a third generic assumption; namely, delinquency is the result of a *deficiency* in something, the *absence* of a working control mechanism. Delinquents are seen neither as driven nor as perfectly "normal." They are simply seen as youth who are relatively uncontrolled or unattached, psychologically or socially.

The specific type of control factor or system deemed absent or faulty among delinquents is what distinguishes various types of control theories. In the main, there are two general types of control systems, personal and social. Personal control systems involve individualistic factors, especially psychological ones. They are best exemplified by psychoanalytic concepts and the notion of self-concept or esteem. Social control variables involve attachments to basic social institutions, such as families, schools, and religious practices. Attachments are often measured in a variety of ways but typically are conceptualized as emotional (such as the amount of affection between parent and child) and behavioral (such as grades in school).

A fourth assumption of control theories is that there is general societal consensus concerning conventional beliefs and norms, especially as these are associated with various institutions in society.

The assumptions of control theories lead to the diagrammatic explanation of delinquency shown in Figure 11.

From Figure 11, one could state that the weakened personal or social control factors contribute to delinquency through socialization (basically child-

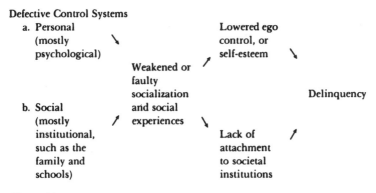

Figure 11

hood) experiences and current social situations. The defective control systems affect the learning of social norms and the implementation of norms in terms of appropriate behavior. It is also possible, of course, that weakened personal and social controls may be interconnected. Lowered self-concepts and antisocial attitudes may stem from negative family and school experiences, and vice versa. This possibility, however, is not a necessary component of control theory.

PERSONAL CONTROLS

Psychoanalysis Revisited

Psychoanalysis can readily be viewed as a control perspective. The emphasis on early childhood socialization experiences, especially within the family, and the focus on the superego, holding sway over instinctive id impulses, are consistent with the control conceptualization of delinquency.

Psychoanalysis, however, offers problems to some who would categorize it as a control theory. To some extent, this concern is a reflection of the individualistic nature of the psychoanalytic approach. Nonetheless, the assumptions of psychoanalytic theory fall within the general assumptions of control theories.

Containment Theory

Other than psychoanalysis, the "containment" perspective, developed by Walter Reckless, has probably attracted the greatest attention as a personal control theory of delinquency. Properly classified as a social-psychological explanation of delinquency, similar to Sutherland's differential association, containment is linked to the idea of self-concept.[1] Unlike differential association, however, containment theory stresses the importance of the personalized feelings of youth rather than their associations.

Specific Assumptions

Containment theory is based on the assumption that delinquency is a result of poor self-concepts. This view is in contrast with that of the labeling perspective, which argues that negative self-concepts are the result of having been labeled delinquent.

Besides the view that negative self-images contribute to delinquency, containment theory is based on the assumption that a boy's positive view of himself provides an insulation against the pressures and the pulls toward delinquency, regardless of social class or other environmental conditions.

Third, containment theory is based on a multifaceted image of behavior. That is, people are conceptualized as being composed of several layers of drives, pressures, pulls, and insulators or buffers. All of these forces affect the individual simultaneously, and they come from both within and outside of the person. The most important of these forces, however, is the internal insulator, the self-concept.

Key Concepts

Containment   The principal concept of this explanation is that drives and pulls (forces in general) toward delinquency must somehow be contained—that is, checked or controlled—if delinquency is to be averted.

Self-concept   This concept usually refers to an image, whether of one's place in society or of one's value to others or to society in general. The most typical way of measuring self-concept is through the use of attitude and personality scales, including subjective and limited-response scale items.

Discussion

Although Reckless began to investigate the relationship between self-concept and delinquency in the mid-1950s (Reckless et al., 1956), the theory of containment was not published in systematic form until the early 1960s. According to Reckless, containment theory is essentially a theory of the *middle range.* By this, Reckless means that it is designed to explain those forms of delinquent and criminal behavior that fall outside the highly personalized acts resulting from organic and personality disorders, such as brain damage, on the one hand,

and organized criminality, such as organized crime and delinquent gangs, on the other hand. According to Reckless, these behaviors constitute from one-fourth to one-third of the acts of crime and delinquency. The rest, the bulk of criminal and delinquent activity, he terms the "middle range of norm violation," the range to which containment theory applies (Reckless, 1961).

During the 1960s, the theory became couched in terms of pressures, pulls, pushes, and containments or buffers, all focused on the individual. Reckless identified four types of pressures and containments: (1) outer, or social, pressures and pulls; (2) external containments; (3) inner containments; and (4) inner pushes, that is, organic or psychological forces (Reckless, 1967). These four factors are conceptualized by Reckless as circles, or layers, emanating from the self. Thus, the self serves as a container of internal pushes, while prosocial contacts serve as buffers against external pressures and containers against external pulls.

External pressures include "adverse living conditions" such as poverty, unemployment, minority group status, and discrimination. Outer pulls consist of bad companions, deviant prestige figures, juvenile gangs (subcultures), and mass media inducements. Internal pushes include a veritable host of faults and problems, such as tensions and frustrations, aggressiveness, need for immediate gratification, rebelliousness, feelings of inadequacy, compulsions, phobias, brain damage, and psychoses.

With all of these pushes and pulls operating on juveniles, it is a wonder that they do not all become delinquent and remain that way. Society, however, offers various external or outer constraints on lawbreaking behavior. The most important of these outer containments, according to Reckless, are "nuclear groups," such as the family and community, whose influences people experience in varying degrees. Two other aspects of external containment are the structure of roles and expectations in society and the sense of acceptance and belonging relative to a group or society.

The inner restraint on delinquent behavior is associated with the self-concept. The theory maintains that a low or negative self-concept contributes to delinquency. Reckless also mentions three other types of inner containment: goal orientation, frustration tolerance, and norm commitment and retention. Orientation to long-range, socially approved goals, high frustration tolerance, and high levels of norm commitment and tolerance are all thought to inhibit delinquency.

Of the two general types of containment, inner and outer, Reckless clearly feels that inner containment is more important for the control of delinquency, at least in industrialized societies. In less developed societies, external pressures toward crime and deviance are not very great. In addition, Reckless reasons that "undisturbed and developing" countries are tightly structured, particularly by religious restraints, and the individualized component of the self is rarely developed.

In summary, containment theory proposes that delinquency can be produced by a variety of forces and factors, both internal and external. That such behavior does *not* occur is attributable to insulations or buffers, both social and personal. Of these two types of containment, the most important in inhibiting delinquency is inner containment, especially self-concept.

Evaluation

Reckless felt that containment theory offered a better explanation of delinquency than other theories for the following reasons: (1) it can be applied to particular individuals; (2) the various external and internal constraints can be observed and measured, both qualitatively and quantitatively; (3) the theory explains both delinquency and conformity; (4) it likewise explains a wide variety of criminal or delinquent activity; and (5) it is a possible basis for the treatment and prevention of delinquency (Reckless, 1967).

The connection between negative self-concepts and delinquency has been fairly uniformly established through empirical research. Reckless and his associates, for example, have presented evidence from studies of juveniles in Columbus, Ohio, which demonstrates that predicted delinquents ("bad" boys) have lower self-concepts than predicted nondelinquents ("good" boys), as measured by official records (Reckless et al., 1956; Reckless et al., 1957). Furthermore, "good" boys not only remain freer of official contacts with police and courts than do "bad" boys, but they consistently evidence more positive levels of self-concept, from the age of 12–13 well into adolescence (Scarpitti et al., 1960; Dinitz et al., 1962).

The data reported by Reckless and his students were characterized by the following conditions: (1) the "good" and "bad" boys were initially selected by teachers' predictions, and (2) the measures of the boys' self-concepts were cross-validated by their teachers and mothers. Although these conditions can be defended, taken together they call into question the validity of self-concept or containment as an explanation of delinquency. Some have argued, for example, that cross-validation of personally expressed self-concept with teachers' and mothers' judgments confuses the issue between what a person actually thinks of himself and what he thinks others think or expect of him (Schwartz and Tangri, 1965; Orcutt, 1970).

Michael Schwartz and Sandra Tangri (1965) examined the issue of self-concept by utilizing a semantic differential test, whereby juveniles were asked to rate themselves on a "good-bad" continuum along several dimensions. These perceptions were then correlated with judgments of how respondents felt mothers, friends, and teachers thought of them. The research was conducted on 101 school-nominated "good" and "bad" sixth-grade boys in an all-black school in a high delinquency area of Detroit. The results lent some support to containment theory in that those designated as "good" boys had higher personal self-concepts than those felt to be "bad" boys. Comparisons of self-concept with perceptions of opinions of others, however, indicated that self-image was correlated with different significant others (meaningful people in one's life) and these significant others tended to vary between "good" and "bad" boys. The self-concepts of "good" boys, for instance, were influenced by perceived teachers' images, while "bad" boys' self-images were strongly associated with perceived mothers' judgments (see also, Schwartz and Stryker, 1970).

Besides the issue of self-concept, some have questioned the validity of identifications of delinquency by teachers and principals (Orcutt, 1970). A critical question is the accuracy of the predictions. The original reports of the Columbus students indicated substantial agreement between group predictions and subsequent official contact with the police or the courts (Scarpitti et al., 1960; Dinitz et al., 1962). Additional investigations, however, question the accuracy of such predictions. In a longitudinal study of delinquency prevention, for example, Reckless and Simon Dinitz (1972) found that of more than 1000 predicted delinquents (bad boys) over 40 percent had had no police contact within four years. If nominations or predictions of future delinquency are to be used as a primary measure of delinquency, there must be consistent and substantial agreement between the prediction and the subsequent behavior for the procedure to be acceptable.

In addition to conceptual and methodological concerns involving attempts to test containment theory, some investigators have raised the issue of relative importance. It is generally conceded in these studies that self-concept measures can distinguish between delinquents and nondelinquents, but that other factors may be more important in the explanation of delinquency. These findings have tended to occur, furthermore, when self-report measures of delinquency have been employed. Several studies (for example, Voss, 1969; Jensen, 1973; and Rankin, 1977) present data that suggest that inner containment may be less powerful as an explanation of delinquency than other factors, such as peer group associations (differential association), family relationships, and social class. At the same time, these investigations suggest that self-concept measures be combined with other variables to improve the explanation of delinquency.

An emerging proposition is that self-concept is indirectly related to delinquency. This view argues that a negative self-concept, as indicated by self-rejection, *along with* experiences of failure at home or school and/or in the community, create a disposition or tendency toward delinquency. This "disposition to deviance," in turn, directly contributes to subsequent involvement in delinquent activity (Kaplan et al., 1986. See also, van Welzenis, 1997). Furthermore, it is maintained that delinquent action, or perhaps participating in groups which commit delinquent behavior, *increases self-esteem* (Kaplan, 1978. See also, Rosenberg et al., 1989).

The ideas of Kaplan and associates are based on analyses of self-report data gathered from junior high students over a three-year period in the early 1970s. Other longitudinal data analyses, utilizing samples of older youth, refute the influence of self-concept as an explanation of delinquency (Wells and Rankin, 1983; McCarthy and Hoge, 1984). However, there is some support for an increase in self-esteem subsequent to committing delinquent acts among those with low self-esteem scores (Kaplan, 1980; McCarthy and Hoge, 1984). Also, Wells and Rankin report a *decrease* in self-esteem among African-American delinquents, but this effect was not observed by McCarthy and Hoge. Furthermore, a study of 20 black and 20 white delinquents in England noted a higher level of self-acceptance among blacks than among whites, but this study was not longitudinal (Emms et al., 1986).

Part of the inconsistency in this research may be the result of differing interpretations of self-concept. Ross (1992), for example, suggests that most of the research on self-esteem (which some differentiate from self-concept) and delinquency ignores a group referent to the concept, particularly as applied to race (pp. 619–620). For some, identification of self with a racial group may actually enhance self-esteem. Consequently, the relationship between self-esteem and behavior may not always follow predicted patterns.

For example, Ross (1994b) argues that *personal* identity must be differentiated from *group* identity, primarily race identity, as a measure of self-esteem. Personal identity refers to such characteristics as academic achievement, sociability, feelings of hopelessness, and confidence in becoming successful. In Ross' study, African-Americans had *higher* total levels of self-esteem than did whites. In addition, personal identity *and* self-esteem attached to race were inversely associated with delinquency among African-Americans. Among whites, however, race esteem was moderately associated with delinquency while only one measure of personal identity, feeling that things are hopeless, was related to delinquency (p. 122).

However, Wells (1989) reports a strong and consistently positive association between "self-enhancement" and self-reported delinquency among a national, longitudinal sample of *white* youth (the Youth-in-Transition survey). Wells' conclusions also suggest that delinquency "enhances" self-concept primarily among juveniles who have the lowest levels of self-esteem, to the point of being "pathological," as well as for those youth who have the highest levels of self-esteem (p. 249). The conjecture Wells offers for this seeming paradox is that delinquency can increase self-esteem among juveniles who have "less to lose" by engaging in delinquency, particularly for those with extremely low levels of self feelings (pp. 249–250).

Another possible reason for inconsistent research results on this topic is the varied meanings of self-concept (Rosenberg, 1979; Ross, 1992). In a study of self-concept and self-reported delinquency among Chinese youth in Hong Kong, for example, Leung and Lau (1989) report a positive association between delinquency and self-concept, when self-concept is conceptualized relative to social and physical abilities. However, when self-concept is measured relative to school abilities, there is an inverse relationship with delinquency.

Many who use the idea of a social self in connection with criminality refer to a negative or positive conception of oneself, and often use the phrase self-esteem to convey the same notion. However, labeling theory suggests that it is not just self-esteem which is important, but also self-identification, the conceptualization of oneself as a delinquent, criminal, deviant, or whatever. Self-identity as a delinquent *could* be interpreted positively. Thus, a higher self-esteem might result not from having committed delinquent activity, but from identifying oneself as a delinquent. The topic of criminal or delinquent identification is partially addressed in Chapter 9, which concerns labeling theory. This theory focuses on the consequences of being officially labeled a criminal or delinquent, including the effects on a person's self-concept or self-identity.

In summary, it cannot be denied that self-concept has an effect on behavior, delinquent or nondelinquent, deviant or nondeviant (Wells, 1978). Changes in self-concept can lead, directly or indirectly, to changes in behavior.[2] While various conceptual and methodological problems have characterized containment theory and attempts to test it, the theory has generally been supported with empirical investigation. Self-concept, however, appears to be less important as an explanation of delinquency than other factors, particularly when unofficial measures of delinquency are used. One such influence, peer group associations, has already been discussed. Another set of conditions, social control or bond variables, is considered next.

SOCIAL CONTROLS—THE SOCIAL BOND

Specific Assumption

The difference between personal and social control theories of delinquency lies in the assumption of social control theory that social bonds and attachments are a stronger protection against delinquency than are personality characteristics.

Key Concept

Social Bond Essentially, this concept refers to the connection between the individual and the society, usually through social institutions. Travis Hirschi

(1969) conceptualizes the social bond as consisting of four parts: attachment, commitment, involvement, and belief.

Discussion

According to Hirschi, the four elements of the social bond collectively explain the social control theory of delinquency. *Attachment* refers to the psychological and emotional connection one feels toward other persons or groups and the extent to which one cares about their opinions and feelings. According to Hirschi, attachment is the social counterpart to the psychoanalytic concept of superego or conscience.

Commitment is the result of a cost-benefit approach to delinquency. It refers to the investments accumulated in terms of conformity to conventional rules (such as time, money, effort, and status) versus the estimated costs, or losses, of investments associated with nonconformity. Commitment, therefore, is viewed as a rational aspect of the social bond, the social counterpart to the psychoanalytic concept of the ego.

Involvement refers to participation in conventional and legitimate activity. In a school, for example, it would include extracurricular activities such as school plays, clubs, organizations, and athletic events.

Belief involves the acceptance of a conventional value system. In the logic of control theory, it is argued that a weakening of conventional beliefs, for whatever reason, increases the chances of delinquency.

Although Hirschi recognizes several possibilities of the interconnectedness of these four elements of the social bond, he suggests that they generally vary together. It is possible, for example, for attachment and commitment to vary inversely. In other words, attachment to parents and peers may prevent a juvenile from developing commitments to school and legitimate occupational pursuits, particularly if he is from a lower- or working-class environment. Hirschi contends, however, that attachment and commitment are *positively* associated, regardless of social class position. Moreover, he maintains that commitment, involvement, attachment, and belief are also positively associated with one another. No component is theoretically more important than another, although research may suggest the ascendancy of one over another under specified conditions. (See, for example, Wiatrowski et al., 1981.)

Evaluation

The evaluation of social control theory will be conducted according to the relationship between delinquency and three institutional settings: religion, the family, and the school. The focus will be on the extent to which bonds (in a general sense) to these institutions are associated with delinquency.

Religion and Delinquency   For some time, criminologists have been interested in the connection between religious participation and beliefs and criminality. Since the 1930s, research has been conducted on the relationship between religious variables and delinquency. Earlier studies, which focused on officially defined delinquents, tended to yield conflicting results. Some studies found delinquents to be *more* involved with religion than nondelinquents; others found delinquents to be *less* active in religious behavior than nondelinquents; and still another group of results found no relationship between religious variables and delinquency (Jensen and Rojek, 1992).

Despite the inconsistencies of systematic research on the subject, popular opinion has held that there exists an inverse relationship between religion and delinquency; that is, delinquents are less religiously active than nondelinquents.

The view that delinquency and "religiosity" are inversely related did have some support in the literature. One of these studies was the previously discussed comparative analysis of 500 delinquents and 500 nondelinquents (Glueck and Glueck, 1950). The Gluecks noted that less than 40 percent of the delinquents attended church regularly, as compared with over 67 percent of nondelinquents. At the same time, neither delinquents nor nondelinquents were markedly negligent of their "church duties," that is, not attending church at all. The Gluecks, though, paid scant attention to the relationship between church attendance and delinquency, presumably because their findings did not clash with general expectations.

A few years after the Glueck study, F. Ivan Nye reported an intensive investigation of the relationship between family factors and self-reported delinquency (1958). Part of that investigation included the relationship between other variables and delinquency, including church attendance. Basically, Nye found that nondelinquents, and their parents, attended church significantly more often than delinquents. Similar to the Gluecks, however, Nye found that the biggest separation between delinquents and nondelinquents occurred at the regular attendance point. The differences between delinquents and nondelinquents, while apparent, were not as large among those who never or only occasionally attended church as among those who attended church regularly. The socialization value of church attendance was questioned in the Nye study because he could find no association between delinquency and length of church attendance.

The Nye study also found religion to be connected with delinquency through family relationships. Nondelinquents, for example, tended to discuss religious issues with their parents. The importance of these relationships lies more in their description of the connection between family factors and delinquency than of the connection between religion and delinquency.

The investigation of religious factors and delinquency lay virtually dormant until the late 1960s when a study called "Hellfire and Delinquency" was published (Hirschi and Stark,1969). Using both a self-report delinquency scale with over 4000 junior and senior high school students in California and police records, Travis Hirschi and Rodney Stark measured the association between delinquency and church attendance, acceptance of moral values, respect for law and the police, and belief in the existence of a supernatural power and sanctions in life after death. Their results were as follows: (1) there was little or no association between church attendance and either an acceptance of moral values or respect for law and the police; (2) there was a strong, positive association between church attendance and belief in supernatural sanctions; (3) there were strong inverse associations between both self-report and official delinquency and acceptance of moral values and respect for law and the police; (4) there was no association between either measure of delinquency and belief in supernatural sanctions; and (5) there was no relationship between either type of delinquency and church attendance. These results led Hirschi and Stark to conclude that religion and church attendance had no effect on delinquency, particularly in the face of worldly influences.

The report by Hirschi and Stark left several issues unresolved. For example, is religion unrelated to delinquency in all locations, for all faiths and denominations, and for all types of delinquency? These and other issues were addressed by a plethora of investigations in the 1970s, many of which were attempted replications or extensions of the Hirschi and Stark research. For the most part, these studies tended to reveal some association between religion and delinquency, but the association depended on various situations.

In one extension of Hirschi and Stark's research, Steven Burkett and Mervin White (1974) investigated the relationship between self-reported delinquency and religion among a sample of 750 high school students in the Pacific Northwest. Although the same measures of religion were used as in the Hirschi and Stark study, the measure of delinquency was extended to include alcohol (beer) and marijuana offenses (no official records of delinquency were used). In virtually all particulars, the results of the study were consistent with those of Hirschi and Stark. When the offenses of alcohol and marijuana use were considered, however, Burkett and White found strong inverse relationships with church attendance, moral values, and respect for "worldly authority"—that is, those who exhibited such behavior and attitudes were relatively less involved with drug use.

Burkett and White concluded from their study that religious participation does seem to deter some delinquency, especially those acts for which there is no consistent condemnation in the secular society. Interestingly, they further concluded that rather than religion being one of the *least* effective institutions for controlling delinquency, it may be one of the *most* effective, since its influence tends to be greater for those offenses for which secular controls have weakened.

In a partial replication of the Hirschi and Stark study, Paul Higgins and Gary Albrecht (1977) examined the relationship between church attendance and self-reported delinquency among 1400 high school students in Atlanta. They concluded that, contrary to Hirschi and Stark, delinquency was inversely related to church attendance. This relationship, furthermore, was influenced by the variable of respect for the juvenile court system (except for nonwhite females). That is, the greater the church attendance, the more respect for the juvenile court, and the less delinquency. Higgins and Albrecht speculated that their findings might have reflected the inclusion of more serious offenses than Hirschi and Stark had investigated, but discounted this explanation in favor of a geographical one. In other words, they ultimately concluded that religion has more of an influence on behavior in areas where religion occupies a more central place in the lives of people, such as in the South. This view is also shared by Stark et al. (1982), who conclude that in "secular communities" no connection exists between religion, or church attendance, and delinquency. However, a different conclusion is reached by Tittle and Welch (1983), who argue that religious factors exert a negative influence on "deviance" when competing secular controls are weak. Thus, in areas where most people are nonreligious (Stark et al.'s "secular communities"), the negative impact of religion on delinquency is greatest.

Furthermore, some research suggests that the impact of religion on adolescent drug use is not direct, but operates indirectly through peer associations (Burkett and Warren, 1987). That is, youth who have little religious commitment are more apt to select as friends others who are likely to use marijuana. These friendships, in turn, are directly related to marijuana use among youth with low religious conviction (see also, Ross, 1994a).

Other research has indicated some relationship between religion and delinquency, usually drug use and status offenses (Linden and Currie, 1977, Jensen and Rojek, 1992). Some would contend, then, that the conclusion of Hirschi and Stark was based on incomplete evidence. There *does* seem to be some connection between religious factors and delinquency, particularly drug and status offenses, and particularly in the South. Furthermore, to some extent, the lack of connection between delinquency and religion may be a result of insensitive statistical measures. When different procedures are used, such as assessing the odds or relative probabilities of church attendance versus delinquency, a strong connection between the two exists (Sloane and Potvin, 1986). However, research continues to find significant, although statistically modest, inverse connections between religious variables and delinquency, particularly alcohol and marijuana use (Cochran and Akers, 1989; Free, 1994; Evans et al., 1996), although some find no such correlations between religiosity and *antiascetic offenses,* that is, status or drug offenses (Benda, 1995).

To make matters more interesting, Lee Ellis (1987) asserts that clear and consistent inverse relationships between delinquency and church attendance and belief in an afterlife have been noted in the literature. These associations are particularly strong with respect to drug use and less predatory criminal acts. A possible reason for these connections, Ellis maintains, is the existence of a "suboptimal arousal" state in offenders (see Chapter 3). This condition renders delinquents, especially psychopaths, bored with traditional religious ceremonies and attracted to the more stimulating prospects associated with committing unlawful acts, particularly those associated with drug use. In a study of self-reported delinquency among high school students, Cochran et al. (1994) find support for this "arousal" theory, except for tobacco and alcohol use. However, their extended analysis suggests that social control factors offer a stronger explanation for delinquency, including drug use, than does the arousal theory (p. 113), although estimates of arousal in this study are based on nonbiological measures. Overall, these authors are supportive of arousal theory not only in connection with religion and delinquency but also as an explanation of delinquency, particularly more serious acts of criminality (pp. 114–115).

In addition, it should be noted that religion (church attendance, church membership) may have various inhibiting effects on behaviors other than delinquency. William Bainbridge (1989), for example, notes that church attendance is negatively associated with serious crime rates, but is relatively unconnected with suicide rates and participation in homosexual organizations.

The relationship between delinquency and *particular* religious faiths is also an issue. Many of the earlier investigations either did not specify a particular faith or considered only Christian faiths as a single category. Some studies have found delinquency rates to be lower among Jews than among Catholics or Protestants (Ellis, 1985; Jensen and Rojek, 1992). On the other hand, Hirschi and Stark, as well as Burkett and White, reported no differences in delinquency rates by denomination, although no data were presented in support of these conclusions. Another analysis indicated that church attendance and delinquency were more inversely related among "fundamentalistic" or "highly ascetic" faiths, such as the Church of Christ or Church of God, than among other religions (Jensen and Erickson, 1979). It would appear more accurate to argue at this point that the religious convictions of members are more central to an explanation of their behavior than the fact that they belong to or attend one denomination or another.

In summation, it may be unrealistic to expect the influence of religion on juvenile delinquency to be greater than that of competing secular forces. At the same time, it would be equally unrealistic to suppose that religion has no effect on juvenile behavior. Most of the recent research discussed above indicates that there *is* an association between the two variables, especially in areas where religion is still generally influential and with delinquent offenses for which secular sanctions have become ambivalent.

Family Factors Perhaps one of the most persistent explanations of delinquent behavior is the breakdown of the family. From the concerns of those in the Child-Saving Movement of the nineteenth century (Platt, 1977) to the present, the family has been regarded as a major variable in the presence or absence of delinquency. This interest in the family as a factor in delinquency is shared by students of sociology and psychology. Many of the individualistic theories of delinquency, such as psychoanalytic explanations, for example, incorporate aberrations in family interaction as these occur early in life. Shaw and McKay's social disorganization theory of delinquency also viewed the breakdown of family controls as an important contribution to the development of social disorganization in a neighborhood.

The centrality of family relationships in the explanation of delinquency, however, has not always been accepted, particularly among sociologists. Karen Wilkinson (1974) argues that interest in the "broken home"[3] and delinquency among sociologists can be divided into three periods: (1) a period of keen interest and research activity (1900–1932); (2) a period of rejection of the relationship between the broken home and delinquency (1933–1950); and (3) a period of renewed interest in the connection between the broken home and delinquency (1951–1970s).

Partly, this fluctuation reflects various interpretations of empirical analyses of the relationship. Wilkinson argues, however, that the emphasis, or deemphasis, on family conditions is also related to other matters, such as ideological biases of researchers, political views about the state of the family and the effects of divorce, and disputes between such fields as psychology and sociology over the importance of family intactness versus social class or other sociological concepts in the explanation of delinquency.

The interest in family factors and delinquency has typically involved both the structure of the family and the nature of relationships occurring within the family (see Geismar and Wood, 1986; and Wright and Wright, 1994, for reviews of some of this literature). The structure of the family includes the broken home—that is, a home where one (or both) natural parent is permanently absent because of events such as death, desertion, or divorce—but, as a force influencing the behavior of youths, this may be changing. The quality of family relationships involves such factors as parental conflicts, parent-child relationships, and discipline and supervision patterns. Both of these factors—the structure of the family and the nature of family relationships—are now discussed in connection with delinquency.

BROKEN HOMES. The relationship between delinquency and a home broken by divorce, desertion, or death has been extensively investigated. For the most part, these studies have found that delinquents come from broken homes significantly more often than nondelinquents. Martin Haskell and Lewis Yablonsky (1982), for example, report the findings of eight studies from 1929 to 1971 that investigated the relationship between broken homes and delinquency. The range of delinquents from broken homes was 23.6 percent to 61.5 percent, while the range for nondelinquents was from 12.9 to 36.1 percent.

Similarly, Lawrence Rosen and Kathleen Neilson (1978) reported small but statistically significant *associations* between broken homes and male delinquency for 15 studies conducted between 1932 and 1975.

One of the clearest differences between delinquents and nondelinquents concerning broken homes is provided by Sheldon and Eleanor Glueck's comparison of 500 delinquents and 500 nondelinquents (1950) previously discussed. Over 60 percent of the delinquents came from broken homes, as compared with slightly more than one-third of the nondelinquents.

From a review of several studies of broken homes and delinquency and an analysis of over 44,000 official delinquents in Philadelphia, Thomas Monahan (1957) concluded that the broken home is definitely related to delinquency.

Although the evidence seems clear that the broken home is associated with delinquency, several doubts exist concerning the importance of this relationship. First, virtually all of the studies supporting a relationship between broken homes and delinquency have used official police, court, or institutional records as the measure of delinquency. The reported relationships may thus reflect the decisions of juvenile justice officials to report and process juveniles from broken homes more often than juveniles from intact homes. That this bias might exist is supported by the observation that there is only a small relationship between the broken home and *self-reported* delinquency (Nye, 1958; Hirschi, 1969). There is some indication that single-parent families (especially mother only) are associated with higher rates of self-report delinquency (Dornbusch et al., 1985), but this relationship is sometimes restricted to status offenses (Van Voorhis et al., 1988) or self-reported legal "trouble" (Johnson, 1986). In addition, some researchers conclude that self-reported delinquency, especially among males, is related to the presence of a stepfather in the home (Dornbusch et al., 1985; Johnson, 1986; Pagani et al., 1998). The influence of stepparents, or the existence of marital separation, may influence youth deviance through mechanisms such as weak, or inconsistent, parental support, a point which is addressed below. In addition, all of these factors might be influenced by psychological problems of parents, or "multiple-problem" families

(Johnson et al., 1995). Overall, however, research continues to reveal a relatively weak and inconsistent relationship between self-report delinquency and broken homes.

Second, not all of the studies that have examined the relationship between official measures of delinquency and the broken home have concluded that a significant association exists. In the period between 1933 to 1950, rejection of this relationship, for example, was partially based on Shaw and McKay's (1932) analysis of official delinquency and broken homes. Essentially, they found the relationship to be insignificant, particularly when controlling for such variables as age and ethnicity.

Third, the relationship between broken homes and delinquency has almost always been investigated from the point of view of delinquents rather than broken homes. As a causal variable, however, the broken home should also be analyzed relative to the proportion of juveniles from broken homes who are delinquent. Rosen and Neilson (1978) have attempted just such an analysis. They found that the overall probability of finding a *delinquent* (officially identified) from a broken home was less than the probability of finding a broken home among delinquents. The *relative* probabilities, however, were the same. That is, delinquents were about three times as likely to be found among broken homes as among intact homes, and broken homes were about three times more likely to be found among delinquents as among nondelinquents.

More recent reviews of research on the connection between broken homes and delinquency conclude that there is some connection between the two variables, but the relationship is neither universal nor particularly strong. In an analysis of 68 published reports on the relationship between broken homes and delinquency, for example, Free (1991) concludes that this relationship is decidedly more evident for status offenses, such as running away, truancy, and disobeying parents, than it is for more serious offenses. In a review of over 50 studies, dating from the 1920s to the late 1980s, Wells and Rankin (1991) conclude that the overall relationship between delinquency and broken homes is weak, particularly when delinquency is measured by self-report methods. Among all the factors concerning the connection between broken homes and delinquency addressed in this analysis, factors such as time period, age, gender, race, and type of family "break," the one which emerged as having the strongest relationship was the measurement of delinquency. Specifically, Wells and Rankin conclude that the strongest association between broken homes and delinquency appears when delinquency is defined as "officially contrived" samples of delinquents; that is, among populations of youth who have been placed in institutions or subjected to court-ordered treatment programs. In these situations, the incidence of broken homes is particularly high. Otherwise, the connection between broken homes and delinquency is weak (p. 88).

FAMILY RELATIONSHIPS. While some doubt exists concerning the connection between broken homes and delinquency, there is considerable evidence that points to a correlation between family relationships and delinquency. Family relationships, in this context, are usually measured in terms of interaction, affection, supervision, and discipline between and among parents and children.

Many investigators who have found a correlation between official delinquency and broken homes have also concluded that an association exists between delinquency and a variety of family relationships. The Gluecks, for example, concluded that future delinquency in a young boy (preschool age) could be predicted from knowledge of five family factors, not including the broken home: (1) discipline by father (overstrict, erratic, or lax discipline was positively associated with delinquency); (2) supervision by mother (classified as "suitable," "fair," or "unsuitable" with unsuitable supervision connected with delinquency); (3) affection of father for son (hostile or indifferent attitudes were positively related to delinquency); (4) affection of mother for son; and (5) cohesiveness of family (inversely related to delinquency; Glueck and Glueck, 1950:260–261).[4]

The importance of family relationships, such as supervision and affection patterns, does not necessarily preclude a contribution of the broken home to delinquency. However, the importance of the broken home may be in its effect on family relationships, which, in turn, have a more forceful impact on delinquency. It is the nature of what goes on in the family, therefore, that influences delinquency more than whether or not one parent is absent from the home.

As indicated earlier, the relative influence of family relationships over the broken home is illustrated in studies utilizing self-report measures of delinquency. Nye (1958), for example, closely examined numerous family factors, including the broken home, and self-reported delinquency among 780 high school students in several medium-sized Washington (state) communities. In all, he tested over 70 associations separately for mother-daughter, mother-son, father-daughter, and father-son relationships. Nearly 95 percent of the associations were consistent with the assumptions of control theory, and about 50 percent of these associations were statistically significant. These parent-child relationships covered such topics as the acceptance or rejection of parents by children, and vice versa, methods of parental discipline and punishment, family recreational patterns, and so on. In general, those adolescents whose parents treated them firmly but with love and respect tended to be considerably less delinquent than those juveniles whose parents continually nagged or scolded them or treated them as pawns by making expressions of love or acceptance contingent on good behavior.

Interestingly, Nye found little relationship between the physically, or legally, broken home and delinquency. He did, however, find a significant inverse association between delinquency and happiness and marital adjustment, regardless of whether the home was physically broken.

Hirschi's (1969) analysis of self-report delinquency among 4077 junior and senior high school students in California also failed to demonstrate an association between broken homes and delinquency. Hirschi did find, however, associations between delinquency and several measures of family relationships, such as affectional identification with parents, intimacy of communication with father, and identification with father. In general, Hirschi found that delinquency was inversely related to the bonds of attachment within the juvenile's family. This relationship was supported, moreover, regardless of race or social class. Furthermore, Hirschi's data led to the conclusion that ties to the family were inversely related to delinquency, even when parents were "unconventional" (on welfare or unemployed) and regardless of the existence of delinquent friends. Attachments to parents and delinquent companions, however, were independently related to delinquency, which supports both social control theory and differential association.[5]

Hirschi's findings were generally replicated by Michael Hindelang (1973) in a study of self-report delinquency among 900 adolescents in a rural area of upstate New York. Specifically, attachment to parents was inversely related to delinquency (the broken home was not investigated in this study).

In addition, Yablonsky and Haskell (1988) devote considerable attention to the connection between family factors and delinquency. They conclude that internal patterns of interaction within the family are more important in the explanation of delinquency than are structural features of the family, such as broken homes, although the broken home does play some causal role.

The dynamics of family relationships continue to be studied, in connection with delinquent behavior. In a survey of over 900 youth aged 12–19, for example, Cernkovich and Giordano (1987) conclude that seven different "family interaction patterns" have various impacts on self-report delinquency. These patterns are both indirect (that is, emotional and communicative factors) and direct (that is, control and supervising behavior). While all but one of the seven dimensions, "intimate communication," were found to have significant associations with delinquency, the more delinquent youth in the sample were "more likely to have conflicts with their parents," and to have difficulties with parents over friendship choices (p. 305). The findings of Cernkovich and Giordano applied across all types of home status, broken and unbroken, suggesting again that the significant contribution of family life to delinquency lies in the quality of relationships in the home, not in the structure of the family. (See also, Wells and Rankin, 1988, for a discussion of the relationship between self-report delinquency and adolescent perceptions of parental punishment and supervision.)

In addition, evidence continues to suggest some specification of the relationship between family relationships and delinquency according to demographic characteristics, such as race and gender. The potential negative impact of stepfathers upon stepsons has already been noted. In addition, Cernkovich and Giordano (1987) found that intimate communications were significantly related to delinquency (interestingly enough, in a *positive* direction) only among white males. On the other hand, identity support from parents was particularly inhibitive of delinquency among females. Also, Rosen (1985) concludes that "father-son interaction" was highly associated with delinquency among a sample of black male 13- to 14-year-olds. However, among whites social class was more highly related to delinquency than any measure of family structure or interaction. Finally, family size and presence of father in the household did exert some influence on delinquency within this sample, especially for the white youth categorized as lower class.

In a more general sense, the conclusions of Loeber and Stouthamer-Loeber (1986) suggest differing racial and socioeconomic effects of family factors on delinquent behavior. Based on an extensive review of the literature, these authors categorized the deleterious effects of family living and interaction patterns into four models, or paradigms: neglect; conflict; deviant behavior and attitudes; and disruption. Their interpretation of the research evidence relative to these four paradigms leads Loeber and Stouthamer-Loeber to conclude that several conditions operate to produce an "at risk" delinquent child, especially if the conditions become cumulative. These conditions include a behaviorally disruptive child (impulsive, overactive, and so forth), poor parenting skills, marital disharmony, lack of support from relatives or community agencies, and ill physical and/or mental health of parents (p. 97). Sometimes, however, the authors argue that these conditions can be overcome by families who have additional resources, such as large family income or high occupational status, or who are "white affluent families" (p. 96).

As it becomes increasingly clear that patterns of family interaction contribute to delinquency, as well as to other behavioral problems among youth, research is focusing on the nature of these interactions, and the connections between family conflicts, school problems, peer associations, and delinquency (Sampson and Laub, 1993:Chapter 4). As mentioned previously, some studies distinguish between direct and indirect family controls. Direct controls include attempts to restrain the movements of children through curfews, strict rules, punishments and rewards for disobedience, and so forth. On the other hand, indirect controls include the constraining effects of strong emotional attachments and positive attitudes which children feel toward their parents. When these positive attitudes and feelings exist, it is argued that youth will hesitate to commit acts which might bring shame, embarrassment, or disappointment to their parents and other family members, as well as to themselves (Nye, 1958:6–7; Rankin and Wells, 1990:141–142; Seydlitz, 1991:177).

This research points to complex interactions between these types of controls and their influence on delinquency (Rankin and Wells, 1990). In addition, the impact of parental methods of control on delinquency is affected by age, gender, and type of delinquency. In analyses of direct and indirect control patterns and delinquency among a national sample of white male and female youth living with *both* biological parents, for example, Seydlitz (1991, 1993) concludes that direct controls may increase tensions and the rebellious behavior of children, when indirect controls are weak. Furthermore, this relationship seems particularly likely for females in the mid-adolescent age range (especially in interactions with mothers) and for status offenses, such as parental disobedience, and "substance abuse." Using current terminology, Seydlitz suggests that the combination of low attachment of children to parents and strict parental control may be indicative of "dysfunctional families," and thus connected with more behavioral problems than status offending among the children in the family (1993:265). Similarly, Marc LeBlanc's research suggests that internal constraints are most important in controlling criminality among older youth, and that a principle component of internal constraint (which LeBlanc identifies as a direct control mechanism) is belief in, and respect for, the validity of the law (LeBlanc, 1995).

Other studies suggest that ineffective parental behavior (including parental infighting) may not lead directly to rebellion and control problems of youth. Rather, these difficulties in familial relationships may indirectly lead to delinquency by negatively affecting a child's performance in school and/or increasing the likelihood for developing deviant peer associations (DiLalla et al., 1988; Simons et al., 1991). Some research indicates that peer relationships may be affected more by the amount of time spent with the family than by a juvenile's emotional attachments to parents (Warr, 1993).

In Chapter 6, the prevalence of single-parent families, especially single mothers, living within or near the poverty level was discussed. Within the context of the present topic, broken homes and delinquency, it should be noted that the connection between poverty, single parenthood, and delinquency has not escaped the attention of researchers (Sampson, 1987; Wright and Wright, 1994). In many cases, however, the conclusions of this research point to the impact of poverty on parental resources as an important factor in the control single parents may be able to exercise on children (McLanahan and Booth, 1989:558–560). In addition to lack of economic resources, for example, poverty may inhibit effective supervision of youth such that single parents are unable to afford day care or other supervisory arrangements while they are working, shopping, or performing other necessary parental duties (McLanahan and Booth, 1989:566; Sampson and Laub, 1994). Also, living in poverty may be associated with the social disorganization of neighborhoods, and the connections of these living conditions with delinquency (Sampson, 1987; McLanahan and Booth, 1989:568; see also, Chapter 5 in this volume). Sampson (1992) makes the interesting observation that broken homes in a neighborhood may alter adult patterns of supervision and other forms of social control of children in the area, which may in turn contribute to greater levels of delinquency in these neighborhoods, whether the delinquents are residing in single-parent homes.

In addition, officials in a community may react to family structures in ways that may contribute to higher rates of delinquency for youth living in single-parent homes. Single mothers may be particularly vulnerable to the biases and prejudices of others in the community, such as school authorities, the police, courts, and social service workers, which may lead to intervention from these authorities and to higher rates of arrest, court referral, and other legal actions against their children (Wright and Wright, 1994:11–12). These conditions may be even more pronounced for younger single mothers (Morash and Rucker, 1989).

While these intervening and connecting factors might contribute to delinquency in single-parent families, it should be remembered that the overall relationship between broken homes and self-report delinquency is relatively weak. Furthermore, evidence consistently points to the importance of parent-child relationships as a key factor in the explanation of delinquency, in any kind of family situation. Seydlitz's conclusions, for example, were based on a sample of youth living with both parents. Furthermore, her conclusion that direct controls contributed to delinquency among females specified that this relationship was particularly strong when indirect controls were weak. Using national survey data (the National Youth Survey), Rankin and Kern (1994) indicate that strong attachments of youth to both parents are associated with lower rates of delinquency, as compared with strong attachment to one parent, but this relationship is discussed simply in terms of general social bond theory. Rankin and Kern do not distinguish between direct and indirect parental controls. Nor do they evaluate their findings relative to competing theoretical perspectives or within various contexts.

Some research concludes that economic hardships, even among parents living together and in rural areas, can contribute to parental conflicts and poor "parenting," and consequently to delinquency and other behavioral problems among the children in these families (Conger et al., 1992). Thus, while it may be informative and helpful to know why single-parent family situations may contribute to delinquency, it should not be forgotten that it is not the legal status of the marriage which matters most in this situation. Rather, of greater importance is the socio-emotional status of the patterns of interaction among the members of the family (McCord, 1991).

Overall, it would appear that the association between delinquency and broken homes is as much a reflection of intervening factors and the attitudes and decisions of juvenile justice personnel as it is a reflection of the delinquency-producing tendencies of broken homes. However, the nature of parent-child interactions and the general atmosphere within the home, whether broken or intact, have been consistently related to delinquency. Accordingly, it would be a mistake to accept the conclusions of many sociologists during the middle of this century—namely, that family-connected variables have no place in the explanation of delinquency. Clearly, family relationships are important and it is logical to locate the etiological significance of these factors within the framework of social control theory.

School Experiences and Delinquency   Achievement, participation, and overall involvement in school-related activities have been connected with delinquency for a long time. The negative association between grades in school (achievement) and delinquency was discussed in Chapter 6, in connection with Albert Cohen's middle-class measuring rod theory of delinquency. The influences of intelligence and learning disabilities have also been discussed in earlier chapters. It would appear that little more could be added to establish the significance of school situations in the explanation of juvenile delinquency. Because school activities constitute such a large focal point for adolescent behavior (Jensen and Rojek, 1992), and because attachment and commitment to school represent another major component of the social control theory of delinquency, it is appropriate to reconsider such issues at this point. The purpose of the following discussion is to comment on the *comparative* influence of these conditions, since the primary influence has already been established.

One of the clearest comparative assessments of the influence of school factors on delinquency is provided by Hirschi (1969). In particular, Hirschi compared "attachment to parents (father)" with "attachment to school" and found that those who were unattached to their parents were also disaffiliated with school (including their teachers). He also found that possessing favorable attitudes toward school, including favorable attitudes toward teachers, was associated with lower rates of delinquency, regardless of the strength of attachments to the father (Hirschi, 1969:131–132). In other words, while attachment to parents is definitely related to delinquency, its effects tend to be overshadowed by affiliations with school (see also, Johnson, 1979:115–120; LeBlanc, 1994; and Jenkins, 1995).

In a study of 482 official delinquents and 185 nondelinquents in Utah and Los Angeles, Lamar T. Empey and Steven G. Lubeck (1971) found that both family variables (broken homes, parental harmony, relations with parents) and school factors (particularly grades in school) were highly associated with delinquency in both settings. When the two sets of conditions were simultaneously compared, however, the data clearly indicated that school (as measured by dropouts) had a stronger direct effect on delinquency than family (as measured by boy-parent harmony) in Los Angeles. In Utah, the direct effect of dropout was somewhat stronger than the effect of harmony with parents, but the differences were not as pronounced as in Los Angeles.

A retrospective study of violent behavior among male prison inmates in Minnesota examined the potential impact of family, school, and media experiences on the violent crimes of the prisoners (Kruttschnitt et al., 1986). While noting the impact of parental violence, poor family relationships, and parental absence on violent behavior, the authors concluded that these negative associations were most pronounced among minority inmates. However, for *both* African-American and white prisoners the only factor associated with violent crime was their assessment of how important doing well in school was to them during adolescence (p. 258).

While the comparative assessments described above point to the greater impact on delinquency of school factors, compared to family variables, these comparisons are based on limited sample sizes within specific geographical settings. The research reviewed in this chapter, and in Chapter 6, suggests strong connections between delinquency and both negative family and school experiences (see also, Sheu, 1986:Chapter 5). In addition, some suggest that parental attachment affects delinquency, which then affects school performance, which then affects parental attachment (Liska and Reed, 1985:556–557). Furthermore, differing effects may be related to racial and subcultural settings. Poor family attachment, for example, may be more predictive of delinquency among minority youth, whereas white juveniles may be more negatively affected by unhappy school experiences (although Liska and Reed, 1985, offer a different conclusion).

In a study of school bonding and delinquency, Cernkovich and Giordano (1992) conclude that attachment and commitment to school and teachers are negatively associated with self-reported delinquency. This relationship, moreover, holds when controlling for race, gender, parental communication, perceptions of opportunity, and SES (pp. 275–279). Overall, the authors conclude that school bonding is moderately associated with delinquency, but that nevertheless school factors are no less important in the understanding of delinquency than are other variables, such as parental and peer attachments (p. 280). However, their analysis did find some differences by race. In particular, among African-American males, the greater the involvement in school activities, the higher the level of delinquency (p. 278). This finding, and others, lead the authors to suspect that the connection between school bonding and race is more complex than their basic results suggest, and that racial comparisons should continue to be investigated (pp. 283–286).

Zingraff et al. (1994) report that neglected and physically abused (but not sexually abused) children are more likely to appear in official records of delinquency than nonabused youth. However, in an interesting analysis, their data demonstrate that good academic performance (as indicated by grades, attendance, and lack of in-school behavior problems) reduces the risk of delinquency among all youth, including abused children. Their results suggest that attempts to keep youth in school and to encourage good academic performance can lead to lower rates of delinquency, regardless of child abuse and neglect (pp. 83–85; see also, Hirschi, 1969:Chapter 7).

Some suggest that strong social bonds can operate to provide "at risk" youth—those with disadvantaged family and early childhood environmental circumstances—with "resilience" to resist opportunities and temptations to commit acts of delinquency and misconduct. In particular, it is suggested that school factors, such as commitment and attachment to school, provide the strongest resilience for these otherwise "disadvantaged" youth (Smith et al., 1995:233–238). Others remind us that a strong social bond to the school environment can also result in less delinquency committed *at* school (Jenkins, 1997).

Future investigations in these areas should continue to provide more answers concerning the relative impact of family and school associations on delinquency among all youth, as well as young people of different age, racial, social class, and gender categories.

Other Considerations   The foregoing discussions lead to the general conclusion that religious, family, and school variables are associated with both official and self-report measures of delinquency. In this sense, therefore, social control theory is supported by the data.

Social control theory also argues that delinquency is related to delinquent attitudes and beliefs. This position has received considerable support in the formulations and testing of differential association and neutralization theory, as discussed in Chapter 7. In addition, empirical assessments of social control theory per se have clearly supported the hypothesized relationship between delinquent attitudes and delinquent behavior (Hirschi, 1969; Hindelang, 1973).

Moreover, attempts to compare various elements of social control theory with structural theories of delinquency (such as anomie and lower-class culture theories) have indicated that social control variables are at least as powerful as structural variables in the explanation of delinquency, and often more so (Cernkovich, 1978; Eve, 1978; Kornhauser, 1978; Knox, 1981; Joseph, 1995).

In numerous ways, therefore, the assumptions of social control theory have received considerable support in the literature. By no means have all of the issues and associated questions relative to social control theory been resolved.

First, not all investigations of delinquency have supported the tenets of social control, especially with respect to the topic of conformity (Rankin, 1977).

Second, the strength of institutional attachments of conformity (or the lack of such attachments in relation to delinquency) must be considered in terms of cultural and historical values and conditions. A study of official delinquency and family factors in Israel, for example, found the two to be unrelated (Rahav, 1976). In addition, an analysis of self-reported delinquency indicated that youth in rural areas were less delinquent than youth in urban locations. Moreover, delinquents in general exhibited weaker social bonds than did nondelinquents. However, rural youths were no more committed to the legitimacy of authority and institutions in society than were urban juveniles. Commitment, or social bonds, therefore, did not explain the differences in delinquency rates between rural and urban youngsters (Lyerly and Skipper, 1981).

A rural-urban comparative analysis of self-reported delinquency indicated that social bond variables provided a good explanation of delinquency among the youth living in the rural area, but not among urban juveniles, although these results were confounded by the high percentage of African-American youth in the urban location and the equally high percentage of white juveniles in the rural area (Gardner and Shoemaker, 1989). Other research indicates racial/ethnic impacts, within the United States, on the relationship between delinquency and the social bond (Weber et al., 1995).

In addition, a study of self-reported delinquency in the Philippines indicated that social bond factors accounted for approximately 20 percent of the variance of delinquency, particularly minor forms of delinquent conduct, among male youth. On the other hand, these same factors provided little understanding of delinquency among the females in the sample (Shoemaker, 1994).

Other cross-cultural research suggests that social bond variables may be of limited power in the explanation of delinquency, particularly female delinquency, in societies which are characterized by high levels of informal control, such as Japan (Tanioka and Glaser, 1991) and India (Hartjen and Kethineni, 1993). Of course, delinquency in these countries *may* be explained by a lack of strong bonds to important institutional figures, such as parents, teachers, and so on. It would seem from these analyses, however, that such controls are so strong within the culture, particularly among females, that relatively little variance in delinquency is to be explained by weakened social bonds.

One interesting aspect of such cultural effects is provided in Tanioka and Glaser's research on self-reported delinquency in Japan. Their study suggests that the wearing of school uniforms (among students in private schools) contributes to the "web of control" exercised by adults in Japanese communities. Students are easily recognized and identified by their school uniforms. Consequently, acts of delinquency, particularly criminal acts, are associated with not wearing school uniforms (pp. 62–70).

However, not all cross-cultural studies conclude that the impact of the social bond on delinquency is culturally specific. A comparative analysis of delinquency among youth from four ethnic groups living in the Netherlands (Junger and Marshall, 1997) found consistent patterns of social bonding and delinquency across all four ethnic categories (Turkish, Surinamese, Moroccan, and Dutch). This topic clearly needs to be more thoroughly investigated.

Third, the importance of other factors in the explanation of delinquency is indicated by the proportion of delinquent behavior explained by social control variables (when this assessment has been possible to ascertain). Few estimates exceed 50 percent, a figure which is impressive relative to other explanations of delinquency but far from allowing one to conclude that social control factors *determine* delinquency.

Fourth, the specific qualities of religious participation, family interactions, and school activities that foster delinquency are far from having been consistently identified. Certain situations are now strongly suggestive of delinquency, such as lax, inconsistent, or physically abusive parental discipline techniques. The thrust of previous research, however, has been on the general influence on delinquency of ties and affections with social institutions rather than on specific types of attachments, commitments, or activities that might more or less contribute to delinquency.

Fifth, evidence suggests that the effect of the social bond on delinquency is age specific, as mentioned earlier. Some research concludes, for example, that the social bond is a stronger inhibitor of delinquency among 15-year-olds (those in the "middle" of adolescence) than among other youth (LaGrange and White, 1985), while other studies suggest that the effect of the bond may be greater among younger juveniles and for less serious offenders in general (Agnew, 1985; LeBlanc, 1992:342–343). In addition, some conclude that the impact of the social bond on delinquency may vary in content with age such that family variables are more important among younger children, while school factors become more salient with middle adolescents, and conventional beliefs assume a greater inhibitory role for older youth (Thornberry, 1987; Shoemaker and Gardner, 1988).

Sixth, longitudinal studies are beginning to appear, and some results indicate that there is a *reciprocal* effect on the connection between the social bond and delinquency. That is, when juveniles are surveyed over several points in time, it has been found that delinquency can weaken the social bond, and vice versa (Liska and Reed, 1985), and that a weak social bond may explain initial instances of delinquency but not continued occurrences (Agnew, 1985).

More recent longitudinal studies indicate the need not only to assess the impact of delinquency on weakened social bonds, but also the impact of social bond factors on each other (Thornberry, 1987; Agnew, 1991; Thornberry et al., 1994), as well as the idea that the reciprocal interactions between parental behavior and delinquency can be influenced by the juvenile's age. Patterns of discipline and supervision which may work for younger children may not be effective for older adolescents (Jang and Smith, 1997:326–328). These views extend earlier conceptualizations which argue that weakened social bonds precede, or occur simultaneously with, delinquent behavior (Hirschi, 1969; Empey and Lubeck, 1971; Jensen, 1972; Linden and Hackler, 1973; Hepburn, 1977; Phillips and Kelly, 1979). In addition, newer analyses indicate that peer associations, and other factors such as strain theory (see Chapter 6), modify the impact of social bond on delinquency (see, for example, the insightful critique of social control theory offered by Greenberg, 1999). Agnew (1993), for example, contends that weakened social bonds contribute to delinquency primarily among those youth who feel angry and frustrated with their situations in school or at home, and/or who associate with delinquent peers. These kinds of interactions were also identified in the preceding discussions of family- and school-related factors. The whole issue of reciprocity and interaction between delinquency and its assumed antecedents will be discussed again, in the last chapter of this book, under the topic of integrated theories.

The overall assessment of the social control theory of delinquency, despite these issues and concerns, is that it has generally been supported by research. The idea that a social bond to conventional activities and values inhibits delinquency is persuasive in its empirical support, although clearly this explanation of delinquency cannot stand alone. In particular, current research suggests a strong link between both peer associations and institutional attachments and delinquency. Continued investigation into these two areas of interest promises to yield significant contributions to a further understanding of delinquent behavior.[6]

SUMMARY

Control theories of delinquency, including those of Reckless, Hirschi, and others, have much empirical support. They consist of concepts that are measurable and that are based on logical properties which have informed popular and scientific opinions regarding delinquency for decades. While many questions relative to these theories remain unsolved, the research conducted thus far suggests that control theories are supported and worthy of continued investigation. This conclusion is particularly valid for the proposition that attachments and commitments to conventional institutions in society (the social bond) are associated with low rates of delinquency.

Of course, control theories cannot explain all acts of delinquency, nor can they predict what specific types of delinquency will develop. In addition, even though it has been established that positive self-concepts and attachments to conventional beliefs and institutions in society "protect," or "insulate," one from delinquent involvement, a key question still remains: "How are self-concepts and attachments produced and changed?" Containment and social control theories must yield to other explanations for an answer to this question, and it has been shown that numerous theories have approached this issue from many different viewpoints. In essence, control theories assume an intermediate, intervening position between delinquency and a variety of preconditions. Regardless of specific contributing factors, therefore, it would appear appropriate and potentially more fruitful to focus attention on more immediate precursors to delinquency—namely, self-concepts and social bonds, including those associated with peers.

Notes

1. Others have viewed Reckless' theory as an example of a *social* control theory of delinquency (Gibbons and Krohn, 1986). Using the conceptualizations developed in the current text, however, containment theory is more appropriately classified as an example of personal control theories.

2. On this point, it should be noted that Reckless and Dinitz (1972) conducted an extensive delinquency prevention program, based on self-concept improvement. While no significant differences appeared between experimental and control subjects, containment theory per se was not rejected because the treatment program also produced no significant changes in self-concept.

3. The term "broken homes" is used in this context to refer to an operational component of a large body of research. Its use is not meant to imply the existence, or advocacy, of any particular standard or ideal family constellation. In fact, the position advocated in this text is that family structure is less important as a determinant of social relationships, or of socialization patterns, than is the nature of the relationships among the members of any family context.

4. Another investigation of official delinquency also found support for an association between "intrafamily problems," including broken homes, and delinquency, particularly in an urban area (Los Angeles) as compared to the state of Utah (Empey and Lubeck, 1971). Multivariate analysis, furthermore, indicated that family relationships, especially as measured by "boy-parent harmony," were more predictive of delinquency than was parental separation. Furthermore, a reanalysis of the Gluecks' data, using multivariate techniques, confirmed the strength of family relationships in the explanation of delinquency (Laub and Sampson, 1988).

5. In another analysis, Hirschi (1983) contends that criminal parents tend to have a disproportionate number of delinquent children. This relationship may be true, and its existence may be explained by several factors. In particular, Hirschi maintains that criminal parents may not "recognize" patterns of criminality in their own children (p. 8). Thus, the sons and daughters of criminal parents are not taught that stealing, for instance, is wrong. In effect, they are not punished for their misdeeds, not because their parents do not want to punish bad behavior, but because these parents literally do not see their youngsters' behavior as wrong. In this scenario, attachment to criminal parents may actually be associated with higher rates of delinquency, although attachment to parents and recognition of criminality in children's behavior are not necessarily related.

6. A good review of the empirical literature on social control theory is found in Kempf (1993). Also, in that same volume, LeBlanc and Caplan (1993) present a formal analysis of social control theory, one which should stimulate more critical conceptualization of this explanation of delinquency in future research.

References

Adler, Freda and William S. Laufer (eds.), 1993, New Directions in Criminological Theory. New Brunswick, N.J.: Transaction.

Agnew, Robert, 1985, "Social Control Theory and Delinquency: A Longitudinal Test." Criminology 23:46–61.

———, 1991, "A Longitudinal Test of Social Control Theory and Delinquency." Journal of Research in Crime and Delinquency 28:126–156.

———, 1993, "Why Do They Do It? An Examination of the Intervening Mechanisms Between 'Social Control' Variables and Delinquency." Journal of Research in Crime and Delinquency 30:245–266.

Bainbridge, William Sims, 1989, "The Religious Ecology of Deviance," American Sociological Review 54:288–295.

Benda, Brent B., 1995, "The Effect of Religion on Adolescent Delinquency Revisited." Journal of Research in Crime and Delinquency 32:446–466.

Burkett, Steven R. and Bruce O. Warren, 1987, "Religiosity, Peer Associations, and Adolescent Marijuana Use: A Panel Study of Underlying Causal Structures." Criminology 25:109–131.

Burkett, Steven R. and Mervin White, 1974, "Hellfire and Delinquency: Another Look." Journal for the Scientific Study of Religion 13:455–462.

Cernkovich, Steven A., 1978, "Evaluating Two Models of Delinquency Causation: Structural Theory and Control Theory." Criminology 16:335–352.

Cernkovich, Steven A. and Peggy C. Giordano, 1987, "Family Relationships and Delinquency." Criminology 25:295–319.

———, 1992, "School Bonding, Race, and Delinquency." Criminology 30:261–291.

Cochran, John K. and Ronald L. Akers, 1989, "Beyond Hellfire: An Exploration of the Variable Effects of Religiosity on Adolescent Marijuana and Alcohol Use." Journal of Research in Crime and Delinquency 26:198–225.

Cochran, John K., Peter B. Wood, and Bruce J. Arneklev, 1994, "Is the Religiosity-Delinquency Relationship Spurious? A Test of Arousal and Social Control Theories." Journal of Research in Crime and Delinquency 31:92–123.

Cohen, Albert K., 1966, Deviance and Control. Englewood Cliffs, N.J.: Prentice-Hall.

Conger, Rand D., Katherine J. Conger, Glen H. Elder, Jr., Frederick O. Lorenz, Ronald L. Simons, and Les B. Whitbeck, 1992, "A Family Process Model of Economic Hardship and Adjustment of Early Adolescent Boys." Child Development 63:526–541.

DiLalla, Lisabeth Fisher, Christina M. Mitchell, Michael W. Arthur, and Pauline M. Pagliocca, 1988, "Aggression and Delinquency: Family and Environmental Factors." Journal of Youth and Adolescence 17:233–246.

Dinitz, Simon, Frank R. Scarpitti, and Walter C. Reckless, 1962, "Delinquency Vulnerability: A Cross Group and Longitudinal Analysis." American Sociological Review 27:515–517.

Dornbusch, Sanford M., J. Merrill Carlsmith, Steven J. Bushwall, Philip L. Ritter, Herbert Leiderman, Albert H. Hastorf, and Ruth T. Gross, 1985, "Single Parents, Extended Households, and the Control of Adolescents." Child Development 56:326–341.

Ellis, Lee, 1985, "Religiosity and Criminality: Evidence and Explanations of Complex Relationships." Sociological Perspectives 28:501–520.

———, 1987, "Religiosity and Criminality from the Perspective of Arousal Theory." Journal of Research in Crime and Delinquency 24:215–232.

Emms, T. W., R. M. Povey, and S. M. Clift, 1986, "The Self-Concepts of Black and White Delinquents: A Comparison Within an English Youth Custody Centre." British Journal of Criminology 26:385–393.

Empey, Lamar T., 1982, American Delinquency, revised edition. Homewood, Ill.: Dorsey.

Empey, Lamar T. and Steven G. Lubeck, 1971, Explaining Delinquency. Lexington, Mass.: D. C. Heath.

Evans, T. David, Francis T. Cullen, Velmer S. Burton, Jr., R. Gregory Dunaway, Gary L. Payne, and Sesha R. Kethineni, 1996, "Religion, Social Bonds, and Delinquency." Deviant Behavior 17:43–70.

Eve, Raymond A., 1978, "A Study of the Efficacy and Interactions of Several Theories for Explaining Rebelliousness Among High School Students." Journal of Criminal Law and Criminology 69:115–125.

Free, Marvin D., Jr., 1991, "Clarifying the Relationship Between the Broken Home and Juvenile Delinquency: A Critique of the Current Literature." Deviant Behavior 12:109–167.

———, 1994, "Religiosity, Religious Conservatism, Bonds to School, and Juvenile Delinquency Among Three Categories of Drug Users." Deviant Behavior 15:151–170.

Gardner, Robert LeGrande and Donald J. Shoemaker, 1989, "Social Bonding and Delinquency: A Comparative Analysis." Sociological Quarterly 30:481–500.

Geismar, Ludwig L. and Katherine Wood, 1986, Delinquent Behavior, fourth edition. Englewood Cliffs, N.J.: Prentice-Hall.

Gibbons, Don C. and Marvin D. Krohn, 1986, Delinquent Behavior, fourth edition. Englewood Cliffs, N.J.: Prentice-Hall.

Glueck, Sheldon and Eleanor Glueck, 1950, Unraveling Juvenile Delinquency. Cambridge, Mass.: Harvard University Press.

Greenberg, David F., 1999, "The Weak Strength of Control Theory." Crime & Delinquency 45:66–81.

Hartjen, Clayton A. and Sesharajani Kethineni, 1993, "Culture, Gender, and Delinquency: A Study of Youths in the United States and India." Women & Criminal Justice 5:37–69.

Haskell, Martin R. and Lewis Yablonsky, 1982, Juvenile Delinquency, third edition. Boston: Houghton Mifflin.

Hepburn, John R., 1977, "Testing Alternative Models of Delinquency Causation." Journal of Criminal Law and Criminology 67:450–460.

Higgins, Paul C. and Gary L. Albrecht, 1977, "Hellfire and Delinquency Revisited." Social Forces 55:952–958.

Hindelang, Michael J., 1973, "Causes of Delinquency: A Partial Replication and Extension." Social Problems 20:471–487.

Hirschi, Travis, 1969, Causes of Delinquency. Berkeley: University of California Press.

———, 1983, "Crime and Family Policy." Journal of Contemporary Studies 6:3–16.

Hirschi, Travis and Rodney Stark, 1969, "Hellfire and Delinquency." Social Problems 17:202–213.

Jang, Sung Joon and Carolyn A. Smith, 1997, "A Test of Reciprocal Causal Relationships Among Parental Supervision, Affective Ties, and Delinquency." Journal of Research in Crime and Delinquency 34:307–336.

Jenkins, Patricia H., 1995, "School Delinquency and School Commitment," Sociology of Education 68:221–239.

———, 1997, "School Delinquency and the School Social Bond." Journal of Research in Crime and Delinquency 34:337–367.

Jensen, Gary F., 1972, "Parents, Peers, and Delinquent Action: A Test of the Differential Association Perspective." American Journal of Sociology 78:562–575.

———, 1973, "Inner Containment and Delinquency." Journal of Criminal Law and Criminology 64:464–470.

———, 1993, "Power-Control vs. Social-Control Theories of Common Delinquency: A Comparative Analysis." Pp. 363–380 in Freda Adler and William S. Laufer (eds.), q.v.

Jensen, Gary F. and Maynard L. Erickson, 1979, "The Religious Factor and Delinquency: Another Look at the Hellfire Hypothesis." Pp. 157–177 in Robert Wuthnow (ed.), The Religious Dimension. New York: Academic Press.

Jensen, Gary F. and Dean G. Rojek, 1992, Delinquency and Youth Crime, second edition. Prospect Heights, Ill.: Waveland.

Johnson, Richard E., 1979, Juvenile Delinquency and Its Origins: An Integrated Theoretical Approach. Cambridge: Cambridge University Press.

———, 1986, "Family Structure and Delinquency: General Patterns and Gender Differences." Criminology 24:65–84.

Johnson, Robert A., S. Susan Su, Dean R. Gerstein, Hee-Choon Shin, and John P.

Hoffman, 1995, "Parental Influences on Deviant Behavior in Early Adolescence: A Logistic Response Analysis of Age- and Gender-Differentiated Effects." Journal of Quantitative Criminology 11:167–193.

Joseph, Janice, 1995, "Juvenile Delinquency Among African Americans." Journal of Black Studies 25:475–491.

Junger, Marianne and Ineke Helen Marshall, 1997, "The Interethnic Generalizability of Social Control Theory: An Empirical Test." Journal of Research in Crime and Delinquency 34:79–112.

Kaplan, Howard B., 1978, "Deviant Behavior and Self-Enhancement in Adolescence." Journal of Youth and Adolescence 7:253–277.

———, 1980, Deviant Behavior in Defense of Self. New York: Academic Press.

Kaplan, Howard B., Steven S. Martin, and Robert J. Johnson, 1986, "Self-Rejection and the Explanation of Deviance: Specification of the Structure Among Latent Constructs." American Journal of Sociology 92:384–411.

Kempf, Kimberly L., 1993, "The Empirical Status of Hirschi's Control Theory." Pp. 143–185 in Freda Adler and William S. Laufer (eds.), q.v.

Knox, George W., 1981, "Social Disorganization Models of Deviance." Pp. 78–92 in Gary F. Jensen (ed.), Sociology of Delinquency. Beverly Hills, Calif.: Sage.

Kornhauser, Ruth Rosner, 1978, Social Sources of Delinquency. Chicago: University of Chicago Press.

Krisberg, Barry and James Austin (eds.), 1978, The Children of Ishmael: Critical Perspectives on Juvenile Justice. Palo Alto, Calif.: Mayfield.

Kruttschnitt, Candace, Linda Heath, and David A. Ward, 1986, "Family Violence, Television Viewing Habits, and Other Adolescent Experiences Related to Violent Criminal Behavior." Criminology 24:235–267.

LaGrange, Randy L. and Helene Raskin White, 1985, "Age Differences in Delinquency: A Test of Theory." Criminology 23:19–45.

Laub, John H. and Robert J. Sampson, 1988, "Unraveling Families and Delinquency: A Reanalysis of the Gluecks' Data." Criminology 26:355–380.

LeBlanc, Marc, 1992, Family Dynamics, Adolescent Delinquency, and Adult Criminality." Psychiatry 55:336–353.

———, 1994, "Family, School, Delinquency and Criminality: The Predictive Power of an Elaborated Social Control Theory for Males." Criminal Behaviour and Mental Health 4:101–117.

———, 1995, "The Relative Importance of Internal and External Direct Constraints in the Explanation of Late Adolescent and Adult Criminality." Pp. 272–288 in Joan McCord (ed.), Coercion and Punishment in Long-Term Perspectives. New York: Cambridge University Press.

LeBlanc, Marc and Aaron Caplan, 1993. "Theoretical Formalization, a Necessity: The Example of Hirschi's Bonding Theory." Pp. 237–336 in Freda Adler and William S. Laufer (eds.), q.v.

Leung, Kwok and Sing Lau, 1989, "Effects of Self-Concept and Perceived Disapproval of Delinquent Behavior in School Children." Journal of Youth and Adolescence 18:345–359.

Linden, Eric and James C. Hackler, 1973, "Affective Ties and Delinquency." Pacific Sociological Review 16:27–46.

Linden, Rick and Raymond Currie, 1977, "Religiosity and Drug Use: A Test of Social Control Theory." Canadian Journal of Criminology and Corrections 19:346–355.

Liska, Allen E. and Mark D. Reed, 1985, "Ties to Conventional Institutions and Delinquency: Estimating Reciprocal Effects." American Sociological Review 50:547–560.

Loeber, Rolf and Magda Stouthamer-Loeber, 1986, "Family Factors as Correlates and Predictors of Juvenile Conduct Problems and Delinquency." Pp. 29–149 in Michael Tonry and Norval Morris (eds.), Crime and Justice: An Annual Review of Research, Vol. 7. Chicago: University of Chicago Press.

Lyerly, Robert Richard and James K. Skipper, Jr., 1981, "Differential Rates of Rural-Urban Delinquency: A Social Control Approach." Criminology 19:385–399.

McCarthy, John D. and Dean R. Hoge, 1984, "The Dynamics of Self-Esteem and Delinquency." American Journal of Sociology 90:396–410.

McCord, Joan, 1991, "Family Relationships, Juvenile Delinquency, and Adult Criminality." Criminology 29:397–417.

McLanahan, Sara and Karen Booth, 1989, "Mother-Only Families: Problems, Prospects, and Politics." Journal of Marriage and Family 51:557–580.

Monahan, Thomas P., 1957, "Family Status and the Delinquent Child: A Reappraisal and Some New Findings." Social Forces 32:250–258.

Morash, Merry with Lila Rucker, 1989, "An Exploratory Study of the Connection of Mother's Age at Childbirth to Her Children's Delinquency in Four Data Sets." Crime & Delinquency 35:45–93.

Nye, F. Ivan, 1958, Family Relationships and Delinquent Behavior. New York: Wiley.

Orcutt, James D., 1970, "Self-Concept and Insulation Against Delinquency: Some Critical Notes." Sociological Quarterly 2:381–390.

Pagani, Linda, Richard E. Tremblay, Frank Vitaro, Margaret Kerr, and Pierre McDuff, 1998, "The Impact of Family Transition on the Development of Delinquency in Adolescent Boys: A 9-Year Longitudinal Study." Journal of Child Psychology and Psychiatry 39:489–499.

Phillips, John C. and Delos H. Kelly, 1979, "School Failure and Delinquency: Which Causes Which?" Criminology 17:194–207.

Platt, Anthony, 1977, The Child Savers, second edition. Chicago: University of Chicago Press.

Rahav, Giora, 1976, "Family Relations and Delinquency in Israel." Criminology 14:259–270.

Rankin, Joseph H., 1977, "Investigating the Interrelations Among Social Control Variables and Conformity." Journal of Criminal Law and Criminology 67:470–480.

Rankin, Joseph H. and Roger Kern, 1994, "Parental Attachments and Delinquency." Criminology 32:495–515.

Rankin, Joseph H. and L. Edward Wells, 1990, "The Effect of Parental Attachments and Direct Controls on Delinquency." Journal of Research in Crime and Delinquency 27:140–165.

Reckless, Walter C., 1961, "A New Theory of Delinquency and Crime." Federal Probation 25:42–46.

———, 1967, The Crime Problem, fourth edition. New York: Appleton-Century-Crofts.

Reckless, Walter C. and Simon Dinitz, 1972, The Prevention of Juvenile Delinquency. Columbus: Ohio State University Press.

Reckless, Walter C., Simon Dinitz, and Barbara Kay, 1957, "The Self Component in Potential Delinquency and Potential Nondelinquency." American Sociological Review 22:566–570.

Reckless, Walter C., Simon Dinitz, and Ellen Murray, 1956, "Self-Concept as an Insulator Against Delinquency." American Sociological Review 21:744–746.

Rosen, Lawrence, 1985, "Family and Delinquency: Structure or Function?" Criminology 23:553–573.

Rosen, Lawrence and Kathleen Neilson, 1978, "The Broken Home and Delinquency." Pp. 406–415 in Leonard D. Savitz and Norman Johnston (eds.), Crime in Society. New York: Wiley.

Rosenberg, Morris, 1979, Conceiving the Self. New York: Basic Books.

Rosenberg, Morris, Carmi Schooler, and Carrie Schoenbach, 1989, "Self-Esteem and Adolescent Problems." American Sociological Review 54:1004–1018.

Ross, Lee E., 1992, "Blacks, Self-Esteem, and Delinquency: It's Time for a New Approach." Justice Quarterly 9:609–624.

———, 1994a, "Religion and Deviance: Exploring the Impact of Social Control Elements." Sociological Spectrum 14:65–86.

———, 1994b, "The Impact of Race-Esteem and Self-Esteem on Delinquency." Sociological Focus 27:111–129.

Sampson, Robert J., 1987, "Urban Black Violence: The Effect of Male Joblessness and Family Disruption." American Journal of Sociology 93:348–382.

———, 1992, "Family Management and Child Development: Insights from Social Disorganization Theory." Pp. 63–93 in Joan McCord (ed.), Facts, Frameworks, and Forecasts. New Brunswick, N.J.: Transaction.

Sampson, Robert J. and John H. Laub, 1993, Crime in the Making: Pathways and Turning Points Through Life. Cambridge, Mass.: Harvard University Press.

———, 1994, "Urban Poverty and the Family Context of Delinquency: A New Look at Structure and Process in a Classic Study." Child Development 65:523–540.

Sanders, Wiley B. (ed.), 1970, Juvenile Offenders for a Thousand Years. Chapel Hill, N.C.: University of North Carolina Press.

Scarpitti, Frank R., Ellen Murray, Simon Dinitz, and Walter C. Reckless, 1960, "The 'Good' Boy in a High Delinquency Area: Four Years Later." American Sociological Review 25:555–558.

Schwartz, Michael and Sheldon Stryker, 1970, Deviance, Selves and Others. Washington, D.C.: American Sociological Association.

Schwartz, Michael and Sandra S. Tangri, 1965, "A Note on Self-Concept as an Insulator Against Delinquency." American Sociological Review 30:922–926.

Seydlitz, Ruth, 1991, "The Effects of Age and Gender on Parental Control and Delinquency." Youth & Society 23:175–201.

————, 1993, "Complexity in the Relationships Among Direct and Indirect Parental Controls and Delinquency." Youth & Society 24:243–275.

Shaw, Clifford R. and Henry D. McKay, 1932, "Are Broken Homes a Causative Factor in Juvenile Delinquency?" Social Forces 10:514–524.

Sheu, Chuen-Jim, 1986, Delinquency and Identity: Juvenile Delinquency in an American Chinatown. New York: Harrow and Heston.

Shoemaker, Donald J., 1994, "Male-Female Delinquency in the Philippines: A Comparative Analysis." Youth & Society 25:299–329.

Shoemaker, Donald J. and Robert LeGrande Gardner III, 1988, "Social Bonding, Age, and Delinquency: Further Evidence." Journal of Sociology 19:195–210.

Simons, Ronald L., Les B. Whitbeck, Rand D. Conger, and Katherine J. Conger, 1991, "Parenting Factors, Social Skills, and Value Commitments as Precursors to School Failure, Involvement with Deviant Peers, and Delinquent Behavior." Journal of Youth and Adolescence 20:645–664.

Sloane, Douglas M. and Raymond H. Potvin, 1986, "Religion and Delinquency: Cutting Through the Maze." Social Forces 65:87–105.

Smith, Carolyn, Alan J. Lizotte, Terence P. Thornberry, and Marvin D. Krohn, 1995, "Resilient Youth: Identifying Factors That Prevent High-Risk Youth from Engaging in Delinquency and Drug Use." Pp. 217–247 in John Hagan (ed.), Current Perspectives on Aging and the Life Cycle, Vol. 4. Greenwich, Conn.: JAI Press.

Stark, Rodney, Lori Kent, and Daniel P. Doyle, 1982, "Religion and Delinquency: The Ecology of a 'Lost' Relationship." Journal of Research in Crime and Delinquency 19:4–24.

Tanioka, Ichiro and Daniel Glaser, 1991, "School Uniforms, Routine Activities, and the Social Control of Delinquency in Japan." Youth & Society 23:50–75.

Thornberry, Terence P., 1987, "Toward an Interactional Theory of Delinquency." Criminology 25:863–891.

Thornberry, Terence P., Alan J. Lizotte, Marvin D. Krohn, Margaret Farnworth, and Sung Joon Jang, 1994, "Delinquent Peers, Beliefs, and Delinquent Behavior: A Longitudinal Test of Interactional Theory." Criminology 32:47–83.

Tittle, Charles R. and Michael R. Welch, 1983, "Religiosity and Deviance: Toward a Contingency Theory of Constraining Effects." Social Forces 61:653–682.

Toby, Jackson, 1957, "Social Disorganization and Stake in Conformity: Complementary Factors in the Predatory Behavior of Hoodlums." Journal of Criminal Law, Criminology, and Police Science 48:12–17.

Van Voorhis, Patricia, Francis T. Cullen, Richard A. Mathers, and Connie Chenoweth Garner, 1988, "The Impact of Family Structure and Quality on Delinquency: A Comparative Assessment of Structural and Functional Factors." Criminology 26:235–261.

van Welzenis, Ingrid, 1997, "The Self-Concept of Societally Vulnerable and Delinquent Boys Within the Context of School and Leisure Activities." Journal of Adolescence 20:695–705.

Voss, Harwin L., 1969, "Differential Association and Containment Theory: A Theoretical Convergence." Social Forces 47:381–391.

Warr, Mark, 1993, "Parents, Peers and Delinquency." Social Forces 72:247–264.

Weber, Linda R., Andrew Miracle, and Tom Skehan, 1995, "Family Bonding and Delinquency: Racial and Ethnic Influences Among U.S. Youth." Human Organization 54:363–372.

Wells, L. Edward, 1978, "Theories of Deviance and the Self-Concept." Social Psychology 41:189–204.

———, 1989, "Self-Enhancement Through Delinquency: A Conditional Test of Self-Derogation Theory." Journal of Research in Crime and Delinquency 26:226–252.

Wells, L. Edward and Joseph H. Rankin, 1983, "Self-Concept as a Mediating Factor in Delinquency." Social Psychology Quarterly 46:11–22.

———, 1988, "Direct Parental Controls and Delinquency." Criminology 26:263–285.

———, 1991, "Families and Delinquency: A Meta-Analysis of the Impact of Broken Homes." Social Problems 38:71–93.

Wiatrowski, Michael D., David B. Griswald, and Mary R. Roberts, 1981, "Social Control Theory and Delinquency." American Sociological Review 46:525–541.

Wilkinson, Karen, 1974, "The Broken Home and Juvenile Delinquency: Scientific Explanation or Ideology?" Social Problems 21:726–739.

Wright, Kevin N. and Karen E. Wright, 1994, Family Life, Delinquency, and Crime: A Policymaker's Guide. Washington, D.C.: Office of Juvenile Justice and Delinquency Prevention.

Yablonsky, Lewis and Martin R. Haskell, 1988, Juvenile Delinquency, fourth edition. New York: Harper & Row.

Zingraff, Matthew T., Jeffrey Leiter, Matthew C. Johnson, and Kristen A. Myers, 1994, "The Mediating Effect of Good School Performance on the Maltreatment-Delinquency Relationship." Journal of Research in Crime and Delinquency 31:62–91.

9

Labeling Theory

HISTORICAL OVERVIEW

The view that formal and informal societal reactions to delinquency can influence the subsequent attitudes and behavior of delinquents was recognized early in this century. Frederick Thrasher's work on juvenile gangs in Chicago (1927) was one of the first instances in which the consequences of official labels of delinquency were recognized as potentially negative. A few years later, Frank Tannenbaum (1938) introduced the term "dramatization of evil," in which he argued that officially labeling someone as a delinquent can result in the person *becoming* the very thing he is described as *being*. A few years after Tannenbaum's book was published, Edwin Lemert (1951) developed the concepts of *primary* and *secondary* deviance (to be defined below), which became the central elements of the first systematic development of what has come to be known as labeling theory.[1] The theoretical "legacy" of this line of reasoning within sociology may be traced to the work of Charles Horton Cooley and George Herbert Mead (Matsueda, 1992). Cooley is credited with the term "looking glass" self (1964:184–185), and Mead is associated with the notion of the "generalized other" (Strauss, 1964:216–228). Both of these concepts stress the importance of social interactions in the development of self–feelings and social identities. The conceptualization of self-concept, per se, is often traced to the work of William James (Rosenberg, 1979).

Interest in labeling theory was dormant during the 1950s, since numerous structural theories were introduced to explain delinquency, particularly lower-class gang delinquency (see Chapter 6). Increasing dissatisfaction with these, and other, theories and the growing awareness of middle-class delinquency, much of which was not officially recorded, prompted many criminologists to return to the earlier views of Thrasher, Tannenbaum, and Lemert. This renewed interest was particularly spawned by Howard Becker's analysis of deviance in the early 1960s (later revised in 1973). Essentially, Becker proposed that deviance was "created" by rule enforcers, who often acted with bias against the poor and powerless members of society. This idea, coupled with the earlier notion of changing self-images, during the 1960s and early 1970s became a central topic of much research and commentary that focused on the subjects of crime, delinquency, and deviant acts.

GENERIC ASSUMPTIONS

One of the basic assumptions of labeling theory is that initial acts of delinquency are caused by a wide variety of factors. These factors, however, are relatively unimportant in the scheme of things, which leads to a second assumption. That is, the primary factor in the repetition of delinquency is the fact of having been formally labeled as a delinquent. This assertion is accompanied by another idea, which may be presented as a third assumption. Repeated acts of delinquency are influenced by formal labels because such labels eventually alter a person's self-image to the point where the person begins to identify himself as a delinquent and act accordingly. Contrary to Reckless' containment theory, therefore, the view of the labeling perspective is that a negative, or delinquent, self-image *follows* the act of delinquency rather than precedes delinquency. A fourth assumption of the labeling approach is that the official application of the label of delinquent is dependent on a host of criteria in addition to, or other than, the behavior itself, such as the offender's age, sex, race, and social class, as well as the organizational norms of official agencies and departments. These assumptions are diagrammed in Figure 12.

Of course, one does not have to be officially labeled criminal or delinquent in order to label himself as such. Moreover, an official label that calls one delinquent can be applied *irrespective* of any nonconformist act. For the most part, however, the advocates of the labeling approach to delinquency have maintained that usually some type of nonconformity precedes an official label and that most self-labeling occurs after official labeling.

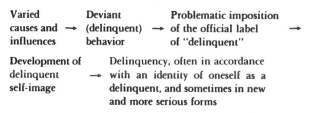

Figure 12

Key Concepts

The focus of this chapter is on the *effects* of labeling on delinquent self-images and behavior rather than on the antecedents of the labeling per se. Two concepts that are important in this regard are *primary* and *secondary* deviance, as introduced by Lemert (1951).

Primary Deviance   This term refers to original acts of nonconformity that may be caused by any of a number of factors. Primary deviance is generally considered to be undetected, or not recognized, as deviant by others. Primary deviants have not adjusted their behavior to accommodate societal reactions to their deviance.

Secondary Deviance   On the other hand, this term refers to deviance that is committed *as the result* of the problems of self-identity and social interaction, which are generated by the identification of the actor as a deviant. It is a new and often more serious form of deviance that is committed, in addition to the original causes of the primary deviance. Thus, secondary deviance is nonconformity created by the "pains of labeling."

Discussion

Lemert's (1951) discussion of the labeling, or "societal reaction," theory was applied to deviant behavior in general. Lemert conceived of such behavior, which he termed "sociopathic," as meaningful only in the sense that it elicited an "effective" form of social disapproval. Deviation is neither *inherently* good or bad; such descriptions emanate only from the societal response to the behavior.

Lemert conceptualized the reaction process from two angles: the members of society and the deviant. The members of society are considered important in this process from the standpoint that it is they, particularly agents of social control, who are responsible for the labeling in the first place.

The second component of the labeling process, the deviant, is considered important because of the consequences the label of deviant produces for the labelee. It is with this aspect of the labeling process that Lemert introduced the concepts of primary and secondary deviation, and on which he concentrated his discussion.

The term "process" becomes meaningful in Lemert's discussion with the view that secondary deviation is reached through a series of steps, beginning with primary deviation, progressing through a series of penalties, to further deviance, then increased penalties, and eventually an acceptance by the actor of a deviant status.

The process of moving from primary to secondary deviance is conceived of as very complex. Numerous issues have been raised concerning the steps involved, and these issues have influenced considerable discussion regarding the logical adequacy of labeling theory (see, for example, Sagarin, 1975; Montanino, 1977; Gove, 1980a; and Dotter and Roebuck, 1988).

One of the most central issues in the process of becoming a secondary deviant is the connection between behavior and the societal reaction to it. While labeling theorists may not be overly concerned with the basic causes of delinquency, those who advocate this theory must be able to distinguish between behavior which is caused by some "primary" (pre-label) factor and that which is committed largely in response to a label or an identification of one as a delinquent.

Howard Becker (1973) has attempted to deal with this question by conceptualizing three situations of deviant (or delinquent) behavior: the pure deviant, the falsely accused deviant, and the secret deviant. The pure deviant is a norm violator and is recognized as such by others. Falsely accused deviants are those whose acts are actually conforming, but who are incorrectly thought by others to be deviant (the victims of the "bum rap," so to speak). In the secret deviant situation, one violates a rule or a law but is not noticed or perceived by others as having committed an act of deviance.

It might appear that the term "secret deviance" is a contradiction within the assumptions of labeling theory (Gibbs, 1966). If an act is not to be considered deviant unless it is so recognized and labeled by others, as Becker maintains, then how is secret deviance possible? Becker addresses this question by suggesting that we call nonconformist behavior that is not reacted to by members of society "rule-breaking" behavior. Deviant behavior, however, is that which is so recognized in society, and secret deviance is behavior that would very likely be labeled as deviant if it were observed.

The use of a new term to answer a strong question does not always resolve the problem. If a considerable amount of undetected delinquency occurs, for example, it could suggest that delinquency is as much in response to primary factors as to the effects of labeling, if not more so. In fact, research does suggest that a great deal of "hidden" delinquency exists. It is still possible, of course, to argue that repeated delinquency occurs primarily because of the problems generated by official detection and labeling. But the existence of a significant amount of hidden delinquency, or "rule-breaking" behavior, questions the extent to which delinquency can be attributed to the effects of labeling (Hirschi, 1980).

Another issue with labeling theory is the matter of how the label is handled by the labelee. Does one resist the negative effects of labeling or become positively influenced by the label? Some people are able to deny the "deviant" implications that the judgments of others may denote. In addition, it is possible, some may say even likely, that being labeled a delinquent would lead to reformed behavior—the juvenile would decide to "mend his ways" to avoid further problems and adjustments occasioned by a label (Thorsell and Klemke, 1972; Becker, 1973). The list of possibilities is lengthy and demonstrates again the complexities of the theory.

The consideration of the labelee's reactions to his identification as a deviant leads many to associate labeling theory with an interactionist perspective (Becker, 1973; Lemert, 1974; Sagarin, 1975); that is, labeling theory attempts to account for the mutual effects of the actor and his audience. Thus, the theory is concerned not only with what the actor and reactor do, but with how each one's actions affect the behavior of the other.

In addition to conceptualizing deviant behavior in terms of personal interaction, some commentators on labeling theory have noted the importance of groups and associations in the actor's acceptance of societal reactions to his behavior. Becker, for example, argues that a "final step in the career of a deviant" is the identification with an "organized deviant group" (pp. 37–39). Others (Sagarin, 1969; Trice and Roman, 1970) have also acknowledged the influence that social groups with a deviant label may have on one's accepting a personal label of deviance. These authors have suggested that group support of a labeled deviant may either nudge him further into an identity as a deviant or serve as a catalyst for a transformation from an unacceptable role, in society's eyes, to a more positive social status. An example of the latter situation would be an alcohol abuser who joins Alcoholics Anonymous and pronounces himself an alcoholic in order to handle the problem (Trice and Roman, 1970).

Evaluation

Despite numerous debates and discussions, several have argued that there are essentially two basic issues with which labeling theory is concerned: (1) the development and enforcement of rules and laws, and (2) the effects of labeling one a delinquent in terms of one's subsequent self-concept or identity and behavior (Schur, 1971; Gove, 1980b; Kitsuse, 1980). The first issue concerns the various influences that shape society's laws and the manner in which they are enforced. With respect to the study of delinquency, these questions have typically been addressed to the demographic characteristics of the juvenile (for example, age, sex, race, or social class), the organizational climate of social control agencies (such as police departments and juvenile courts), and the interaction between juveniles and agents of social control (police, judges, probation officers, and so on). Some contend that this issue has become a dominant area of concern in criminology, but that it has become associated with conflict theory, particularly neo-Marxist, or radical theory (Hirschi, 1980). Because the question of discrimination against minorities is so important, its evaluation is placed in the following chapter, which addresses the radical theory of criminality.

The second basic issue of labeling theory, the consequences of labeling on one's self-image and behavior, has received considerable attention in the literature and is definitely accessible to evaluation. It is recognized that concentrating on self-concepts and attitudes and visible behavior does not do full justice to the complexities of labeling theory and to the process of moving from primary to secondary deviance or of becoming enmeshed in a life of criminality, a "career" deviant (Becker, 1973). A systematic assessment of these factors, however, will provide some information concerning the validity of labeling theory.

Labeling and Self-Concept The relationship between a formal delinquency label and consequent identity problems has been analyzed through both qualitative and quantitative research problems. Qualitatively, the connection between labeling a juvenile a delinquent and the development of a delinquent identity, or antiauthority attitudes, has been established by examinations of the court processing of juveniles (Emerson, 1969; Cicourel, 1976) as well as observations of juvenile gangs (Werthman, 1970). Thrasher and Tannenbaum also qualitatively assessed the connection between self-concept and formally being labeled, or "tagged," as a delinquent. In addition, Matza's view that delinquents develop a cynical and disrespectful attitude toward the police and juvenile courts was based essentially on qualitative assessments of juvenile reactions (see Chapter 7).

A quasi-experimental participant observation study of delinquency in a small town reported a connection between official (and unofficial) labeling and delinquent self-images. William Chambliss (1973) conducted a longitudinal study of two juvenile gangs—eight children of respectable, upper-middle-class families who formed a gang called the "Saints" and six youths from lower-class families who belonged to a gang called the "Roughnecks."

Although none of the Saints had ever been arrested, their observed involvement in delinquency was as thorough (although not for violent offenses) as the Roughnecks, who had been arrested repeatedly. Furthermore, the overall reputation of the Saints, in the community and among school officials, was generally good. The acknowledged transgressions of the Saints were often passed off as "pranks" and mischievousness to be expected of boys. The Roughnecks, on the other hand, were viewed by the police, school officials, and other members of the community as headed for "trouble," a "bad bunch of boys" (Chambliss, 1973:27–28).

More to the point of this discussion, Chambliss' observations indicated that the juveniles generally adopted, or lived up to, their reputations in the community. The Saints never saw themselves as delinquents. Instead, they saw themselves as merely out to have a good time, to raise a little hell, as it were, all of which never really hurt anyone. The Roughnecks, however, made their delinquency quite visible to the public and openly flouted their hostility toward the respectable members of the community. According to Chambliss, members of the Roughnecks not only viewed themselves as delinquents, but they also sought out as friends and associates other juveniles with similar self-concepts.

It would appear from qualitative analyses that official labels do produce, or at least contribute to, a delinquent self-image. More empirical or quantitative measures of self-concept, however, have provided only mixed support for the contention that a formal delinquency label produces a delinquent identity.

Jack Foster and his colleagues (1972), for example, interviewed 196 male youths who had either been arrested or referred to juvenile court. The juveniles were interviewed in their homes within 20 days after their arrest or court appearance. Basically, the boys reported no changes in personal relationships or parental attitudes toward them as a result of their involvement with the law. In addition, over 90 percent of the boys felt no difficulties would develop with respect to finishing school as a result of their official records of delinquency. About 40 percent of the boys felt that their chances of getting a suitable job might have been hurt by their legal involvements, but this feeling seemed more pronounced among those boys who had been sent to court. Overall, the investigators concluded that the labeled youths either did not feel any great liabilities as a result of their labels or were able to minimize, in their own minds, the possible effects of such labels because of their age, generally good behavior, and the current practice of keeping juvenile records confidential in the United States.

While the Foster study did not specifically address the issue of self-concept, the results clearly lent no support to the contention that associations and identities are affected by a formal label of delinquency (see also, Giordano, 1976). Other research has, however, concluded that a formal delinquency label has no direct effect on self-concept. Leonard Gibbs (1974) compared the delinquent images and levels of self-esteem of a sample of 21 juveniles who had been arrested and subsequently referred to juvenile court for auto theft with a sample of 56 officially nondelinquent high school students. He found that the official delinquents looked on themselves as more delinquent after an arrest than after a court appearance. At both stages of processing, however, the official delinquents viewed themselves as more delinquent than the nondelinquents. With respect to self-esteem, Gibbs reported that the levels were higher after court processing, but not after arrest. Altogether, in five of eight comparisons the results ran counter to the assumptions of the labeling perspective.

In another comparative study, John Hepburn (1977) analyzed the self-concepts and attitudes of 105 nondelinquent males versus 96 officially delinquent (arrested) males. Hepburn found that the delinquents, compared to the nondelinquents, had greater definitions of themselves as delinquents and greater commitment to future delinquency and to delinquent others, but lower self-concepts and less respect for the police. However, when the effects of several variables were considered simultaneously, such as socioeconomic status and self-reported delinquency, it was found that an arrest record had no direct effect on self-concept or delinquent identification. Hepburn concluded that whatever association may exist between a formal label of delinquency and a negative or low self-concept is spurious, in that self-image is best explained by the overall situation of a juvenile's life, including his self-reported delinquency.

In spite of the somewhat negative impression one may have after a review of this literature, in terms of the validity of the labeling perspective, there have been some conclusions in support of labeling, particularly with respect to certain categories of juveniles (Jensen, 1972; Ageton and Elliott, 1974). Using the same data base as in Travis Hirschi's study, Gary Jensen (1972) found that among adolescent males official delinquency (as measured by police records) was much more strongly related to having a delinquent self-concept among whites than among African-Americans. Furthermore, the lack of a relationship among African-Americans between an official label and a delinquent self-concept persisted among all social class levels. Among African-Americans, Jensen concludes, an official label of delinquency might not carry much significance for a delinquent identity either because such labels are fairly common or because the label is applied by "outsiders" (see also, Gould, 1969).

On the assumption that a delinquent identity does not always mean a low self-esteem, Jensen also compared self-esteem with official delinquency, by race. This analysis showed no relationship at all, for either blacks or whites. However, the relationship did vary by social class among African-Americans. It was positive (the greater the official delinquency, the higher the self-esteem) among lower-class African-Americans but negative among middle- and upper-middle-class African-Americans. In this instance, Jensen argues, a delinquency label carries no negative value for lower-class blacks but is a stereotype that middle-class minorities wish to avoid or renounce.

Suzanne Ageton and Delbert Elliott (1974) extended Jensen's analysis by examining the relationship between official delinquency (police contact) and delinquent orientation over a six-year time period (the same data base used in the Elliott and Voss study discussed earlier). The authors concluded that a greater change toward a delinquency orientation, subsequent to police contact, occurred among males, both lower- and upper-class youths (which negated the effect of social class generally), and whites. Furthermore, Ageton and Elliott concluded that the *most* significant factor in the development of a delinquent orientation was police contact, as opposed to sex, class, and race. Even this conclusion must be tempered by the finding that the relationship between police contact and delinquent orientation, although statistically significant, was rather low.

In an effort to clarify the seeming contradictions of three earlier studies, Jensen (1980) reaffirmed his conclusion, and that of Ageton and Elliott, that official labels have more impact on the self-images and attitudes of those less heavily involved in delinquency. It may be that juveniles who have had previous contact with juvenile justice officials have come to terms with whatever effect such contact has upon their self-images. Future arrests or court appearances are thus unlikely to have a significant impact on a juvenile's self-concept, especially in comparison with youth who are arrested or sent to court for the first time.

Studies of those released from juvenile reformatories also report inconsistent findings relative to the effects of incarceration on self-concepts and attitudes. There is some evidence that suggests that a *treatment*-oriented institution is related to the development of *positive* self-images, while *custody*-oriented facilities tend to foster *negative* self-images and cynical attitudes toward staff members and authority figures in general (Street et al., 1966). Other studies, however, have not consistently documented any pronounced attitudinal or identity changes among youth as a result of confinement in juvenile detention centers or reformatories (Eynon and Simpson, 1965; O'Connor, 1970; Gibbons and Krohn, 1986), although the length of confinement in these institutions is, on average, less than one year (Children in Custody, 1985:6).

In summary, it is true that labeled delinquents do have negative or delinquent self-concepts (see Chapter 8) and that qualitative analyses suggest that such self-images are the product of official labeling. Quantitative analyses, however, have failed to confirm consistently the existence of measurable changes in identity or attitude as a result of official labeling, at any stage of processing. These studies do suggest, though, that the effects of official labeling that do exist are strongest among those least involved in delinquent activity (see also, Lipsitt, 1968; Snyder, 1971; Mahoney, 1974; Jensen and Rojek, 1992).

The studies thus far reported have not lent themselves to a careful comparison of the effects of official labeling on juveniles because they have been unable to take a cohort of youths and follow them up for a considerable period of time, including those years *before* they were labeled. To varying degrees, research has approximated this ideal design. Nonetheless, most studies have allowed for a "labeling effect" to appear more often than would a thorough longitudinal design. Given these circumstances, a truly inconsistent set of findings casts considerable doubt on the significance of formal labels on the identities and attitudes of juveniles.

Labeling and Delinquent Behavior   In Chapter 7, it was noted that a common finding in the literature on juvenile delinquency is the tendency for miscreant juveniles to become more conformist with age, to "mature out" of delinquency. Studies of juvenile arrests and referrals to juvenile court indicate that the peak age of delinquency is around 16 (Wolfgang et al., 1972; Smith et al., 1980). Marvin Wolfgang and co-workers (1972), for example, studied the arrest records of over 10,000 males born in 1945 who lived in Philadelphia between their 10th and 18th birthdays (a "cohort" study). They noted that nearly all arrest rates, for both whites and minorities, peaked at age 16 for both serious and nonserious offenses (see also, Tracy et al., 1990).

On the surface, it would appear that being arrested or sent to court would have only limited behavioral effects on delinquency, inasmuch as most official delinquents mature out of their law-breaking activities around the age of 16. The effects of an official label might be greatest, however, if applied early in a child's life. This view is consistent with the previous observation that official labeling is harsher among less-delinquent youth. It is also in agreement with the often-noted tendency for the rate of official delinquency to be inversely related to the age of the first official record of delinquency (Wolfgang et al., 1972; Tracy et al., 1990).

Of course, it is possible to argue, in support of labeling theory, that a small proportion of juveniles continue to violate the law in response to the problems of having a record of delinquency. Wolfgang's cohort study provides some support for this contention. Whereas half of the boys with an arrest record had been arrested only once, and many two or three times, a small group of "chronic offenders," defined as youths who had five arrests or more, was identified. While these boys represented only 18 percent of all those arrested, they accounted for over half of all the arrests (Wolfgang et al., 1972; see also, Shannon, 1982; Tracy et al., 1990). Attempts to connect the chronic offenders specifically with official labeling, however, proved inconclusive. An analysis of another cohort study, gathered from police records in Racine, Wisconsin, also concludes that arresting youth does not lead to the prevention of future arrests of these juveniles (Smith and Gartin, 1989). However, this study did uncover possible labeling effects when the official reactions to criminality included more severe actions, such as incarceration (p. 103).

Nonetheless, the authors note that the true effects of arrests, and other punitive responses to offending behavior, are difficult to assess when examining official records because "The inherent problem is that not all future offenses result in detection" (p. 102).

Additional research on the topic has yielded conflicting results. Some have found that juveniles who have been sent to court have lower rates of subsequent delinquency than those handled less formally (McEachern, 1968). Others have found that juveniles referred to court have higher subsequent rates of delinquency than others (Meade, 1974). Studies of those released from juvenile institutions indicate that about half (particularly males) violate parole or are referred to court within 12 to 15 months (Gibbons and Krohn 1986; Ohlin et al., n.d.). The rates for females, however, tend to be lower. These findings suggest that the behavioral effects of institutionalization are not pronounced, in any direction, at least for males.

Part of the reason for these inconsistent results is the fact that delinquency is indeed related to a host of factors other than official labels. In addition, as long as delinquent behavior is measured in terms of official records, the results are likely to be influenced by a self-fulfilling prophecy—in which the label generates a suspicion of future misdeeds, which leads to a higher probability of official processing, which affirms the original label, and so on.

Another consideration with respect to labeling is the subject of waiver, or transfer, of cases from juvenile court to criminal court. Presumably, the goal of such transfers is to punish youth in the criminal system, youth who might otherwise avoid punitive consequences in the juvenile system. Aside from the merits of such an assumption (Whitehead and Lab, 1999:221–222), another aspect of transfers is the impact such a decision has on the future behavior of those youth transferred to the criminal court system. Donna Bishop and colleagues studied the effect of transfers in Florida, using a comparative and longitudinal research design (Bishop et al., 1996). Over 2700 transferred youth were studied, and compared with a matched sample (in terms of criminal history and offense, age, and gender) of over 2700 juveniles whose cases were not waived to criminal court. Upon studying the records of these youth from 1987 through 1988, Bishop et al. concluded that those who were waived to criminal court were *more* delinquent than the nontransfers (pp. 179–183). The researchers speculated the increased recidivism (return to crime or delinquency) among the transferred youth might have been caused by feelings of unfair treatment by authorities (labeling?), but this conclusion can only be speculative, since the juveniles were not interviewed. A longer follow-up analysis indicated that rates of reoffending among both groups became more similar (Winner et al., 1997), but, still, the earlier impact of higher recidivism among the transferred youth lends support to labeling theory.

One way to offset the influences of the self-fulfilling prophecy is to examine the association between labeling and self-report delinquency. Such studies have often noted a small but direct relationship between official records of delinquency and the frequency or seriousness of self-reported delinquency (Williams and Gold, 1972; Elliott and Ageton, 1980; Hindelang et al., 1981). To some extent, therefore, those who are caught and labeled as delinquent are indeed already delinquent, by their own admission. The label may thus be as much a reaction to delinquent behavior as it is a cause of delinquency. The difficulty with accepting such assessments is, again, the fact that they are not based on longitudinal investigations that measure behavior *before* a label has been applied. Moreover, specific attempts to compare the subsequent self-reported delinquency of those who have been labeled delinquent versus those who have not been so labeled have yielded inconclusive results (Jensen and Rojek, 1992).

The conclusion with respect to the behavioral effects of labeling is essentially the same as with the attitudinal effects of labeling. That is, what results may develop are more likely to occur among originally less delinquent youth and are more likely if the label is applied earlier in life. Otherwise, a strong connection between officially labeling a juvenile a delinquent and subsequent delinquent behavior is unsubstantiated.

It is possible that the effects of labeling one a delinquent would not be noticeable over the short term, but would be more pronounced with repeated contacts with juvenile justice authorities over time (Klein, 1974; Thornton et al., 1982). In fact, this situation appears to be the contention of some of the earlier developers of labeling theory, such as Lemert and Becker. As indicated earlier, research that compares behavioral and attitudinal differences among juveniles who have reached various stages of juvenile justice processing would cast doubt on such a conclusion. Again, however, the issue would be better addressed with longitudinal research or by studying groups of youngsters over an extended period of time.[2]

Some efforts to assess self-reported attitudinal and behavioral consequences of labeling, both formal and informal, among youth in the general population have failed to establish clear support for the predictions of labeling theory (Thomas and Bishop, 1984; Ray and Downs, 1986). While both studies are termed longitudinal, they only cover a time span of one year. The study by Ray and Downs uses a small sample size (N = 188) and addresses only drug offenses. The results of this study, however, do report some evidence of secondary deviance among the males in the sample. The research by Thomas and Bishop is unable to separate the ordering of follow-up indications of delinquency and reported societal responses to previous reports of delinquent behavior.

Other longitudinal studies of self-reported delinquency, however, do provide evidence in support of labeling theory. Kaplan and associates, for example, have analyzed the impact of negative labeling in their longitudinal data concerning the integrated model of delinquency (see Chapter 8). The results of these analyses indicate that negative reactions from others are associated with feelings of self-rejection, dispositions toward deviance, associations with deviant peers, and self-reported delinquent and drug-use behavior (Kaplan and Johnson, 1991; Kaplan and Fukurai, 1992). In these analyses, negative reactions (or sanctions) include school expulsion or other punishments, run-ins with authority figures, and psychological or psychiatric referrals. While the data do not clearly demonstrate that self-rejection is a direct consequence of these sanctions, the strength of the statistical relationships and the temporal ordering of the variables in the explanatory model suggest that this is the case.

Matsueda (1992) offers additional support for the impact of negative sanctions on self-appraisals and subsequent delinquency, also using data from a longitudinal self-report study of delinquency (the National Youth Survey). In Matsueda's analysis, the focus is on negative labeling from *parents*. One of the conclusions is that such labels are strongly connected with negative self-appraisals and with delinquency, particularly among those youth who report high levels of delinquency. These associations occur despite the rather modest measurement of parental labels (essentially asking parents to agree or disagree with statements concerning whether their child is well liked, distressed, is likely to be a success, or gets into trouble). While these results offer some support for labeling theory, Matsueda also suggests that delinquency among youth may lead to parental alienation, which leads to more delinquent behavior. Or a criminal parent may see a child as antisocial or as a trouble-maker, and withhold affection, thereby contributing to future delinquency by the youth. Both of these scenarios, moreover, could occur without the child reevaluating his or her self-image, or the reactions of others (p. 1604), and both suggest a weakened social bond between parent and child as an important contributing factor in the explanation of delinquency (see also, Triplett and Jarjoura, 1994).

Additional analyses of the National Youth Survey data by Heimer and Matsueda (1994) conclude that the effects of labeling, by parents, teachers, and others, are transformed into additional acts of crime and delinquency by youth taking the roles of deviant actors; that is, by behaving in accordance with the presumed role(s) associated with a label of deviant or delinquent. These role-taking behaviors, or "reflected appraisals," furthermore, may be influenced by gender identities of youth. In particular, Bartusch and Matsueda (1996) conclude that the negative impact of informal labels is more pronounced among males than among females, particularly for males who identify with a male gender. Perhaps this is another way of expressing the adage, "boys will be boys." In this scenario, however, boys who think of themselves as boys will act as they feel boys should act, especially when parents and other significant others around them label them as delinquent or troublemakers.

The tendency for negative labels to lead to increased delinquent behavior may also be influenced by associations with delinquent peers (Adams, 1996), which is the heart of differential association theory (Chapter 7). In this case, however, the causal arrow points to the impact of informal labels on one's peer associations, which then affect delinquency.

SUMMARY

The significance of labeling juveniles as delinquent appears to be questionable, as far as subsequent identities and behavior are concerned. The rapid rise in the popularity of labeling theory during the 1960s perhaps reflects more the dissatisfaction among social scientists and criminologists with extant explanations of deviance and criminality than the validity of the labeling perspective's assumptions. In this period, assumptions were accepted without careful empirical examination. Subsequent analyses, however, have cast doubt on the validity of many of those assumptions.

In retrospect, the view that a label creates behavior appears oversimplified. While it is true that many of the assumptions of the more popular theories of delinquency are not empirically supported, the alternate view proposed by labeling theorists is also not supported.

The assumptions of the labeling perspective, however, are not totally indefensible. Several studies, both qualitative and quantitative, suggest the existence of an effect of official labels on delinquent identities and behavior. In addition, research indicates a relatively strong effect of official labels among those less committed to antisocial behavior at the time the label was applied, and this would be truer of juveniles than of adult criminals. Furthermore, most of these conditions have been assessed relative to *official* labels. Had unofficial labels been more thoroughly examined, it is possible that the changes would have been more pronounced (see also, Mahoney, 1974; Paternoster and Iovanni, 1989). Some of the more recent research seems to be addressing the impact of these informal labels, and the results are encouraging for the proponents of labeling theory. Even these studies, however, include the negative impact of labeling along with other, often more important, connecting variables in the explanation of delinquency (see also, Rosenbaum, 1989).

The arguments of labeling theorists have provided important issues and views concerning the understanding of delinquency. The somewhat negative overall assessment of this theory, however, stems primarily from the inconsistent results that have been derived from research so designed as to reveal even weak labeling effects. Although such effects obviously occur, they are neither as inevitable nor as dramatic as the assumptions of the theory would predict.[3]

Notes

1. To some, the views of this approach are not accepted as a "theory" but, instead, as a perspective or an orientation. Using the definition of theory given in Chapter 1, however, the assumptions of "labeling" are within the realm of a theory and thus to call this approach a theory is appropriate for the purposes of this book.

2. The obverse of labeling theory would lead one to expect lower recidivism rates among offenders who are reintegrated into the community, rather than pushed away from interactions with "conformists." Braithwaite argues that shaming can be an important part of successful rehabilitative efforts, if incorporated into an overall theme of reintegration (1989). Braithwaite and Mugford (1994) offer support for this conceptualization in an observational analysis of "reintegrative ceremonies" for juvenile offenders in Australia and New Zealand. However, other investigations and analyses raise issues and considerations, including societal and judicial acceptance of shaming, which question the potential efficacy of reintegrative efforts, in Western nations or in Asian societies, such as Hong Kong (Bazemore, 1998; Schiff, 1998; Vagg, 1998).

3. A discussion of many of the issues and research directions concerning labeling theory is found in Wellford and Triplett (1993).

References

Adams, Mike S., 1996, "Labeling and Differential Association: Towards a General Social Learning Theory of Crime and Deviance." American Journal of Criminal Justice 20:147–164.

Ageton, Suzanne, and Delbert Elliott, 1974, "The Effects of Legal Processing on Self-Concept." Social Problems 22:87–100.

Bartusch, Dawn Jeglum and Ross L. Matsueda, 1996, "Gender, Reflected Appraisals, and Labeling: A Cross-Group Test of an Interactionist Theory of Delinquency." Social Forces 75:145–177.

Bazemore, Gordon, 1998, "Crime, Victims and Restorative Justice in Juvenile Courts: Judges as Obstacle or Leader?" Western Criminology Review 1 (1) [Online]. Available: http://wcr.sonoma.edu/v1n1/bazemore.html.

Becker, Howard S., 1973, Outsiders. New York: Free Press. Originally published in 1963.

Bishop, Donna M., Charles E. Frazier, Lonn Lanza-Kaduce, and Lawrence Winner, 1996, "The Transfer of Juveniles to Criminal Court: Does It Make a Difference?" Crime & Delinquency 42: 171–191.

Braithwaite, John, 1989, Crime, Shame and Reintegration. Cambridge: Cambridge University Press.

Braithwaite, John and Stephen Mugford, 1994, "Conditions of Successful Reintegration Ceremonies." British Journal of Criminology 34:139–171.

Chambliss, William, 1973, "The Saints and the Roughnecks." Society 11:24–31.

Children in Custody, 1985. Washington, D.C.: U.S. Government Printing Office.

Cicourel, Aaron, 1976, The Social Organization of Juvenile Justice, second edition. New York: Wiley.

Cooley, Charles Horton, 1964, Human Nature and the Social Order. New York: Schocken. Originally published in 1902.

Dotter, Daniel L. and Julian B. Roebuck, 1988, "The Labeling Approach Re-Examined: Interactionism and the Components of Deviance." Deviant Behavior 9:19–32.

Elliott, Delbert S. and Suzanne S. Ageton, 1980, "Reconciling Race and Class Differences in Self-Reported and Official Estimates of Delinquency." American Sociological Review 45:95–110.

Emerson, Robert M., 1969, Judging Delinquents. Chicago: Aldine.

Eynon, Thomas G. and Jon E. Simpson, 1965, "The Boy's Perception of Himself in a State Training School for Delinquents." Social Service Review 39:31–37.

Foster, Jack D., Simon Dinitz, and Walter C. Reckless, 1972, "Perceptions of Stigma Following Public Intervention for Delinquent Behavior." Social Problems 20:202–209.

Gibbons, Don C. and Marvin D. Krohn, 1986, Delinquent Behavior, fourth edition. Englewood Cliffs, N.J.: Prentice-Hall.

Gibbs, Jack P., 1966, "Conceptions of Deviant Behavior: The Old and the New." Pacific Sociological Review 9:9–14.

Gibbs, Leonard, E., 1974, "Effects of Juvenile Legal Procedures on Juvenile Offenders' Self-Attitudes." Journal of Research in Crime and Delinquency 11:51–55.

Giordano, Peggy C., 1976, "The Sense of Injustice? An Analysis of Juveniles' Reactions to the Justice System." Criminology 14:93–112.

Gould, Leroy C., 1969, "Who Defines Delinquency? A Comparison of Self-Reported and Officially Reported Indices of Delinquency for Three Racial Groups." Social Problems 16:325–336.

Gove, Walter R. (ed.), 1980a, The Labeling of Deviance, second edition. Beverly Hills, Calif.: Sage.

———, 1980b, "The Labeling Perspective: An Overview." Pp. 9–26 in Walter R. Gove (ed.), q.v.

Heimer, Karen and Ross L. Matsueda, 1994, "Role-Taking, Role Commitment, and Delinquency: A Theory of Differential Social Control." American Sociological Review 59:365–390.

Hepburn, John R., 1977, "The Impact of Police Intervention upon Juvenile Delinquents." Criminology 15:235–262.

Hindelang, Michael, Travis Hirschi, and Joseph G. Weis, 1981, Measuring Delinquency. Beverly Hills, Calif.: Sage.

Hirschi, Travis, 1980, "Labeling Theory and Juvenile Delinquency: An Assessment of the Evidence: Postscript." Pp. 271–302 in Walter R. Gove (ed.), q.v.

Jensen, Gary F., 1972, "Delinquency and Adolescent Self-Conceptions: A Study of the Personal Relevance of Infraction." Social Problems 20:84–103.

———, 1980, "Labeling and Identity: Toward a Reconciliation of Divergent Findings." Criminology 18:121–129.

Jensen, Gary F. and Dean G. Rojek, 1992, Delinquency and Youth Crime, second edition. Prospect Heights, Ill.: Waveland.

Kaplan, Howard B. and Hiroshi Fukurai, 1992, "Negative Social Sanctions, Self-Rejection, and Drug Use." Youth & Society 23:275–298.

Kaplan, Howard B. and Robert J. Johnson, 1991, "Negative Social Sanctions and Juvenile Delinquency: Effects of Labeling in a Model of Deviant Behavior." Social Science Quarterly 72:98–122.

Kitsuse, John I., 1980, "The 'New Conception of Deviance' and Its Critics." Pp. 381–392 in Walter R. Gove (ed.), q.v.

Klein, Malcolm W., 1974, "Labeling, Deterrence, and Recidivism: A Study of Police Dispositions of Juvenile Offenders." Social Problems 22:292–303.

Lemert, Edwin M., 1951, Social Pathology. New York: McGraw-Hill.

———, 1974, "Beyond Mead: The Societal Reaction to Deviance." Social Problems 21:457–468.

Lipsitt, Paul, 1968, "The Juvenile Offender's Perception." Crime & Delinquency 14:49–62.

Mahoney, Anne R., 1974, "The Effect of Labeling upon Youths in the Juvenile Justice System: A Review of the Evidence." Law & Society Review 8:583–614.

Matsueda, Ross L., 1992, "Reflected Appraisals, Parental Labeling, and Delinquency: Specifying a Symbolic Interactionist Theory." American Journal of Sociology 97:1577–1611.

McEachern, A. W. (ed.), 1968, "The Juvenile Probation System: Simulation for Research and Decision-Making." American Behavioral Scientist 11:1–48.

Meade, Anthony C., 1974, "The Labeling Approach to Delinquency: State of the Theory as a Function of Method." Social Forces 53:83–91.

Montanino, Fred, 1977, "Directions in the Study of Deviance: A Bibliographic Essay, 1960–1977." Pp. 277–304 in Edward Sagarin (ed.), Deviance and Social Change. Beverly Hills, Calif.: Sage.

O'Connor, Gerald G., 1970, "The Impact of Initial Detention upon Male Delinquents." Social Problems 18:194–199.

Ohlin, Lloyd E., Alden D. Miller, and Robert B. Coates, n.d., Juvenile Correctional Reform in Massachusetts. Washington, D.C.: U.S. Government Printing Office.

Paternoster, Raymond and Lee Ann Iovanni, 1989, "The Labeling Perspective and Delinquency: An Elaboration of the Theory and Assessment of the Evidence." Justice Quarterly 6:359–394.

Ray, Melvin C. and William R. Downs, 1986, "An Empirical Test of Labeling Theory Using Longitudinal Data." Journal of Research in Crime and Delinquency 23:169–194.

Rosenbaum, Jill Leslie, 1989, "Family Dysfunction and Female Delinquency." Crime & Delinquency 35:31–44.

Rosenberg, Morris, 1979, Conceiving the Self. New York: Basic Books.

Sagarin, Edward, 1969, Odd Man In. Chicago: Quadrangle.

———, 1975, Deviants and Deviance. New York: Prager.

Schiff, Mara F., 1998, "Restorative Justice Interventions for Juvenile Offenders: A Research Agenda for the Next Decade." Western Criminology Review 1 (1) [Online]. Available: http://wcr.sonoma.edu/v1n1/schiff.html.

Schur, Edwin M., 1971, Labeling Deviant Behavior. New York: Harper & Row.

Shannon, Lyle, 1982, Assessing the Relationship of Adult Criminal Careers to Juvenile Careers: A Summary. Washington, D.C.: U.S. Department of Justice.

Smith, Daniel D., Terrence Finnegan, and Howard N. Snyder, 1980, Delinquency 1977: United States Estimates of Cases Processed by Courts with Juvenile Jurisdiction. Pittsburgh, Pa.: National Center for Juvenile Justice.

Smith, Douglas A. and Patrick R. Gartin, 1989, "Specifying Specific Deterrence: The Influence of Arrest on Future Criminal Activity," American Sociological Review 54:94–106.

Snyder, Eloise C., 1971, "The Impact of the Juvenile Court Hearing on the Child." Crime & Delinquency 17:180–190.

Strauss, Anselm (ed.), 1964, George Herbert Mead on Social Psychology: Selected Papers. Chicago: University of Chicago Press. First published in 1934.

Street, David, Robert D. Vinter, and Charles Perrow, 1966, Organization for Treatment. New York: Free Press.

Tannenbaum, Frank, 1938, Crime and the Community. New York: Ginn and Company.

Thomas, Charles W. and Donna M. Bishop, 1984, "The Effect of Formal and Informal Sanctions on Delinquency: A Longitudinal Comparison of Labeling and Deterrence Theories." Criminology 75:1222–1245.

Thornton, William E., Jennifer A. James, and William G. Doerner, 1982, Delinquency and Justice. Glenview, Ill.: Scott, Foresman.

Thorsell, Bernard A. and Lloyd W. Klemke, 1972, "The Labeling Process: Reinforcement or Deterrent?" Law & Society Review 6:393–403.

Thrasher, Frederick M., 1927, The Gang. Chicago: University of Chicago Press.

Tracy, Paul E., Marvin E. Wolfgang, and Robert M. Figlio, 1990, Delinquency Careers in Two Birth Cohorts. New York: Plenum.

Trice, Harrison M. and Paul Michael Roman, 1970, "Delabeling, Relabeling, and Alcoholics Anonymous." Social Problems 17:538–546.

Triplett, Ruth A. and G. Roger Jarjoura, 1994, "Theoretical and Empirical Specification of a Model of Informal Labeling." Journal of Quantitative Criminology 10:241–276.

Vagg, Jon, 1998, "Delinquency and Shame: Data from Hong Kong." British Journal of Criminology 38:247–264.

Wellford, Charles F. and Ruth A. Triplett, 1993, "The Future of Labeling Theory: Foundations and Promises." Pp. 1–22 in Freda Adler and William S. Laufer (eds.), New Directions in Criminological Theory. New Brunswick, N.J.: Transaction.

Werthman, Carl, 1970, "The Function of Social Definitions in the Development of Delinquent Careers." Pp. 9–44 in Peter G. Garabedian and Don C. Gibbons (eds.), Becoming Delinquent. Chicago: Aldine.

Whitehead, John T. and Steven P. Lab, 1999, Juvenile Justice, third edition. Cincinnati: Anderson.

Williams, Jay R. and Martin Gold, 1972, "From Delinquent Behavior to Official Delinquency." Social Problems 20:209–229.

Winner, Lawrence T., Lonn Lanza-Kaduce, Donna M. Bishop, and Charles E. Frazier, 1997, "The Transfer of Juveniles to Criminal Court: Re-Examining Recidivism over the Long Term." Crime & Delinquency 43:548–563.

Wolfgang, Marvin E., Robert M. Figlio, and Thorsten Sellin, 1972, Delinquency in a Birth Cohort. Chicago: University of Chicago Press.

10

The Radical Theory
of Delinquency

HISTORICAL OVERVIEW

The radical theory of criminality argues that criminal behavior is a result of the repressive efforts of the ruling class to control the subject class. The effects of this repression are not only higher instances of crime and delinquency among the subjugated class (the lower class, generally), but also greater tendencies among the middle and upper classes to label the actions of the lower class as criminal in order to facilitate their control. Basically, this view is a more specific statement of a general conflict interpretation of criminality (see Lynch and Groves, 1986).

A conflict perspective of society stresses the existence of different value systems and norms that influence the efforts of people to establish rules and to regulate behavior. This perspective, as it relates to criminal and delinquent behavior, is implied or incorporated in the theories of Shaw and McKay, Merton, Sellin, and Sutherland (see Chapters 5 and 7). In addition to these contributions, others have developed theories of crime and delinquency that are conflict oriented. George Vold (1979), for example, notes that laws are passed in response to the struggles of competing interest groups. Furthermore, he contends that some criminal behaviors are committed in accordance with norms that were previously acceptable, but that have become illegal because of the successful efforts of competing interest groups.

Austin Turk (1969) contends that value conflicts can influence the eventual identification of one as a criminal or delinquent, particularly if the conflicts appear threatening to society's officials. This theory basically places the significance of value conflicts at the point of interaction between citizens and authority figures. Turk argues that among the groups most likely to be identified as delinquent are the juvenile gangs, because they are likely to be in open conflict with the police who often perceive the juveniles' behavior as threatening and hostile.

Another aspect of conflict theory is included in the assumptions of labeling theory (see Chapter 9). One part of labeling theory is conflict oriented—the aspect that examines the reasons why some individuals are labeled as criminals or delinquents and others are not, when both sets of people have committed essentially the same acts (see also, Meier, 1980).

Most conflict theories of crime and delinquency assume that laws are developed and enforced because some people have a virtual monopoly on power and others are essentially powerless (Quinney, 1970; Chambliss, 1974). The nature of power conflicts is variously interpreted. The development of radical theory is seen by some as the culmination of thinking that views delinquency in terms of rule making and enforcement rather than as an individualistic tendency (Empey, 1982). Radical theory differs from other conflict theories in that it proposes that capitalism is the root cause of much criminal behavior, particularly that committed by the lower class. As such, the proper solution to the problem of crime is to eliminate capitalism and replace it with something more socialistic; to some, a radical solution indeed. The economic emphasis of radical theory is associated with Karl Marx and, accordingly, some argue that this approach should be called "Marxist" (a view which will be challenged later in this chapter).

The somewhat recent popularity of this perspective stems from the persistence of social ills, such as war, racism, poverty, social unrest, political and governmental corruption, and urban decay, which have plagued America and other Western societies for decades. The persistence and exacerbation of these problems, it is argued, have created a "crisis of legitimacy" in America that has promoted a fertile atmosphere for the growth of a radical perspective on crime and social problems in general (Sykes, 1974; Meier, 1980; Empey, 1982). But this does not mean that Marxist theories of crime are recent innovations; in fact, they were proposed in the early part of this century by Willem Bonger (1916).

Basic Assumptions[1]

The first and foremost assumption of the radical approach to delinquency is that most behavior is the product of a struggle among the classes within society, particularly between those who own the tools of production (the bourgeoisie) and those who do not (the proletariat).

Second, radical theory assumes that the economic system of capitalism is primarily responsible for the class divisions within society.

Third, it assumes that the bourgeoisie, either directly or through its agents, such as the State, controls the proletariat, economically, institutionally, or legally. For example, the occupational choices, educational opportunities, familial arrangements, and legality of customs and behavior among the proletariat are controlled by the bourgeoisie in order to protect the interests of the ruling class and to keep the proletariat in a subordinate position in society.

A fourth assumption of this theory is that most official crime and delinquency is committed by the lower and working classes as a form of accommodation to the restraints placed on them by the bourgeoisie. In addition, some "criminal" acts of the proletariat are artifactual judgments imposed by the agents of the bourgeoisie to keep certain people or certain situations under control.

Figure 13 schematically illustrates the assumptions of radical theory.

Key Concepts

Class Conflict   While Marx and the radical criminologists indict capitalism as the root of most criminality, the major concept in this view of delinquency is class conflict, based on economic considerations. Without this conflict, and the attendant efforts of the bourgeois class to protect its interests, criminal behavior among the proletariat would not be necessary, either as a response of accommodation or as a mechanism of bourgeois control.

Surplus Labor   A second key concept in this perspective is surplus labor, the major instrument by which the ruling class in a capitalist society exploits the working, propertyless classes. Essentially, it is argued that a worker's labor produces a greater value in goods than the wage earned for work. The capitalist, or employer, can use the laborer to produce commodities whose value far exceeds the cost to the employer of the laborer's work (the wages). The capitalist can thus accumulate greater amounts of wealth with limited investment or risk. Laborers, if they are to work at all, must work the amount of hours assigned to them by their capitalist employers. Those hours employees are

The economic system of capitalism	→	Class divisions and struggles	→	Overt and covert attempts of the ruling class (bourgeoisie) to control the powerless class (proletariat)	→	Delinquency, either in the form of accommodations to bourgeois controls or the direct "criminalization" of certain norms and behavior

Figure 13

required to work over and above what is needed to replace their wages are called surplus labor. Surplus labor is one means by which the capitalist exploits the working class (Marx, 1950b; Hirst, 1975; Gintis, 1976).

Discussion

Although the radical perspective draws heavily on the ideas of Karl Marx, it would be inaccurate to characterize all of the assumptions listed above as purely Marxist for the simple fact that Marx himself had little to say about the subjects of crime and delinquency. As a matter of fact, Marx classified most criminals as "lumpenproletarians," or the "dangerous class," the déclassé "scum" who had abdicated their class positions and could not be counted on for revolutionary purposes (Marx and Engels, 1950; Marx, 1950a, c). Criminals, in other words, had little place in Marx's heart or in his visions of a just society. For this reason it would be more appropriate to refer to radical theory as *neo-Marxist* (Friedrichs, 1980a).[2]

Borrowing, then, from some of the tenets of Marx, radical criminologists have built a number of theoretically important statements concerning the issue of criminality in capitalist societies. Notable among these efforts is the work of William Chambliss (1975), who lists a "Marxian paradigm" of propositions concerning crime and the law. The paradigm is divided into three sections: the nature of criminal law, the consequences of crime for society, and the causes of criminal behavior. Each section contains three propositions. An example of a proposition concerning the nature of criminal law is, "As capitalist societies industrialize and the gap between the bourgeoisie and the proletariat widens, penal law will expand in an effort to coerce the proletariat into submission." On the consequences of crime for society, Chambliss proposes that, "Crime diverts the lower class's attention from the exploitation they experience, and directs it toward other members of their own class rather than toward the capitalist class or the economic system." With regard to the causes of crime, Chambliss argues that "Criminal and non-criminal behavior stem from people acting rationally in ways that are compatible with their class position. Crime is a reaction to the life conditions of a person's social class" (1975:152–153).

Richard Quinney, well known for his contributions to the radical perspective, discusses in *Class, State, and Crime* (1980) both the basic reasons for criminality among the oppressed and the injustices committed by, or in the name of, the capitalist (ruling) class against the noncapitalist classes.

Utilizing this framework, Quinney envisions two broad categories of criminality: crimes of domination and repression and crimes of accommodation and resistance. Crimes of domination and repression are committed by agents of the capitalist class to keep this class in a position of supremacy. Thus, crime control policies of the government serve to criminalize those of the working class who appear to threaten the existing order. These agencies may even break the law in order to obtain the more important goal of maintaining order (crimes of control and crimes of government). In addition, Quinney argues that the domination of the noncapitalist classes occurs through the manipulation of criminal values to the extent that those in the working class accept as legitimate the very laws and policies established to control *them*. Finally, under crimes of domination and repression, Quinney lists crimes of economic domination. Examples of these crimes include the white-collar offenses, environmental pollution, and organized crime, which is joined with the interests of the capitalists in preserving the capitalist system.

Crimes of accommodation and resistance are crimes committed mainly by the working class in order to survive the repressive and oppressive tactics of the capitalist class. Included in this category of crimes are predatory (economically oriented) crimes, such as burglary, robbery, and drug dealing. Second, there are the personal crimes of murder, assault, and rape, which are typically committed against members of the same class and not specifically against the capitalist system. In addition, Quinney lists crimes of clandestine assembly-line sabotage, political resistance, and open rebellion, committed by the working class as a means of resisting the control efforts of the capitalist class.

To Quinney and other Marxist criminologists (Spitzer, 1975), an inherent characteristic of capitalism is the existence of contradictions, stemming basically from the problem of surplus labor. Capitalism, it is argued, cannot create a situation in which the value of human labor is consonant with the needs of the capitalists. Consequently, "problem populations" emerge that must be continually guarded and controlled. This concern over problem populations creates among capitalists a greater dependence on the State and numerous social institutions to handle and control these people. Over time, the State assumes a major role in the criminalization of the working class and the management of those institutions established to control legally those of the working class (Gordon, 1973; Quinney, 1980). Quinney (1979) also argues that even criminologists have been co-opted by the State in the study and control of crime among lower-class people.

The contradictions of capitalism continue to grow as capitalism advances. Even the institutions designed to handle the problem populations for the ruling class begin to develop their own identities and functions, which are not always identical with the interests of capitalism and which further add to the problems and contradictions of capitalism (Spitzer, 1975). In addition, the growth of problem populations in advanced capitalism extends the oppressed or ruled classes to include even the petty bourgeoisie, such as professionals and middle-management bureaucrats (Quinney, 1980).

Not all spokespersons for the radical perspective, of course, agree on every point regarding crime and delinquency (Friedrichs, 1980b). David Gordon (1973), for example, argues that basic institutions within capitalist societies must be altered substantially if crime is to be prevented. While he contends that capitalism is the fundamental cause of crime, the system is so entrenched in society that its abolition cannot be a realistic mechanism of crime prevention. Instead, the institutions that serve capitalism must be changed to serve the needs of all the people. Gordon suggests that a "Family Model of the Criminal Process" (1973:185) be considered in which the criminal is viewed as a transgressor of family rules and trust. The proper response would be a loving, supportive concern for the well-being of the transgressor, a response designed not only to admonish and correct the offender, but also to examine the family's contribution to his or her misdeeds.

Steven Spitzer (1975) contends that the transformation of a "bothersome population" into a group deemed in need of control is neither a simple nor an automatic process. Instead, the transformation depends on a variety of situations and circumstances that involve both the control system and the potential target population, such as the relative power of the State in the control system, the perceived size and degree of threat of the population, the degree of organization of this population, the availability and effectiveness of alternatives to control and domination, and the utility of the problem population to the capitalist system.

Evaluation

As Ronald Akers suggests (1979), the evaluation of the radical perspective must carefully distinguish between the *theory* of Marx and the *ideology* of Marxist philosophy. It is sometimes difficult to distinguish between what is thought to be an observation of the societal contributions to crime and a description of what societal conditions *ought* to be relative to crime. Moreover, in some treatises, the topic of crime becomes secondary to the issues of humanitarianism and human rights and how these relate to capitalism and socialism (Taylor et al., 1973). In an earlier edition of *Class, State, and Crime,* for example, Quinney (1977) concludes his discussion with the statement, "We are engaged in socialist revolution" (1977:165). In other words, capitalism must be destroyed and the contradictory and unjust way in which criminality is handled in capitalist societies is just another reason why capitalism should be eliminated.

If one concentrates on the social theory of Marx as it pertains to criminality, two fairly distinct issues emerge: (1) how capitalism contributes to criminality, especially among the lower classes, and (2) how capitalist interests are served by the identification and legal control of individuals, groups, or social categories of people.

The influence of capitalism and the capitalist class on crime and delinquency rests largely on the assumption that delinquency is a lower-class phenomenon (Klockars, 1979). To reiterate a point made in Chapter 6, evidence points to a significant amount of delinquency among youth from lower *and* middle social classes (see also, Schwendinger and Schwendinger, 1976), although delinquency among lower-class youth seems to be relatively more violent, and probably committed by a small segment of young males. The existence of middle- or upper-middle-class delinquency creates a problem for the argument that class-based conflicts and oppressions generate criminality within the subordinate or powerless class. If the ruling class creates the rules and determines the economic course of society, how is it that some (perhaps many) of those in the ruling class themselves resort to crime and delinquency? If it is assumed that greed and conflict among the bourgeoisie contribute to their criminality, then the same *intraclass* factors may be presumed to operate on the proletariat as well. Attempts to expand the definition of the oppressed class to include all but a very few members of society in effect explain nothing from a class standpoint, because the variation among classes has been virtually eliminated.[3]

The focus of the radical perspective on the economic domination of the lower class has been previously discussed under the topic of delinquency and opportunity (Chapter 6). To restate the general conclusion of that discussion, evidence demonstrating the influence of economic issues and concerns on *delinquent* behavior is at best inconsistent and often weak. Juveniles are concerned with many other things, besides their economic position in society, including personal status among peers, school status, and parental relationships. It may be the case that modern youth are becoming more pragmatic and economically motivated than their counterparts in previous generations. This possibility is in need of further investigation. If children and adolescents are becoming more economically oriented, however, the relationship between delinquency and social class position would not necessarily be better interpreted from a radical perspective. It might be, for example, that strain theories, such as Cloward and Ohlin's differential opportunity thesis, would best explain delinquency. Perhaps new theories would have to be formulated if it were found that pragmatism and economic concerns characterized youth from all social class levels.

In addition, some, such as Duster (1987), Oliver (1989), Irvine (1990), and West (1993) maintain that school failure, social problems, unemployment, and criminality are connected with racial identities and experiences, not necessarily with social class. Of course, these observations concerning the impact of race and ethnicity, compared to social class, on identities and patterns of criminality, do not completely negate the tenets of radical theory. However, it is becoming increasingly clear that society operates on a much more complicated system of social patterning than is depicted in neo-Marxist theories of crime and delinquency.

Not all of the advocates of the radical perspective feel that capitalism has a direct economic effect on delinquency. Some find that capitalism exerts numerous indirect effects on delinquency by directly affecting the social institutions that influence the lives of juveniles (Schwendinger and Schwendinger, 1976; Liazos, 1979). David Greenberg (1977) suggests that the age structure of capitalist societies results in depressed economic opportunities for juveniles. At the same time, the period of adolescence is stressful on peer relations, and the inability in essence to "buy" friends and good times forces many juveniles to steal. In addition, stigmatizing school experiences and degrading work opportunities (among the few jobs which are available) are particularly focused on working- and lower-class youth, creating even greater incentives for delinquency among these adolescents in capitalist societies.

The importance of institutional factors in the explanation of delinquency has already been examined (see Chapter 8). Indeed, such factors do have considerable influence on delinquency and their incorporation into radical theory is laudable. The contention that adolescence is a period of status anxiety and peer concern, however, is hardly novel, nor is it *necessarily* linked to capitalism (a point which Greenberg himself makes; Greenberg, 1977). Similarly, the connection between capitalism and degrading school experiences, mentioned earlier, has been neither logically nor empirically demonstrated. Thus, Greenberg's ideas are somewhat accurate, but their connection with capitalism is tenuous at best.

In summary, the connection between capitalism and delinquency is questionable because of several factors: (1) the existence of widespread delinquency among middle- and upper-middle-class juveniles; (2) the relative lack of concern for economic and workforce status among juveniles; (3) the influence of racial and ethnic factors, as opposed to social class variables, on crime and deviance; and (4) the lack of a necessary connection between capitalism per se and institutional or demographic conditions within a society.

The second point raised in radical theory is the influence of the capitalist, ruling, upper class (the exact composition of this class is not universally accepted) on the identification or handling of the lower or oppressed classes.[4] This topic has been investigated from two general approaches: historical analysis and contemporary investigations of juvenile justice decisions. Historically, several observations have indicated the influence of middle-class values and capitalistic interests in the establishment of the juvenile court and the philosophy of juvenile justice in eighteenth- and nineteenth-century America (Platt, 1974; Schwendinger and Schwendinger, 1976; Platt, 1977; Krisberg and Austin, 1978). Anthony Platt (1977) further indicates that the values of middle-class housewives heavily influenced policies and legislation affecting juvenile delinquents in the nineteenth century.

The accounts of these developments, however, do not demonstrate that ruling-class interests were the only considerations involved in the development of a juvenile justice system. A term often applied to mid-nineteenth-century juvenile reform efforts is the "Child-Saving Movement" (Platt, 1977; Krisberg and Austin, 1978). Although Platt and others debate the issue, it seems reasonable that some of the motivations of these reforms were aimed at humanitarian accomplishments in addition to, or apart from, the protection of middle- and upper-class interests (see also, Mennel, 1973).[5]

Lamar Empey (1982) asserts that the concept of childhood preceded the invention of delinquency (see also, Ariès, 1962). The modern concept of childhood embodies sentiments of fragility and innocence, yet arrogance and susceptibility. This view of the child, according to Empey, gradually emerged over many centuries and was influenced by the events of "the Renaissance, the Protestant Reformation, the colonization of the New World, and eventually the Industrial Revolution" (Empey, 1982:38). Moreover, the specific influences that led to the creation of the legal concept of delinquency in 1899 included a host of factors besides those of economics and social class. Empey indicates that religious (particularly Puritan) influences were most important in nineteenth-century reform efforts, which eventually led to the development of separate confinement facilities and legal proceedings for children (see also, Rothman, 1971). Furthermore, changes in attitudes and in family and community structures in the aftermath of the Declaration of Independence also contributed heavily to the separate confinement of juveniles and to creation of the juvenile court.

Moreover, an examination of the development of delinquency legislation in Canada concluded that the emergence of probation agencies was more responsible for this legislation than the contradictions of capitalism or the political maneuverings of a ruling class (Hagan and Leon, 1977).

At best, therefore, it would seem that a neo-Marxist historical view of delinquency is incomplete and only partially valid. Of course, class divisions exist in society. It is also certain that some laws are enacted to protect interests that may be identified with certain social class positions. To contend that class factors influence the making of all laws, or even the bulk of them, however, is assuming something that has yet to be conclusively demonstrated.

Contemporary studies of the processing of delinquents by police and court officials also yield limited support for the neo-Marxist approach. The significance of social class in the decisions of these officials is questionable. There is some evidence that social class does indeed exert an influence on the official handling of juveniles (Thornberry, 1973; McCarthy and Smith, 1986; Sampson, 1986), particularly when social class is measured according to the *perceptions* of juvenile justice officials (Carter, 1979) or when the type of delinquency under consideration involves moral or status offenses (Carter and Clelland, 1979).

Many studies, however, have found that social class has little significance on the official handling of juveniles, especially in comparison to variables such as offense severity and number of prior offenses (Arnold, 1971; Scarpitti and Stephenson, 1971; Thomas and Sieverdes, 1975; Cohen and Kluegel, 1978; Johnstone, 1978; Hindelang et al., 1979; Sieverdes et al., 1979; Horwitz and Wasserman, 1980).

Besides the importance of offense-related variables in the handling of juveniles, some investigations have pointed to the influence of other non-offense-related factors besides social class. Studies of police decisions have often indicated that situational, "curbside" considerations and departmental norms and regulations have an influence on the processing of juveniles (Piliavin and Briar, 1964; Black and Reiss, 1970; Weiner and Willie, 1971; Lundman et al., 1978). Donald Black and Albert Reiss (1970) maintain that what might appear to be racial (and to some extent class) discrimination on the part of the police is actually a reflection of the complainant's visible preference for the police to make an arrest. The preference for police action, furthermore, is greater among African-American complainants, who are more often victimized by black juveniles than by white youth. This study was replicated several years later in another location, and the results were the same (Lundman et al., 1978).

The importance of juvenile court norms and organizational procedures on the processing of youth was mentioned in the previous chapter. Additional research indicates that juvenile court judges are strongly influenced by the recommendations of the caseworkers working with the court (Kraus, 1975; Warner, 1981), and the recommendations of these officers are not necessarily associated with the social class of the juveniles referred to court.

Bortner (1984) places most of this literature, and the surrounding controversies, in perspective by noting that much of what is decided in the juvenile justice system, especially the juvenile court system, is individualized according to the specifics of a case, and individual stereotypes of decision makers (pp. 243–249). In an analysis of the processing of youth in one juvenile court system, Bortner offers evidence that legal factors such as number of prior referrals, detention decisions, and presence of an attorney exert greater influence on the outcomes of cases than do "socioeconomic" variables, such as gender, age, and race (but not social class). However, the relative power of all these factors, in terms of explaining decisions, is not very great (pp. 253–258). This means that many other factors, presumably individualistic, operate to influence decision making among probation officers, judges, and others working in juvenile courts. In addition, this "individualized justice" inhibits a fuller examination of the social and political contexts within which juveniles are processed and treated. Thus, while individual decisions may be just, they are rendered "within an unequal and unjust context" (p. 251). This last point seems to be what radical criminologists are making, but often within the realm of the deleterious effects of capitalism. (See Mahoney, 1987, for another view of the social and political contexts within which decision making occurs in the juvenile justice system.)

The empirical support for the assumption that social control officials discriminate against lower-class (and often nonwhite) juveniles is inconsistent. While it is obviously true that such discrimination does exist, its extent and overall significance in the processing of juveniles are variable. The data suggest that social class exerts an influence in the making and enforcing of some laws, at various times, in different locations, and in connection with other factors. The specification of all of these conditions, however, has not been systematically identified, nor have these qualifiers been formally incorporated into radical theory.

BEYOND "RADICAL" THEORY

The discussion and dialogue concerning radical theory as an explanation of criminality has created several divisions or positions, some of which have moved well beyond a Marxist base. In part, these newer conceptualizations are the result of reactions to some of the earlier criticisms of radical theory, as well as to reflective reinterpretations of the relationship among society, patterns of criminality, and reactions to crime and delinquency. Some of these newer positions tend to focus on female crime and delinquency, and will be discussed in the following chapter (see also, Lilly et al., 1995: Chapter 7).

While there are too many views and scholarly positions within the framework of radical theory to discuss in this volume, one division in particular has relevance for the present discussion. This division contrasts what has become known as a "left realist" position, as opposed to a "left idealist" point of view (Schwartz and DeKeseredy, 1991; Young and Mathews, 1992; Lilly et al., 1995:192–195).

There are several points along which the debate regarding left realism and left idealism may be argued. However, one essential element seems to be the concern for left realists to devise meaningful crime intervention strategies. The left realist position maintains that crime and delinquency cannot be resolved simply by advocating the dismantling of capitalism, or of attempts to disarm the negative effects of capitalism by discourse and dialogue. Left idealism, by implicative contrast, is thus placed in a kind of traditional, rather naive mold, in which crime control is to be accomplished by quixotic, idealist calls for the elimination of capitalism.

This is not to say that capitalism is not a problematic factor in a "leftist" explanation of crime, whether the left is realist or idealist. For the realists, however, the concern would appear to be with the more pressing, practical results of crime, including the negative effects of crime on the oppressed. The deeper roots of crime, traced to capitalism, are to be dealt with at a later date (Lynch and Groves, 1989:126–130).

Certainly, not all criminologists, including conflict theorists, who might adopt this approach to crime control identify their position as left realist (Groves and Sampson, 1987). Furthermore, the crime prevention strategies consistent with a left realist position are hard to distinguish from more traditional theoretical perspectives, such as strain or social disorganization theory, or even social control theory. This point is not lost on Groves and Sampson (1987), who present various ways in which these perspectives, and other "traditional" theories, overlap radical theory (although radical and traditional theories remain conceptually distinct).

One reason there seems to be convergence between radical theory and more traditional theories of crime and delinquency is the recognition among left realists that lower-class crime is not only a reality, but a source of concern among lower-class victims of crime committed by lower-class offenders (Schwartz and DeKeseredy, 1991). Thus, left realists are not content with describing criminality strictly from a class oppression point of view. Even if the pressures for crime among the lower class are generated from middle- and upper-class attempts to control workers, which is a point not forgotten by left realists, the fact remains that crime among the lower classes is a reality, and must be incorporated into explanations of crime.

These "realist" conceptualizations certainly address many of the concerns with neo-Marxist views of criminality. Moreover, left realists, and other conflict theorists who advocate realist perspectives, seem to be as interested in explaining crime and delinquency as with controlling it, and with accomplishing these goals using "empirical" methods. This direction within radical theory would seem to augur more favorable reaction among criminologists in general, as well as within the public, for the questions asked and answers proposed have a more direct, practical referent. In addition, the left realist perspective is in keeping with the Marxist orientation of merging theory, and history, with action, or practice, that is, "praxis" (Groves and Newman, 1993:242–244). One rather ironic result of the left realist position, however, is its distance from a "radical" solution to the control of crime (even though the idea that crime is ultimately caused by capitalism is a domain assumption within radical theory). Future developments within this perspective may begin to address this contradiction and its implications for radical theory (see, for example, the interesting debate between Schwartz and DeKeseredy, as proponents of left realism, and Henry, as an opponent of the theory, found in Fuller and Hickey, 1999:128–148).

SUMMARY

The neo-Marxist or radical approach to delinquency is based on broad conceptualizations of juvenile behavior and societal responses. Perhaps because of the generalizations which often accompany such an approach, efforts to assess the validity of its assumptions have yielded inconclusive results. Some feel that radical criminologists find unacceptable any attempt to quantify the decisions of police and court officials and the behavior of juveniles (Jensen, 1981). This type of approach to criminology is thought to serve only the ruling class and the State, at the expense of the oppressed masses. From this perspective, no amount of empirical evidence could dissuade one from Marxist assumptions, although such an approach is not necessarily incompatible with a radical view of criminality (Groves and Sampson, 1987). To become a viable theoretical perspective, however, the radical approach must begin to adopt the usual tenets of the scientific, or at least empirical, approach to discovery. To deny the value of empirical assessments of a perspective is to deny the theoretical process altogether. One is left having to decide what is acceptable on the subjective grounds of faith and belief. However, to an increasing extent, the methodological implications of radical theorists, particularly within left realism, do incorporate empiricism in the study of crime and delinquency. This criticism of radical theory, therefore, is becoming less valid (see also, Lynch and Groves, 1989:51).

In some ways the subjective nature of the radical position is its most appealing characteristic. The assumption that delinquency and its treatment (or punishment) are influenced by class considerations is based on traditional sociological conceptions (see Chapters 5 and 6) and is, therefore, certainly not without precedent. Calls for changes in the processing of delinquents based on their social class position are praiseworthy, even if such reforms are not solidly based on empirical findings. It is precisely this distinction between theory and action that must be maintained in the overall evaluation of radical theory. The assumptions of this perspective are questionable, considering research findings. The stronger value of this approach would appear to lie with its attention to social injustices and the need to correct them.

As an *explanation* of delinquency, radical theory has several deficiencies: (1) the existence of crime and delinquency, in varying degrees, in socialist countries, such as the former U.S.S.R., Cuba, and China (Connor, 1970, 1972; Hinners, 1973; Liazos, 1979; Rosner, 1986; Curran and Cook, 1993); (2) the presence of middle-class delinquency; (3) the relative strength of other factors, besides social class and economics, in the explanation of delinquency and reactions to it; and (4) the problem of documenting *class-linked* motives for behavior, both on the part of juveniles and social control officials, such as the police and judges. Until these issues are resolved within the framework of the radical perspective, the importance of radical theory will likely remain within the realm of identifying and correcting social injustices rather than within the category of explanations of delinquency.

Notes

1. The following discussion is based on a number of sources, including Marx and Engels (1950), Bottomore (1956), Gordon (1973), Chambliss (1975), Spitzer (1975), Quinney (1980), Empey (1982), and Empey and Stafford (1991).

2. To be sure, Marx advocated political revolution throughout much of his writing. In this sense, one could argue that he actually championed criminality. By and large, however, Marx did not envision himself as a criminal and he certainly did not categorize himself with street criminals, the scum he so derisively excluded from his revolutionary plans.

3. It is certainly plausible to assume that social and economic conditions may have adverse consequences for members of all social classes. The point here is that the economic frustrations and related criminal accommodations thought to be generated by capitalism are likely to be relatively more pronounced for those in the lower classes. Nonetheless, radical theory is placed in the position of having to account both for the existence of crime among all social classes and for the relative ability of those in higher social classes to handle the negative economic effects of capitalism in noncriminal ways.

4. A general issue here is the question of who *rules* versus who controls or manages wealth and corporate power. It is begging the question to assume the two are one and the same. At any level of society, decisions, policies, and laws are made that may reflect various interests or class positions. The important task is to determine more precisely which interests are involved in which decisions or laws and the processes whereby one set of interests prevails over another. Such concerns as these are beyond the topic of juvenile delinquency, but their investigation is central to the conflict and radical positions.

5. Sutton (1985) argues that the establishment of juvenile courts and specialized delinquency laws in the twentieth century served to formalize and protect the inter-

ests of child-saving efforts which had already appeared. Thus, the interests of child savers, and their ideology of "progressive reform," were served by the formal development of the juvenile justice system in the United States at the turn of the twentieth century.

References

Akers, Ronald L., 1979, "Theory and Ideology in Marxist Criminology: Comments on Turk, Quinney, Toby, and Klockars." Criminology 16:527–544.

Ariès, Phillippe, 1962, Centuries of Childhood. New York: Knopf.

Arnold, William R., 1971, "Race and Ethnicity Relative to Other Factors in Juvenile Court Dispositions." American Journal of Sociology 77:221–227.

Black, Donald J. and Albert J. Reiss, Jr., 1970, "Police Control of Juveniles." American Sociological Review 35:63–77.

Bonger, Willem, 1916, Criminality and Economic Conditions. Reprinted, Bloomington, Ind.: University of Indiana Press, 1969.

Bortner, M. A., 1984, Inside a Juvenile Court: The Tarnished Ideal of Individualized Justice. New York: New York University Press.

Bottomore, T. B. (trans.), 1956, Karl Marx. New York: McGraw-Hill.

Braithwaite, John, 1981, "The Myth of Social Class and Criminality Reconsidered." American Sociological Review 46:36–57.

Carter, Timothy J., 1979, "Juvenile Court Dispositions: A Comparison of Status and Nonstatus Offenders." Criminology 17:341–359.

Carter, Timothy J. and Donald Clelland, 1979, "A Neo-Marxian Critique, Formulation, and Test of Juvenile Dispositions as a Function of Social Class." Social Problems 27:96–108.

Chambliss, William J., 1974, "Functional and Conflict Theories of Crime." MSS Modular Publications 17:1–23.

————, 1975, "Toward a Political Economy of Crime." Theory and Society 2:149–170.

Cohen, Lawrence E. and James R. Kluegel, 1978, "Determinants of Juvenile Court Dispositions: Ascriptive and Achieved Factors in Two Metropolitan Courts." American Sociological Review 43:162–176.

Connor, Walter D., 1970, "Juvenile Delinquency in the U.S.S.R.: Some Quantitative and Qualitative Indicators." American Sociological Review 35:283–297.

————, 1972, Deviance in Soviet Society. New York: Columbia University Press.

Curran, Daniel J. and Sandra Cook, 1993, "Growing Fears, Rising Crime: Juveniles and China's Justice System." Crime & Delinquency 39:296–315.

Duster, Troy, 1987, "Crime, Unemployment, and the Black Underclass." Crime & Delinquency 33:300–316.

Empey, Lamar T., 1982, American Delinquency, revised edition. Homewood, Ill.: Dorsey.

Empey, Lamar T. and Mark Stafford, 1991, American Delinquency, third edition. Belmont, Calif.: Wadsworth.

Friedrichs, David O., 1980a, "Radical Criminology in the United States: An Interpretive Understanding." Pp. 35–60 in James A. Inciardi (ed.), q.v.

————, 1980b, "Carl Klockars vs. the 'Heavy Hitters': A Preliminary Critique." Pp. 149–160 in James A. Inciardi (ed.), q.v.

Fuller, John R. and Eric W. Hickey (eds.), 1999, Controversial Issues in Criminology. Boston: Allyn and Bacon.

Gintis, Herbert, 1976, "The Nature of Labor Exchange and the Theory of Capitalist Production." Review of Radical Political Economics 8:36–54.

Gordon, David M., 1973, "Capitalism, Class, and Crime in America." Crime & Delinquency 19:163–186.

Greenberg, David F., 1977, "Delinquency and the Age Structure of Society." Contemporary Crisis 1:189–223.

Groves, W. Byron and Graeme R. Newman, 1993, "Marx, Sartre, and the Resurrection of Choice in Theoretical Criminology." Pp. 231–245 in Graeme Newman, Michael J. Lynch, and David H. Galaty (eds.), Discovering Criminology: From W. Byron Groves. New York: Harrow and Heston.

Groves, W. Byron and Robert J. Sampson, 1987, "Traditional Contributions to Radical Criminology." Journal of Research in Crime and Delinquency 24:181–214.

Hagan, John and Jeffrey Leon, 1977, "Rediscovering Delinquency: Social History, Political Ideology, and the Sociology of Law." American Sociological Review 42:587–598.

Hindelang, Michael J., Travis Hirschi, and Joseph G. Weis, 1979, "Correlates of Delinquency." American Sociological Review 44:995–1014.

Hinners, James E., 1973, "Soviet Correctional Measures for Juvenile Delinquency." British Journal of Criminology 13:218–226.

Hirst, Paul Q., 1975, "Marx and Engels on Law, Crime and Morality." Pp. 203–232 in Ian Taylor, Paul Walton, and Jock Young (eds.), Critical Criminology. London: Routledge and Kegan Paul.

Horwitz, Allen and Michael Wasserman, 1980, "Some Misleading Conceptions in Sentencing Research: An Example and a Reformulation in the Juvenile Court." Criminology 18:411–424.

Inciardi, James A. (ed.), 1980, Radical Criminology. Beverly Hills, Calif.: Sage.

Irvine, Jacqueline Jordan, 1990, Black Students and School Failure: Policies, Practices, and Prescriptions. New York: Greenwood.

Jensen, Gary F., 1981, "The Sociology of Delinquency: Current Issues." Pp. 7–19 in Gary F. Jensen (ed.), Sociology of Delinquency. Beverly Hills, Calif.: Sage.

Johnstone, John W. C., 1978, "Social Class, Social Areas, and Delinquency." Sociology and Social Research 63:49–72.

Klockars, Carl B., 1979, "The Contemporary Crises of Marxist Criminology." Criminology 16:477–515.

Kraus, Jonathan, 1975, "Decision Process in the Children's Court and the Social Background Report." Journal of Research in Crime and Delinquency 12:17–29.

Krisberg, Barry and James Austin (eds.), 1978, The Children of Ishmael: Critical Perspectives on Juvenile Justice. Palo Alto, Calif.: Mayfield.

Liazos, Alexander, 1979, "Capitalism, Socialism, and Delinquency." Pp. 336–379 in Lamar T. Empey (ed.), The Future of Childhood and Juvenile Justice. Charlottesville, Va.: University Press of Virginia.

Lilly, J. Robert, Francis T. Cullen, and Richard A. Ball, 1995, Criminological Theory: Context and Consequences, second edition. Thousand Oaks, Calif.: Sage.

Lundman, Richard J., Richard E. Sykes, and John P. Clark, 1978, "Police Control of Juveniles: A Replication." Journal of Research in Crime and Delinquency 15:74–91.

Lynch, Michael J. and W. Byron Groves, 1986, A Primer in Radical Criminology. New York: Harrow and Heston.

———, 1989, A Primer in Radical Criminology, second edition. New York: Harrow and Heston.

Mahoney, Anne Rankin, 1987, Juvenile Justice in Context. Boston: Northeastern University Press.

Marx, Karl, 1950a, "The Eighteenth Brumaire of Louis Bonaparte." Pp. 225–311 in Karl Marx and Frederick Engels, q.v.

———, 1950b, "Wages, Price and Profit." Pp. 361–405 in Karl Marx and Frederick Engels, q.v.

———, 1950c, "Manifesto of the Communist Party." Pp. 21–61 in Karl Marx and Frederick Engels, q.v.

Marx, Karl and Frederick Engels, 1950, Selected Works, Vol. 1. London: Lawrence and Wishart.

McCarthy, Belinda R. and Brent L. Smith, 1986, "The Conceptualization of Discrimination in the Juvenile Justice Process: The Impact of Administrative Factors and Screening Decisions on Juvenile Court Dispositions." Criminology 24:41–64.

Meier, Robert F., 1980, "The New Criminology: Continuity in Criminological Theory." Pp. 372–387 in Stuart H. Traub and Craig B. Little (eds.), Theories of Deviance, second edition. Itasca, Ill.: F. E. Peacock.

Mennel, Robert M., 1973, Thorns and Thistles. Hanover, N.H.: University Press of New England.

Oliver, William, 1989, "Black Males and Social Problems: Prevention Through Afrocentric Socialization." Journal of Black Studies 20:15–39.

Piliavin, Irving and Scott Briar, 1964, "Police Encounters with Juveniles." American Journal of Sociology 70:206–214.

Platt, Anthony, 1974, "The Triumph of Benevolence: The Origins of the Juvenile Justice System in the United States." Pp. 356–389 in Richard Quinney (ed.), Criminal Justice in America. Boston: Little, Brown.

———, 1977, The Child Savers, second edition. Chicago: University of Chicago Press.

Quinney, Richard, 1970, The Social Reality of Crime. Boston: Little, Brown.

———, 1977, Class, State, and Crime. New York: David McKay.

———, 1979, "The Production of Criminology." Criminology 16:445–457.

———, 1980, Class, State, and Crime, second edition. New York: Longman.

Rosner, Lydia S., 1986, The Soviet Way of Crime: Beating the System in the Soviet Union and the U.S.A. South Hadley, Mass.: Bergin and Garvey.

Rothman, David J., 1971, The Discovery of the Asylum. Boston: Little, Brown.

Sampson, Robert J., 1986, "Effects of Socioeconomic Context on Official Reaction to Juvenile Delinquency." American Sociological Review 51:876–885.

Scarpitti, Frank R. and Richard M. Stephenson, 1971, "Juvenile Court Dispositions: Factors in the Decision-Making Process." Crime & Delinquency 17:142–151.

Schwartz, Martin D. and Walter S. DeKeseredy, 1991, "Left Realist Criminology: Strengths, Weaknesses, and the Feminist Critique." Crime, Law and Social Change 15:51–72.

Schwendinger, Herman and Julia R. Schwendinger, 1976, "Delinquency and the Collective Varieties of Youth." Crime and Social Justice 5:7–25.

Sieverdes, Christopher M., Donald J. Shoemaker, and Orville Cunningham, 1979, "Disposition Decisions by Juvenile Court Probation Officers and Judges: A Multivariate Analysis." Criminal Justice Review 4:121–132.

Spitzer, Steven, 1975, "Toward a Marxian Theory of Deviance." Social Problems 22:638–651.

Sutton, John R., 1985, "The Juvenile Court and Social Welfare: Dynamics of Progressive Reform." Law & Society Review 19:107–145.

Sykes, Gresham M., 1974, "The Rise of Critical Criminology." Journal of Criminal Law and Criminology 65:206–213.

Taylor, Ian, Paul Walton, and Jock Young, 1973, The New Criminology. New York: Harper & Row.

Thomas, Charles and Christopher M. Sieverdes, 1975, "Juvenile Court Intake: An Analysis of Discretionary Decision-Making." Criminology 12:413–434.

Thornberry, Terence P., 1973, "Race, Socioeconomic Status and Sentencing in the Juvenile Justice System." Journal of Criminal Law and Criminology 64:90–98.

Turk, Austin T., 1969, Criminality and Legal Order. Chicago: Rand McNally.

Vold, George, 1979, Theoretical Criminology, second edition, prepared by Thomas J. Bernard. New York: Oxford University Press.

Warner, Jerry T., 1981, "Disposition Decisions by Court Officials in a Rural Setting." Unpublished Master's Thesis. Blacksburg, Va.: Virginia Polytechnic Institute and State University.

Weiner, Norman L. and Charles V. Willie, 1971, "Decisions by Juvenile Officers." American Journal of Sociology 77:199–210.

West, Cornell, 1993, Race Matters. Boston: Beacon.

Young, Jock and Roger Mathews, 1992, Rethinking Criminology: The Realist Debate. Newbury Park, Calif.: Sage.

11

Female Delinquency

HISTORICAL OVERVIEW

The subject of female involvement in crime, delinquency, and deviant behavior has been relegated to secondary importance, although special attention was given to it by Cesare Lombroso (Lombroso and Ferrero, 1895), W. I. Thomas (1925), Sheldon and Eleanor Glueck (1934), and Otto Pollak (1950), in the period from the turn of the century to World War II. With the advent of the new feminism, a new focus on this subject was made by Freda Adler (1975), Rita Simon (1975), and others, and a controversy was ignited that has not abated.

Virtually all of the theories discussed thus far have focused on male participation in delinquent acts. This inattention to women is partly attributed to their perceived limited involvement in crime and delinquency. In addition, some feel that males have controlled the accumulation and dissemination of information concerning crime and have collectively perpetuated the myth of low female involvement in crime as one means of dominating women (Pollak, 1950), while others feel that the relatively greater male criminality is far from mythical, whether it be rooted in biological or sociocultural factors (Sutherland and Cressey, 1978).

References to female patterns of delinquency have been made throughout this book. It would be tempting to leave the issue of female delinquency to brief discussions of applications to one theory or another, but the subject is too complex and too important for that kind of treatment. Accordingly, the purpose of the present chapter is to present discussions of several explanations of female juvenile offending, from traditional to modern perspectives.

Several categories of explanations for female criminality are discussed in this chapter: (1) innate, or basic, sexual characteristics; (2) gender roles; (3) the women's movement, or female emancipation; (4) power-control theory; and (5) feminist views.

For the most part, these explanations of female criminality have tended to ignore demographic differences, such as age, and to account for criminal behavior among females in general. Accordingly, the following discussions concentrate on the theories themselves, with special reference to adolescent behavior where possible.

BASIC BIOLOGICAL AND PSYCHOLOGICAL APPROACHES

Many students of human behavior, deviant or conforming, contend that behavior is at least partially a product of natural, inborn traits or tendencies—that is, predispositions. This applies to all human behavior, acts of males and females, and to people of different races, nationalities, or other sociological divisions. As discussed in Chapter 3, a proponent of this point of view, with respect to criminality, was Cesare Lombroso.

Although Lombroso's analyses of criminals were largely confined to the male sex, he did produce one volume reflecting on female criminality (Lombroso and Ferrero, 1895). In this work, Lombroso maintained that females, as a category, were lacking in sensitivity, compared to men; he also found females more childlike, morally deficient, jealous, and vengeful. Ordinarily, Lombroso reasoned, these traits of vengeance and cruelty are balanced by maternity, lack of passion, and low intelligence. In some women, however, these neutralizers are absent, for a variety of reasons, and the innate cruel tendencies of such women are released to yield a "born criminal more terrible than any man," a "double exception" to civilized behavior (Lombroso and Ferrero, 1895:151).

Lombroso reasoned, however, that the majority of female delinquents, like males, could be classified as "occasional criminals" whose physical features contain no signs of degeneration and whose moral character is similar to that of their "normal sisters" (Lombroso and Ferrero, 1895:193–195). In addition, he argued that occasional female criminals could be encouraged to commit crime because of the increased frustrations they would meet in life upon the broadening of their education. Lombroso, therefore, recognized the influences of female criminality that have gained popularity in recent years.

Another explanation of female criminality was given by Sigmund Freud, who suggested that females have a natural tendency to envy the symbol of male dominance in society (penis envy). This situation becomes a type of "castration complex" for girls. Penis envy is present in young children of both sexes, but Freud felt that it is of more importance for females than males (Freud, 1933). As with other significant events in the psychosexual development of children,

Freud proposed that penis envy does not necessarily lead to problems of adjustment and deviant behavior. Sometimes the girl becomes sexually normal and passes through the self-doubt and mother rejection that accompany the castration complex. Some girls, however, become sexually inhibited or neurotic, while still others develop a masculinity complex, an identity with maleness, so to speak, in which the girl refuses to recognize her feminine sexuality. Both sexual inhibition and masculine identity can create behavioral problems for females. Freud suggested that the masculinity complex can lead to homosexuality, and presumably to patterns of delinquency, among girls. Furthermore, he maintained that the development of a masculinity complex was probably related to a biological cause, thus linking female criminality with some type of natural condition.

Freud, however, had little to say about female criminality, adolescent or adult. He acknowledged the small amount of information that existed on female personality characteristics in general and suggested that his ideas were rather speculative (Freud, 1933).

The views of W. I. Thomas on the female personality and female delinquency represent a combination and extension of the ideas of Lombroso and Freud. In *Sex and Society* (1907), Thomas proposed that women were basically *anabolic* in constitution, while men were essentially *katabolic*. By this, he meant that women tended to accumulate body fat and fluid, while men tended to release such bodily products. Consequently, women were seen as more passive and more capable of constitutionally adapting to stresses and strains than men, who were considered more energetic and less able to resist the biological complications of environmental stress. By extension, Thomas further suggested that the inherent nature of the male is to be both "the hero and the criminal" (Thomas, 1907:168), while the female is destined to be concerned about morality and stability and behavioral acquiescence to the rules of men.

In *The Unadjusted Girl* (1925), Thomas argued that people behave according to four basic wishes: new experience, security, response, and recognition. With respect to female delinquency, Thomas felt that it basically starts with the wish for new experience and excitement, which girls ultimately learn they can achieve by manipulating their "capital"—that is, their sexuality. Thomas argued that the concern with excitement and amusement in delinquent girls largely occurred among lower-class girls, whom he characterized as "amoral"—in other words, neither immoral nor moral—who manipulate their sexual capital for personal excitement and perceived gain. In this way, also, Thomas argued that female delinquency was a result of "adjustment" problems, similar to the Freudian view but without the concept of castration complex. At the same time, it appears that Thomas foreshadowed the later explanations of female crime and delinquency, which have stressed the importance of sex roles on such behavior.

Later, theorists sought to explain biological and psychological properties of female offenders in a variety of ways. Thus, female delinquency has been related to abnormal chromosomal configurations (Cowie et al., 1968), overweight and physical overdevelopment problems (Healy, 1915; Pollak, 1950), and biopsychological problems associated with menstruation and puberty (Konopka, 1966). The relationship of menstruation to delinquency has also been considered by Otto Pollak (1950), who used a Freudian framework. Essentially, Pollak argues that menstruation adds to the anxiety girls experience over their sexual identities. If they are going through a castration complex and are attempting to resolve it through male identification, the event of menstruation destroys this type of resolution. Thus, menstruation heightens female adolescent problems of identity (stemming from the castration complex), apart from the other biological and psychological complications it may produce.[1]

These other biological and psychological factors, however, represent relatively minor modifications of the basic themes of female criminality which were proposed at the turn of the century. The dominant image from this perspective remains that of inherent differences between males and females that influence the degree and type of female involvement in crime and delinquency.

GENDER ROLES AND DELINQUENCY

According to some, the major explanation of female deviance up to the 1960s was the Freudian perspective (Simon, 1975), although the specific concept of castration complex was not always given as the major underlying cause of such behavior. Actually, beginning in the 1950s, another explanation of female offenses began to appear—the influence of gender roles. Essentially, this explanation argues that women act and think in accordance with the roles in society they have been taught and are expected to play. From this perspective it is reasoned that women are expected to be passive, orderly, motherly, and, if ambitious, wily and cunning, inasmuch as women are not likely to be freely given occupational responsibilities and social power outside of the home and family.

In some discussions, it is hard to distinguish between sex roles considered *natural* and sex roles that are *learned* or acquired. The importance of this perspective, however, lies in its contention that sex roles are taught and learned, not biologically influenced. While it is certainly true that biological differences between males and females exist, this approach maintains that acting as a male or female is *expected* to behave is not necessarily inborn or biologically predisposed but, instead, is influenced by cultural and social definitions that one learns from early childhood. In other words, traits such as *maleness* and *femaleness* are biological, whereas the concepts of *masculinity* and *femininity* are socially learned roles (Smart, 1976; Klein, 1979).

An earlier example of this approach to female criminality was offered by Otto Pollak (1950), who argued that female involvement in crime was greater than official estimates indicate because female criminality is essentially masked or hidden. Besides being accorded a more chivalrous or protective attitude by criminal justice officials, females are given roles in society that tend to isolate them from public view. In some cases, the criminal behavior of women is private indeed, such as with illegal abortions. In addition, Pollak argued that women participate in crimes as accomplices, particularly with respect to property offenses. Violent crimes by females, he maintained, are often committed within the privacy of the home and involve methods that are hard to detect, such as poisoning.

Ruth Cavan and Theodore Ferdinand (1975) assert that delinquent behavior among girls is associated with cultural values and social roles. These values and roles, moreover, are influenced by social class and ethnic background. The authors suggest that among middle-class girls the previously taught values of sexual chastity and domestic happiness are being challenged, thus giving these girls and their parents confusing ideas about what constitutes proper supervision and appropriate behavior. Should the girl be allowed to spend the night with a boy, with or without the company of peers? Is it all right to let the juvenile experiment with drugs, especially with other youth? Such issues as these may not only allow the middle-class female adolescent to entertain new role expectations and social norms, but they may also serve to generate conflicts between her and her parents, teachers, and more "conventional" peers. These conflicts may lead or further push the teenage female into delinquency.

According to Cavan and Ferdinand, deviations from social expectations of sexual and moral conformity are more accepted among lower-class female juveniles than among middle-class girls. Delinquent acts such as running away, sexual promiscuity, and ungovernability are thus somewhat expected of lower-class girls. However, they assert that among some ethnic groups, such as Italians, sexual standards and morals are rigidly enforced, even among those in the lower class, and sexual delinquencies among girls in Italian-American neighborhoods are relatively rare.

These two examples of a sex-role perspective of female criminality are tinged with various considerations that tend to merge them with other explanations. Pollak's analysis suggests that some of the characteristics of female crime are biologically influenced. Cavan and Ferdinand essentially describe female delinquency in terms of sexual and moral behavior, similar to the "adjustment" problems seen by Freud, Thomas, and others to be so predominant among delinquent girls.

More sociological sex-role explanations of female delinquency have been offered by George Grosser (cited by Gibbons, 1981:239–241) and Albert J. Reiss (1960). According to Grosser, delinquent boys are predominantly involved in theft because stealing is daring and risky, masculine, as it were, and that is what males are supposed to be. In addition, stolen goods can be used to help support the masculine role of provider, such as paying the way on dates. Females, on the other hand, tend to steal less often than males because stealing does not directly express the qualities of femininity (although the incidence of theft among adolescent females is increasing). Some girls may steal, however, because stolen property may help them to maintain female appeal. Of course, these gender-role behavior patterns are traditional, and not universal. Sutherland contends, for example, that among Gypsies the woman is considered to be the primary economic provider for the family, even if this means "hustling" for a living (1975:71–91).

Sexually promiscuous behavior among female adolescents was not explained by Grosser in role terms. However, Reiss contends that sexual offenses among females and males (particularly in the lower class) are a means of expressing approved social roles with peers in the peer-oriented adolescent society. Males engage in (consensual) sex acts with females because they gain status and prestige by so doing. Females engage in sex because relationships with males are the primary source of status and prestige among girls, and to develop relationships with boys, girls have to often "give in" to the sexual demands of boys. The sexual behavior of girls becomes a problem when complications result, such as pregnancy or venereal disease, or when the behavior becomes too visible in other ways. At that point, the girl risks losing her status and reputation among both male and female peers, and additional involvement in delinquency may result. In essence, sexual promiscuity is generally seen as a problem or an instance of delinquency when it is committed by females more than when it pertains to males. While this last scenario is reminiscent of Thomas' unadjusted girl syndrome, the role implications of Reiss' explanation are clear.

WOMEN'S EMANCIPATION

During the 1970s, a number of books and articles appeared that attributed an increase in female crime in the United States to the increased participation of women in the labor force, as well as to the general emancipation and liberation of women from traditional domestic and sexual behavior roles (Adler, 1975; Simon, 1975; Smart, 1976; Klein and Kress, 1979). The argument in essence has been that, as women become freer to develop their individual potentials and to achieve their goals in life, they simultaneously become exposed to the crime-inducing frustrations and stresses of life that have characterized the male experience for years, as well as to increased opportunities to commit crime. The current "women's movement," as such, is generally regarded as having started in the early to mid-1960s, contemporaneously with civil rights and antiwar demonstrations (Adler, 1975; Simon, 1975), although most accounts recognize earlier efforts to allow women greater economic and political involvement, such as the suffrage movement of the late nineteenth and early twentieth centuries.

Indeed, the recognition of the effects of increased freedom for women on female crime rates is evident in the work of Lombroso, as mentioned above, as well as others writing around that time (Bonger, 1916). In addition, the previously discussed work of Pollak directed considerable attention to the criminological effects of increased participation of women in the labor force. In fact. Pollak asserts that a rise in female crime because of the emancipation of women has been predicted by criminologists since at least the 1870s.

Discussions of the connection between increased freedom for women and a subsequent rise in crime rates have often suggested that the increase will largely occur with property crimes, although some contend that an increase in other crimes, by females, including drug offenses and violence, can be expected to occur as the women's liberation movement continues (Adler, 1975; Smart, 1976).

For the most part, these accounts of the relationship between female criminality and the emancipation of women leave out the connection with juvenile delinquency. Freda Adler (1975), however, maintains that the results of increased freedom and changing gender roles for women can be seen among girls as well. To a large extent, Adler suggests that younger females emulate their mothers or older sisters in their quest for increased freedom. Thus, all of the different types of crime that may be expected of adult women may be expected of girls as well.

While she argues that one of the changes the liberation movement has created for adolescent girls is in the area of sexual behavior (recall the previous discussion of Cavan and Ferdinand's analysis of middle-class female delinquency), Adler claims that the effects have been most notable in two areas: (1) a general imitation of masculine behavior, as evidenced in greater involvement in fighting and gang behavior, and (2) an increased rate of delinquency in general, as the confusion accompanying liberation adds to the turmoil and uncertainty of an already troubled period of life—adolescence. In connection with violent crime and delinquent behavior changes, Adler indicates an increase in gang involvement among girls, both in their traditional role as accomplices to male gangs and as members of exclusive female gangs or cliques. In addition, she points to numerous and varied violent episodes among girls in general, such as reformatory rioting and aggressive political protesting.

In summary, whether girls are seen as becoming more violent, the general hypotheses of the emancipation explanation of female delinquency are that rates of female delinquency will be greater in more industrialized and technologically "advanced" societies and that increases in these rates can be traced to the rise of the women's liberation movement, especially as this movement has blurred the traditional distinctions between masculine and feminine roles.

EVALUATION

The idea that females and males behave according to innate characteristics has been challenged for some time. That females are innately passive, naive, cunning, or anything else is arguable with respect to the various learning theories of the social and behavioral sciences. Of course, modern biological theories stress that an interaction between physical predispositions and sociocultural conditions produce behavior. Even this position, however, is not totally accepted by those who emphasize the importance of environmental factors in the explanation of behavior.

A common notion of the naturalistic explanation of female delinquency is that such behavior is caused, or associated with, adjustment problems, particularly those stemming from the home environment. To some extent, the literature supports this view. Numerous accounts of female delinquency have stressed what may be called a "wayward girl" syndrome, in which the delinquent girl is characterized as having difficulties at home, becoming incorrigible or "ungovernable," running away from home, becoming or suspected of becoming sexually promiscuous, and perhaps ultimately becoming involved in various acts of criminal behavior (Glueck and Glueck, 1934; Konopka, 1966; Vedder and Somerville, 1975). In addition, several studies have noted that there is a stronger relationship between broken homes and family relationships and official measures of delinquency among females than males (Gibbons and Griswold, 1957; Monahan, 1957; Toby, 1957). Other investigations have found that female delinquency (as measured by self-reports) is more strongly related to family factors than is male delinquency, especially for status offenses, such as ungovernability and running away (Nye, 1958; Datesman and Scarpitti, 1975; Norland et al., 1979).

The validity of the wayward girl syndrome ultimately rests on the extent to which girls actually do commit status offenses. Official estimates of female delinquency have consistently associated the delinquent girl with such offenses as running away and incorrigibility, offenses which fit the pattern of being wayward (Barton, 1976; Cernkovich and Giordano, 1979a; Gibbons, 1981; Richards, 1981; Empey, 1982; Weis, 1982). While the results of self-report surveys indicate that, overall, males are more delinquent than females, the difference is mostly attributable to the greater involvement of males in property and violent offenses. Differences between males and females with respect to status offenses are negligible or indicate greater involvement among males than females. In a study of delinquency among a sample of nearly 600 middle-class high school students in Connecticut, for example, Nancy Wise (1967) found that the proportion of males admitting to sex and alcohol offenses was about the same as for females, one-third and between 50 and 60 percent, respectively. The percentage of males who admitted to being ungovernable, however, was nearly twice the figure for females, 26.6 to 13.7 percent. The percentages of boys involved in theft and violent offenses were greater than for females, which yielded a higher overall rate of delinquency for males than for females (see also, Hindelang, 1971). A comparative analysis by Rachelle Canter (1982b) suggests that the findings of Wise and others have been replicated in different parts of the country and over a period of at least 10 years (see also, Barton and Figueira-McDonough, 1985; Chesney-Lind and Shelden, 1992).

The results of these self-report surveys suggest that the official data concerning female delinquency are correct, but incomplete. Female delinquents do often commit status offenses, but no more than do males. Certainly, many female delinquents have difficulties at home and become involved in numerous status offenses in connection with those problems. The high proportions of female status offenders in juvenile courts and institutions, however, must be accounted for in terms of societal reactions to the behavior, as well as the behavior itself. It could well be that a stereotype of the delinquent girl as wayward and promiscuous is associated not only with the theoretical explanation of psychological and biological problems of adjustment but, also, with official decisions concerning what to do with disobedient or runaway girls. Clearly, the data suggest that additional theories and information are needed for a fuller understanding of female delinquency.

To some extent, the gender-role explanation of female delinquency has been supported with research that investigates social expectations of behavior as these are differentiated by sexual status. Ruth Morris (1965), for example, studied the connection between social role expectations and delinquency among males and females. Overall, Morris found that girls expressed more shame and guilt than boys over having been in trouble with the police. In addition, she found that girls were more critical of delinquency than boys, especially delinquency committed by boys. These findings suggest that females are socialized into greater conformity and less delinquency than males. When females commit acts of delinquency, they are essentially violating feminine social role expectations.

A more specific test of female delinquency from a social role perspective is provided by a test of the "masculinity hypothesis," which suggests that females who commit delinquent acts are conforming to the masculine role more than are nondelinquent girls (Cullen et al., 1979). Numerous tests of the masculinity hypothesis have provided conflicting results. A study of self-reported delinquency among male and female midwestern university students, for example, found that those who scored high on such "masculine" traits as aggressiveness, dominance, competition, and independence tended to have high levels of delinquency (Cullen et al., 1979). The relationship between delinquency and masculine traits, moreover, was stronger for males than for females. Being male and having relatively high levels of masculinity were more likely to coincide with delinquent behavior than were being female and having masculine expectations. A similar conclusion was reached in another self-report study of delinquency in Nashville (Thornton and James, 1979). Additional analysis of these data indicated, however, that masculine views (including such items as who will pay the way on dates and who will provide the most income and make "major" family decisions in marriage) were less related to delinquency than the possession of feminine characteristics (such as expecting to do housework and caring for a family, telling parents about one's whereabouts on dates, and relocating according to a spouse's work). Accepting feminine expectations was associated with low rates of self-admitted property offenses for both males and females and with lower rates of aggressive offenses for females. Masculine role attitudes were not significantly related to delinquency for either sex (Shover et al., 1979).

One of the difficulties of the sex-role explanation of delinquency, however, is that it cannot account for the *changes* in gender-role orientations and expectations and, thus, for changes in patterns of delinquency. Basically, it is the attempt to account for such variations that separates the gender-role explanation of female delinquency from the emancipation theory.

A central issue of the emancipation argument is whether female crime rates have increased during the years the contemporary women's liberation movement is thought to have occurred (1960s to the present). Assessments of both official and self-report measures of crime and delinquency support the contention that female involvement in criminality has increased during the last 30 years or so (Adler, 1975; Simon, 1975; Steffensmeier and Steffensmeier, 1980; Empey, 1982; Leonard, 1982; Chesney-Lind and Shelden, 1992). Most of this increase has occurred in the areas of theft and drug use, contrary to Adler's prediction that female crime rates would rise for several different types of crime. Furthermore, reports of widespread increases in female participation in violent *gang* behavior are unconfirmed by studies that have attempted to document this type of delinquent activity (Miller, 1975; Chesney-Lind and Shelden,

1992, 1998: Chapter 4; Steffensmeier and Allan, 1996).[2] As Chesney-Lind and Shelden observe, female delinquency has not changed much in the past two decades, whether delinquency is measured according to self-report studies or according to official statistics. Females still typically commit nonviolent offenses (1998:239–241).

To attribute this increase in female crime and delinquency to the women's movement, however, is debatable for several reasons. First, the increase occurred largely before the 1970s, when the effects of the movement would not have been at their height, and leveled off in subsequent years, when the impact of the movement would be expected to have increased (Steffensmeier and Steffensmeier, 1980). This conclusion is also reached by researchers examining arrest data in England and Wales over the years 1951–1979 (Box and Hale, 1983).

Second, no consistent evidence has appeared that connects rising female crime rates with rising levels of industrialization and socioeconomic development (Simon, 1975; Steffensmeier et al., 1989).

Third, the unique connection between liberation attitudes toward the feminine role and female delinquency has not been established (Smart, 1976). In order to establish a specific connection between a social movement and behavior changes, it is important, although not necessary, to document the influence of the movement's ideas and goals on those whose behavior is thought to be associated with them. With respect to the women's movement and female delinquency, it has been pointed out that some indices of female liberation, such as employment opportunities, may have relatively little relevance for girls (Giordano and Cernkovich, 1979). In addition, the association between self-reported delinquency and liberated attitudes toward female roles has not been consistently documented. In fact, in some instances, those girls who express traditional female sex-role views are *more* delinquent than females who espouse liberated opinions (Giordano and Cernkovich, 1979; see also, Giordano, 1978). Of course, it is possible for a movement to influence general behavior patterns without affecting any particular individual. In the present case, however, a presumed consequence of the women's movement—liberated attitudes among females—is found not to be associated with relatively high rates of female delinquency.[3]

Thus, while the women's liberation movement offers a general explanation of changing female gender roles and increases of crime and delinquency among women, a documented connection between the two has not been established (Chesney-Lind and Shelden, 1998:22). Indications of increasing arrest rates of juvenile females in the United States may alter these conclusions regarding the validity of the emancipation theory of female delinquency. These increases in arrest rates, however, may be no more than a temporary trend. In addition, changes in female crime and arrest rates may be attributable to a number of factors other than to the liberation thesis, as Steffensmeier and Streifel cogently argue (1993:75–94). The overall interpretation of this theory of female criminality is still relatively pessimistic, but not yet moribund.

In the course of sorting out the influence of gender-role changes on female criminality, several commentators have suggested the importance of other factors that have traditionally been associated with male delinquency. The previously discussed study by Peggy Giordano and Stephen Cernkovich, for example, indicated that peer relations, especially in mixed-sex group contexts, play a more important part in the explanation of female delinquency than do liberated attitudes (1979).[4] In another study of female delinquency, Cernkovich and Giordano indicate that the perception that there are fewer general opportunities for advancement is more related to delinquency than are blocked opportunities that result from sex discrimination (1979b; see also, Datesman et al., 1975). However, feelings of strain are not necessarily linked with liberated attitudes (Leiber et al., 1994).

In addition, evidence exists in support of social control factors as an important part in the explanation of female delinquency. Besides the influence of family factors, some research suggests that other control variables, such as lack of commitment to conventional goals and attachment to school, contribute significantly to delinquency among females (Duke and Duke, 1978; Thornton and James, 1979).

Since adjustment problems stemming from family situations have been associated with female delinquency for a long time, it is logical that control variables in general are presumed to be strongly related to delinquency among girls, especially since social control theory has become the subject of considerable interest (see Chapter 8). The specific effect of control variables on female delinquency, however, may still not account for differences in rates of delinquency between males and females. For example, Gary Jensen and Raymond Eve (1976) utilized the same data set on which Hirschi developed his social control theory of delinquency among males and analyzed the data for females. While their analysis supported control theory hypotheses (that is, girls who are more attached to family and school admitted to fewer acts of delinquency), males were more involved in delinquency than females *regardless* of the degree of attachment to families, schools, and so on. A similar conclusion is reached by Barton and Figueira-McDonough (1985). Obviously, many other factors, certainly including those previously discussed in this chapter, must be considered if an adequate understanding of the etiology of female delinquency is to be obtained.

The search for an explanation of male and female delinquency that can explain the "gender gap" continues. The particular theoretical explanation, however, is not uniformly identified by scholars. Some, for example, make a

strong case for the power of differential association theory, or peer relationships (see Chapter 7), as the critical variable in the explanation of delinquency
among boys and girls (Mears et al., 1998). Other research indicates that the
key factor is role-taking, or gender identification (Heimer, 1996). Some argue
that the explanation of the gender gap is to be found in Agnew's revised strain
theory, which was discussed in Chapter 6 (Broidy and Agnew, 1997; Hoffman
and Su, 1997), while others (Burton et al., 1998; LaGrange and Silverman, 1999)
analyze the gender gap using self-control theory (see Chapter 12). Still others
feel there are several factors, such as a strong social bond, associations with
delinquent peers, and negative sanctions in the school or by the police, that
explain the gender gap (Liu and Kaplan, 1999).

Most of these explanations conclude that while there may be a single—or a
single combined—explanation of male and female delinquency, the gap in
offender rates, which consistently indicates higher incidences of delinquency
among males, particularly for serious criminal offenses, can be explained by
how males and females differ in handling a particular contributing factor. For
example, in presenting a case for the influence of role-taking in the explanation
of delinquency, Karen Heimer (1996) maintains that factors such as associations with deviant peer groups, commitments to family and friends, and attachments to family all contribute to delinquency, but indirectly, through role-taking
behaviors. More specifically, Heimer says that identification with a female
gender role reduces delinquency among girls, but identification with a masculine identity, or definition, does not reduce delinquency among males (p. 56).

Mears et al. (1998) argue that association with delinquent peers is one of
the stronger explanations of male and female delinquency. However, these
authors suggest the influence of delinquent peers is offset, at least partially,
among young women by their prior socialization, which stresses the acceptance
of moral values, even in the face of deviant peer pressure. Using the logic of
control theory (see Chapter 8), it could be argued that females have a stronger
sense of internal controls protecting against delinquency, even when powerful
prodelinquency forces are present in their lives.

In a related vein, Agnew and Brezina (1997) suggest that young men are
more susceptible to the strains and pressures of delinquent peers than are girls.
The speculation is that males resent peer pressure, and react negatively to it, in
the form of "moral outrage," while females tend to internalize these pressures,
or to see the side of others, in ways that reduce delinquency (pp. 104–105).
This position is similar to the conclusions of Chandy et al. (1996), who examined the effects of sexual abuse on juvenile males and females. According to
this study, sexual abuse is internalized among women, and can lead to suicide
ideation (thoughts of killing oneself), drug use, and eating disorders. Among
males, however, reactions to sexual abuse tended to be externalized more in

the form of delinquent behavior, academic problems, and more frequent and unsafe sex practices (pp. 1222–1228). Thus, there may be common factors underlying the explanation of male and female delinquency, but the gender gap is to be explained by the manner in which males and females adjust to or react to those contributing factors (see also, Steffensmeier and Allan, 1996).

Despite the interest in seeking a "common" cause of delinquency among males and females, some, such as Chesney-Lind and Shelden (1998), continue to remind us that behavior among young women must be understood from the context of growing up female in a male-dominated world (pp. 111–123, 242–243). They, too, maintain that socialization into the "feminine" role tends to prevent delinquency, but experiences which are more common among women can be the catalyst for delinquency among girls. In particular, Chesney-Lind and Shelden identify sexual abuse against a girl as a major factor in the explanation of female delinquency. In addition, these authors suggest that girls from disadvantaged backgrounds have a more difficult time living up to the "middle-class" standard of femininity, including beauty and popularity, especially among school peers. Subsequent attempts to negotiate the objective of becoming feminine, and of handling other adolescent pressures, may result in delinquent behavior for these girls (p. 123).

POWER-CONTROL THEORY

John Hagan and his associates, A. R. Gillis and John Simpson, have advanced what they call a "power-control theory" to explain female delinquency or, more appropriately, relatively less serious, "common" types of illegal activity (Hagan et al., 1985, 1987).

Essentially, the argument is that the structure of the occupational system divides the populace into those who control and those who are controlled. Furthermore, the theory argues that mothers are the primary socializing agents of children in the family, especially girls. However, what is taught to children is influenced by the economic, power position the household head has in the workplace. When one has power over others at work, she or he and her or his spouse will also be in *control* of children (especially girls) at home. However, because of the power exercised at work, these parents will be *more* likely to excuse deviant behavior by their children and to increase the "taste for risk" among their offspring, especially male youth. According to Hagan et al., power and control are thought to be directly related to social class, "freedom to deviate is directly related to class position," and "males are freer to deviate than are females"; therefore, "males are freest to deviate in the higher classes" (Hagan et al., 1985:1155). These males will be free to deviate not only because their influential parents allow them greater latitude of behavior, but also because these youth will not perceive sanctions for their deviance to be a realistic threat.

These ideas were tested by Hagan et al. (1985) on a sample of 458 Canadian adolescent students, using a self-report survey of delinquency. The occupational position of the head of the household was categorized as employer, manager (both considered controllers), workers and surplus population, or the unemployed (both considered controlled).

The results of their analysis lead Hagan et al. to conclude that no relationship exists between delinquency and socioeconomic status per se (1985:1167–1168). However, they did find that the difference in the rate of delinquency *between* males and females was greatest in families headed by employers, and this difference narrowed with each occupational classification (1985:1170). This finding is supportive of the predictions of Willem Bonger, a neo-Marxist criminologist writing in the early twentieth century (see Chapter 10). These results are also supportive of power-control theory.

Further analyses added additional support to the theory. For example, Hagan and his associates found that mothers were the principal control figures in the home, especially for daughters (p. 1172). In addition, they conclude that adolescent males in the employer class are the most delinquent (and more delinquent than females) because "they are less controlled by their mothers and less likely to perceive the risks of getting punished as threatening" (p. 1173).

Overall, the statement and test of power-control theory by Hagan et al. in 1985 was more an exposition of the differences between male and female rates of delinquency by class position. The conclusions they reached, furthermore, addressed the motivations for delinquency among upper-middle-class males.

In an effort to extend power-control theory more specifically to female delinquency, Hagan, Simpson, and Gillis reconceptualized their data by concentrating on the power relations of occupational positions of husband *and* wife, and of female-headed households (Hagan et al., 1987). The reconceptualization divided families into patriarchal and egalitarian structures. Patriarchal families are headed by males who are employed in a position of authority (or power) while the wife is not employed outside the home. The egalitarian family is one in which both husband and wife have jobs encompassing authority over others. The prediction relative to these family divisions is that female delinquency (common delinquency) will increase, and become more equal to the extent of male delinquency within egalitarian families. In addition, Hagan et al. suggest that female delinquency will be higher in female-headed households because females will be freer to deviate in these families (since there would be a lack of "power imbalance between parents," p. 793). As stated, this version of power-control theory represents an extension of the liberation theory of female delinquency, discussed earlier in this chapter, by pointing to the relationship between employment conditions and socialization patterns of mothers, relative to fathers—the "class dynamics of the family," as Hagan et al. (p. 791) put it.

This version of power-control theory was tested by Hagan and his colleagues through follow-up contacts with the parents of the youth surveyed in the earlier analysis, in an effort to collect employment information about the mothers. Based on the new conceptualization of employment, Hagan et al. divide the patriarchal and egalitarian families into several subtypes. Patriarchal families, for example, include those in which the father is employed, regardless of level of authority, while the mother is not employed. Egalitarian families include those in which both father and mother are employed in occupations that involve similar levels of authority. The situations of an unemployed father and an employed mother or of father-only homes are not considered because of the small number of such cases.

The basic assumption of the power-control theory, again, is that "authority in the workplace is translated into power in the household" (p. 798). Furthermore, the theory assumes that the treatment of boys and girls will be similar in egalitarian homes, and that female rates of delinquency will be correspondingly high among these families, regardless of the overall socioeconomic status of the family. As such, this variant of power-control theory is less concerned with Marxist conceptualizations of the overall influence of the marketplace than with the *relative* locations of father and mother vis-à-vis the market and the home (p. 815).

Power-control theory further proposes that mothers are the major sources of socialization in the patriarchal family, and that the primary object of control in this family is the daughter. This control and supervision are thought to decrease a "taste for risk" in the child, and also to increase the youth's perception of punishment as a threat to his or her behavior. These factors are conceived as intervening between the structure of the family and delinquency. They are used to explain the associations between family occupational situation, gender, and delinquency.

The results of the analysis by Hagan et al. (1987) tend to verify the power-control theory of female delinquency. In the patriarchal families, mothers were the primary instruments of control and daughters were the main objects of supervision. In egalitarian and female-headed households, mothers were still important instruments of control, and daughters were the objects, but the relationships were not as strong as within patriarchal families. In addition, taste for risk and perceptions of punishment were associated with delinquency, in predicted directions. Daringness was higher among males than females, and girls perceived greater risk from delinquency than did boys (pp. 802–803). However, these relationships were particularly strong within patriarchal families. Finally, differentials in delinquency rates between males and females were much greater for patriarchal families than for egalitarian or female-headed households, and this primarily occurred because female delinquency increased within the latter two types of families (pp. 803–807, 810). The authors conclude, "The implication is that daughters are freest to be delinquent in families in which mothers either share power equally with fathers or do not share power with fathers at all" (p. 812).[5]

A replicative test of power-control theory presented evidence which supported many of its predictions, but extended the scope of analysis (Singer and Levine, 1988). This study addressed the influence of peer relations on delinquency, specifically by examining "group risk" (p. 629). The study was conducted with 705 public and private American suburban high school youth and 560 parents. Measures of family structure, risk orientation, and delinquency were similar to those used by Hagan et al., with the exception of adding a "measure of attitudes toward group risk-taking" (p. 630).

The results of Singer and Levine's analysis were similar to those of Hagan and his associates. Several of the predictions of power-control theory were supported. Boys were subject to less control than were girls, maternal control was more pronounced with girls than with boys, and boys had a greater "risk preference" and less perceived risk compared with girls (1988:635). However, contrary to Hagan et al., Singer and Levine found these relationships were stronger in egalitarian families, rather than in patriarchal ones (p. 635, 637). Moreover, girls expressed a *higher* level of group risk than did boys in patriarchal families, contrary to power-control theory (p. 637). In addition, boys were more delinquent than girls in egalitarian households (p. 639), again contrary to predictions.

Essentially, Singer and Levine's study provides mixed support for power-control theory. As a possible explanation of the contradictory results, they suggest that group risk taking (or subcultural) factors may influence an adolescent's reaction(s) to control and supervision efforts utilized by parents. For example, in egalitarian, or balanced, families males might resent the intrusive power of mothers, and women in general, in their lives. Their dissatisfaction with this type of female dominance might contribute to higher rates of delinquency among such males, particularly within a group context. Power-control theory may generally be accurate, therefore, but applicable in different ways in varying social contexts.

In an effort to specify the types of familial control exercised relative to males and females, Hill and Atkinson (1988) examined a part of power-control theory by using such concepts as parental support (paternal and maternal), appearance rules, and curfew rules. Support is measured by indications of a juvenile's relationship with a father or mother (such as perceived parental understanding). Appearance and curfew rules refer to parental expectations relative to a juvenile's personal appearance and homebound schedule, respectively.

Using a self-report delinquency scale with a sample of 3110 adolescent youth in Illinois, Hill and Atkinson conclude that parental support is inversely related to delinquency among males, while maternal support inhibits female delinquent behavior. Furthermore, parental support is more strongly associated with delinquency (inversely) than is either set of rules. However, boys are more deterred by appearance rules, while girls' behavior is more affected by curfew expectations (1988, 137–140). Thus, they argue that females are *not* the objects of control efforts more than are males; rather, girls and boys are subject to different types of controls, enforced by same-sex parents (p. 143).

Another feature of power-control theory is its assumption that common forms of delinquency are positively related to social class for both males and females. As mentioned in the previous chapter, many scholars are of the opinion that class plays a relatively small role in the explanation of delinquency. A similar conclusion has been reached by Jensen and Thompson, who maintain that patterns of delinquency among national samples of youth in the United States simply do not correspond to the class-related predictions of power-control theory (Jensen and Thompson, 1990), although Hagan et al. (1990) challenge this conclusion.

Furthermore, Morash and Chesney-Lind (1991) challenge some of the basic assumptions of power-control theory, as well as its class-related implications. Their contention is that, from a feminist perspective, nurturing parents and caregivers to children, including female youth, may be more common among women, but not necessarily so. Fathers, for example, might be more actively involved than mothers in the control of daughters' movements and relationships with males. In their view, power-control theory needs to be "reformulated" to accommodate these kinds of differences and the implications of these patterns for delinquency.

Upon examining a national sample of over 1400 youth, Morash and Chesney-Lind conclude that mother's place in the workforce has relatively little to do with delinquency, for males or females. However, family structure influences types of controls for both sexes, particularly when stepfathers are present. Also, girls are consistently less delinquent than boys, regardless of social class position or type of family system. Actually, delinquency among females is greater in lower-class families than in higher-status situations, although controls are decreased for girls in upper-class families (pp. 368–370). An interesting finding of this study is that child-rearing by mothers who are nurturing results in greater identification with the mother and reduced involvement in delinquency, while child-rearing by fathers tends to generate negative sanctions, which are related to higher rates of delinquency. Furthermore, the pattern of father involvement in child-rearing, followed by negative sanctions and then delinquency, is associated with both male and female delinquency (pp. 365–374).

All these studies certainly call for modifications and reconceptualizations in power-control theory as originally presented by Hagan and associates. In fairness to Hagan et al., some of these studies, such as those by Jensen and Thompson and Morash and Chesney-Lind, do not always use workplace classifications, or family structure measures, in strict accordance with the conceptualizations and methodologies proposed in power-control theory, and these inconsistencies could distort the findings of these studies (Hagan et al., 1990). It would seem evident at this point in time, however, that power-control theory, while offering an interesting perspective, needs to be considerably revised and more thoroughly examined before any definitive conclusions can be reached regarding its contribution to the explanation of female delinquency. One possible modification would be to examine the tenets of power-control theory within the context of social control or bond theory (Hagan et al., 1993).

Continued investigations into the validity of power-control theory indicate that the original notion of Hagan and associates, that the single-mother family is an example of an egalitarian family, is questionable. Leiber and Wacker (1997), for instance, studied the predictions of power-control theory with two samples of juveniles living in single-mother households, one in Seattle, Washington, and the other in Iowa. In neither sample did the results support the theory. Rather, in both cases, the data support the importance of peer associations in the explanation of delinquency (pp. 342–344).

There are still many family-related issues to be addressed, such as joint-custody arrangements, sibling interactions, and the like. Furthermore, more precise specifications of influences on parental control methods need to be introduced in order to assess more accurately the particular influence(s) of occupational position on parenting. Included here would be background characteristics such as education, age, geographical location, race and ethnicity, and other social factors which are known to affect behavior. In addition, thus far, the theory has been applied mainly to relatively minor acts of delinquency. To what extent it would contribute to an understanding of serious criminal activity is not known.

FEMINIST EXPLANATIONS OF FEMALE DELINQUENCY

The development of what have become known as "feminist" theories has also contributed to a greater understanding of female delinquency. According to Meda Chesney-Lind (1989:20), a feminist theory of female criminality is based on the idea that females are positioned in society in ways which produce vulnerability to victimization by males, including abuse and the negative effects of poverty (see also, Chesney-Lind and Shelden, 1992:80–81). Moreover, a feminist perspective addresses the reactions of females to male domination, from the context of women.

However, the literature on this subject indicates the presence of several varieties of "feminist" explanations of female delinquency (Simpson, 1989; Messerschmidt, 1993). One issue is the source of the domination and oppression of women by men. If the disadvantaged position of women is attributed to gender-role differences, then the feminist perspective is often referred to as "liberal" feminism (Simpson, 1989:607; Steffensmeier et al., 1989; Messerschmidt, 1993:23–25). A "radical feminist" perspective emphasizes the structured domination, often physical, of men over women, in a patriarchal society (Simpson, 1989:607–608; Messerschmidt, 1993:32–54). Marxist-feminist theory focuses on the negative impact of capitalism on male-female relationships, and the pressures on women to resort to criminal behavior in an attempt to gain greater control of their lives relative to males (Radosh, 1993). Others, however, such as Greenberg (1993), maintain that the term "Marxist-feminist" is a misnomer because Marx never developed a theory of female behavior, feminist or otherwise, although Greenberg does see some utility in pursuing an analysis of female crime and delinquency from a labor-force perspective.

Socialist-feminist theory attempts to synthesize Marxism (class) and patriarchy to focus on the structured domination and oppression of women by men, regardless of the capitalistic nature of the society. The socialist-feminist position maintains that in patriarchal societies men control not only important decisions and policies affecting both men and women, but that they also physically control the lives and decisions of women in interpersonal relationships (Simpson, 1989:607; Messerschmidt, 1993:54–66). From this perspective, female delinquency may be seen as a defensive reaction to male efforts to control and dominate their lives economically, emotionally, and/or physically.

In many ways, feminist theories address the reactions of social control officials, such as the police and court figures, to the behavior of females (Chesney-Lind, 1989; Simpson, 1989; Chesney-Lind and Shelden, 1992). While this is certainly an important subject, differential or discriminatory practices within the juvenile justice system are not the focus of this volume (with the partial exception of labeling theory; see Chapter 9). This position is similar to the one taken in Chapter 10, in connection with the radical theory of delinquency. However, with respect to explanations of illegal behavior among females, feminist theories offer promising avenues for future exploration and examination.

The utility of feminist theory as an explanation of criminality more likely rests with its overall position that behavior is gender contextualized and should be examined from this perspective (Chesney-Lind, 1989; Baskin and Sommers,

1990:especially p. 153; Carlen, 1990:118; Chesney-Lind and Shelden, 1992: Chapter 5), rather than in conceptualizing several varieties of this position. Also of importance are the methodological implications of qualitatively examining the contextual situations of behavior, in both industrialized societies and developing countries, where records and statistical information may not be available or reliable, although a feminist perspective does not necessarily equate with qualitative methods (Simpson, 1989:608–609). Actually, the use of ethnographic and other qualitative methods is needed to develop more basic information on criminality in general, whether this research is influenced by a feminist perspective.

The need to utilize more qualitative and contextualized assessments of female behavior is illustrated in the study of male-female patterns of self-reported delinquency in the Philippines (Shoemaker, 1994), which was mentioned in Chapter 8. In that study, it may be recalled, social bond factors explained virtually none of the variations in female delinquency within the sample studied. Perhaps part, or maybe even most, of the problem here is that the use of predetermined questions based on theoretical constructs generated in the West, with limited response options, is simply not sufficient to generate meaningful descriptions of behavioral patterns among females in developing countries. Again, this conclusion may well apply to general studies of crime and delinquency in geographical areas or among populations which have received relatively little attention from scholars in the past.

Thus, it seems appropriate to encourage further investigations into causal patterns of female delinquency from a feminist point of view, utilizing qualitative techniques of analysis. Besides generating more meaningful information on female criminality, research influenced by this perspective may also contribute to clearer understandings of male patterns of delinquency, and perhaps ultimately to an understanding of common factors in the explanation of crime and delinquency among males and females, which some argue should be the primary focus of attention in this area of research (Steffensmeier and Streifel, 1993:71–72).

SUMMARY

With the accumulation of evidence on the contributing factors to female criminality, it becomes increasingly clear that no simple answers are to be found for the explanation of female delinquency, any more than for an understanding of male offenses. Certainly, it would appear that we have come a long way from the simple, often paternalistic view of women and their transgressions which prevailed less than a century ago.

In the search to understand the delinquent behavior of people, theories that have been developed to explain male criminality are now being applied to female deviance as well. Because these theories seem to be appropriate for both sexes, some have called for the discontinuation of lines of inquiry that posit explanations of crime or delinquency among males as separate from females (Harris, 1977; Smith, 1979; Barton and Figueira-McDonough, 1985; Smith and Paternoster, 1987; Steffensmeier and Streifel, 1993).

While the investigation of factors that contribute to a *general* understanding of crime and delinquency is defensible, it may be too early to abandon the search for unique clues to an understanding of male behavior as distinct from female behavior (Farnworth, 1984). Not only are males and females biologically different but, even now, boys are socialized differently from girls. The influence of gender roles on behavior, for example, may be an important link between biological factors and a host of environmental factors that have been offered as explanations of behavior, and yet research on this topic is only just beginning to expand. In discussing sex-related behavior, both biologically and psychologically oriented accounts acknowledge the influence of environmental factors, such as parent-child interactions, on sexual identities and gender-role behavior (Money and Ehrhardt, 1972; Maccoby and Jacklin, 1974; Baucom et al., 1985; Ruble and Martin, 1998). Gender identification and sex-related behavior are very complex phenomena. It would thus be a mistake to ignore the investigation of gender-role perceptions and identifications in female (and male) delinquency, regardless of whether these are associated with the emancipation of women, *in favor* of continued explorations into general patterns of delinquency.

Notes

1. Pollak discusses the biological sources of female criminal behavior according to three major events: menstruation, pregnancy, and menopause (1950). Clearly, menopause lies outside the realm of adolescence and, for the most part, Pollak's discussion is focused on adult women more than adolescent girls. For additional information concerning the connection between menstruation and crime, see Shah and Roth, 1974.

2. Campbell (1986) reports a relatively high incidence of self-reported fighting among females in British schools, and in institutions for juvenile and adult offenders. The severity of injuries in such fights was usually limited to cuts and bruises, inflicted with hands and feet, not weapons (most felt it inappropriate to use a knife). Furthermore, the violence among these women and girls was not specifically associated with gang activity, female emancipation attitudes, or other forms of violent activity, such as robbery or murder. Thus, while fighting among females is more common than official records may indicate, it does not necessarily reflect a tendency toward committing more serious acts of violent crime, nor is it directly linked to liberated attitudes.

3. Austin (1982) argues that female liberation in America, as measured by changes in divorce rates and female labor force participation rates, cannot be overlooked as a possible cause of increased female crime rates (juvenile and adult) that started in the mid-1960s, especially for the crimes of robbery and auto theft. However, he acknowledges that other factors besides female emancipation may be responsible for this increased crime, such as an increase in self-service businesses and increased female exposure to television advertising and programming. Furthermore, although his crime data did include juveniles, his measures of emancipation (divorce and employment statistics) would appear to be more relevant for adults than for adolescents.

4. Canter (1982a) argues that family factors may be more significant as an explanation of male delinquency than female delinquency, especially for serious offenses. She also contends, however, that peer influences may be more important than family bonds in the etiology of female delinquency. The influence of peer group orientations on female delinquency is also found in research by Morash (1986).

5. An expanded discussion of power-control theory, including its potential to explain a wider range of deviance among females, is presented in Hagan, 1989, especially pp. 145–255.

References

Adler, Freda, 1975, Sisters in Crime. New York: McGraw-Hill.

Adler, Freda and William S. Laufer (eds.), 1993, New Directions in Criminological Theory. New Brunswick, N.J.: Transaction.

Adler, Freda and Rita James Simon (eds.), 1979, The Criminology of Deviant Women. Boston: Houghton Mifflin.

Agnew, Robert and Timothy Brezina, 1997, "Relational Problems with Peers, Gender, and Delinquency." Youth & Society 29:84–111.

Austin, Roy L., 1982, "Women's Liberation and Increases in Minor, Major, and Occupational Offenses." Criminology 20:407–430.

Barton, William H., 1976, "Youth in Correctional Programs." Pp. 20–53 in Robert Vinter (ed.), with Theodore M. Newcomb and Rhea Kish, Time Out. Ann Arbor, Mich: National Assessment of Juvenile Corrections.

Barton, William H. and Josefina Figueira-McDonough, 1985, "Attachments, Gender, and Delinquency." Deviant Behavior 6:119–144.

Baskin, Deborah R. and Ira B. Sommers, 1990, "The Gender Question in Research on Female Criminality." Social Justice 17:148–156.

Baucom, Donald H., Paige K. Besch, and Steven Callahan, 1985, "Relation Between Testosterone Concentration, Sex Role Identity, and Personality Among Females." Journal of Personality and Social Psychology 48:1218–1226.

Bonger, Willem, 1916, Criminality and Economic Conditions. Reprinted, Bloomington, Ind.: Indiana University Press, 1969.

Box, Steven and Chris Hale, 1983, "Liberation and Female Criminality in England and Wales." British Journal of Criminology 23:35–49.

Broidy, Lisa and Robert Agnew, 1997, "Gender and Crime: A General Strain Perspective." Journal of Research in Crime and Delinquency 34:275–306.

Burton, Velmer S., Jr., Francis T. Cullen, T. David Evans, Leanne Fiftal Alarid, and R. Gregory Dunaway, 1998, "Gender, Self-Control, and Crime." Journal of Research in Crime and Delinquency 35:123–147.

Campbell, Anne, 1986, "Self-Report of Fighting by Females: A Preliminary Study." British Journal of Criminology 26:28–46.

Canter, Rachelle J., 1982a, "Family Correlates of Male and Female Delinquency." Criminology 20:149–167.

———, 1982b, "Sex Differences in Self-Report Delinquency." Criminology 20:373–393.

Carlen, Pat, 1990, "Women, Crime, Feminism, and Realism." Social Justice 17:106–123.

Cavan, Ruth Shonle and Theodore N. Ferdinand, 1975, Juvenile Delinquency, third edition. Philadelphia: Lippincott.

Cernkovich, Stephen A. and Peggy C. Giordano, 1979a, "A Comparative Analysis of Male and Female Delinquency." Sociological Quarterly 20:131–145.

———, 1979b, "Delinquency, Opportunity, and Gender." Journal of Criminal Law and Criminology 70:301–310.

Chandy, Joseph M., Robert Wm. Blum, and Michael D. Resnick, 1996, "Gender-Specific Outcomes for Sexually Abused Adolescents." Child Abuse & Neglect 20:1219–1231.

Chesney-Lind, Meda, 1989, "Girls' Crime and Woman's Place: Toward a Feminist Model of Female Delinquency." Crime & Delinquency 35:5–29.

Chesney-Lind, Meda and Randall G. Shelden, 1992, Girls, Delinquency, and Juvenile Justice. Pacific Grove, Calif.: Brooks/Cole.

———, 1998, Girls, Delinquency, and Juvenile Justice, second edition. Belmont, Calif.: West/Wadsworth.

Cowie, John, Valerie Cowie, and Eliot Slater, 1968, Delinquency in Girls. London: Heinemann.

Cullen, Francis T., Kathryn M. Golden, and John B. Cullen, 1979, "Sex and Delinquency: A Partial Test of the Masculinity Hypothesis." Criminology 17:301–310.

Culliver, Concetta C. (ed.), 1993, Female Criminality: The State of the Art. New York: Garland.

Datesman, Susan K. and Frank R. Scarpitti, 1975, "Female Delinquency and Broken Homes: A Reassessment." Criminology 13:33–35.

Datesman, Susan K., Frank R. Scarpitti, and Richard M. Stephenson, 1975, "Female Delinquency: An Application of Self and Opportunity Theories." Journal of Research in Crime and Delinquency 12:107–123.

Duke, Daniel Linden and Paula Maguire Duke, 1978, "The Prediction of Delinquency in Girls." Journal of Research and Development in Education 11:18–33.

Empey, Lamar T., 1982, American Delinquency, revised editon. Homewood, Ill.: Dorsey.

Farnworth, Margaret, 1984, "Male-Female Differences in Delinquency in a Minority-Group Sample." Journal of Research in Crime and Delinquency 21:191–212.

Freud, Sigmund, 1933, New Introductory Lectures on Psychoanalysis, translated and edited by James Strachey. New York: Norton.

Gibbons, Don C., 1981, Delinquent Behavior, third edition. Englewood Cliffs, N.J.: Prentice-Hall.

Gibbons, Don C. and Manser Griswold, 1957, "Sex Differences Among Juvenile Court Referrals." Sociology and Social Research 42:106–110.

Giordano, Peggy C., 1978, "Guys, Girls, and Gangs: The Changing Social Context of Female Delinquency." Journal of Criminal Law and Criminology 69:126–132.

Giordano, Peggy C. and Stephen A. Cernkovich, 1979, "On Complicating the Relationship Between Liberation and Delinquency." Social Problems 26:467–481.

Glueck, Sheldon and Eleanor Glueck, 1934, Five Hundred Delinquent Women. New York: Knopf.

Greenberg, David F., 1993, "The Gendering of Crime in Marxist Theory." Pp. 405–442 in David F. Greenberg (ed.), Crime and Capitalism: Readings in Marxist Criminology. Philadelphia: Temple University Press.

Hagan, John, 1989, Structural Criminology. New Brunswick, N.J.: Rutgers University Press.

Hagan, John, A. R. Gillis, and John Simpson, 1985, "The Class Structure of Gender and Delinquency: Toward a Power-Control Theory of Common Delinquent Behavior." American Journal of Sociology 90:1151–1178.

———, 1990, "Clarifying and Extending Power-Control Theory." American Journal of Sociology 95:1024–1037.

———, 1993, "The Power of Control in Sociological Theories of Delinquency." Pp. 381–398 in Freda Adler and William S. Laufer (eds.), q.v.

Hagan, John, John Simpson, and A. R. Gillis, 1987, "Class in the Household: A Power-Control Theory of Gender and Delinquency." American Journal of Sociology 92:788–816.

Harris, Anthony R., 1977, "Sex and Theories of Deviance: Toward a Functional Theory of Deviant Type-Scripts." American Sociological Review 42:3–16.

Healy, William, 1915, The Individual Delinquent. Boston: Little, Brown.

Heimer, Karen, 1996, "Gender, Interaction, and Delinquency: Testing a Theory of Differential Social Control." Social Psychology Quarterly 59:39–61.

Hill, Gary D. and Maxine P. Atkinson, 1988, "Gender, Familial Control, and Delinquency." Criminology 26:127–149.

Hindelang, Michael J., 1971, "Age, Sex and the Versatility of Delinquent Involvements." Social Problems 18:522–535.

Hoffman, John P. and S. Susan Su, 1997, "The Conditional Effects of Stress on Delinquency and Drug Use: A Strain Theory Assessment of Sex Differences." Journal of Research in Crime and Delinquency 34:46–78.

Jensen, Gary F. and Raymond Eve, 1976, "Sex Differences and Delinquency: An Examination of Popular Sociological Explanations." Criminology 13:427–448.

Jensen, Gary F. and Kevin Thompson, 1990, "What's Class Got to Do with It? A Further Examination of Power-Control Theory." American Journal of Sociology 95:1009–1023.

Klein, Dorie, 1979, "The Etiology of Female Crime." Pp. 58–81 in Freda Adler and Rita James Simon (eds.), q.v.

Klein, Dorie and June Kress, 1979, "Any Woman's Blues." Pp. 82–90 in Freda Adler and Rita James Simon (eds.), q.v.

Konopka, Gisela, 1966, The Adolescent Girl in Conflict. Englewood Cliffs, N.J.: Prentice-Hall.

LaGrange, Teresa C. and Robert A. Silverman, 1999, "Low Self-Control and Opportunity: Testing the General Theory of Crime as an Explanation for Gender Differences in Delinquency." Criminology 37:41–72.

LeBlanc, Marc and Aaron Caplan, 1993, "Theoretical Formalization, a Necessity: The Example of Hirschi's Bonding Theory." Pp. 237–336 in Freda Adler and William S. Laufer (eds.), q.v.

Leiber, Michael J., Margaret Farnworth, Katherine M. Jamieson, and Mahesh K. Nalla, 1994, "Bridging the Gender Gap in Criminology: Liberation and Gender-Specific Strain Effects on Delinquency." Sociological Inquiry 64:56–68.

Leiber, Michael J. and Mary Ellen Ellyson Wacker, 1997, "A Theoretical and Empirical Assessment of Power-Control Theory and Single-Mother Families." Youth & Society 28:317–350.

Leonard, Eileen B., 1982, Women, Crime, and Society. New York: Longman.

Liu, Xiaoru and Howard B. Kaplan, 1999, "Explaining the Gender Difference in Adolescent Delinquent Behavior: A Longitudinal Test of Mediating Mechanisms." Criminology 37:195–215.

Lombroso, Cesare and Guglielmo Ferrero, 1895, The Female Offender. New York: Appleton.

Maccoby, Eleanor Emmons and Cary Nagy Jacklin, 1974, The Psychology of Sex Differences. Stanford, Calif.: Stanford University Press.

Mears, Daniel P., Matthew Ploeger, and Mark Warr, 1998, "Explaining the Gender Gap in Delinquency: Peer Influence and Moral Evaluations of Behavior." Journal of Research in Crime and Delinquency 35:251–266.

Messerschmidt, James W., 1993, Masculinities and Crime: Critique and Reconceptualization of Theory. Lanham, Md.: Rowman & Littlefield.

Miller, Walter B., 1975, Violence by Youth Gangs and Youth Groups as a Crime Problem in Major American Cities. Washington, D.C.: U.S. Government Printing Office.

Monahan, Thomas P., 1957, "Family Status and the Delinquent Child: A Reappraisal and Some New Findings." Social Forces 35:250–258.

Money, John and Anke A. Ehrhardt, 1972, Man and Woman: Boy and Girl. Baltimore: Johns Hopkins University Press.

Morash, Merry, 1986, "Gender, Peer Group Experiences, and Seriousness of Delinquency." Journal of Research in Crime and Delinquency 23:43–67.

Morash, Merry and Meda Chesney-Lind, 1991, "A Reformulation and Partial Test of the Power Control Theory of Delinquency." Justice Quarterly 8:347–377.

Morris, Ruth R., 1965, "Attitudes Toward Delinquency by Delinquents, Non-Delinquents and Their Friends." British Journal of Criminology 5:249–265.

Norland, Stephen, Neal Shover, William E. Thornton, and Jennifer James, 1979, "Intrafamily Conflict and Delinquency." Pacific Sociological Review 22:223–240.

Nye, F. Ivan, 1958, Family Relationships and Delinquent Behavior. New York: Wiley.

Pollak, Otto, 1950, The Criminality of Women. Philadelphia: University of Pennsylvania Press.

Radosh, Polly F., 1993, "Women and Crime in the United States: A Marxian Explanation." Pp. 263–289 in Concetta C. Culliver (ed.), q.v.

Reiss, Albert J., 1960, "Sex Offenses: The Marginal Status of the Adolescent." Law and Contemporary Problems 25:309–333.

Richards, Pamela, 1981, "Quantitative and Qualitative Sex Differences in Middle-Class Delinquency." Criminology 18:453–470.

Ruble, Diane N. and Carol Lynn Martin, 1998, "Gender Development." Chapter 14 in William Damon and Nancy Eisenberg (eds.), Handbook of Child Psychology, fifth edition, Vol. 3. New York: Wiley.

Shah, Saleem A. and Loren H. Roth, 1974, "Biological and Psychophysiological Factors in Criminality." Pp. 101–173 in Daniel Glaser (ed.), Handbook of Criminology. Chicago: Rand McNally.

Shoemaker, Donald J., 1994, "Male-Female Delinquency in the Philippines: A Comparative Analysis." Youth & Society 25:299–329.

Shover, Neal, Stephen Norland, Jennifer James, and William E. Thornton, 1979, "Gender Roles and Delinquency." Social Forces 58:162–175.

Simon, Rita James, 1975, The Contemporary Woman and Crime. Washington, D.C.: U.S. Government Printing Office.

Simpson, Sally S., 1989, "Feminist Theory, Crime, and Justice." Criminology 27:605–631.

Singer, Simon I. and Murray Levine, 1988, "Power-Control Theory, Gender, and Delinquency: A Partial Replication with Additional Evidence on the Effects of Peers." Criminology 26:627–647.

Smart, Carol, 1976, Women, Crime and Criminology. London: Routledge and Kegan Paul.

Smith, Douglas A., 1979, "Sex and Deviance: An Assessment of Major Sociological Variables." Sociological Quarterly 20:183–195.

Smith, Douglas A. and Raymond Paternoster, 1987, "The Gender Gap in Theories of Deviance: Issues and Evidence." Journal of Research in Crime and Delinquency 24:140–172.

Steffensmeier, Darrell and Emilie Allan, 1996, "Gender and Crime: Toward a General Theory of Female Offending." Annual Review of Sociology 22:459–487.

Steffensmeier, Darrell, Emilie Allan, and Cathy Streifel, 1989, "Development and Female Crime: A Cross-National Test of Alternative Explanations." Social Forces 68:262–283.

Steffensmeier, Darrell J. and Renee Hoffman Steffensmeier, 1980, "Trends in Female Delinquency: An Examination of Arrest, Juvenile Court, Self-Report, and Field Data." Criminology 18:62–85.

Steffensmeier, Darrell J. and Cathy Streifel, 1993, "Trends in Female Crime, 1960–1990." Pp. 63–101 in Concetta C. Culliver (ed.), q.v.

Sutherland, Anne, 1975, Gypsies: The Hidden Americans. London: Tavistock.

Sutherland, Edwin H. and Donald R. Cressey, 1978, Criminology, tenth edition. New York: Lippincott.

Thomas, William I., 1907, Sex and Society. Chicago: University of Chicago Press.

———, 1925, The Unadjusted Girl. Boston: Little, Brown.

Thornton, William E. and Jennifer James, 1979, "Masculinity and Delinquency Revisited." British Journal of Criminology 19:225–241.

Toby, Jackson, 1957, "The Differential Impact of Family Disorganization." American Sociological Review 22:505–512.

Vedder, Clyde B. and Dora B. Somerville, 1975, The Delinquent Girl, second edition. Springfield, Ill.: Charles C. Thomas.

Weis, Joseph G., 1982, "The Invention of the New Female Criminal." Pp. 152–167 in Leonard D. Savitz and Norman Johnston (eds.), Contemporary Criminology. New York: Wiley.

Wise, Nancy Barton, 1967, "Juvenile Delinquency Among Middle-Class Girls." Pp. 179–188 in Edmund W. Vaz (ed.), Middle-Class Juvenile Delinquency. New York: Harper & Row.

12

Delinquency Theory: An Integrative Approach

INTEGRATED THEORIES: SOME CONSIDERATIONS AND A PROPOSED MODEL

The search for the causes of delinquency has covered several centuries and numerous viewpoints. While we should despair of ever finding *the* answer, it is possible to point to promising theoretical positions that should provide valuable information on the understanding of delinquency.

Many of the discussions in the previous chapters provide examples of efforts to combine two or more theories, including cross-disciplinary perspectives, into a more complete explanatory model of delinquency. The purpose of the present chapter is to elaborate on this approach to an understanding of delinquent behavior. First, there is a discussion of some theoretical and methodological concerns with respect to theory integration. Then, one example of an integrated theory of delinquency is presented, based largely on the conclusions and interpretations presented throughout the other chapters in this book.

There have been several attempts to present multiple theoretical descriptions of crime and/or delinquency causation. Often, these efforts are depicted as "integrated" (Aultman and Wellford, 1979; Elliott et al., 1979; Empey, 1982; Colvin and Pauly, 1983; Pearson and Weiner, 1985; Buikhuisen and Mednick, 1988b), although the degree to which the theoretical model is integrated, including feedback loops, varies. Several other adjectives could be used to depict the kind of multiple explanatory efforts suggested here, such as mixed, synthetic, and convergent, to name a few. Whatever the name chosen, an important point is that the effort to combine different theoretical perspectives into an explanation of delinquent behavior is tempting to many, and an idea that needs to be explored further.[1]

Some theorists address more general patterns of crime and deviance, including delinquency (Kaplan et al., 1983, 1986; Kaplan, 1985; Wilson and Herrnstein, 1985; Gottfredson and Hirschi, 1990). Of these efforts, the work of Kaplan and his associates is a good example of an integrative approach, and his theory focuses on the general patterns of youth deviance (see discussions of Kaplan's work in Chapters 8 and 9 of this book).

Of the general explanations of criminality, one which is creating considerable interest among criminologists is proposed by Gottfredson and Hirschi (1990). Although this theory is not truly "integrative," it proposes that, generally, delinquent and criminal offenders lack "self-control," and it is this lack of self-control, combined with opportunity for committing crime, which contributes most significantly to antisocial behavior, although low self-control does not always lead to deviance (Gottfredson and Hirschi, 1990:especially Chapter 5). In this conceptualization, low self-control is viewed in constructs such as impulsivity, pursuit of pleasure, insensitivity to pain, adventuresomeness, and, frankly, many of the terms used to describe criminal personalities and tendencies which were discussed in Chapters 3 and 4 of this volume (see also, Arbuthnot et al., 1987: 147–151; Quay, 1987b:130). However, low self-control is not inborn, according to these authors. Rather, it is acquired from faulty patterns of socialization in the family and the school, a view which is reminiscent of the social control (bond) theory which Hirschi earlier espoused (see Chapter 8), but which is not invoked in this theoretical approach (Akers, 1991). Once developed, low self-control is viewed by Gottfredson and Hirschi as likely to continue, along with the associated tendency to commit acts of crime and delinquency.

This view is a comprehensive one, and, not surprisingly, has received a certain amount of criticism for lack of conceptual clarity in its current state of presentation (Akers, 1991). In addition, it is in contrast to the general view that, at least to some degree, separate causal explanations are needed for juvenile delinquency, as opposed to adult crime (McCord, 1991). Nonetheless, this theory of criminality is likely to spark continued interest and research on the causes of crime and delinquency. Some attempts to test the theory have provided support for its tenets (Grasmick et al., 1993; Wood et al., 1993). Moreover, the identification of low self-control as an explanation of delinquency is consistent with the inclusion of "arousal" constructs in the examination of various social controls, such as religiosity, on delinquency (see Chapter 8), and with the "risk-taking" component of power-control theory (see Chapter 11). Perhaps theory development in crime and delinquency is entering into a "continuum of controls" paradigm (Cochran et al., 1994:115). In this event, Gottfredson and Hirschi's ideas may be on the cutting edge.

Recent efforts to test this theory, however, raise doubts and qualifications regarding the applicability of low self-control as a predictor of delinquency in various sociocultural contexts, including populations of adult offenders (Creechan, 1995; Longshore et al., 1996; Arneklev et al., 1998; Piquero and Rosay, 1998; Katz, 1999). Some research casts doubt on the assumptions of the theory that age and gender differences in criminality are invariant (Jang and Krohn, 1995; Bartusch et al., 1997; Tittle and Grasmick, 1998; LaGrange and Silverman, 1999). Others, however, find the major tenets of the theory to be supported (Evans et al., 1997; Gibbs et al., 1998). All of these studies make the case for continued investigation into this theory, with longitudinal samples, modifications on measures of low self-control, applications to various sub-samples of the population, and in comparison to other explanations of delinquency (see also, Longshore et al., 1998).

Theoretical explanations of delinquency should account for why youth not only become involved in such activity, but also why they cease this type of behavior as they get older (Loeber et al., 1991; Smith and Brame, 1994). Of course, this task also faces the student of criminal behavior, for most adult criminals eventually cease committing illegal acts. However, the shift in patterns seems less abrupt among adults as compared to juveniles. Delinquency seems to be more common during the mid-to-late adolescent years (see Chapter 9). However, some delinquents continue their criminal activity into adulthood. Additionally, some adult criminals have no record of juvenile delinquency, although in all likelihood they did commit delinquent acts. Adult criminals, however, despite their backgrounds, eventually become more conformist, especially during middle age. General health changes may be used to explain, at least partially, the decline in criminality with increased age, but this physical process would not apply to adolescents, who, as a group, would be presumed to be in the prime of health. For the discussions to follow, the theoretical approaches will be those which pertain to delinquent behavior. This book is specifically a discourse on delinquency and, as noted above, there are valid reasons to focus on the illegal behavior of youths separately from adults (McCord, 1991).

Attempts to combine several theoretical explanations of delinquency into a coherent sequence of connecting events and outcomes face a number of major issues and concerns. For example, many current efforts to build integrated theories of delinquent behavior are, in part, informed by widely used multivariate methods of statistical analysis, such as multiple regression and path analysis. These techniques help to determine the relative influence different factors, including those constituent to varying theoretical positions, may have on delinquency. These assessments help to explain the comparative strength of competing factors in accounting for the outcome. However, as Hirschi

(1979) notes, such efforts are not always successful because different theories may themselves be separated into distinct units which are used to explain acts other than those measured in a multiple statistical analysis. Furthermore, if variables are strung out, in sequential fashion, toward the ultimate explanation or prediction of a designated behavioral pattern, the last factor examined may appear to be the only correct one, to the exclusion of the other events in the model (Hirschi, 1979), although this is not necessarily the case (Elliott, 1985). These possibilities are important to consider in developing combined theoretical explanations of delinquency because in nearly all of these efforts the factors proposed were originally used to explain delinquency *in and of themselves*.

Another issue facing integrative theories is the specific form of delinquent behavior to be explained. Many of the theoretical positions discussed in this volume were developed to explain delinquency in general. Yet, attempts to test these theories have often found them to be more applicable to some types of delinquency than to others. Social bond theory, for example, has been proposed as a general explanation of delinquency. Yet, as the discussion in Chapter 8 of this volume indicates, tests of the theory have tended to find it particularly useful as an explanation of more common and less serious acts of youth misconduct.

An illustration of the differential focus of multiple theory efforts is provided by Delbert Elliott and his colleagues. Building on an earlier statement of integrative theories to explain delinquency (Elliott et al., 1979), Elliott, Huizinga, and Ageton (1985) offer an integrated approach which includes strain (anomie) theory, inadequate socialization, and social disorganization as immediate precursors to weak conventional bonding to societal norms and institutions. Weak conventional bonding, in turn, leads to greater associations with delinquent and deviant peers. Delinquent peer association is conceptualized as the proximate cause of delinquency, but the other factors, especially weak social controls, are also important. This model was tested on a national "probability sample" of over 1700 American youth aged 11–17 (pp. 91–92). These people were interviewed three different times between 1977 and 1979. The focus of the interviews was on the youths' involvement in delinquency and drug use, using the explanatory model described above. The results of the surveys led Elliott et al. to conclude that their model was useful in explaining and predicting delinquency. However, variations in the power and utility of the integrated theory occurred with respect to different types of delinquent activity. For example, the theory explained 59 percent of the variation in marijuana use but only 29–34 percent of the distribution of hard drug use (p. 135).

A third issue facing mixed theoretical explanations of delinquency is the question of which factors to use as representations of different theories used in the model. Differential association, for example, is divided into nine propositions, each of which can be further subdivided into more discrete constructs.

Social bond or control theory has at least four major components, with several potential categories within each unit. If one were to include all major components of these two theories in one comprehensive model, there would be at least 13 variables, and most likely more than double that amount, in the theory. If other theoretical explanations were included, such as anomie, social disorganization, psychological, and biological theories, the number of potential variables in the analysis would soon approach 50! To test such a theory, a very large sample size would be necessary, in order to account for the influence of each variable, or set of variables, in the model. Large sample sizes are not easily garnered, particularly when voluntary responses from youth are being sought.

One way researchers have dealt with this issue is to limit the number of variables thought to be representative of each theoretical statement being considered. This solution is also partly reflective of the potential for overlapping explanation among variables within a theory, or between theories. Whatever the motivation(s), selection of "representative" theoretical variables involves decision-making procedures which are not standardized across research efforts. The aforementioned examination of the integrated theoretical proposal of Elliott et al., for example, ultimately used 8 measures, of a potential number of 25, to represent three theories in their model—strain, social control, and deviant peer bonding (1985:94, 141). The selection of these 8 variables was justified on the basis of statistical procedures, and the purpose of this discussion is not to challenge these procedures. However, other researchers not only might have conceived of alternative measures of these three theories besides the 25 presented, but they may have chosen different ones to be representative of these theories. In such instances, the results might be different from those found by Elliott and his colleagues (see, for example, Edwards, 1992).

A fourth concern regarding synthesis efforts is the generalizability of the theory to all segments of the population (Coie and Dodge, 1998:838). This issue is a troubling one for specific explanations of delinquency. Recall, for example, the focus on working- and/or lower-class youth which characterizes much of the literature on strain or anomie theory. This problem does not disappear when considering multiple theoretical explanations of delinquency; if anything, it becomes larger. The examination of the integrated model of Elliott et al. is based on the total sample of approximalely 1700 youth surveyed. Subgroups were not analyzed separately and, as the researchers acknowledge, the results of the analysis might have been different if different "subtypes" had been studied (1985:148).

To underscore this point further, Matsueda and Heimer (1987) report that learning theory (differential association) is a better explanation of delinquency among males than is social control theory. Attachments to parents and peers were indirectly related to delinquency through the variable of learning definitions favorable to violation of law, a central component of differential association theory (pp. 831–837). Furthermore, this process applied to both African-American and white youth. However, among African-American males in the sample, the effect of broken homes on delinquency (as measured by a self-report questionnaire) was significantly stronger than for whites, thus providing more support for social control theory for this subsample (p. 836). Since there is little reason to believe specific theories of delinquency apply equally well to all categories of youth, there should be similar misgivings regarding the generalizability of integrated theories to all subsamples of a population.

Not all research, of course, concludes that separate theories are needed for specific categories of juveniles. Segrave and Hastad (1985), for example, conclude that male and female patterns of self-reported delinquency are explained equally well by strain, subcultural, and control theories, particularly when all three perspectives are combined. Nevertheless, such convergence is not consistently found in studies which compare patterns of delinquency by categories such as race, ethnicity, and gender (see, for example, the discussion in Chapter 11). Consequently, the explanatory power of any particular integrated theory of delinquency cannot be presumed to be equally distributed across all social categories.

Another concern with mixed explanations of delinquency is the different basic assumptions each included theory may have with respect to motivations, attitudes, and the specific contributing factor to delinquency, as has repeatedly been demonstrated in this book. This situation may be even more pronounced when integrated theories are interdisciplinary. In essence, it becomes a matter of what is being explained, individual behavior or rates of criminality (Short, 1979, 1985, 1989). For example, strain or anomie theory assumes that delinquent youth basically strive for success and achievement through legitimate avenues but become frustrated when unable to do so, and instead turn to illegal methods of achieving success and recognition. In addition, this process is thought to be particularly relevant for youth in *lower socioeconomic positions* in society. On the other hand, social control, or bond, theory maintains that delinquency is more pronounced for youth who have lost their desire for achievement and recognition. In essence, these young people are more *alienated* from, and *less attached* to, society and its representatives than are less delinquent youth, and this situation applies to *all* people. Since these two theories offer opposing views on basic feelings and attitudes of delinquent children, and address different levels of explanation, it may be wondered how they could be combined to provide a unified explanation of delinquency.

However, these seeming incompatibilities need not sound the death knell for integrative theoretical proposals. It is becoming increasingly clear that such structural factors as anomie or social disorganization may be contributing to delinquency in indirect, albeit important, ways by rendering the lives of certain juveniles more susceptible to *detachment from* parents, schools, and conformist others in general and *attachment to* peers and those who are less conformist (Aultman and Wellford, 1979; Johnson, 1979; Elliott et al., 1985). Thus, one may generally desire to be successful through legitimate activity. However, when these avenues of achievement become difficult to pursue, identities and self-feelings are protected by rejecting those elements of society which promote conformity. These are complicated processes to be sure, but then people, young ones included, can be very complicated and perplexing to understand, particularly when confusing and frustrating events are occurring in their lives.

Others have taken structural theories and attempted to combine them with social control and learning theories to explain delinquency, but in ways different from the present discussion. In an integrated theory similar to the power-control theory of Hagan et al. (see Chapter 11) Colvin and Pauly (1983) provide an explanation of delinquency which starts with a radical, neo-Marxist set of assumptions and proceeds to examine the effects of the capitalist economy on work situations, family socialization patterns, and, ultimately, delinquency. These commentators suggest, as have others, that the more direct causes of delinquency lie in the patterns of parental socialization, and family relations in general, and subsequently in the peer associations of juveniles. Family relations, however, are more directly shaped by the occupational positions of parents, which are influenced by the economic system (a structural factor) of society, particularly capitalism. The particular links between capitalism, occupational norms, and authority structures and child-rearing practices are not clearly made by Colvin and Pauly, and they present no empirical tests of their theory. Messner and Krohn (1990) provide one example of a test of this theory, using the data from the Richmond Youth Survey (but excluding African-American youth from this particular report). Their analysis confirms significant relationships between delinquency and coercive family (and school) experiences and delinquent peer associations, which provides some support for Colvin and Pauly's theory. However, Messner and Krohn fail to identify any specific connections between social class (as conceptualized by Colvin and Pauly) and juveniles' attitudes toward family or school, or delinquent peer associations, a conclusion which fails to support the basic tenets of this theory.

While the contributions of a capitalist production system to occupational structure, and ultimately to socialization patterns, are speculative, and probably unrealistic (see Chapter 10), the attempt to reconcile these competing theoretical positions again illustrates how integrative theories might combine what may appear to be incompatible explanations of delinquency into a more unified vision of what is occurring.

While these issues and concerns may seem insurmountable to some, and lead them to reject integrative efforts to explain delinquency (Hirschi, 1979, 1989), others encourage such attempts despite these pitfalls and shortcomings (Short, 1979, 1989, 1998; Elliott, 1985; Greenberg, 1999). The trend in the literature concerning explanations of delinquency is in the direction of pursuing integrative efforts. What is to follow is an effort to combine many of the theoretical approaches discussed in this book into an "integrative" explanation of delinquency.

The first point to be made about the model to be presented is that it is focused on the origins of delinquency. Others, such as Elliott et al. (1985:137–148), have noted that present acts of delinquency are often good predictors of future illegal behavior, up to the point of maturation. Indeed, this process is one of the principle contentions of labeling theory, although the reasoning may not be accurate, as was indicated in Chapter 9. Nonetheless, a model of delinquency which proposes that delinquent behavior causes delinquent behavior does not explain much if there is little offered to help understand why the illegal activity occurred in the first place.

A second point to be made is that the model concerns delinquency in general, with due recognition of the complexities associated with explaining all types of delinquent behavior. Since no one theory, combined or otherwise, is going to explain the totality of youthful misconduct, one relatively useful alternative would be to focus on more general patterns of illegal activity. Consequently, the integrated approach to be discussed will be referenced to status offenses (again, acts which are illegal only for minors) and less serious forms of criminality. It may well be the case that the model is reasonably indicative of more serious acts, such as violent crimes, but these would not be the major target of attention.

Coie and Dodge (1998) present an outstanding review of the literature on interdisciplinary explanations of juvenile violence and antisocial behavior. While their interpretation of the underpinnings of juvenile offending is sequential and longitudinal, and supports a life-course or developmental perspective (see below), it is not integrated in the sense this term is used in the present chapter.

The proposed model of delinquency (Figure 14) is similar to other integrative attempts, especially Johnson (1979), Empey (1982:289–296), Elliott et al. (1985), and Hawkins and Lishner (1987). In this regard, the present suggestion is not entirely new. However, the purpose here is to demonstrate a sequential, and at points integrative, explanation of delinquency based on the analyses and conclusions presented in previous chapters. The causal factors are listed in horizontal fashion, with solid arrows depicting hypothesized strong connections between two factors in the sequence. Broken lines represent weaker as-

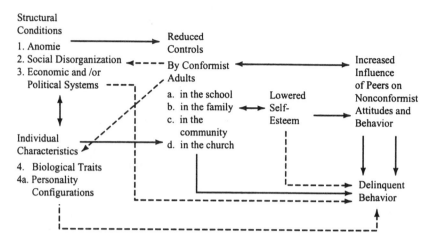

Figure 14

sociations. Double arrows indicate a *mutual* influence between two variables. For example, although many studies and several integrative proposals position lack of social controls before low self-esteem and increased peer associations, there is evidence to posit a feedback influence between self-concept and social attachments, particularly to conformist adults, and between peer associations and controls by adults. A solid double line is used to indicate a strong reciprocal influence between reduced adult controls and lowered self-esteem, as well as the connection between reduced controls and negative peer influence.

The explanatory model presented in Figure 14 incorporates three levels of conceptualization, structural (that is, pertaining to societal conditions), individual (biological and psychological), and social-psychological (social controls, self-esteem, and peer associations). To a very large extent, each set of factors corresponds to particular theories, but the connection is not absolute or complete. Structural conditions, for example, include variables related to anomie, social disorganization, and neo-Marxist or radical theories of delinquency. Social control factors pertain to the social bond. Self-esteem is associated, in part, with containment theory. Peer influences deal mainly with differential association but also include drift theory. Biological and personality trait conditions include numerous theoretical constructs discussed in Chapters 3 and 4. Among biological factors, no one particular theoretical position is advanced over another, although certain traits may be more feasibly examined. One "biosocial" explanation of adolescent sexual behavior, for example, postulates a connection between age, hormonal and pubertal development, social controls, and sexuality (Udry, 1988).[2] Psychological characteristics, however, are considered best represented by personality configurations. While other psychological variables may be used in integrative theories, the conclusion in this volume is that a more prudent approach would be to incorporate personality *attributes (not* a core personality) into the explanation of delinquency.

The leftmost factors in the figure are further demarcated with a numbering system which indicates the relative strength the corresponding item has, or is predicted to have, as an explanation of reduction in social controls. Thus, structural factors, in general, are depicted as having more of an impact on social bonding than are individualistic variables. Additionally, among structural conditions, anomie and social disorganization are thought to have stronger influences on social attachments than are economic and/or political systems. Among individual characteristics, biological and psychological factors are given equal weight in terms of their effect on social attachments. They may operate independently of societal conditions, although the two sets of variables could be interactive. If more serious forms of illegal behavior were to be the explained factor, individual characteristics would weigh more heavily in the model (see, for example, Buikhuisen, 1988; Peters et al., 1992). As demonstrated in Figure 14, structural and individual conditions usually indirectly influence delinquency, first through social controls and subsequently relative to self-esteem, and peer associations. At times, however, there may be a direct connection between delinquency and either societal factors or personal characteristics.

The weakened social controls occasioned by structural and/or individualistic situations occupy a major explanatory position in the model. A connection between the social bond and delinquency is predicted to occur through lowered self-concept and increased (negative) peer associations. However, there is ample evidence to justify positing a direct relationship between delinquency, especially less serious forms, and a weakened social bond, and this possibility is indicated in the model. Rather than focusing on specific elements of the social bond, the proposed integrative interpretation lists social, basically institutional, components of society. This listing is not haphazard. The particular situations of weakened controls by adults are listed in *descending* order of importance relative to delinquency, to self-esteem, and to peer connections. Also, the listing can be additive, such that weakened ties to two or more of these societal components would yield greater tendencies toward negative self-images and peer relations and/or delinquency than would any one unit separately.

The figure is based on the assumption that the first societal attachments for youth are with adults, usually in conformist institutional settings. Weakened ties to these adult figures decrease self-esteem and increase the likelihood of oppositional peer influences on a youth's attitudes and behavior, especially an adolescent youth. Either factor, weakened social bonds, lowered self-concept, or negative peer influences, can contribute directly to delinquency, but in combined form, the effect is powerful. Most likely, self-concept is determined, or at least largely influenced, by relationships with adults and/or peers. A negative self-image may logically be expected from poor relationships with *either* adults or youths, and bad experiences with both would only exacerbate the problem. A poor self-image may further erode positive relationships with adults and conformist peers, enhancing the likelihood of associating with nonconformist others, particularly delinquent peers, perhaps in an effort to restore damaged egos. In effect, the juvenile who has a weak or negative self-image, born of negative, rejecting relationships with adults, may seek alternative relations with other people, probably other peers, who will "accept" him/her more openly; at least this would be the youth's perception. This type of new acceptance, of course, may come from those who have been similarly rejected and now have delinquent, or deviant, values and attitudes, which they may attempt to pass along to the new "friend" or associate. Whether the youth's self-image improves from these new relationships is problematic (as the broken arrow suggests, the self-concept may become lower still), but his/her chances of engaging in delinquent conduct have now increased. Thus, this model of delinquency proposes that poor self-esteem most often *indirectly* contributes to delinquency, through negative experiences with conformist adults and/or strong associations with nonconformist peers, a position which is at variance with the assumption of containment theory. Still, it is acknowledged that having a low self-concept may sometimes directly lead to delinquent conduct.[3]

The proposed integrated model is a modest one, with restricted explanatory foci. It does not adequately address the situation in which one's original associations are with nonconformist adults and peers. In areas characterized by high rates of crime, deviance, and social disorganization, for example, associations, perhaps role models, of some youth may well be with nonconformists. Even in these areas, however, many prosocial settings involving adults and youth exist, as was discussed in Chapter 5. Furthermore, among deviant adults there has been noted the wish to impart conformist values to their children, and presumably to other youth in the area. Being rejected by deviant others, however, does not necessarily mean one will turn to conformists for support. Perhaps the search for acceptance would lead one to associate with other deviants, and the model being proposed would also fit these youth.

As has been stressed throughout this volume, more contemporary thinking in the literature concerning explanations of delinquency is incorporating feedback effects from delinquency to its suggested "causal" antecedents. This interactional conceptualization from delinquency to its suspected antecedents is missing in the present example of an integrated theory of delinquency, but it is becoming the subject of theory and research in this field. Sampson and Laub (1994), for example, contend that the relationship between parenting skills and delinquency should incorporate the situation wherein "difficult" children contribute to "ineffective parenting" of these juveniles (p. 534; see also, Agnew, 1991). However, one of the more systematically developed interactive theories of delinquency is offered by Terence Thornberry.

An earlier paper by Thornberry (1987) conceptualizes delinquency in integrated terms, but with the addition of an interactional connection between delinquency and disconnections to societal institutions. Essentially, the model proposed by Thornberry suggests that delinquency is better viewed as the result of events which occur in a developmental fashion, with some factors affecting illegal behavior at certain ages and other variables exerting a greater influence at later ages, or stages of development (see also, Matsueda, 1989).

Furthermore, delinquency is not viewed as the end product in this scheme; rather, delinquency leads to the formation of delinquent values, which in turn contribute to disconnections in social bonds, more attachments to delinquent peers, and further involvement in delinquency. For example, Thornberry proposes that lack of attachments to parents is a significant contributor to delinquency among those in "early adolescence" (11-13 years old), while attenuations in school bonds and associations with peers assume greater significance in the lives of juveniles in the stage of "middle adolescence" (15-16 years old). In addition, in middle adolescence, delinquent values become more important, particularly in terms of causation of further involvement in delinquency (pp. 870–879). In "later adolescence" (ages 18–20), "criminal" behavior is shaped more by lack of commitment to "conventional" activities, such as "employment, attending college, and military service," than by parental and school factors (pp. 879–881).

Thornberry et al. (1991, 1994) offer some support for this theoretical perspective in examinations of a longitudinal study of youth in New York (the Rochester Youth Development Study). In one study, their analysis suggests that weakened bonds to parents and school contribute to delinquency, but that delinquent behavior also contributes to a further weakening of these bonds (1991:19–25). In another examination of these data, Thornberry et al. conclude that peer influences are of primary importance in the development of delinquent behavior patterns, delinquent beliefs (or values), and the *interactions* among these variables (1994:74). The importance of peers would be consistent with the integrated theory proposed in this chapter.

Moreover, the developmental implications of this theory fit within the criminological debate which has been discussed throughout this book. That is, are there underlying, persistent personal characteristics, such as lack of self-control, which contribute to delinquency early in life, and which continue to influence criminal and deviant behavior into adulthood (Gottfredson and Hirschi, 1990)? Or are manifestations of criminal and delinquent behavior changeable and subject to alterations throughout the life course (Sampson and Laub, 1993)?

Clearly, Thornberry's interactional theory does not identify personal traits, such as lack of self-control, as the underlying factor in the explanation of delinquency. Rather, this perspective emphasizes attenuations in the social bond and delinquent peer relationships in the initial explanation of delinquency. However, the developmental trajectories proposed in this theory suggest that the interaction among weak social bonds, associations with delinquent peers, delinquent behavior, and delinquent beliefs assumes a spiraling, cumulative effect. Thus, in this view, delinquency is reinforced and would be expected to continue, even into adult crime (Thornberry, 1987:882–884). Furthermore, this interactive network is discussed in terms of structural factors such as social class, and it is contended that the cumulative interactions which contribute to delinquency are likely to be more common among the "lowest classes," while the opposite trajectory is predicted for middle-class adolescents (p. 885).

While police statistics report the overrepresentation of lower-class youth (Thornberry, 1987:885), this scenario fails to address the rather substantial presence of middle-class delinquency (see Chapter 6). Moreover, the prediction that delinquency will persist throughout adolescence and into adulthood is consistent with the projected life patterns of delinquency and crime proposed by some, such as Gottfredson and Hirschi (1990) and Hagan (1993), but it is inconsistent with the views of others, such as Sampson and Laub (1993). In addition, racial and gender issues concerning developmental patterns of delinquency and criminal behavior have not been thoroughly incorporated into this theory, as Thornberry acknowledges (1987:887), although the examinations of the theory by Thornberry et al. fail to locate any significant racial or gender variations in the results (1991:27–29; 1994:67).

Despite the inconsistencies relative to the predictions of this theory, and the lack of clear specification concerning its accuracy for diverse categories of people, Thornberry's interactional perspective seems to make sense of much of the existing literature on explanations of delinquency, particularly from an environmental perspective. Furthermore, interactional conceptualizations are becoming more common among researchers, and are being incorporated into interdisciplinary studies as well. Most importantly, interactional theories are consistent with the actual settings in which humans live and interact with others and with their environment in general (Thornberry et al., 1994:76). Future conceptualizations and investigations of explanations of delinquency will undoubtedly address this perspective in more detail and with increasing precision, thus contributing significantly to a greater understanding of the total causal nexus of delinquent behavior. For example, Matsueda and Anderson (1998) make a strong case for linking interactional theory with learning theory (peer relationships) and delinquency. Others suggest that interactional theory be integrated with a developmental perspective on delinquency (LeBlanc et al., 1992).

Throughout this book, reference has been made to the view that delinquency is a product of complicated "multiple pathways," with many turns and twists that contribute to delinquency. Sometimes, these events are the result of labeling, as discussed in Chapter 9. Sampson and Laub (1993) make a strong case for the influence of social and environmental life-course events, particularly familial socialization and marriage, in the shaping of deviant or conforming behavior patterns. Moffitt (1993, 1997), Patterson and Yoerger (1993), and others present convincing evidence that there are at least two "developmental" paths to delinquency, one occurring before adolescence, which is more persistent, and another which develops in adolescence and seems to be relatively short-lived (see Chapters 3 and 4 in this volume).

Of course, the multiple pathway, or developmental, perspective seems to be at odds with more basic explanations of crime and delinquency, currently being espoused by Gottfredson and Hirschi's general (low self-control) theory of crime. A considerable amount of research has been devoted to this debate in the past few years, with examinations of different longitudinal data sets. The weight of the evidence and conclusions presented in these studies favors the life-course, or multiple pathways, perspective over the general trait view of delinquency (Bartusch et al., 1997; Paternoster and Brame, 1997; Simons et al., 1998; Warr, 1998).

Loeber et al. (1998) present what may be a compromise view concerning this debate. They summarize the major findings of a longitudinal study of male delinquency, the Pittsburgh Youth Study. Among the many conclusions of this research is the notion that there are at least three pathways to serious forms of delinquency: (1) the "Authority Conflict Pathway," which is associated with defiance and challenges to authority; (2) the "Covert Pathway," which includes "lying, vandalism, and theft"; and (3) the "Overt Pathway," the most aggressive and violent of the three. Furthermore, these patterns of delinquency seem to develop sequentially, from less serious to more serious behaviors, beginning before adolescence (pp. 149–151). However, an individual trait which is strongly associated with delinquency, presumably with all developmental models, is impulsivity (pp. 151–153), a finding which is consistent with the general theory of crime.

As with all debates, the final resolution of these competing perspectives awaits additional research, and perhaps a further modification of the existing explanatory models. It is fairly certain, however, that a dynamic depiction of delinquency causation will ultimately be the more accepted explanatory model, even if it contains a more singular "latent" individual trait, or constellation of traits, as one of the pathways to youthful offending.

What is needed in delinquency theory and research is continued understanding of how delinquency develops and is either maintained or discontinued, whether for a short period of time or more permanently (Loeber et al., 1991; Elliott, 1994; Smith and Brame, 1994). At this point it would seem that the way to approach this goal is to attempt to amalgamate existing theories, building on the relative strengths of each and increasing their explanatory power.

We should not pretend to be so knowledgeable of human behavior as to unequivocally cast aside any effort to explain it. The informed student of delinquency should know what various theories offer, their strengths, their weaknesses, and their interconnections. If this is accomplished, more sophisticated interpretations of juvenile delinquency become possible, and the eventual management of such behavior comes more within our reach.

Notes

1. One edited work compiles several papers prepared for discussion at a conference held in 1987 at SUNY Albany, concerning problems and prospects of theoretical integration for explanations of crime and deviance (Messner et al., 1989). Generally, the authors of the papers tend to favor efforts to develop and/or test integrative theories, but with the awareness that such attempts face many problematic issues. Also, see Akers (1994:181–197) for an excellent discussion of integrative theories and several examples of such theories, including those of Elliott et al., Kaplan, and Thornberry.

2. C. Ray Jeffery (1989) advocates an interdisciplinary approach which would more carefully incorporate biological factors into an explanation of delinquency. Jeffery argues that many sociological concepts and theories have biological bases, but these are not explored. To emphasize this point he states, "No muscle has ever been moved by a social bond or a self-concept" (p. 85). See also, Jeffery (1994). Others call for more inclusion of psychological and social-psychological concepts in theories of crime and delinquency (Gibbons, 1989; Wood et al., 1993:125–126). It would seem from the discussions in Chapters 3 and 4 that current research is, indeed, becoming more interdisciplinary, and perhaps cognizant of the view that while no muscle may have ever been moved by a social bond, individual characteristics and environmental factors combine, and sometimes interact, to produce behavior, conformist or illegal.

3. Again, it should be emphasized that self-esteem, or self-concept, as used in the present context is conceptualized in positive or negative terms. It is possible that one may *identify* with criminal attitudes, commit criminal acts accordingly, and possess a *positive* self-concept (see the discussions in Chapters 8 and 9). The position taken in this volume, however, is that delinquency is more often associated, indirectly, with low self-esteem.

References

Agnew, Robert, 1991, "A Longitudinal Test of Social Control Theory and Delinquency." Journal of Research in Crime and Delinquency 28:126–156.

———, 1995, "Testing the Leading Crime Theories: An Alternative Strategy Focusing on Motivational Processes." Journal of Research in Crime and Delinquency 32:363–398.

Akers, Ronald L., 1991, "Self-Control as a General Theory of Crime." Journal of Quantitative Criminology 7:201–211.

———, 1994, Criminological Theories: Introduction and Evaluation. Los Angeles: Roxbury.

Arbuthnot, Jack, Donald A. Gordon, and Gregory J. Jurkovic, 1987, "Personality." Pp. 139–183 in Herbert C. Quay (ed.), q.v.

Arneklev, Bruce J., John K. Conklin, and Randy R. Gainey, 1998, "Testing Gottfredson and Hirschi's 'Low Self-Control' Stability Hypothesis: An Exploratory Analysis." American Journal of Criminal Justice 23:107–127.

Aultman, Madeline G. and Charles F. Wellford, 1979, "Towards an Integrated Model of Delinquency Causation: An Empirical Analysis." Sociology and Social Research 63:316–327.

Bartusch, Dawn R. Jeglum, Donald R. Lynam, Terrie E. Moffitt, and Phil A. Silva, 1997, "Is Age Important? Testing a General Versus a Developmental Theory of Antisocial Behavior." Criminology 35:13–48.

Buikhuisen, Wouter, 1988, "Chronic Juvenile Delinquency: A Theory." Pp. 27–47 in Wouter Buikhuisen and Sarnoff A. Mednick (eds.), q.v.

Buikhuisen, Wouter and Sarnoff A. Mednick (eds.), 1988a, Explaining Criminal Behavior: Interdisciplinary Approaches. Leiden, The Netherlands: E. J. Brill.

Buikhuisen, Wouter and Sarnoff A. Mednick, 1988b, "The Need for an Integrative Approach to Criminology." Pp. 3–7 in Wouter Buikhuisen and Sarnoff A. Mednick (eds.), q.v.

Cochran, John K., Peter B. Wood, and Bruce J. Arneklev, 1994, "Is the Religiosity-Delinquency Relationship Spurious? A Test of Arousal and Social Control Theories." Journal of Research in Crime and Delinquency 31:92–123.

Coie, John D. and Kenneth A. Dodge, 1998, "Aggression and Antisocial Behavior." Chapter 12 in William Damon and Nancy Eisenberg (eds.), q.v.

Colvin, Mark and John Pauly, 1983, "A Critique of Criminology: Toward an Integrated Structural-Marxist Theory of Delinquency Production." American Journal of Sociology 89:513–551.

Creechan, James H., 1995, "A Test of the General Theory of Crime: Delinquency and School Dropouts." Pp. 226–244 in James H. Creechan and Robert A. Silverman (eds.), Canadian Delinquency. Scarborough, Ontario: Prentice-Hall Canada.

Damon, William and Nancy Eisenberg (eds.), 1998, Handbook of Child Psychology, fifth edition, Vol. 3. New York: Wiley.

Edwards, Willie J., 1992, "Predicting Juvenile Delinquency: A Review of Correlates and a Confirmation by Recent Research Based on an Integrated Theoretical Model." Justice Quarterly 9:553–583.

Elliott, Delbert S., 1985, "The Assumption That Theories Can Be Combined with Increased Explanatory Power: Theoretical Interpretations." Pp. 123–149 in Robert F. Meier (ed.), q.v.

———, 1994, "Serious Violent Offenders: Onset, Developmental Course, and Termination—The American Society of Criminology 1993 Presidential Address." Criminology 32:1–21.

Elliott, Delbert S., Suzanne S. Ageton, and Rachelle J. Canter, 1979, "An Integrated Theoretical Perspective on Delinquent Behavior." Journal of Research in Crime and Delinquency 16:3–27.

Elliott, Delbert S., David Huizinga, and Suzanne S. Ageton, 1985, Explaining Delinquency and Drug Use. Beverly Hills, Calif.: Sage.

Empey, Lamar T., 1982, American Delinquency, revised edition. Homewood, Ill.: Dorsey.

Evans, T. David, Francis T. Cullen, Velmer S. Burton, Jr., R. Gregory Dunaway, and Michael L. Benson, 1997, "The Social Consequences of Self-Control: Testing the General Theory of Crime." Criminology 35:475–501.

Gibbons, Don C., 1989, "Comment—Personality and Crime; Non-Issues, Real Issues, and a Theory and Research Agenda." Justice Quarterly 6:311–323.

Gibbs, John J., Dennis Giever, and Jamie S. Martin, 1998, "Parental Management and Self-Control: An Empirical Test of Gottfredson and Hirschi's General Theory." Journal of Research in Crime and Delinquency 35:40–70.

Gottfredson, Michael R. and Travis Hirschi, 1990, A General Theory of Crime. Stanford, Calif.: Stanford University Press.

Grasmick, Harold G., Charles R. Tittle, Robert J. Bursik, Jr., and Bruce J. Arneklev, 1993, "Testing the Core Empirical Implications of Gottfredson and Hirschi's General Theory of Crime." Journal of Research in Crime and Delinquency 30:5–29.

Greenberg, David F., 1999, "The Weak Strength of Control Theory." Crime & Delinquency 45:66–81.

Hagan, John, 1993, "The Social Imbeddedness of Crime and Unemployment." Criminology 31:465–491.

Hawkins, J. David and Denise M. Lishner, 1987, "Schooling and Delinquency." Pp. 179–221 in Elmer J. Johnson (ed.), Handbook on Crime and Delinquency Prevention. Westport, Conn.: Greenwood Press.

Hirschi, Travis, 1979, "Separate and Unequal Is Better." Journal of Research in Crime and Delinquency 16:34–38.

———, 1989, "Exploring Alternatives to Integrated Theory." Pp. 37–49 in Steven F. Messner, Marvin D. Krohn, and Allen E. Liska (eds.), q.v.

Hodgins, Sheilagh (ed.), 1993, Mental Disorder and Crime. Newbury Park, Calif.: Sage.

Jang, Sung Joon and Marvin D. Krohn, 1995, "Developmental Patterns of Sex Differences in Delinquency Among African American Adolescents: A Test of the Sex-Invariant Hypothesis." Journal of Quantitative Criminology 11:195–222.

Jeffery, C. Ray, 1989, "An Interdisciplinary Theory of Criminal Behavior." Pp. 69–87 in William S. Laufer and Freda Adler (eds.), Advances in Criminological Theory. New Brunswick, N.J.: Transaction.

————, 1994, "Biological and Neuropsychiatric Approaches to Criminal Behavior." Pp. 15–28 in Gregg Barak (ed.), Varieties of Criminology: Readings from a Dynamic Discipline. Westport, Conn.: Praeger.

Johnson, Richard E., 1979, Juvenile Delinquency and Its Origins. Cambridge: Cambridge University Press.

Kaplan, Howard B., 1985, "Testing a General Theory of Drug Abuse and Other Deviant Adaptations." Journal of Drug Issues 15:477–492.

Kaplan, Howard B., Steven S. Martin, and Robert J. Johnson, 1986, "Self-Rejection and the Explanation of Deviance: Specification of the Structure Among Latent Constructs." American Journal of Sociology 92:384–411.

Kaplan, Howard B., Cynthia Robbins, and Steven S. Martin, 1983, "Toward the Testing of a General Theory of Deviant Behavior in Longitudinal Perspective: Patterns of Psychopathology." Research in Community and Mental Health 3:27–65.

Katz, Rebecca S., 1999, "Building the Foundation for a Side-by-Side Explanatory Model: A General Theory of Crime, the Age-Graded Life-Course Theory, and Attachment Theory." Western Criminology Review 1 (1) [Online]. Available: htpp://wcr.sonoma.edu/v1n2/katz.html.

LaGrange, Teresa C. and Robert A. Silverman, 1999, "Low Self-Control and Opportunity: Testing the General Theory of Crime as an Explanation for Gender Differences in Delinquency." Criminology 37:41–72.

LeBlanc, Marc, Evelyne Vallieres, and Pierre McDuff, 1992, "Adolescents' School Experience and Self-Reported Offending: An Empirical Elaboration of an Interactional and Developmental School Social Control Theory." International Journal of Adolescence and Youth 3:197–247.

Loeber, Rolf, David P. Farrington, Magda Stouthamer-Loeber, Terrie E. Moffitt, and Avshalom Caspi, 1998, "The Development of Male Offending: Key Findings from the Pittsburgh Youth Study." Studies in Crime and Crime Prevention 7:141–171.

Loeber, Rolf, Magda Stouthamer-Loeber, Welmoet van Kammen, and David P. Farrington, 1991, "Initiation, Escalation, and Desistance in Juvenile Offending and Their Correlates." The Journal of Criminal Law and Criminology 82:36–82.

Longshore, Douglas, Judith A. Stein, and Susan Turner, 1998, "Reliability and Validity of a Self-Control Measure: A Rejoinder." Criminology 36:175–182.

Longshore, Douglas, Susan Turner, and Judith A. Stein, 1996, "Self-Control in a Criminal Sample: An Examination of Construct Validity." Criminology 34:209–228.

Matsueda, Ross L., 1989, "The Dynamics of Moral Beliefs and Minor Deviance." Social Forces 68:428–457.

Matsueda, Ross L. and Kathleen Anderson, 1998, "The Dynamics of Delinquent Peers and Delinquent Behavior." Criminology 36:269–308.

Matsueda, Ross L. and Karen Heimer, 1987, "Race, Family Structure, and Delinquency." American Sociological Review 52:826–840.

McCord, Joan, 1991, "Family Relationships, Juvenile Delinquency, and Adult Criminality." Criminology 29:397–417.

Meier, Robert F. (ed.), 1985, Theoretical Methods in Criminology. Beverly Hills, Calif.: Sage.

Messner, Steven F. and Marvin D. Krohn, 1990, "Class, Compliance Structures, and Delinquency: Assessing Integrated Structural-Marxist Theory." American Journal of Sociology 96:300–328.

Messner, Steven F., Marvin D. Krohn, and Allen E. Liska (eds.), 1989, Theoretical Integration in the Study of Deviance and Crime: Problems and Prospects. Albany, N.Y.: State University of New York Press.

Moffitt, Terrie E., 1993, "Life-Course-Persistent and 'Adolescent-Limited' Antisocial Behavior: A Developmental Taxonomy." Psychological Review 100:674–701.

———, 1997, "Adolescence-Limited and Life-Course-Persistent Offending: A Complementary Pair of Developmental Theories." Pp. 11–54 in Terence P. Thornberry (ed.), Developmental Theories of Crime and Delinquency. New Brunswick, N.J.: Transaction.

Paternoster, Raymond and Robert Brame, 1997, "Multiple Routes to Delinquency? A Test of Developmental and General Theories of Crime." Criminology 35:49–84.

Patterson, Gerald R. and Karen Yoerger, 1993, "Developmental Models for Delinquent Behavior." Pp. 140–172 in Sheilagh Hodgins (ed.), q.v.

Pearson, Frank S. and Neil Alan Weiner, 1985, "Toward an Integration of Criminological Theories." Journal of Criminal Law and Criminology 76:116–150.

Peters, Ray DeV., Robert J. McMahon, and Vernon L. Quinsey (eds.), 1992, Aggression and Violence Throughout the Life Span. Newbury Park, Calif.: Sage.

Piquero, Alex R. and Andre B. Rosay, 1998, "The Reliability and Validity of Grasmick et al.'s Self-Control Scale: A Comment on Longshore et al." Criminology 36:157–173.

Quay, Herbert C. (ed.), 1987a, Handbook of Juvenile Delinquency. New York: Wiley.

———, 1987b, "Patterns of Delinquent Behavior." Pp. 118–138 in Herbert C. Quay (ed.), q.v.

Sampson, Robert J. and John H. Laub, 1993, Crime in the Making: Pathways and Turning Points Through Life. Cambridge, Mass.: Harvard University Press.

———, 1994, "Urban Poverty and the Family Context of Delinquency: A New Look at Structure and Process in a Classic Study." Child Development 65: 523–540.

Segrave, Jeffrey O. and Douglas N. Hastad, 1985, "Evaluating Three Models of Delinquency Causation for Males and Females: Strain Theory, Subculture Theory, and Control Theory." Sociological Focus 18:1–17.

Short, James F., Jr., 1979, "On the Etiology of Delinquent Behavior." Journal of Research in Crime and Delinquency 16:28–33.

———, 1985, "The Level of Explanation Problem in Criminology." Pp. 51–72 in Robert F. Meier (ed.), q.v.

———, 1989, "Exploring Integration of Theoretical Levels of Explanation: Notes on Gang Delinquency." Pp. 243–259 in Steven F. Messner, Marvin D. Krohn, and Allen E. Liska (eds.), q.v.

————, 1998, "The Level of Explanation Problem Revisited—The American Society of Criminology 1997 Presidential Address." Criminology 36:3–36.

Simons, Ronald L., Christine Johnson, Rand D. Conger, and Glen Elder, Jr., 1998, "A Test of Latent-Trait Versus Life-Course Perspectives on the Stability of Adolescent Antisocial Behavior." Criminology 36:217–243.

Smith, Douglas A. and Robert Brame, 1994, "On the Initiation and Continuation of Delinquency." Criminology 32:607–629.

Thornberry, Terence P., 1987, "Toward an Interactional Theory of Delinquency." Criminology 25:863–891.

Thornberry, Terence P., Alan J. Lizotte, Marvin D. Krohn, Margaret Farnworth, and Sung Joon Jang, 1991, "Testing Interactional Theory: An Examination of Reciprocal Causal Relationships Among Family, School and Delinquency." Journal of Criminal Law and Criminology 82:3–35.

————, 1994, "Delinquent Peers, Beliefs, and Delinquent Behavior: A Longitudinal Test of Interactional Theory." Criminology 32:47–83.

Tittle, Charles R. and Harold G. Grasmick, 1998, "Criminal Behavior and Age: A Test of Three Provocative Hypotheses." Journal of Criminal Law and Criminology 88:309–342.

Udry, J. Richard, 1988, "Biological Predispositions and Social Control in Adolescent Sexual Behavior." American Sociological Review 53:709–722.

Warr, Mark, "Life-Course Transitions and Desistance from Crime." Criminology 36:183–216.

Wilson, James D. and Richard J. Herrnstein, 1985, Crime and Human Nature. New York: Simon and Schuster.

Wood, Peter B., Betty Pfefferbaum, and Bruce J. Arneklev, 1993, "Risk-Taking and Self-Control: Social Psychological Correlates of Delinquency." Journal of Crime and Justice 16:111–130.

AUTHOR INDEX

Abbott, Robert D., 131
Abrahamsen, David, 70
Adams, Mike S., 209
Adams, Reed, 142, 155
Adams, Stuart N., 64, 66, 71
Adler, Freda, 43, 100, 106, 131, 188, 213, 232, 237, 238–9, 241, 254
Ageton, Suzanne S., 52, 71, 128, 132, 156, 203–4, 207, 210, 211, 263, 264, 276
Agnew, Robert, 67, 70, 98, 100, 101, 130, 131, 153, 155, 185, 186, 188, 244, 254, 275
Aichhorn, August, 56, 57, 58, 70
Akers, Ronald L., 7, 8, 10, 17, 19, 128, 131, 133, 142, 155, 172, 188, 219, 228, 261, 274, 275
Alarid, Leanne Fiftal, 255
Albada-Lim, Estefania, 148, 155
Albanese, Jay, 129, 131
Albrecht, Gary L., 171, 190
Alexander, Franz, 56, 57, 70
Allan, Emilie Anderson, 120, 131, 135, 242, 245, 258
Anderson, Kathleen, 273, 277
Andrews, David W., 155, 156
Arbuthnot, Jack, 261, 275
Ariès, Phillippe, 222, 228
Arneklev, Bruce J., 189, 262, 275, 276, 279
Arnold, William R., 223, 228
Arthur, Michael W., 189
Aseltine, Robert H., Jr., 146, 155
Atkinson, Maxine P., 248–9, 256
Aultman, Madeline G., 260, 266
Austin, James, 12, 19, 48, 73, 159, 191, 222, 229
Austin, Roy L., 51, 66, 71, 127, 131, 254
Austin, W. Timothy, 19
Ayers, William, 5, 10

Bahr, Stephen J., 156, 157
Bainbridge, William Sims, 172, 188
Baker, Daniel, 91, 101
Ball, Richard A., 11, 152, 155, 230
Banfield, Edward C., 125, 131
Bank, Lou, 74
Barak, Gregg, 104, 277
Barkley, Russell A., 36, 42
Barton, William H., 240, 243, 253, 254
Bartusch, Dawn Jeglum, 208, 262, 273, 275
Baskin, Deborah R., 251, 254
Battin, Sara R., 105, 131
Baucom, Donald H., 253, 254
Bazemore, Gordon, 210
Beccaria, Cesare, 4, 13–14, 19
Becker, Gary S., 16, 19
Becker, Howard S., 196–7, 199, 200, 201, 207, 210
Beker, Jerome, 64, 66, 71
Benda, Brent B., 172, 188
Bender, Doris, 68, 71
Benson, Michael L., 276
Bentham, Jeremy, 4, 15, 19
Berger, Alan S., 127, 131
Bernard, Thomas J., 4, 11, 12, 14, 15, 20, 24, 28, 46, 51, 65, 130, 131
Besch, Paige K., 254
Beyer, J. Arthur, 46
Binet, Alfred, 49
Bishop, Donna M., 206, 207, 210, 213
Black, Donald J., 223, 227
Blalock, Hubert M., Jr., 7, 10
Blesecker, Gretchen, 74
Block, Jack, 64, 71
Block, Jeanne H., 71
Block, N. J., 49, 71
Blum, Robert Wm., 255
Bonger, Willem, 215, 228, 238, 246, 254
Booth, Alan, 42

SUBJECT INDEX